Business to Business

Englische Geschäftskorrespondenz und Kommunikation
im Büro

von
Ruth Feiertag
Dr. Richard Hooton
Dr. Otto Maderdonner

Ernst Klett Verlag
Stuttgart Düsseldorf Leipzig

Business to Business

Englische Geschäftskorrespondenz und Kommunikation im Büro

von
Ruth Feiertag
Dr. Richard Hooton
Dr. Otto Maderdonner

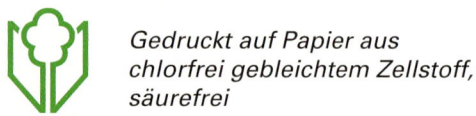
Gedruckt auf Papier aus
chlorfrei gebleichtem Zellstoff,
säurefrei

1. Auflage 1 5 4 3 2 1 | 04 03 02 2001
Alle Drucke dieser Auflage können im Unterricht nebeneinander benutzt werden, sie sind untereinander unverändert.
Die letzte Zahl bezeichnet das Jahr dieses Druckes.

© Make Your Way in Business Communication B
öbv & hpt VerlagsgmbH & Co. KG, Wien 1999
Internetadresse: http://www.oebvhpt.at

Für diese Ausgabe:
© Ernst Klett Verlag, Stuttgart und Leipzig 2001
Alle Rechte vorbehalten.
Internetadresse: http://www.klett-verlag.de

Redaktion: Volker Wendland
Umschlaggestaltung: Christine Schneyer
Druck: Schnitzer Druck GmbH, Korb
Printed in Germany.

ISBN: 3-12-808230-8

Vorwort

Mit der rapide zunehmenden Globalisierung in der Geschäftswelt spielt die Vermittlung aktiver Englischkenntnisse für den Beruf eine immer wichtigere Rolle in der Aus- und Weiterbildung.

Ziel von **Business to Business** ist deshalb die erfolgreiche Bewältigung mündlicher und schriftlicher Kommunikationsanlässe in internationalen Geschäftsbeziehungen und daneben der Nachweis dieser Fertigkeit durch eine Fremdsprachenprüfung.

Im Mittelpunkt stehen die sprachlichen Bedürfnisse von Mitarbeitern von Unternehmen in Deutschland, die mit Kunden, Lieferanten, Kollegen oder Mitarbeitern im Ausland auf Englisch kommunizieren müssen.

Inhaltlich liegt das Schwergewicht auf dem Außenhandel, der an einem die moderne Wirtschaft widerspiegelnden Branchenmix vorgestellt wird. Im Außenhandel erforderliche kaufmännische und interkulturelle Kenntnisse werden eigens vermittelt.

Sprachlich bildet die Bekämpfung typisch deutscher Fehler durch gezielte Einsetzübungen und Hervorhebung einen Schwerpunkt. Der selbständige Umgang mit englischen Ausdrucksformen wird durch die Arbeit mit Satzbausteinen gefördert.

Didaktisch basiert **Business to Business** auf Interaktion: Die Vermittlung und Vertiefung des Stoffes wird für die Lernenden durch aktives Bearbeiten möglichst kurzweilig gestaltet. Die 12 Units bestehen aus individuell einsetzbaren Modulen mit vielerlei Geschäftsfällen, Aufgaben (auch zum Hörverständnis), Texten, Satzbausteinen, Redewendungen und Informationen unterschiedlicher Schwierigkeitsgrade. Den Lehrenden steht somit gestuftes Material zur Verfügung, aus dem sie entsprechend den Bedürfnissen ihrer Kurse auswählen können. Farbige Zeichen im Inhaltsverzeichnis zeigen an, ob Module für eine Fremdsprachenprüfung unbedingt notwendig ● ● ●, in Teilen erforderlich ❖ ❖ ❖ oder empfohlen ▲ ▲ ▲ sind.

Aufgebaut ist **Business to Business** wie folgt: Alle Units beginnen mit einer Einführung in das jeweilige Thema der Unit (**Introduction**), dem ein erster Aufgabenblock (**A Activities**) folgt. Im **B**-Teil (**Tool kit**) werden konkrete Hilfestellungen in Form von Satzbausteinen und Hinweisen zur mündlichen und schriftlichen Kommunikation gegeben. Weitere Übungen schließen sich im **C**-Teil (**Additional practice**) an. Wertvolle Hintergrundinformationen – z.B. kaufmännische Grundlagen und interkulturelle Aspekte – finden sich im **D**-Teil (**Background information**). Bis auf Unit 1 schließen alle Units mit Aufgaben zur Vorbereitung auf verschiedene IHK-Prüfungen (**E IHK-Prüfungsvorbereitung**).

Business to Business ist in kaufmännischen Englischkursen aller Art einsetzbar. Darüber hinaus bereitet das Lehrwerk gezielt auf drei Fremdsprachenprüfungen der Industrie- und Handelskammern (IHK) vor:
- Geprüfter Fremdsprachenkorrespondent
- Zusatzqualifikation für kaufmännische Auszubildende
- Fremdsprache im Beruf I

Die Anforderungen der Prüfungsordnungen dieser Prüfungen sind vollständig abgedeckt.

 Hörverständnisaufgabe   Kopieren

➜ 70 Seitenverweis auf z.B. frühere Korrespondenz in einem Geschäftsfall

Autoren und Redaktion wünschen Ihnen viel Erfolg und Freude mit **Business to Business.**

Inhaltsverzeichnis

- Geprüfter Fremdsprachen-korrespondent
- Zusatzqualifikation für kaufmännische Auszubildende
- Fremdsprache im Beruf I

Für die jeweilige Prüfung:
● ● ● unbedingt notwendig
▲ ▲ ▲ empfohlen
◆ ◆ ◆ in Teilen erforderlich

Unit 1 First impressions 7

Introduction ● ● ● 7

A Activities 8
Introducing yourself and your business ● ● ●
Designing business cards ▲ ▲ ▲
Giving names and addresses ● ● ●
Designing business letters ● ● ●

B Tool kit 12
Elements of business letters ● ● ●
Letter format ▲ ▲ ▲
Spelling on the telephone ● ● ●

C Additional practice ● ● ● 16

D Background information 18
Holidays and hours of work in the UK ● ▲ ●
Intercultural aspects of communication ● ▲ ●

Unit 2 Enquiries 19

Introduction ● ● ● 19

A Activities 20
Studying advertisements ● ▲ ▲
Enquiry by telephone, by letter, by e-mail, by fax ● ● ●

B Tool kit 25
Building blocks: Enquiries ● ● ●
Punctuation ● ● ●
Faxes and E-mails ● ● ●
Telephone phrases ● ● ●

C Additional practice ● ● ● 30

D Background information 32
Types of companies ●
Organisation of companies, titles ● ▲ ▲

E IHK-Prüfungsvorbereitung ● ● ● 35

Unit 3 Offers 38

Introduction ● ● ● 38

A Activities ● ● ● 39
Making arrangements
Offer by phone, by letter, by e-mail, by fax

B Tool kit 45
Effective correspondence ● ● ●
Building blocks: Offers ● ● ◆
Dictation ▲ ▲ ▲
Telephone phrases ● ● ●

C Additional practice ● ● ● 52

D Background information 53
Pricing policy ● ● ▲
Risks in foreign trade ●

E IHK-Prüfungsvorbereitung ● ● ● 54

Unit 4 Comparing options 59

Introduction ● ● ● 59

A Activities 59
Comparing written information ▲ ▲ ▲
Comparing information by phone ● ▲ ▲
Making comparisons in memos ● ● ●
Making comparisons in reports ▲
Giving presentations ▲ ▲

B Tool kit 67
Memos and reports ◆ ◆ ◆
Summaries in German ● ● ●
Presentations ▲ ▲

C Additional practice ● ● ◆ 69

D Background information 72
Incoterms 2000 ● ◆

E IHK-Prüfungsvorbereitung ● ● 76

Unit 5 Orders 79

Introduction ● ● ❖ 79

A Activities ● ● ● 79
Order by letter with order form / Order by letter, by fax, by telephone

B Tool kit 85
Building blocks: Orders ● ● ❖
Negotiations ❖ ▲

C Additional practice ● ● ● 90

D Background information 92
Cheques ● ❖ ▲
Bills of exchange ● ❖

E IHK-Prüfungsvorbereitung ● ● ● 96

Unit 6 Order confirmation, dispatch advice 101

Introduction ● ● ▲ 101

A Activities 101
Accepting orders by phone / Order confirmation by letter, by fax ● ● ●
Sales confirmation ●
Cancellation by letter / Informing of delay / Dispatch advice ● ●

B Tool kit 109
Building blocks: Order confirmation/ Dispatch advice ● ● ❖
Telephone phrases ● ● ●

C Additional practice ● ● ❖ 118

D Background information
Trade Unions ●

E IHK-Prüfungsvorbereitung ● ● ● 120

Unit 7 Payment 127

Introduction ● ● 127

A Activities 128
Proforma invoice ● ●
Commercial invoice ● ▲
Payment by bank transfer, by cheque ● ● ▲
Payment by letter of credit ● ❖
Confirming payment ● ● ▲

B Tool kit 140
Building blocks: Payment ● ● ❖
Translation of business texts ●

C Additional practice ● ● ▲ 144

D Background information 145
Methods of payment ● ● ▲
Terms of payment (letter of credit, etc.) ● ❖

E IHK-Prüfungsvorbereitung ● ● ●150

Unit 8 Documents in foreign trade 153

Introduction ● ▲ 153

A Activities 154
Arranging for transport ● ●
Taking out insurance ●
Packagings, shipping and caution marks ● ●
Shipping documents ● ❖

B Tool kit 163
Describing graphs and diagrams ●

C Additional practice ● ❖ 168

D Background information ● ❖ ...169
Transport, Insurance, Documents in foreign trade (bill of lading, etc.)

E IHK-Prüfungsvorbereitung ● ● 174

Unit 9 Complaints 176

Introduction I 176
(Making complaints) ● ●

Introduction II 177
(Adjusting complaints) ●

A Activities 178
Complaints on the telephone, in writing ● ●
Adjusting complaints by letter, by e-mail ● ▲

B Tool kit 184
Building blocks: Complaints ● ●
Building blocks: Replies to complaints ●

C Additional practice ● ❖ 192

D Background information ● 194
International organisations (EU, etc.)
Economic indicators

E IHK-Prüfungsvorbereitung ● ● 197

Unit 10 Reminders 200

Introduction ● ❖ 200

A Activities 201
Collection series / First and second reminder /
Reminder by telephone ● ●
Final reminder / Reply to reminder ●

B Tool kit 207
Building blocks: Reminders ● ●
Builing blocks: Replies to reminders ●

C Additional practice ● ❖ 214

D Background information 216
Banking services ●

E IHK-Prüfungsvorbereitung ● ● 218

Unit 11 Credit enquiries 222

Introduction ● 222

A Activities ● 223
Offering references
Making credit enquiries
Giving credit information

B Tool kit ● 226
Building blocks: Credit enquiries / Credit information

C Additional practice ● 231

D Background information ● 232
Distribution channels (wholesalers, retailers)

E IHK-Prüfungsvorbereitung ● ... 233

Unit 12 Promoting sales 234

Introduction ● ▲ ▲ 234

A Activities 234
Sales letters ● ● ▲
Websites ▲ ▲ ▲
Agencies and co-operation ●
Fairs and exhibitions ● ●
Personal assistants' communication ● ● ●

B Tool kit 243
Building blocks: Agencies ●
Fairs ● ● ●
Secretarial communication / Welcoming
visitors ● ● ●

C Additional practice ● ❖ ❖ 250

D Background information ● 253
Intermediaries in foreign trade (agents, etc.)
Sales promotion (marketing, PR, etc.)
Fairs and exhibitions

E IHK-Prüfungsvorbereitung ● ● 258

Further reading:
Job applications ▲ ▲ ▲ 264
Vokabelverzeichnis 268
Fotokopierbare Formulare 284
Quellenverzeichnis 288

Unit 1 First impressions

Introduction

a Read this text and look up any words you don't know in a dictionary.

There are a number of conflicting views about first impressions - some say you should not rely on them, others say that you should trust them. However, first impressions are lasting and it is important to make a good impression when meeting people for the first time.

Psychologists studying the way in which we see and remember things have shown that we take in far more impressions than we are aware of. These unconscious perceptions may influence what we feel about something. This is true of the way we see both private individuals and firms. When we meet a person, we not only listen to what they say, we are also watching other signals such as the eyes, or the expression on the person's face, which may tell us to what extent we can rely on what is being said or indirectly show an aspect of their personality.

At all events, companies have to make sure that they are creating the impression they actually want to create. They too are judged not only by what they say but also by the layout and design of their publications, by their imaginative and sometimes witty logos and names, and the arresting use of colour in their letterheads or websites. They also have to decide which values they wish to project, for instance, young and dynamic or traditional and solidly reliable. Do the employees of a company make a businesslike, efficient yet friendly impression? Is the company's website really worth visiting? Can the company be bothered to update it? Are these signals saying: our clients are important to us? Or are they saying: whatever we may claim, customers are no more than a necessary evil?

This is an important matter for all companies. Larger companies have marketing and PR (public relations) departments whose role it is to give information and project a particular image. Nearly all companies have at least one person who is responsible for marketing and PR matters. Larger companies use advertising and PR agencies extensively to support their departments and to have a supply of creative ideas from outside.

b Listen to these people introducing themselves and their businesses and take notes on the following points:

- Name
- Company
- Speciality

A Activities

A1 Introducing yourself and your business

a Get together in groups of four. Think of a business you would like to set up and run. Consider these questions:

- What line of business are you going to be in? (fashion, advertising, catering, tourism, PC support, film production, car sales, motor cycle equipment, etc.)
- What are you going to offer your customers or clients to make your business special?
- What name will you give your company to make it stand out?

b Create a good, ten-second introduction to describe yourself and your business. Make it fifteen to twenty-five words long and practise it until it rolls off your tongue, so that you can introduce yourself fluently to the members of the other groups. Use the phrases on the right.

Phrases: Introducing yourself

Hello, I'm … of/from …

We specialize in …

Hi, my name is …

I'm the … of …

We offer …

A2 Designing business cards

a Good business cards can help build relationships between you and your customers and spread the name of your business throughout the community.

Study these cards, read the text and complete it using words from the box on the right.

actually * direct * tear-off
unusual * waterproof * wooden

Business cards can be regarded as "mini hoardings" that may often be the first ❶ contact that a potential customer has with your business. Be creative and design an ❷ card. Some cards are larger than the traditional size (8.8 x 5 cm) and fold out to a width of 12.6 cm. These can serve as "mini brochures" and list the services and products you provide. Here are some examples of attention-catching business cards:

- Thin ❸ cards, for a plywood manufacturing company.
- Distinctive and ❹ plastic cards, for a fly-fishing shop.
- Cards with a ❺ section that is an admission ticket for an amusement park
- A card that is ❻ a photograph, for a photography store.

b Say which card(s) you like best and why. Use the phrases in the box.

Phrases: Likes and dislikes

I like the	Sports Unlimited card Computer Clinic card LeisureCorp card	because …
I prefer … because …			
I like … best because …			
I don't like … because …			

c Get together again in groups and gather ideas on how to design an outstanding business card for your company. Make your business card attractive by using a suitable typeface and artwork, but do not put too many things on your small card!

Your business card should include this information:

- company logo
- company name
- company address
- postcode
- telephone number
- fax number
- company e-mail address
- WWW home page
- full name
- job title
- telephone extension
- e-mail address within company

A 3 Giving names and addresses

a Listen to the people on the telephone and take down the following information:

- first name
- (middle initial)
- last name
- address
- city
- postcode/zip code
- telephone number
- fax number
- e-mail

b Work with a partner. Sit back to back.
Student A closes the book and takes notes on a piece of paper.
Student B reads out the information below. Make sure that Student A reads back all the information. Then change roles.

Patricia Hendricks
FarAway Trips
145 Baker Street
Birmingham
B8 12RB
Tel 0121 689 4694

Philip Carrington
BuyDirect Mail Order
59 North Street
Edinburgh
EH2 2JQ
Tel 013 556 3477
philcarr@buydirect.co.uk

Karl-Heinz Schmidt
PWA Brauereimaschinen AG
Gottlieb-Daimler-Str. 47
63151 Heusenstamm
Germany
Tel   06101 9855334
Fax 06101 9855329
khschmidt@pwa.de

Denise MacGuire
c/o Sierra Club
330 Ocean Street
Santa Cruz
California 95115
Tel (408) 635-8572
dmacguire@sierraclub.org

Activities · Unit 1

A4 Designing business letters

a Stationery can also be the first impression that your business makes on a potential customer. You can give your company a consistent look by using the same logo, typeface etc., as for your business card.

**Look at the ideas that you gathered in exercise c on page 9 and use them to create an attractive letterhead for your business.
Before you start designing your letterhead, study these examples.**

COMPUTER CLINIC

www.compclinic.co.uk

12 Bedford Street   Pembroke SA62 6YE
Tel 01646 873894   Fax 01646 873894

SPORTS UNLIMITED

76 The Mall · Stratford E15 1XD
Tel 020 8226 3112 · Fax 020 8226 3112

Please visit our new web site at
www.sportsul.co.uk

b Some of the words in the box below have a slightly different meaning when they refer to correspondence.
First make sure that you are familiar with these words, and then study the letter on page 11. Next, match the numbers in the letter with the words in the box below.

- body
- complimentary close
- company logo
- company address
- date
- enclosures
- ending
- fax number
- job title
- opening
- postcode
- recipient's name
- recipient's address
- reference
- salutation
- sender's name
- signature
- subject line
- telephone number
- website

10 Unit 1 · Activities

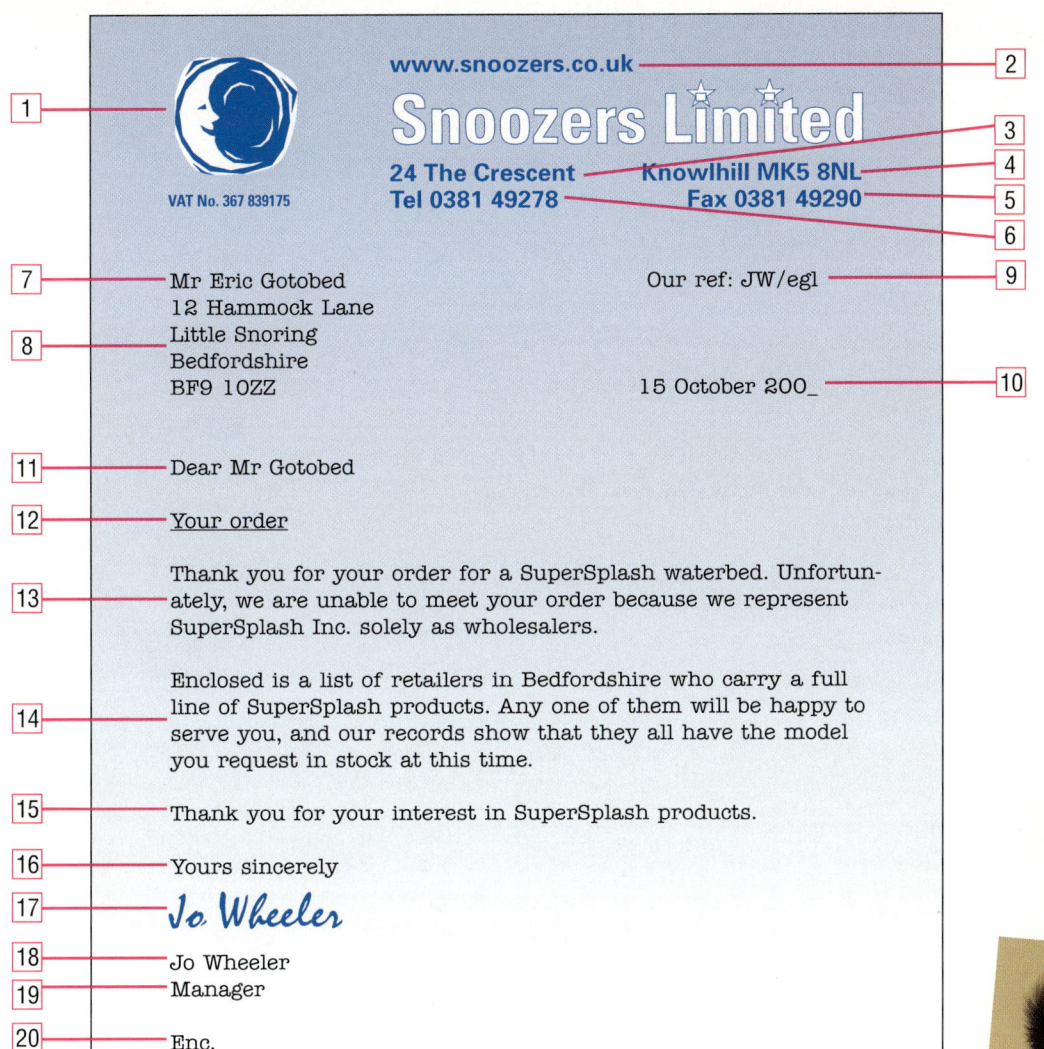

c Philip Aitken, a 21-year-old college graduate, is interested in the job offered by the University of North London.

Study the job advertisements, then read Philip's letter (page 12) and match the numbers with the names of the letter parts on page 10. Also compare the layout with the letter above and find the differences.

Computing Officer

(Help Desk Support)   £17K – £28K

Working within our Information System & Services Department, you will have a wide range of responsibilities providing user support to students and staff. This will include checking computer equipment, providing general advice and assistance, keeping records and identifying user requirements.

You should have a good standard of education and experience of carrying out maintenance procedures on computers and printers. You should also be familiar with a variety of software packages and, ideally, with Apple Mac systems.

You will need good communication skills and the ability to work unsupervised in a busy environment.

Closing date: 31 October 200_

Application forms and further details are available from Mrs A. Hartley, Personnel Services, University of North London, Holloway Road, London N7 8DB or e-mail a.hartley@unl.ac.uk, quoting the reference number LC 972.

Activities · Unit 1   11

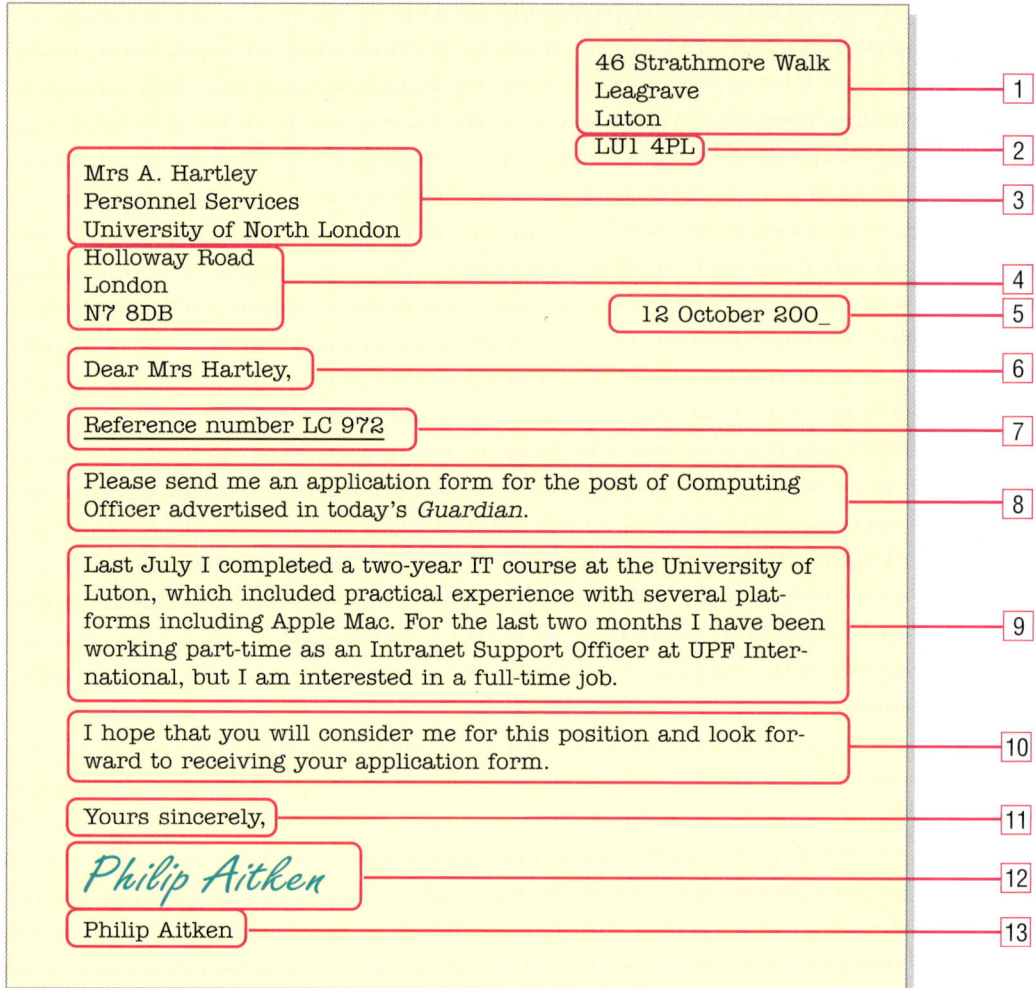

B Tool kit

B 1 Elements of business letters

The **letterhead** shows a company's logo, its name, address, telephone, fax and e-mail numbers and its Internet address.

The **reference** may include the initials of the signatory and of the secretary (e.g. JW/el) or references to files or departments (e.g. Our Ref. D15/a4). Note that the reference is sometimes preceded by "Ref.", whereas the subject line may be preceded by "Re".

The **date** can be written in various different ways:

> 3 August 2002 – 3 Aug 2002 – 3rd August 2002 – August 3, 2002
>
> 3/8/2002 (BrE: day/month/year) – 8/3/2002 (AmE: month/day/year)
> Obviously, this can easily cause confusion so it is often advisable to write out the month. It is also advisable to write out the year in full (i.e. 2001).

The date may be written on the left above the address of the recipient, or on the right in the traditional way.

The **inside address** gives the recipient's full postal address including the country if the letter is going abroad.
Note that *Messrs, Mrs, Ms, Miss* or *Mr* are written on the same line as the name, not above the name as in Germany. In the USA they are often omitted altogether. The order of the various parts of an address in Britain and the USA is different from that in Germany. Study the examples on the right →

> Messrs J. McDream & Co.
> 91 Malvern Road
> Brynmill
> Swansea
> SA3 6AH
> UK

> Samantha Duvet
> 1386 Munras Avenue
> Monterey, CA 93940
> USA

Note that *Messrs* is only used for smaller firms, such as partnerships whose names show that they are not incorporated, for example →

> Messrs J. Vernon & Co.
> Messrs Peter Price & Partners
> Messrs Jennings & Sons

Messrs is, however, never used for companies that are legal entities in their own right, as shown by the abbreviations "Limited", "Ltd", "Plc" or "plc" after the names of British companies and "Inc." or "Corp." with American companies. Examples →

> Snoozers Limited
> J. W. Philips Plc
> Robert Osborne Inc.
> The Mattress Company

Ms should be used whenever the marital status of the female addressee is not known. In contrast to German usage, do not address someone as "Mrs" unless you know for certain that she is married.

An **attention line** ensures that the letter is dealt with by a specific person or – in his or her absence – by a deputy or colleague in charge. You may write "For the attention of Mr John Bull" or "Attention: Miss Jane Doe" or just "Attn. Jane Doe".

Traditionally, the **salutation and complimentary close** in business communication must be in line with each other.

	Salutation (UK)	Complimentary close (UK)
	Dear Sirs, Dear Sir/Madam*	Yours faithfully
	Dear Ms Heavenknows	Yours sincerely
	Dear Customer	Yours sincerely
	Dear Miss Ramsbottom	Yours sincerely, Kind regards
	Dear Margaret	Best regards, Kind regards, Best wishes
	Salutation (USA)	**Complimentary Close (USA)**
	(Ladies and) Gentlemen:	Sincerely, Very truly yours
	Dear Madam Chairperson:	Very truly yours, Sincerely
	To whom it may concern:	Sincerely
	Dear Ms Grey:	Sincerely, Cordially,
	Dear Alf:	Regards, Cordially

* Dear Sir or Madam is also acceptable.

Nowadays "Yours faithfully" is often felt to be too formal and "Yours sincerely" may be used instead. Especially in e-mails and faxes informal endings such as "Best regards" are used.

If at all possible you should address the person you are writing to by name (Dear Mrs McCaghy). "Dear Sir(s)" or "Gentlemen: (USA)" is used for initial contact only when you do not have a name to write to.

The **subject line** briefly tells the recipient what the letter, e-mail, fax or memo is about. As it makes things easier for the reader it is also a means of creating goodwill for the sender's firm. That is why most business letters should have a subject line which may be underlined, or typed in capital letters or bold type. In some firms it is customary to precede the subject line by "Subject:" or "Re:"

In the UK subject lines are normally, but not always, written below the salutation, in the USA above the salutation.

UK	Dear Mrs Lefroy		Overdue account
	Overdue account		Dear Mrs Lefroy
	Thank you for your letter of …		Thank you for your letter of …
USA	Your order no. AB/123 for swimwear		
	Dear Mr Leigh:		
	We are sorry to tell you …		

Note that in English the first word of the body of the letter begins with a capital letter.

The **signature block** often begins with the company's name right below the complimentary close, followed by several blank lines for the signature. The signatory's name is typed below the signature and below that his or her position or department are mentioned as well. Women sometimes indicate in brackets behind their name how they wish to be addressed. →

Yours sincerely
Dot.Com.Ltd.
Julia Bertram
Julia Bertram (Miss)
Customer Relations

If somebody signs the letter on behalf of another person, for instance a personal assistant for his or her boss, the other person's name is typed below the signature, preceded by the abbreviation pp., meaning "on behalf of". →

Jane Rushworth
pp. Mary Crawford
Sales Manager

Whenever **enclosures** are sent with a letter, a reference to the enclosure is required at the bottom of the letter. This can take any of the following forms:

Enc.	Enclosure(s)	Enc. Invoice No. CB/34	Encs.	5 Leaflets

The abbreviation **cc** below the signature is used to indicate that one or more people are going to get a copy of the letter or fax.

cc: William Norris, Chief Financial Officer

Unit 1 · Tool kit

B 2 Letter format

■ First, match the English computer terms with their German translations, and read the information. Next, study the example in reduced size below.

Then start up your word processor, type the letter, and define the settings as shown. Print it out in different fonts, and decide for yourself which one you like best. Save those settings to create your personal style.

1. to align		a. Absatz
2. alignment		b. ausrichten (z.B. zentriert)
3. font		c. Textausrichtung
4. indentation		d. Rand
5. line spacing		e. Schriftart
6. margin		f. speichern
7. paragraph		g. Einrückung
8. to save		h. Formatvorlage
9. style sheet		i. Schriftschnitt (z.B. kursiv)
10. style		j. Zeilenabstand

Enhance your productivity and the appearance of your letters

It is the overall look of the letter that makes the first impression on your prospective customer. Before even reading a single word, the recipient may judge your business from what your letter looks like.

You can create stationery for your business by defining the appropriate settings offered by your software. Note that you can also create style sheets and save your settings in these, which makes it much easier to draft letters!

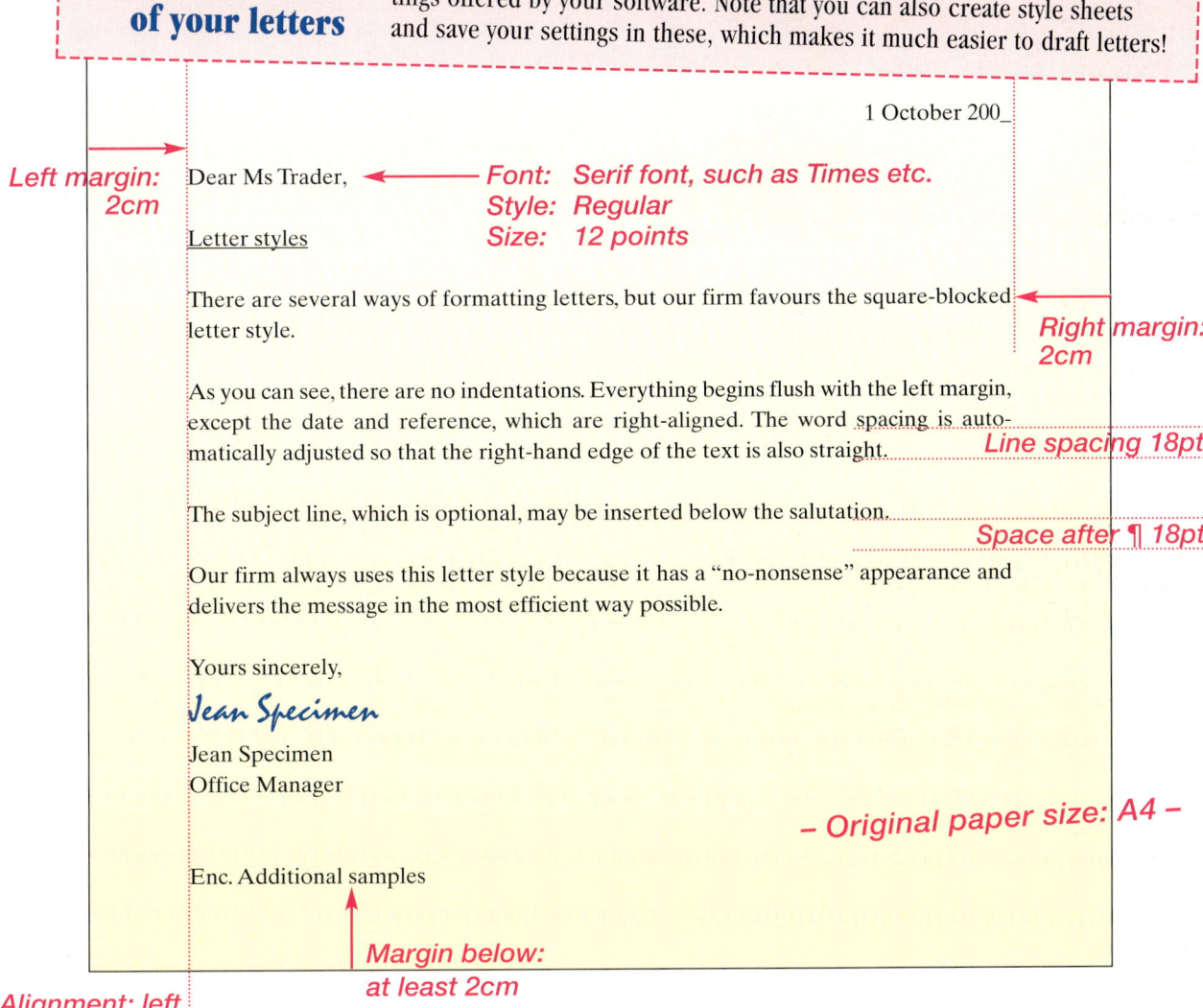

B 3 Telephoning: Spelling on the telephone

The telephone alphabet

When spelling out a name on the telephone, the telephone alphabet helps avoid misunderstandings:

BJ7 – **B** for Benjamin, **J** for Jack. No, not **I**. It's **Y** for yellow.

There are different alphabets in use, and people in Britain often use these words:

Andrew	**N**elly
Benjamin	**O**liver
Charlie	**P**eter
David	**Q**ueenie
Edward	**R**obert
Frederick	**S**ugar
George	**T**om
Harry	**U**ncle
Isaac	**V**ictor
Jack	**W**illiam
King	**X**mas
Lucy	**Y**ellow
Mary	**Z**ebra

Numbers and symbols

In addresses, phone and fax numbers the figures are pronounced individually:

908	*nine oh eight / nine nought eight*
253-8001	*two five three / eight double oh one*
	AmE: ... *eight zero zero one*

Note that in British English
0	is generally pronounced *oh*.
00	is read *double oh*.
33	is *double three*,
44	is *double four* etc.,
777	is *triple seven*.

In e-mail and Internet addresses
@ is given as *at*, . is *dot*, : is *colon*,
/ is *slash*, - is *dash* or *hyphen*.

dwoods@demon.or.uk
d woods at demon dot o-r dot u-k

www.stockmaster.com
double-u double-u double-u dot stockmaster dot com

C Additional practice

a **Describe the ideal business partner using appropriate words from the box. Give the opposites of the words you haven't chosen. Consult a dictionary where necessary.**

> courteous * helpful * inefficient
> incompetent * knowledgeable * rude
> unfriendly * pushy * patient
> informed * tough * unreliable

→ 11/12 b **Study the letters on pages 11 and 12 again and find the right order for these jumbled addresses. Then dictate them to your partner.**

```
134 Redwoods Drive
CA 94039
President
USA
Omega Corporation
Mountain View Village
Karen A. Detweiler
```

```
10 Greycoat Place
SW1P 1SB
Premier House
Mr James Stafford
Marketing Manager
London
e-mail: jstafford@mediacontacts.co.uk
Collins Classics
```

```
24 Modwen Road
e-mail: maryrav@dial.popex.com
Fax: 0161 876 5499
Human Resources Officer
M5 3EZ
Ms Mary Ravenhill
Salford
Tel: 0161 876 5492
UTELL International
```

II/12 **c** Use the letters on pages 11 and 12 as examples and rewrite this letter using the correct spacing and punctuation.

> Mrs Evelyn Strand Weinbauer Ltd. Importer of German wines 105 Deansgate Manchester M60 2IR (today's date) Dear Mrs Strand Wine tasting The members of the Wanstead Club of the British Wine and Food Society would indeed be interested in a presentation of German wines at one of our next meetings Therefore I gladly accept your offer to speak about Germany's wine-growing regions and to bring samples of the best vintages The BWFS meets every other Thursday at 7pm at Bush House in Wanstead The programmes for our next three meetings have already been established However I shall call you next week to arrange a date for your presentation before Christmas The members and I look forward to this event Best regards Sam Purcell

d Identify these letter parts and match them with the layout on the right. Then rewrite the letter.

A As the date of our departure is not too distant, we hope to hear from you soon.

B Simon and Ellen Woodford

C KIWI TRAVEL
Far East Desk

D 34 Harcourt Parkway
Larne
BT40 4JX
Tel 01574 740875

E In particular, we are interested in visiting Malaysia, Singapore and Thailand. We would like to see as much as possible, but avoid the beaten track.

Please let us know if you arrange custom tours of this kind, and when it would be convenient to discuss the details with your representative at your main office.

F Trip to South East Asia

G Kiwi House
North Road
Bloomfield
Belfast
BT5 4AZ

H Yours faithfully,

I 24 October 200_

J Dear Sir or Madam,

1 sender's address

2 recipient

3 recipient's address

4 date

5 salutation

6 subject

7 opening

8 body

9 ending

10 complimentary close

signature

11 sender's name

K We are celebrating our 25th wedding anniversary next month. Therefore, we are planning a three-week journey to the Far East from 1 January to 22 January next year.

Additional practice · Unit **1**   17

D Background information

D1 Holidays and hours of work in the UK

Most full-time employees have a basic working week of between 34 and 40 hours and work a five-day week. The average including overtime was 38.3 hours in 1999. Both male and female employees tend to work more hours than in other EU countries. Many employees (office workers, teachers, banks, for example) work from 9am in the morning to 5pm in the afternoon.

Holiday entitlement has been largely determined by negotiation. At the beginning of 1999 the average paid holiday entitlement for full-time workers was just under five weeks. EU regulations which provide for a minimum annual holiday entitlement of four weeks and a maximum of 48 hours per week came into force in 1998.

Apart from the usual public holidays at Christmas, New Year and Easter there are also "Bank Holidays" – May Day Bank Holiday on 1 May, Spring Bank Holiday at the end of May and Summer Bank Holiday in August.

D2 Intercultural aspects of communication

The British are generally considered to be very polite. Perhaps it is more useful to remember that there are differences in conventions of politeness between different cultures. A failure to realise this may lead to friction or misunderstanding.

Expressions such as "Could you pass the salt", "Could you possibly bring me something from the supermarket", "I wonder if I could possibly ask you a favour", are not considered stiff in English; they are normal conversational style. In German a particle such as "mal" can be used as a downtoner, i.e. to turn a command into a request, e.g: "Reich mir mal das Salz". This possibility does not exist in English, with the result that more polite formulae are used. There are different ways of achieving the same result in German and English: If you wish to leave (say, a party) without sounding too abrupt in German you can say "Ich muss allmählich/langsam gehen". The same effect is achieved in English by using the continuous form: "I must be going, I'm afraid".

When introducing yourself you should always give both your first name and your surname. Do not be surprised if people call you by your first name.

One word answers (particularly yes and no) may sound impolite and suggest that you are not in a particularly communicative mood.
You should say things like,
"Yes, I'd love to", "I'm afraid I can't",
"No, I'm sorry I'm not". "What would you prefer – a Chinese or an Indian restaurant?". "I think I'd prefer Chinese". Don't just answer: "Chinese", which sounds uncommunicative.

Unit 2 Enquiries

Introduction

business letter

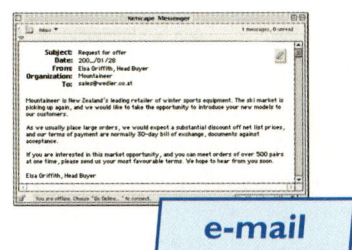
e-mail

FAX

telephone

a Complete the following text using words from the box below.

consist
delivery
discounts
form
pronounced
prospective

Business transactions often start with enquiries. The word *enquiry* is a noun which is derived from the verb *to enquire*, which simply means to ask for information. Note that these words are also spelled *inquiry* and *to inquire*, especially in American English. The noun is ❶ [ɪnˈkwaɪˈrɪ] or, mainly in Scottish and American English, [ˈɪnkwɪrɪ].

There are several ways for ❷ buyers to get the information they want:
- make a telephone call
- send a fax
- send an e-mail message or respond to a website
- write a letter of enquiry

An old English saying goes *if you want good answers, ask good questions*. Therefore, an enquiry should be courteous, complete and concise to ensure a good answer.

An enquiry may ❸ of a simple postcard, a tear-off coupon put into an envelope or a more complex preprinted enquiry ❹ if specific information is required.

An enquiry may ask for
- sales literature, i.e. catalogues, brochures or leaflets
- price lists, quotations or cost estimates
- information on   – prices and ❺, terms of payment
  – terms of ❻ and delivery periods
- samples, patterns, demonstrations, presentations.

b Write a short summary of the text in German.

A Activities

A 1 Studying advertisements

a Study this advertisement and say whether the statements below are true or false.

SPACE AGE TECHNOLOGY AT AN AFFORDABLE PRICE

"A SUPER PACKAGE FOR THE MONEY"

Mountain Bike UK

Hyflyer DX-2000
space-age design features include:
- Aerospace titanium frame tubes
- Titanium fork
- Shimada XTR 24-speed gears
- Shimada XTR Rapidfire SL shifters
- All-new Shimada XTR 'V' brakes
- Shimada XTR levers, rims and hubs
- Ritchey Alfabite 26" tyres

HYFLYER plc

438 Weltmore Industrial Park   Warwick CV43 6TS
Tel: 01926 439523   Fax: 01926 451427
E-mail: info@hyflyer.uk

1. The Hyflyer DX-2000 mountain bike offers excellent value for money.
2. Mountain Bike UK magazine has given the Hyflyer DX 2000 a favourable review.
3. Hyflyer is a British bike manufacturer based in Weltmore.
4. Hyflyer DX 2000 features Shimada gears, shifters, brakes and tyres.

b Study this advertisement and say which answer is appropriate.

This drive's capacity is unlimited.

While technology is making the world smaller, it's also making your applications and files larger. The perfect situation for UltraSpeed™ 1280MB. With ultra-high transfer speeds, it's 400 per cent faster than its closest rival. Which means you can run applications straight off UltraSpeed. Plus you can keep adding cartridges, giving you the flexibility of unlimited capacity.

UltraSpeed™ 1280 — Space is no longer the final frontier

DigiCorp K.K   4–9–37 Takada   Shinjuku-ku   172 Tokyo Japan
Fax (...81) 3–5578–8476   e-mail intlsales@digicorp.co.jp

1. A major problem in computing is
   a. the constant danger of viruses.
   b. limited storage capacity.
   c. software incompatibility.
2. The UltraSpeed has no limits because
   a. it has several drives built in.
   b. its capacity is 1280 GB.
   c. you can add cartridges.
3. Applications can be run straight off the drive because
   a. of its ultra-high transfer speed.
   b. its capacity is unlimited.
   c. space is no longer limited.
4. Traditional disks
   a. are too slow to run applications.
   b. don't have enough capacity.
   c. are made for back-up purposes.
5. The drive maker's name is
   a. UltraSpeed.
   b. IntlSales.
   c. DigiCorp K.K.

A 2 Enquiry by telephone

a LeisureCorp's old office printers break down frequently, and repairs are quite expensive. At a recent meeting, LeisureCorp decided to replace the printers. Therefore, Freddie Murphy, one of LeisureCorp's employees, studies a few magazines to find out what is on the market. These advertisements attract his attention. He decides to ask for information by telephone.

Flexibility at your fingertips …

… the new NECSON 1612
With the new 30 ppm 1200x1200 dpi colour workgroup printer you can turn your hands to almost everything. From postcard size to A3, from tissue paper to board. And it's compatible with PC, Mac and UNIX and all major networks, so you can be sure it works with your favourite systems and applications.

You've got to see it to believe it.

For information on dealers near you, call 0800 5057827.

NECSON UK *Fraser Road, Perivale Middlesex, UB6 7AQ*

If your output could be **close to perfect** or **perfect**, which would you choose?

The new HocusPocus LaserBolt 1200
The new Conan JPF engine is at the heart of this leading-edge colour printer, combining high performance and incredibly crisp output. And for the first time in history, a 1200 dpi colour workgroup printer is available for less than £150.

Hocus **P**ocus

For perfect output at a perfect price – call 020 74894728 ext. 7362

Listen to the telephone call and note down the relevant information (as shown on the right) on a separate sheet of paper.

authorized dealer:
address:
telephone number:
availability of certified technician:

b Work with a partner. Partner A studies the Hocus Pocus advertisement above. Partner B looks up the information about authorized dealers on the next page. Partner A phones Partner B. Partner B answers partner A's questions. Partner A takes down the details as shown in the slip above.

Hocus Pocus
Authorized dealers · Ulster

		Telephone	Fax
Bloggs Bros. sales only	486 King's Road Belfast BT2 4WM	(01232) 776036 bloggs@csi.com	(01232) 776060
Mahoney & Co. sales and repairs	89 Market Square Downpatrick BT20 6RZ	(01396) 81375 mahoney@hpnet.uk	(01396) 81390
HyperOffice no repairs	9 High Street Larne BT40 8EC	(01960) 650357 sales@hyperoffice.co.uk	(01960) 650475

c Kate Paxton, who works for Sports Unlimited, has seen Hyflyer's advertisement and would like to know more about their new product.

Listen to the telephone conversation between Kate and Hyflyer's sales representative, take notes and then complete these sentences:

1. The operator puts Kate through to …
2. Rob Sullivan says that the new Hyflyer range is available …
3. Kate Paxton is also interested in …
4. The DX is not the only Hyflyer model. There are …
5. Rob Sullivan offers to send her a …
6. Kate Paxton's address is …
7. Rob Sullivan promises to …

d Restore the order of this jumbled dialogue. Match the numbers with the letters.

1. Sports Unlimited, Joanne Quinn speaking. Good afternoon. Can I help you?
2. Certainly, madam. For which products?
3. Where should I send it?
4. And the postcode, madam?
5. Thank you, madam. I'll put it in the mail today.

a. B1 4BZ.
b. Thank you very much.
c. Chambers & Partners, 56 Victoria Square, Birmingham
d. Hello. My name is Judy Chambers. I'm enquiring about a price list.
e. Ladies' swimwear.

e Now work with a partner and create similar dialogues using these cues:

A Jim Duffy, who lives at 56 Derby Road, Wanstead, London E11 2PS, calls Metro Bank for a leaflet about their 6.5% savings plan advertised in today's Daily Mirror.

B Samantha Guardian is planning a trip to South Africa, and she calls LeisureCorp for a brochure. Her address is 28 Town Lane, Larne, County Antrim BT40 3SZ.

A 3 Enquiry by letter

a Amanda Jones, the manager of LeisureCorp, also finds an advertisement in a local newspaper and decides to make a written enquiry to PCM.
Complete the letter using words from the box below.

13 November 200_

PCM Office Machines
158 Tredagar Street
Belfast
BT8 13RX

Our ref AJ/ig

Dear Sir or Madam,

We saw your advertisement ❶ PowerComp colour laser printers ❷ today's Limavady Guardian.

We are planning to purchase four new laser printers ❸ the end of the year, and we would like to receive information ❹ all of the suitable models. Each printer will serve five PCs and typically print 4,000 pages a month. We would like one printer to be equipped ❺ a duplex unit so we can print ❻ both sides without having to turn the paper manually.

Could you please send us an offer ❼ with details ❽ your warranty and repair service.

We look forward ❾ hearing ❿ you.

Yours faithfully,

Amanda Jones

Amanda Jones
Manager

> about
> before
> for
> from
> in
> of
> on
> to
> together
> with

b **Cover up Amanda Jones' letter and try to complete these sentences.**

1. Amanda Jones saw an advertisement for …
2. She saw the advertisement in …
3. LeisureCorp is planning to …
4. They would like to receive …
5. Each printer will typically …
6. One printer should be equipped with …

Activities · Unit 2   23

A 4 Enquiry by e-mail

■ Will Duncan, the proprietor of Computer Clinic, also read the advertisement on page 20 and decided to contact DigiCorp. **Study the message below and answer the questions in the box.**

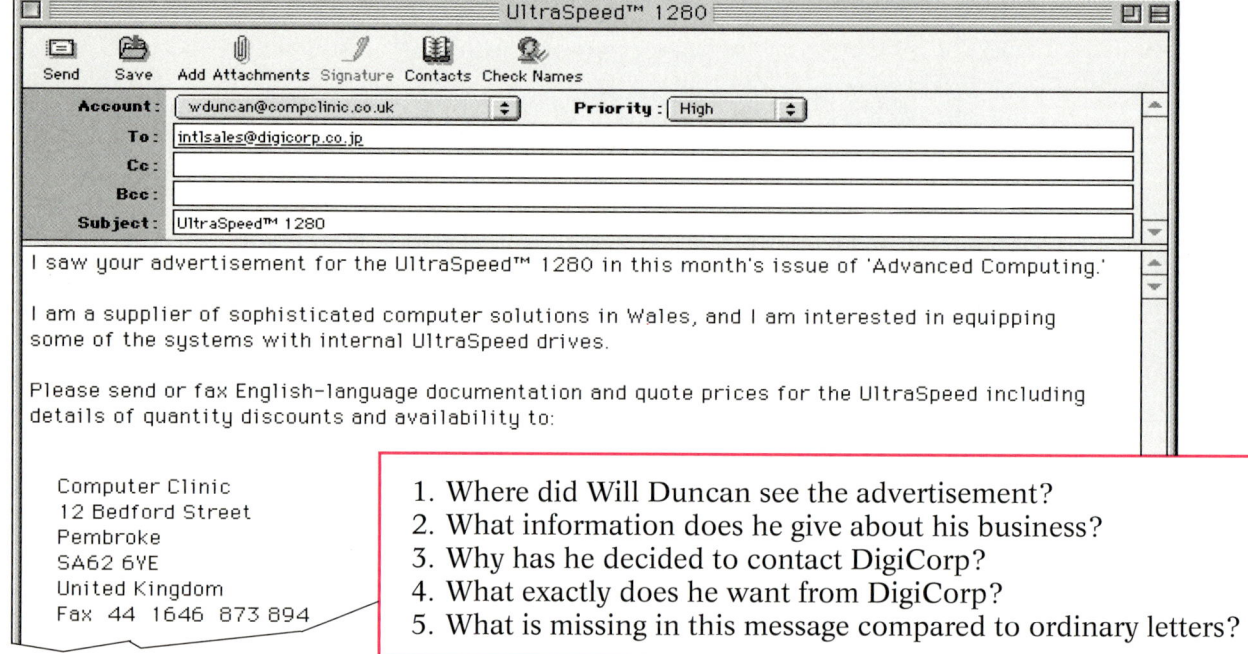

1. Where did Will Duncan see the advertisement?
2. What information does he give about his business?
3. Why has he decided to contact DigiCorp?
4. What exactly does he want from DigiCorp?
5. What is missing in this message compared to ordinary letters?

A 5 Enquiry by fax

■ **Complete this fax using the correct form of the verbs in brackets.**

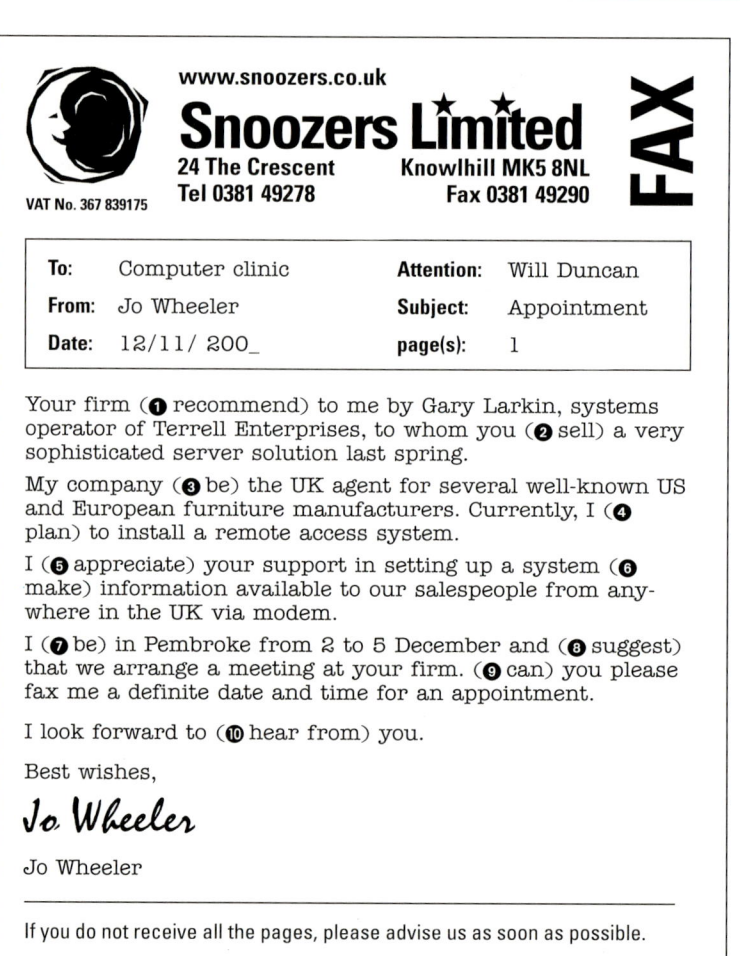

24 Unit 2 · Activities

B Tool kit

B 1 Structure of business communications: Detailed enquiries

Enquiries are standard correspondence and should be structured like this:

Structure	Language to use
1. appropriate salutation	Dear Sir or Madam
2. source of address	We saw your advertisement **for** … **in** this month's issue **of** …
3. introduction of your company	We are a … and specialise **in** …
4. reason for enquiry	We are planning to …
5. request to send • catalogues and price lists • a quotation or cost estimate	Could you please send us …?
6. request for information on • prices and discounts • terms of payment and delivery • delivery periods	We would appreciate information **on** …
7. further requests, if applicable • samples or patterns • a visit by a representative • a demonstration or presentation	We would be glad to receive … Would it be possible **for** your representative to …
8. closing phrase	We look forward **to** hearing **from** you soon.
9. appropriate complimentary close	Yours faithfully

B 2 Building blocks for business communications: Enquiries

1 To mention the source of address

We saw I refer to	your advertisement for	laser printers **in**	the Daily Express **of** 2 October. the October issue **of** PC World.

We have obtained	your address **from**	the Anglo-German Chamber of Commerce. one of our business partners. the Indian Consulate in Munich.

Your	firm has been services have been products have been	recommended **to** us **by** …

We have visited your website and …
We saw your products at the Machine Tools Exhibition in Leeds.

2 To introduce your business

We are a	young and rapidly growing medium-sized well-established	company firm business	producing specialising **in** importing	a wide range of … sophisticated … upmarket …

3 To explain the reason for your enquiry

We are planning to	import market expand our line of	high-quality …

We are	interested **in** importing considering marketing currently expanding our line of	first-class …

4 To say what you require

Could you please Please	send us let us have enclose	information brochures **about** full details **of** a catalogue **of** a price list **for** a quotation **for**	the services you offer. your latest products. your range of … your …
		a cost estimate for	the performance of …

5 To ask for information

We	require would be grateful for	details **of** information **on**	your the	prices and discounts. terms of payment and delivery. delivery periods. quantities available.

What are your terms of payment?
Do you grant any quantity discounts?
Can you deliver ex stock?

6 To ask for other services, if applicable

| A visit by your representative
A demonstration **on** our premises
A presentation of your services | would be appreciated. |

7 To close the communication with a standard phrase

| If your prices are competitive, we may be able to place substantial orders in the near future. |
| We hope to hear from you soon. |

| We | look forward
are looking forward | to | hearing from you soon.
an early reply. |

a Use these building blocks to find equivalents for the following German sentences.

1. Wir haben Ihre Anzeige für Laserdrucker in der Oktoberausgabe der PCWorld gesehen.
2. Wir sind ein junges, aufstrebendes Unternehmen, das sich auf hochwertige PC-Peripherie spezialisiert.
3. Da wir zur Zeit unsere Produktpalette vergrößern, wären wir am Vertrieb Ihrer Drucker interessiert.
4. Könnten Sie uns nähere Einzelheiten über Ihre neuesten Erzeugnisse mitteilen?
5. Wir bitten Sie um Zusendung von Prospekten und Preislisten.
6. Wir haben Ihre Anschrift vom indischen Konsulat in München erhalten.
7. Bitte geben Sie uns Auskunft über Ihre Liefer- und Zahlungsbedingungen.
8. Wir sehen Ihrer Antwort mit Interesse entgegen.
9. Ihr Unternehmen wurde uns von Knightley Brothers in Dublin empfohlen.
10. Wir sind auf den Vertrieb von Kosmetikartikeln spezialisiert.
11. Wir bitten Sie um einen Kostenvoranschlag für die Durchführung der Malerarbeiten.
12. Bitte teilen Sie uns Ihre kürzeste Lieferzeit mit.
13. Wir wären dankbar für nähere Angaben zu den von Ihnen angebotenen Dienstleistungen.
14. Wir bitten Sie daher um ein ausführliches Angebot über Ihre neue Produktlinie.
15. Gewähren Sie Mengenrabatt?
16. Könnte uns Ihr Vertreter im Laufe der nächsten Woche aufsuchen?

b First, listen to the boss giving instructions and take notes.
Then write the letter on a piece of the stationery that you designed in Unit 1. When you have finished, use this checklist to make sure you have included all the items a business letter should contain.

- body
- ending
- postcode
- reference
- complimentary close
- job title
- recipient's name
- salutation
- signature
- date
- opening
- recipient's address
- sender's name
- subject line

B 3 Punctuation

There is a choice of punctuation in some parts of a letter. The punctuation is either

standard:	or open:
David Barratt Ltd., 14 Montpelier Rd., Brighton BN1 2LQ	David Barratt Ltd 14 Montpelier Rd Brighton BN1 2LQ
Dear Mr Barratt,	Dear Mr Barratt
Yours sincerely,	Yours sincerely

Sometimes open punctuation is chosen for the recipient's address and standard punctuation for the salutation (Dear Mr Barratt,) and the close (Yours sincerely,).

Note that in all these cases normal punctuation rules apply to the body of the letter.

B 4 Faxes and e-mails

Letters are still widely used in many business contexts but faxes (occasionally called "facsimiles") and e-mails have become very popular because they are fast and convenient. Sometimes urgent information is sent by fax and then confirmed in a traditional letter, although a fax also has the status of a document.

Obviously, it saves a lot of time (and money!) to type a message on your PC and fax it directly. You do not even have to print it out and the addressee has the information immediately. This means that he or she, in turn, can react more quickly – immediately if they wish.

A further advantage is that you can reduce the level of formality. This also makes for speed. A fax often looks more like a memo than a traditional letter. You can leave out the standard salutation "Dear Sir or Madam" but you can include one if you wish ("Dear James"). The ending is also usually less formal – not "Yours faithfully", but "Regards", "Kind regards", or "Best wishes". However, dispensing with formality does not mean that the overall tone of a fax should be less polite or friendly than a letter!

A fax is usually sent on company stationery with a letterhead. Apart from the the date, subject and addressee it also states how many pages are to be transmitted. At the bottom of the fax cover page there may also be a request to contact the sender if the specified number of pages has not been received.

www.snoozers.co.uk
Snoozers Limited
24 The Crescent Knowlhill MK5 8NL
Tel 0381 49278 Fax 0381 49290
FAX
VAT No. 367 839175

To:	Hotel Europe	Attention:	Reservations
From:	Elsa Yates	Subject:	
Date:	25 November 200_	page(s):	1

Please reserve a single room with business facilities for our manager, Ms Jo Wheeler. She will be arriving on Monday 2 December and staying for three nights to attend the Annual Furniture Fair.

I look forward to receiving your confirmation, including exact cost, by return.

Elsa Yates

If you do not receive all the pages, please advise us as soon as possible.

With the development of the Internet and company intranets, e-mail has also become a rapidly growing means of communication. Like faxes, the style of communication in an e-mail is more economical and less formal.

Avoid using special characters like *ß, ä, ü* or *ö*. They may come out very strangely at the other end! Use *ss, ae, ue* and *oe* instead.

Use capital letters sparingly, otherwise the emphatic effect wears off! For example: Please send us the spare parts by return – we need them URGENTLY.

Some e-mails contain attachments which are referred to at the end of the message. The e-mail header apart from giving date and time and subject may also indicate that the e-mail has been

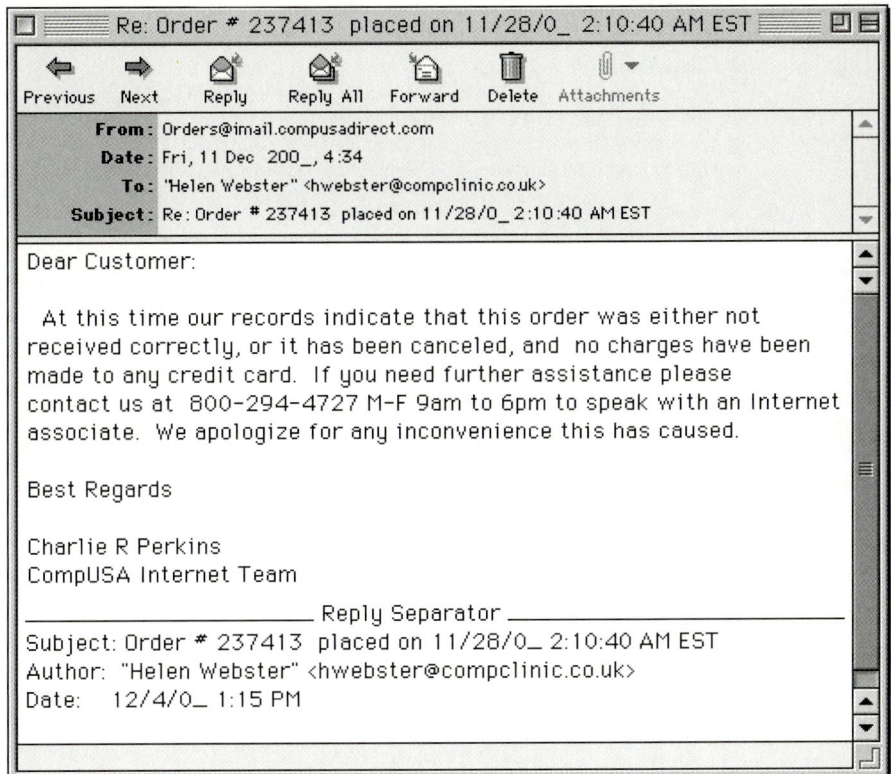

B 5 Telephone phrases: Enquiry

Sunshine Enterprises.
  Good morning (afternoon).
Cathy Turner speaking.
  (How) Can I help you?

~ My name is Nicole Braun.

~ Good morning (afternoon). I saw your ad(vertisement) for … in …
  I'd like to have further information about …

Certainly, madam (sir).
  What information do you require?

~ Specifications, prices and terms. Do you have an information pack?

If you give me your address,
  I'll send it off today.

~ Could you possibly send me …

C Additional practice

a **Study this advertisement and consider what additional information you want to have before ordering one of these publications. Then form three groups and follow these instructions:**

➡ 20 You are the assistants of Pete O'Brien, Export Sales Manager of Hyflyer. Group A drafts a letter of enquiry, Group B drafts a fax. Both have to be ready for Mr O'Brien's signature. Group C sends an e-mail message.

> **SITPRO® MEET THE CHALLENGES OF EXPORT**
>
> You'll find three decades of unrivalled expertise in our updated publications. Designed to guide you through export and customs procedures. Helping you to export more efficiently, more competitively and more profitably.
>
> **The New Export Guide**
> Our new export kit brings together all SITPRO's unique expertise in one easy to digest and comprehensive product. Starting with the basics, it takes you through the procedures and methods of exporting. From preparatory planning, getting your goods to the market through to getting paid. Packaged in a convenient A5 binder with an audio cassette. The Export Guide is a quick access, low cost reference guide for exporters.
>
> **Top Form 2**
> Top Form 2 is the definitive guide to the UK aligned export forms. Containing full scale examples, it clearly sets out and explains the range of UK export documents. Top Form 2 comes as a complete set enclosed in a handy ring binder. And it remains the single best reference source for UK export forms.
>
> **SITPRO®** Making your business more effective.
> The Simpler Trade Procedures Board
>
> SITPRO, 151 Buckingham Palace Road, London SW1W 9SS
> Phone: +44 20 7215 0825, Fax: +44 20 7215 0824
> Email: info@sitpro.org.uk

b **Now analyse what you have written and check which of the following items you have used. Then compare your results in class.**

- recipient's name and address
- salutation
- signature
- reference
- subject line
- sender's name
- date
- complimentary close
- job title

c **Spell out these names and the telephone numbers.**

R. E. Buchanan	D. Yilmaz	W. Maier-Lüttringhaus
Sean McIntyre	J. G. Evans	V. Heiermann
(020) 7842 9631	987 6543	(0044-20) 8659 4726
(01143-1) 774 5694 ext467		(001-212) 792 1482 ext3592

d **Read these e-mail and website addresses.**

pnorstad@t-online.de   compass@pathfinder.com
eva.muster@oebv.co.de   www.nosy.com/home.html
joe.sixpack@aol.com   www.pathfinder.com/time

e **Put these addresses into the correct order.**

Edinburgh	Canada	WC2R 0QU
EH2 9FO	1490 Asquith Street	United Kingdom
King George Hotel	Ms Anita Lopez	The Trade Commissioner
Scotland	V8 R345	London
The Manager	Victoria, B.C.	47 Strand
36 Royal Terrace	WorldWide Shipping Co.	Australia House

f Copy the text on the right and supply the correct punctuation. Then format the letter as shown in unit 1 and print it on a piece of blank paper.

> Costas y Figueras 34 Puerta del Sol 10857 Madrid Spain Hotel Marotti Mozartring 34 1010 Wien (today's date) Dear Sir or Madam Reservation Please reserve two separate rooms with bath from 6 November to 9 November inclusive for Mr Costas and Mr Figueras who will be attending the Annual Euro Congress in Vienna The gentlemen would prefer quiet rooms with a nice view Please charge the deposit to our EXAM card #4845 1218 4860 0423 expiring June 200_ Sincerely Evita Gonzales Head Secretary

g Put the elements of this letter into the correct order and print it out on your own stationery.

① As we are currently expanding our line of table-top games, we are interested in importing your products to Germany.

② Please send us full details on your range of table-top games including your latest price list.

③ We look forward to hearing from you soon.

④ Inquiry for table-top games

⑤ Delta Games
1 Infinite Loop
Cupertino CA 94086
USA

⑥ (your name)
Head Buyer

⑦ Sincerely,

⑧ 7 July 200_

⑨ Ladies and Gentlemen:

⑩ We saw your advertisement for your new sets of trading cards in this month's issue of **Games & More**.

⑪ We are a young and rapidly growing firm marketing a wide range of games.

h You work for Importex, a German company that imports textiles. Importex is based in Modegasse 6, 94034 Passau. Their telephone number is 0851 37 03 01, their fax number 0851 370312 and their website is www.importex.co.de

First, design a logo for your company and create a letterhead for a piece of stationery. Next, study the advertisement for HEADTOTOE's collection of ski caps and sweaters, which you have found in this month's issue of a trade magazine called *Winter Chill*. Then draft an enquiry, introducing your business and asking for full details, prices and samples.

Additional practice · Unit 2   31

D Background information

D1 Types of firms and companies

Strictly speaking, English law differentiates between firms which are represented by at least one *fully liable* individual, and companies, which are separate legal entities in their own right.

A **sole trader** is the sole proprietor of a small business. Such businesses are mainly involved in the provision of services, e.g. small shops, hairdressing, EDP services. Such firms can be set up with few legal formalities and the owner can make independent decisions and retain all the profits. He or she is, however, fully liable, i.e. liable to the full extent of his or her personal fortune for any debts incurred by the firm.

A **partnership** is, according to the Partnership Act 1890 "the relation which subsists between persons carrying on a business in common with a view of profit". Partnerships are usual for firms of accountants, solicitors and doctors etc.. **Ordinary** (or general) **partnerships** carry *unlimited liability* for all partners, with all partners taking part in the management of the firm. In a **limited partnership**, on the other hand, some partners are allowed *limited liability*. This means that their personal assets (house, car etc.) cannot be claimed by the partnership's creditors. Such limited (or sleeping) partners cannot take part in the management of the firm, which is run by the ordinary partners, of which there must be at least one. The ordinary partners are fully liable for the debts and obligations of the limited partnership. Limited partnerships must be registered with the Registrar of Companies.

Unlike the above-mentioned types of firm, **joint stock companies** (private limited companies and public limited companies) are incorporated, which means that they are artificial legal entities that can conclude contracts, sue and be sued. They must be registered with the Registrar of Companies. *Shares* are sold to raise the capital for the company and the *shareholders*, i.e. the owners, enjoy limited liability. The shareholders elect a *board of directors* who run the company on their behalf. Profits are distributed to the owners in the form of *dividends*. In the United States such companies are called **corporations**.

Private limited companies may in many respects be compared with the German GmbH, but are not required to have a minimum share capital. They must use the abbreviation **Ltd.** after their name. Their shares cannot be offered to the general public and cannot, therefore, be traded at the stock exchange. There are certain requirements as far as the publication of accounts is concerned. Many former partnerships now prefer to operate as private limited companies. The US American equivalent is the **closed corporation**, the legal form preferred for smaller and family-owned businesses.

Public limited companies are in many ways the British counterparts of the German AG. The latter is, however, run by two tiers of management, i.e. the executive board (also called board of management) and the supervisory board, whereas, under English law, companies are run by one *board of directors* only, some of whom have executive functions while others play a supervisory role. Public limited companies use the abbreviation **plc.** after their names. They must have a minimum nominal share capital of £50,000 and their shares are traded at the stock exchange. Their results must be published after presentation to the shareholders at the *annual general meeting*. The distribution of profits in the form of dividends must also be approved by the shareholders at this meeting. In the United States similar companies are known as **public/stock corporations** and account for 90% of all turnover.

A **holding company** is formed for the special purpose of administering more than half of the share capital of one or more other companies, called **subsidiaries**. A firm operating a business of its own while holding more than half of the shares of a subsidiary company is the latter's **parent company**.

Increasing **globalisation** of business has led to the formation of big **multinational companies**, operating in many different countries. In order to benefit from the advantages offered by specific **locations**, such as access to foreign markets, availability of cheap labour, reduced transportation costs, government subsidies, softer regulations, tax advantages, cheaper energy or raw materials, and the like, major companies nowadays set up new companies in other countries or try to acquire existing companies. They do so either by means of **mergers**, with both companies forming a new entity, or by means of **take-overs**, where the stronger company takes control of the other one, which stands to lose much of its identity. If a take-over is attempted against the wish of the board of directors and/or some of the shareholders of the company targeted, this is known as a hostile or unsolicited take-over bid.

■ Study the text above and then select the correct legal designation of the businesses described below from the box.

- general partnership
- limited partnership
- parent company
- private limited company
- public limited company
- sole trader
- subsidiary

- Lucy Steele often disagrees with her boss at a software house. She decides to set up a business of her own, specialising in designing websites for small businesses. She will be a ❶.

- Every year Cumbria Steel organises a meeting for its thousands of owners at the Convention Centre in Cardiff. On this occasion the chairman of its board of directors makes a speech, presenting the annual report. Cumbria Steel is a ❷.

- James Mainwaring, a solicitor, and Catherine Vernon, a tax consultant, wish to offer their services jointly to corporate customers. They may form a ❸.

- 40 years ago John Thorpe founded a business manufacturing optical instruments. Thanks to his skills, energy and good fortune the firm became a market leader in the UK. After he died, however, his two sons and three daughters had no inclination to run the firm nor to assume any liability for it. They appointed the chief engineer and the chief accountant as managing directors and transformed the firm into a ❹.

- Mrs Musgrove and Mr Benwick have been running an interior decorating firm that has just gone bankrupt. They will have to sell their houses and cars to satisfy the creditors, whereas the other partners in this firm, Mr Wentworth and Mr Croft, will only lose the money they invested in the firm. This firm is a ❺.

- Wheeling Industries have finally managed to acquire 51 per cent of the shares in Hyflyer plc. Wheeling Industries is Hyflyer's ❻ and Hyflyer plc is Wheeling Industries' ❼.

Lucy Steele
Innovative Websites

J. Thorpe Ltd.
Optical Instruments

Cumbria Steel plc
Cumbria House

D 2 Organisation of companies

The larger a company is the more complex its organisation tends to be. The scope of an individual employee's responsibilities will likewise be smaller and his or her duties be more specialised in a large company than in a small one. Typically, a major company may be organised like this:

Board of Directors Chief Executive Officer (Chairman or Managing Director or President) Directors (Vice-Presidents)														
Company Secretary														
Administration & Finance					Purchasing			Sales				Production		
Accounting	Personnel	Controlling	Legal Matters		Ordering	Delivery Control	Storage	Domestic Sales	Foreign Sales	Marketing	Shipping	Research & Development	Production Planning	Production

D 3 Titles in British and US companies

Titles in British and US companies can be rather puzzling, with increasing globalisation only adding to the confusion. Some knowledge of the legal structure of companies helps to find the German equivalents. The following table merely shows a few generally accepted equivalents.

🇩🇪	🇬🇧	🇺🇸
Aktiengesellschaft	**Public Limited Company (Plc)**	**Stock Corporation (Inc. or Corp.)**
Vorstandsvorsitzender	Chief Executive Officer, Chairman of the Board of Directors	Chief Executive Officer, President
Kaufmännischer Vorstand	Commercial Director	Senior Executive Vice-President Administration
Exportleiter	Export Manager, Head of the Export Department	Export Director
GmbH	**Private Limited Company (Ltd)**	**Closed Corporation**
Geschäftsführer	(Managing) Director	General Manager, Managing Director
Vorsitzender der Geschäftsführung	Chairman of the Board of Directors	Chief Executive Officer (CEO), President
Gesellschafter	Shareholder, Member	Stockholder

34 Unit 2 · Background information

E IHK-Prüfungsvorbereitung

1. Zusatzqualifikation Englisch für kaufmännische Auszubildende Fremdsprache im Beruf I

Geschäftsbrief nach Stichwortangaben (Bearbeitungszeit 45 Minuten)	Hilfsmittel: zweisprachiges Wörterbuch

Situation

Sie sind Auszubildende/r bei der Firma Zischfrisch, Waldweg 8, 73033 Göppingen, die Designergetränke für junge Leute importiert und vertreibt. Frau Kathrin Zab, die Leiterin der Importabteilung Ihrer Firma, hat Ihnen einen Ausschnitt aus einem englischsprachigen Zeitungsartikel über die neuen Produkte der kanadischen Firma Clearly Canadian Beverages, 1700 Water St., Victoria, British Columbia N8C R356, Canada, vorgelegt.

TODAY'S TEENAGERS HAVE fallen in love with lava lamps, those kitschy 1960s artifacts that featured floating lumps. So it's not surprising that the Clearly Canadian company has launched a line of soft drinks that bring the lamps to mind. The noncarbonated fruit-flavored beverages, called Orbitz, contain brightly colored jelly balls that can be sipped through a straw.

Aufgabe

Verfassen Sie für Frau Zab, die den Brief selbst unterschreiben wird, ein Schreiben an Clearly Canadian Beverages.

- Stellen Sie Ihre Firma kurz vor.
- Sie interessieren sich für Orbitz, das neue alkoholfreie Designergetränk.
- In Deutschland ist ein schnell wachsender Markt vorhanden.
- Sie möchten ein Angebot mit Preislisten und Angaben über Mengenrabatte, Lieferbedingungen, Lieferzeiten usw. erhalten.
- Sie würden zunächst nur einen Probeauftrag erteilen.
- Wenn das Produkt einschlägt, würden Sie größere Mengen bestellen.
- Sie hoffen, dass eine gute Geschäftsbeziehung zustande kommt.

Verfassen Sie einen unterschriftsfertigen Brief mit Absenderadresse, Anschrift, Datum, Betreff, Grußformel, Name der Firma und Position des Unterzeichnenden. Der Brief sollte in der äußeren Form englischen bzw. amerikanischen Gepflogenheiten entsprechen.

2. Fremdsprachenkorrespondent/in

Übersetzung Englisch/Deutsch (Bearbeitungszeit 60 Minuten)	Hilfsmittel: zweisprachige Wörterbücher

The struggling retailing giant Global Stores has now presented its new logo and new carrier bags in matching shades of green. It is also promising to adopt a more informal approach towards its customers. GS claims that from now on their "vision is to be the most trusted retailer, wherever we trade, by delivering leading standards of product, service and behaviour to our customers ..."

Until recently GS saw itself as a business managing a chain of stores rather than managing one of the most powerful brands in the UK, possibly in the world. This brand needs to be carefully developed and adapted to changing markets. First and foremost GS needs to ask itself whether it has got its stores in the right place with the right merchandise at the right time. GS won't be changed simply by re-designing a bag or the look of some packaging.

It is in the highly competitive field of fashion that GS is experiencing the greatest difficulties. It plans to drop the Manor House brand which is hardly associated with a cool, fashionable lifestyle and launch a more exciting range. It will not be easy to regain lost ground and compete with both the successful chains and the new e-commerce companies.

3. | **Fremdsprachenkorrespondent/in**

Beantwortung einer Korrespondenz
(Bearbeitungszeit 60 Minuten)

Hilfsmittel:
zweisprachige Wörterbücher

Elton Business Accessories Ltd.

17 Highbury Road
Duffield, Derbyshire DE55 9BR
Tel. 01773 836100
Fax 01773 836200

12 September 200_

Ms Michaela Fetzer
Importex
Modegasse 6
94034 Passau
Germany

Dear Ms Fetzer

In the new millennium business life is as pressurised and fast-moving as ever. It is reassuring to know, therefore, that Elton Diaries can help you – or your friends and customers – to stay organised and composed.

Elton Business Diaries are known to meet the highest standards of craftsmanship and have been styled by leading British designers. It goes without saying that we only use genuine leather for our products. On request all items are supplied either with your initials or your full name.

We offer two collections of diaries to meet different business needs:
- the Global Collection has been developed for the international business traveller and includes a range of sturdy, flexible, light-weight wallet diaries.
- the Traditional Collection comprises a selection of classical, functional desk diaries for quick reference in day-to-day business

Both collections are shown in the leaflet enclosed.

We expect that our diaries will be very much in demand. I would therefore urge you to place your order as soon as possible to guarantee early delivery and avoid disappointment. Simply complete and fax or post the enclosed order form, along with your credit card details. Please indicate if you wish to personalise your order with initials or names.

We look forward to welcoming you as a customer.

Yours sincerely

Augusta Hawkins

Augusta Hawkins
Sales Director

Enc.

Situation

Sie arbeiten bei dem Textilhandelshaus Importex., Fax +49 851 370312, Ihre Chefin, Frau Fetzer, hat Ihnen das Werbeschreiben links zusammen mit der handschriftlichen Notiz unten zur Bearbeitung auf den Schreibtisch gelegt.

Aufgabe

> Bitte eine Fax-Anfrage für mich zur Unterschrift
> - etwas Britisches scheint interessant als Aufmerksamkeit zu Weihnachten
> - auch andere Farben? Welches Leder? Musterexemplar erbitten
> - Kalender müssen in Deutsch sein
> - Preise für 100, 500 Stück?
> - Zahlungsbedingungen für solche Mengen?
> - Lieferzeit? Lieferbedingung?
>
> Fetzer

4.	**Fremdsprachenkorrespondent/in**	
	Zusammenfassung (in Deutsch) einer englischen mündlichen Nachricht (Bearbeitungszeit 30 Minuten)	**Hilfsmittel:** zweisprachige Wörterbücher

Situation

Während der Hannover-Messe wohnen Sie in einer Pension. Die Inhaberin, Frau Schulte, hat eine Nachricht in Englisch auf ihrem Anrufbeantworter vorgefunden, die sie nicht ganz versteht. Sie bittet Sie um Hilfe.

Aufgabe

Fassen Sie die Nachricht für Frau Schulte schriftlich zusammen. Sie werden sie zweimal hören.

Unit 3 Offers

Introduction

■ Read this information and complete the text using words from the box.

> time * cater * reply
> specific * following
> relevant * stopgap * wholesaler

Answering the incoming mail is an important part of handling a company's correspondence. Therefore, the ability to write an appropriate reply to an enquiry is an important skill.

All enquiries should be answered, even those that, for some reason, cannot be responded to in full. An enquiry indicates interest in your business, and a personal, well-worded reply can be the beginning of a lasting business relationship.

A reply should begin by thanking the enquirer for his/her interest in your business. Like an enquiry, a reply should be ❶ and *complete*. It should inform the prospective customer about your product line or services and terms. Needless to say, you must *never make a promise you cannot keep*. In other words, it is far better to *underpromise* and *overdeliver*.

Also, it is essential to answer an enquiry promptly. A prompt reply lets your prospective customer know that you are interested in doing business with him/her and that you want to be *helpful*. In fact, a good ❷ not only answers all questions, but often goes further than the original enquiry. This extra step can turn an interested person into a regular customer.

If, for some reason, you cannot provide all the ❸ information right away, *do not delay your reply until all the information is available*. In such cases, send a so-called stopgap letter that lets the prospective customer know that his/her request has not been ignored and will be handled as soon as possible. A ❹ letter informs the reader that some time is needed to process the enquiry thoroughly.

If you cannot provide the information or service at all, you should explain this in your letter. For example, a manufacturer or ❺ may receive an order from an individual that cannot be fulfilled. In this case, the reply must tactfully explain the reasons for refusing the request and, ideally, refer the customer to a retail business which can ❻ to his/her needs.

When submitting a quotation you should always – at least indirectly, for example by referring to a catalogue or price list – mention the ❼ essentials:

- nature and quality of the product
- quantity
- price(s) and possible discount(s)
- terms of delivery
- terms of payment
- delivery ❽
- validity of the offer, if applicable.

Always remember that you are writing to a very important person: your customer. Whenever possible personalise the salutation by using a proper name. Do not forget to take the opportunity to say something positive about your firm and/or your products. Finish off your communication by some phrase creating good will, i.e. making the customer feel positive towards your firm.

A Activities

A1 Making arrangements

→ 17 a Listen to the telephone conversation between Mr Purcell and Mrs Strand and correct these notes.

> Tuesday, 16 December 200_
> Push House, 70 Derby Street
> Contact person Simon Purcell, Wanstead
> wine tasting at British Food & Wine Society
> arrive at 7.00, preparation 45 minutes
> presentation 8.30 – 9.15

b We often use polite forms when we are making arrangements. Match the jumbled halves of these sentences.

1. Could I speak to
2. I'd like to
3. Would you
4. Would you mind if
5. Both dates
6. Which of the two
7. Do you think you could
8. We would be grateful if

a. be there at 9 a.m.?
b. I came a little later?
c. Mrs Strand, please?
d. speak to Mr Donnell.
e. prefer the 9th or the 14th?
f. would suit me perfectly.
g. would you prefer?
h. you could call on us on Monday.

→ 24 c Complete this fax on a separate sheet of paper.

COMPUTER CLINIC
12 Bedford Street   Pembroke SA62 6YE
Tel 01646 873894   Fax 01646 873894
www.compclinic.co.uk

FAX TRANSMISSION

from Will Duncan

To: Snoozers Ltd
Attn: Jo Wheeler
Subject: Appointment
Date: 12 Nov 200_
No. of pages: 1

Thank ❶ for ❷ interest ❸ company.

We could meet ❹ December 4 ❺ 10 a.m. ❻ discuss details and ❼ lunch ❽ wards. Please contact me ❾ there are any problems.

❿ forward to seeing you.

Will Duncan

Will Duncan

39 **d** First, study the telephone phrases on page 52.
Then work with a partner.

Partner A uses the information in Will Duncan's diary on page 42. **42**
Partner B uses Jo Wheeler's diary below. Study the diaries and
make a phone call to agree on a suitable date for an appointment.

Jo Wheeler's diary:

A 2 Offer by phone

17 **a** In Unit 1 there was an enquiry about custom travel arrangements.
A Kiwi travel representative calls back. Complete the dialogue on a
separate sheet of paper.

A: Hello.
B: Hello. Could I ❶ to Mr Woodford, please.
A: Who's ❷ , please?
B: Helen Johnson from Kiwi Travel.
A: One moment, I'll ❸ Grandpa.
C: Simon Woodford here.
B: Good morning, Mr Woodford. ❹ Helen Johnson from Kiwi Travel. I'm calling about your travel plans.
C: ❺.

B: I'm sorry, but we ❻ individual trips. I'm afraid we can't help you.
C: Oh, that's a pity. Do you ❼ any other agent that does individual tours?
B: Well, I think your best bet would be LeisureCorp. They're in Limavady and their number is 05047 22016. Ask for Amanda Jones. She really knows a lot about Asia.
C: LeisureCorp, Limavady, 05047 22016. Thanks a lot. Goodbye.
B: ❽.

 b Listen to the conversation to check your work in a.

 c You work in the purchasing department of a chain of retailers in Germany selling electronic equipment. You receive the following offer by telephone.

Listen to the conversation and make a note of the main points in German for Bodo Westhoff, the purchasing manager.

A 3 Offer by letter

31 a Read this letter and say which of the words in brackets are correct.

Delta Games
1 Infinite Loop · Cupertino CA 94086
Tel. (0210) 52 22 61 00 · Fax (0210) 6 80 57 63
e-mail: d-games@picnet.com

July 15, 200_

GAMETOYS
Glückstrasse 57
93449 Spielberg
Germany

Dear Mrs. Spielvogel:

Your inquiry (❶ from / dated) July 7, 200_

Thank you for your interest in our table top games. Over the last 15 years we have developed a wide range of fascinating games for every age group. And – what is even more important – our customers get regular updates for our games (❷ at / to) very reduced prices.

For more details on our range of products please refer to the enclosed (❸ prospect / catalogue) and export price list. Our prices are quoted EXW, including export packing. We offer a special 5 percent discount on the list prices. Normally, we require two weeks for delivery. We always do business on the (❹ basis / base) of cash against documents.

We have recently launched a new strategy game, called "Hit and Run", which has become an instant success in the US. We are sending you a sample kit (❺ by / with) separate mail. Test the game and you will be fascinated.

Should you need any further information please contact us at (❻ any / some) time.

We look forward to (❼ receive / receiving) your order which we will carry out promptly and carefully.

Sincerely,
Delta Games

Joe T. Wallis

Joe T. Wallis
Export Manager

Enc.

b In Unit 2 (page 22), Kate Paxton spoke to Hyflyer's sales representative Rob Sullivan. ➡ 22

Take Rob Sullivan's role, go back and check your notes.
In addition, you quote a 10 per cent discount for orders over 200 units.
Choose appropriate phrases from those given below and write a reply to Kate Paxton using the following letter structure:

Dear Kate,

Dear Ms Baxter,

Dear Ms Paxton,

Enclosed are a leaflet about the DX-2000 and a price list.

For orders over 200 we can quote a 10 per cent discount.

Kind regards,

Please reply soon.

We enclose our brochure detailing the entire Hyflyer range and our current price list.

We look forward to hearing from you.

Thank you for your letter of 12 November 200_ , in which you enquired about the Hyflyer.

Thank you for your interest in our new Hyflyer 2000 range.

Yours faithfully,

Yours sincerely,

Letter structure:

HYFLYER plc
438 Weltmore Industrial Park   Warwick CV43 6TS
Tel: 01926 439523   Fax: 01926 451427

recipient
recipient's address
                                                                date
salutation
subject
opening
body
ending
complimentary close
signature
sender's name and job title
enclosures

➡ 39 Will Duncan's diary (see page 40):
➡ 40

DECEMBER 3

10.00 Beaconhead
       maintenance
       (approx. 2 hrs)

14.00 Terrell Ent.
       network install
       w/ Alison
       (poss. 4 hrs?)

DECEMBER 4

10.00 Jo Wheeler
       remote access system
       most interesting!!!
12.00 lunch at Marine Hotel
       (table reservation)

14.00 Dr Turner
15.00 Ms Cameron (Necson)

17.00 Derek MacAdam

DECEMBER 5

09.30 Apricot rep
       (new Ethernet specs)
11.00 Roy Green
12.00 lunch w/ Roy

17.00 meeting w/ Larry & Steve

A4 Offer by e-mail

a When Will Duncan, the proprietor of ComputerClinic, checked his e-mail messages the next morning, there was this reply from DigiCorp K.K (see his enquiry on page 24).

➜ 24

Read the reply.

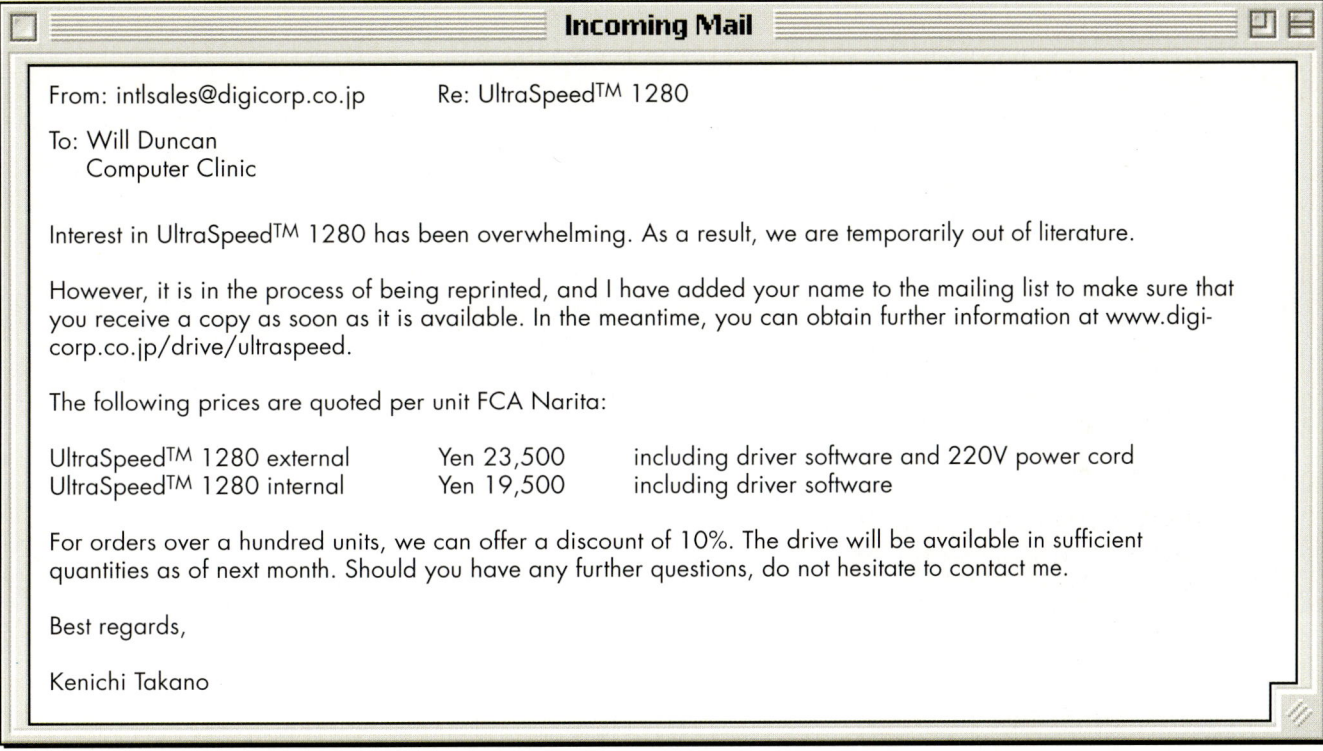

From: intlsales@digicorp.co.jp   Re: UltraSpeed™ 1280

To: Will Duncan
    Computer Clinic

Interest in UltraSpeed™ 1280 has been overwhelming. As a result, we are temporarily out of literature.

However, it is in the process of being reprinted, and I have added your name to the mailing list to make sure that you receive a copy as soon as it is available. In the meantime, you can obtain further information at www.digi-corp.co.jp/drive/ultraspeed.

The following prices are quoted per unit FCA Narita:

UltraSpeed™ 1280 external   Yen 23,500   including driver software and 220V power cord
UltraSpeed™ 1280 internal   Yen 19,500   including driver software

For orders over a hundred units, we can offer a discount of 10%. The drive will be available in sufficient quantities as of next month. Should you have any further questions, do not hesitate to contact me.

Best regards,

Kenichi Takano

b Now say whether these statements are true or false.

1. Customers have shown much more interest in the drive than DigiCorp had anticipated.
2. A completely revised brochure is being prepared and will be available shortly.
3. If Will Duncan wants to know more about UltraSpeed, he can visit DigiCorp's website.
4. The prices quoted by DigiCorp include packaging and delivery to Will Duncan's doorstep.
5. If Computer Clinic orders 50 units next month, they will qualify for a 10% discount.
6. If Will Duncan wants to know more, he can contact Kenichi Takano at intlsales@digicorp.co.uk.

A5 Offer by fax

a First study the Hotel Europe price list. Then listen to the conversation between George King, the Front Office Manager, and Diane Cooper, a trainee. Next, read the fax, find two major errors and correct them.

➡ 28

PRICES	Oct 1 – Mar 31	Apr 1 – Sep 30
Single	£ 69.00	£ 79.00
Single with business facilities	£ 99.00	£ 99.00
Double	£ 89.00	£ 109.00
Triple	£ 119.00	£ 139.00
Executive suite	£ 289.00	£ 319.00

HOTEL EUROPE

FAX TRANSMISSION

To: Elsa Yates
0381 - 49290

From: Diane Cooper

Date: 25 November 200_

Pages (incl. this one): 1

Thank you for your fax this morning.

We have pleasure in confirming your reservation of a single room with business facilities for Ms Wheeler from Sunday 2 December to Tuesday 5 December.

The current price is £69.00 per night, incl. VAT.

If you have any further queries, do not hesitate to contact me.

We look forward to Ms Wheeler's visit.

Kind regards,

Diane Cooper

b Listen to the telephone conversation and take notes. Then use the price list of Hotel Europe and send a fax to confirm the reservation.

B Tool kit

B 1 Effective business correspondence

Writing effective letters, e-mails, faxes and memos is one of the most valued skills in business.

Before you start writing consider who is going to read your correspondence and what **tone** is most appropriate for the message you wish to send. Choose the tone carefully to achieve the desired effect, i.e. a response or action on the part of the recipient. An e-mail sent to a close business associate may be friendly and informal, a letter to an unreliable supplier could be coldly polite and urgent, to mention but a few of many possible tones. It is, however, always unbusinesslike to be rude, impolite, sarcastic or overbearing in business communication. Sexist language should likewise be avoided. For instance, instead of saying "he" when the gender of the person in the sentence is not known the pronoun "he/she" is now often used. Writers who find this awkward put the sentence into the plural and use "they" instead.

Business correspondence must be well organised. The body of the correspondence must be divided into three **essential parts**: the beginning, the middle (main part) and the end.

The **beginning** is either a single sentence or a short paragraph that states the reason why you are writing the letter. For example:

> We wish to inform you that there has been a delay in the shipment of the MF2GD Spray Dryer.

The **middle** contains the details. If two topics are to be discussed, there should be two paragraphs. The first sentence of each new paragraph should introduce a new idea; the final sentence should indicate that the topic is finished. For example:

> According to the terms of the contract the spray dryer was to be delivered no later than 20 Aug 200_. However, there has been no delivery as yet. If there is a reason for the delay, please let us know. We would also like to know if there is a revised delivery date.
>
> If we incur damages due to further delay in delivering the spray dryer, we will advise you of them. We likewise wish to remind you of the penalty clause of $500.00 per day for failure to deliver on time.

The **end** section is a summing up that confirms the expectations of the writer towards the recipient. For example:

> Please let us have your reactions as soon as possible in this matter.

The end is, however, also frequently used to create good will towards the sender in the recipient of the correspondence. For example:

> We look forward to doing business with you and feel sure that you will be satisfied with our services.

Business correspondence is often made up of standard phrases.
For smooth reading of the correspondence such individual building blocks ought to be connected by **linking words** like both … and, as well as, in addition, moreover, further, firstly, secondly, finally etc. which suggest a list:

> We should like to order both model Y2K and Y2Ki.
> Finally, (after listing a number of other points) we should like to confirm the dates for next year's gala fashion show.

Other linking words imply a contrast: whereas, while, in contrast to, although etc.

> Software sales have been very buoyant recently, whereas (or while) hardware sales have been sluggish.

The following linking words indicate that an explanation is being given: that is why, therefore, thus, as, because etc.

> We have recently been dissatisfied with the level of service you have provided. This is why we have decided to instruct a different company.

In many German firms a number of stuffy, outmoded phrases are still being used in English correspondence. Try to replace them by simple **modern language** to convey the image of an efficient modern company.

Old-fashioned	Modern
Please be informed that …	We are pleased to inform you …
Please find enclosed …	We are pleased to enclose … / We are enclosing …
As per your request …	As requested …
We are in receipt of …	We have received …
Thanking you in advance we remain …	Thank you for your assistance.

Some of Germans' favourite phrases for business letters are incorrect, for example "We kindly ask you to …" must be replaced by "We would like to ask you to …" or by "Please be so kind as to …". The phrase "We like to ask you to …" is also definitely wrong; it should be "We would like to ask you to …".

Once you have completed the correspondence, revise it carefully. The **revision** should result in an e-mail, letter, fax, report or memo that uses simple, concise language to convey a clear message. The checklist on the right will help you:

Finally, don't mail your correspondence in haste. The very ease of responding to an e-mail, in particular, may tempt you to make a rash and ill-considered reply which you might later regret.

CHECKLIST: Business correspondence

- What will be the effect of this correspondence on the reader and, indirectly, on my company?
- Are date, name, address, reference numbers etc. correct?
- Is there a subject line, if necessary?
- Is the salutation in keeping with the type, tone and level of formality of the correspondence?
- Is there an introductory sentence or paragraph?
- Does the main part consist of separate paragraphs for different ideas?
- Does the ending consist of a separate sentence or paragraph?
- Is the complimentary close in line with the salutation?
- Is there a reference "Encl." if something is enclosed?

B 2 Structure of business communications: Replies to enquiries, detailed offers

Offers and replies to enquiries should be structured like this:

Structure	Language to use
1. personal salutation	Dear Ms Woodhouse
2. thanks for the enquiry	Thank you for your letter **of** …
3. reference to enclosed information	We are enclosing our catalogue and price list.
4. description of goods or services	We are pleased to quote as follows: 25 high-speed air filters LF7

46 Unit 3 · Tool kit

5. prices (unit and total) and discounts	... **at** a price of DM 205.00 per unit, less 2% introductory discount.
6. terms of delivery	Our prices are quoted EXW Schwerin.
7. terms of payment	Our terms of payment are 30 days net, 10 days 2%.
8. delivery period	Delivery can be effected two weeks after receipt of order.
9. additional information, if necessary	Please note that our prices include VAT.
10. validity of the offer, if applicable	This offer is firm **until** March 15.
11. request for references, if applicable	Please furnish the usual references.
12. further action, if required (visit by agent, demonstration, presentation)	If you wish we can arrange a convenient date for a product demonstration on your premises.
13. goodwill phrase	We look forward to doing business with you.
14. appropriate complimentary close	Yours sincerely
15. enclosure, if applicable	Encs. catalogue, price list

■ What is the purpose of these sentences?
 Find the appropriate numbers in *structure of business communications* above.

1. If you need any further information, please let me know.
2. Dear Mr MacIntyre,
3. Thank you very much for your letter of ... enquiring about ...
4. Our prices include VAT and delivery.
5. Please note that all our products come with an extended warranty.
6. We look forward to hearing from you.
7. Thank you for your letter of ..., in which you enquired about ...
8. Yours sincerely,
9. We have pleasure in sending you our latest brochure about ...
10. Please do not hesitate to contact us if ...
11. We would like to suggest that Ms Anne Morgan, our area representative, should visit you to demonstrate the exceptional quality of our machines.
12. If you have any further questions, we will be pleased to assist you.

B 3 Building blocks for business communications: Replies to enquiries / Making offers

1 To say thank you for an enquiry

Many thanks Thank you	for	your enquiry of 2 October **about** our new range of ... your interest in our products.

We were pleased to hear that you	are interested **in** our ... like our new range of ... were impressed **with** our ...

2 To introduce an unsolicited offer

| The Bristol Chamber of Commerce has been
The Canadian Consulate in Stuttgart has been
Ferrars and Brandon Ltd. have been | so kind **as** to give us your address. |

| May we draw your attention **to** our special offer **for** … |

3 To refer to enclosures or things you are going to send by separate mail

| Enclosed you will find
As requested, we enclose
By separate mail,
　we are sending you | our latest catalogue and price list | for …
quoting prices CIF … |

4 To make an offer

| We are pleased to quote as follows: … |

| We would now like to | give you
enclose
submit | our cost estimate. |

| We take pleasure **in** | submitting
enclosing
making | the following quotation: … |

| **Essential points for an offer:**
Explicitly or implicitly, e.g. by referring to a price list or to previous business, your offer should contain information on the following points:
1　description of the goods/services offered, e.g. article No.
2　quantity
3　prices and discounts
4　terms of delivery
5　terms of payment
6　delivery period
7　validity of the offer |

5 To state your terms of delivery and payment

| Our prices are | quoted

to be understood | EXW Chemnitz.
FOB Rotterdam.
FCA Düsseldorf Airport.
CIF Singapore.
DDU Birmingham. |

| We do business on the basis of payment **by** | sight draft
irrevocable (and confirmed) documentary letter
　of credit **in** our favour, payable **at** … bank. |

48　Unit 3　·　Tool kit

Our usual terms of payment are	cash **with** order. ¹/₃ **with** order, ¹/₃ **on** delivery, ¹/₃ 1 month **after** delivery. cash **against** documents. documents **against** acceptance. 30 days net, 10 days 2%. strictly net **by** the 15th of the month following the month of delivery.
We would request payment by	banker's draft. cheque. bank transfer to our account **with** ... Bank.
Regular customers are granted open account terms.	

6 To refer to the delivery time

Delivery Shipment	can be effected will be made	immediately **on** receipt of order. ex stock. two to three weeks **after** receipt of order.
The delivery period is 6 weeks.		

7 To inform the customer how long the offer is valid

This Our	offer is	valid **until** 7 March. firm **until** the end of the month. subject **to** confirmation. without engagement.
Prices are subject **to** change without notice.		
The offer is subject to prior sale.		

8 To answer specific questions or give additional information

We can	quote offer	a 10% quantity discount **for** orders over 5,000 units. a 15% trade discount **on/off** our list prices. 2% cash discount for payment **within** 10 days. 5% introductory discount.
Please note that		our products come with a three-year warranty. our prices include free set-up and on-site service in the first year.
The	goods articles machinery	will be	packed	**in** cardboard boxes. **in** sturdy wooden crates. **in** styrofoam-padded cases. **in** seaworthy containers.
			transported shipped sent	**by** air (freight). **by** sea, **by** vessel. **by** road, **by** rail.

9 To apologize and explain why you cannot fulfil a request

Unfortunately We are sorry that We regret that	we are unable to supply the article you require	since because as	production has been discontinued.
	the product is temporarily out of stock		demand has been overwhelming.
	we are unable to sell to private customers		we are wholesalers only.

Much to our regret we are not in a position to make you an offer	as we no longer carry this article. because we only sell **through** our agents. since we are unable to execute the work **within** the time stipulated in your enquiry.
Please contact one of our agents in your country, a list of whom is enclosed.	
We would suggest **that** you contact …, who will be able to assist you in this case.	

10 To suggest further contact and encourage further questions

If you wish, we could arrange for	a product presentation on your premises. a visit by our Regional Sales Manager.

Please do not hesitate to	contact us call	if	you have any further questions. you require any further information.

Should If	you have any further queries,	please contact us **on** 789 5356 between 9 a.m. and 5 p.m. our staff will be pleased to assist you **at** any time.

11 To create goodwill

We hope this quotation will	come **up to** your expectations. find your approval. meet your requirements.

We look forward **to**	hearing from you soon. receiving your (trial) order. welcoming you as our customer(s).

We assure you that your order You may rest assured that any order placed	will be	executed dealt **with**	promptly and carefully.

■ Use these building blocks to find equivalents for the following German sentences.

1. Wir freuen uns zu hören, dass Sie an unserer neuen Sommerkollektion interessiert sind.
2. Als Anlage erhalten Sie unseren neuesten Katalog über Brettspiele und unsere Preisliste.
3. Bei Bestellungen von mehr als 500 Stück gewähren wir 10% Mengenrabatt.
4. Unsere Zahlungsbedingungen lauten: 30 Tage netto, 10 Tage 2%.

5. Unsere Preise verstehen sich FCA Flughafen München.
6. Zahlung durch unwiderrufliches und bestätigtes Dokumentenakkreditiv zu unseren Gunsten, zahlbar bei der Handels- und Kreditbank Cottbus.
7. Wir danken Ihnen für Ihre Anfrage bezüglich Luftfiltern.
8. Die Lieferung kann sofort nach Auftragseingang erfolgen.
9. Wir freuen uns Ihnen mitteilen zu können, dass sämtliche Artikel vorrätig sind.
10. Wir bedauern, dass wir das Modell X4 nicht mehr liefern können, weil die Produktion eingestellt wurde.
11. Dieses Angebot ist freibleibend.
12. Für weitere Auskünfte steht Ihnen Frau Streicher, Apparat 345, zur Verfügung.
13. Wir freuen uns Ihnen nachstehendes Angebot unterbreiten zu können.
14. Unsere Lieferzeit beträgt vier bis fünf Wochen.
15. Wir würden uns freuen, einen Probeauftrag von Ihnen zu erhalten.
16. Wir bitten um Zahlung durch Banküberweisung.
17. Wenn Sie es wünschen, können wir einen Besuch unseres Vertreters veranlassen.
18. Wir versichern Ihnen, dass Ihr Auftrag mit der größten Sorgfalt ausgeführt wird.
19. Um die Einführung unserer Software auf dem australischen Markt zu erleichtern, gewähren wir 10% Einführungsrabatt auf unsere Listenpreise.
20. Die gewünschten Muster gehen Ihnen mit getrennter Post zu.

B 4 Dictation

When someone dictates a text they have to provide additional information so that it can be typed correctly. Here are the most important words and phrases for dictating.

Please take a dictation.
Address it to …
(Spell the name and the address of the recipient if you are not sure that the secretary can type it correctly.)
Put today's date and our reference …

In the dictation, also tell the secretary where to put the punctuation marks and where to begin a new paragraph.

Dear M … – comma, new paragraph.
Thank you for your enquiry of 3 October – full stop, new paragraph.

Also indicate a word that begins with a capital letter or is entirely in CAPITAL LETTERS.

Europe – capital E
POWERCOMP – in capital letters

Before you finish, give instructions for the signature, name and job title and other relevant items.

Yours sincerely – comma, new paragraph – my name and job title.
Mention the enclosure(s).

Remember the most important punctuation marks:

.	full stop	*Punkt*
,	comma	*Komma*
;	semi-colon	*Strichpunkt*
:	colon	*Doppelpunkt*
!	exclamation mark	*Ausrufezeichen*
?	question mark	*Fragezeichen*
'	apostrophe	*Apostroph*
/	slash	*Schrägstrich*
-	hyphen	*Bindestrich*
–	dash	*Gedankenstrich*
(…)	in brackets	*in Klammern*
[ ]	square brackets	*eckige Klammern*
(	open bracket	*Klammer auf*
)	close bracket	*Klammer zu*
"…"	quotation marks (inverted commas)	*Anführungszeichen*
"…	quote	*Anführungszeichen vorne*
…"	unquote	*Anführungszeichen hinten*
	space	*Leerzeichen*

B 5 Telephone phrases: Making appointments

Good morning / afternoon.
 I'd like to speak to …

~ Speaking.

Oh, good. This is … I'm calling from …

~ Oh, yes, Mr/Ms … What can I do for you?

Well, it's about our appointment on …
 The thing is, I'll be busy all day. Would it be alright with you if I came on … at …

~ Let me see … No, I'm afraid I'll be away on the … How about the …?

Uhmm, …, you said. Yes, I could make it after … Is that convenient for you?

~ Yes, that'll suit me fine. Now, shall we say 1:30?

Certainly, yes. That's fine.
 So that's at 1:30 on …

~ You know how to get to our shop, don't you?

Yes, I'll take a taxi anyway.

~ Fine, I'll see you soon, then.

Goodbye.

Goodbye, Mr/Ms …

C Additional practice

a Unlimited Horizons Ltd has just received the coupon on the right.

Write a reply thanking the customer for his interest in Garmisch and mention that you are enclosing a 36-page colour brochure and a list of participating travel agents, who could book Mr McAdam's holiday.

»It's cool, it's great – it's Garmisch«

Post to:
Unlimited Horizons Ltd,
35 Great Ormond Street, London WC3 2OL

Name: Walter McAdam
Address: Fairways Lodge
Fairways, Tobermory
Isle of Mull
Postcode: DA75 6DS

b Complete this letter using words from the box.

Dear Ms Owen,
Requests for our new table-top games catalogue have been overwhelming and ❶, we are ❷ out of copies.
❸, the catalogue is being reprinted, ❹ we have added your name to our mailing list to make sure that you receive a copy ❺ it is available.
❻, you may refer to the enclosed list for pricing. ❼ you need further details of the games on offer, please visit our Website at www.deltagames.com.
Yours sincerely,

in the meantime
if
however
and
as a result
as soon as
currently

c   Restore the correct order of these elements and rewrite the letter on a blank piece of paper.

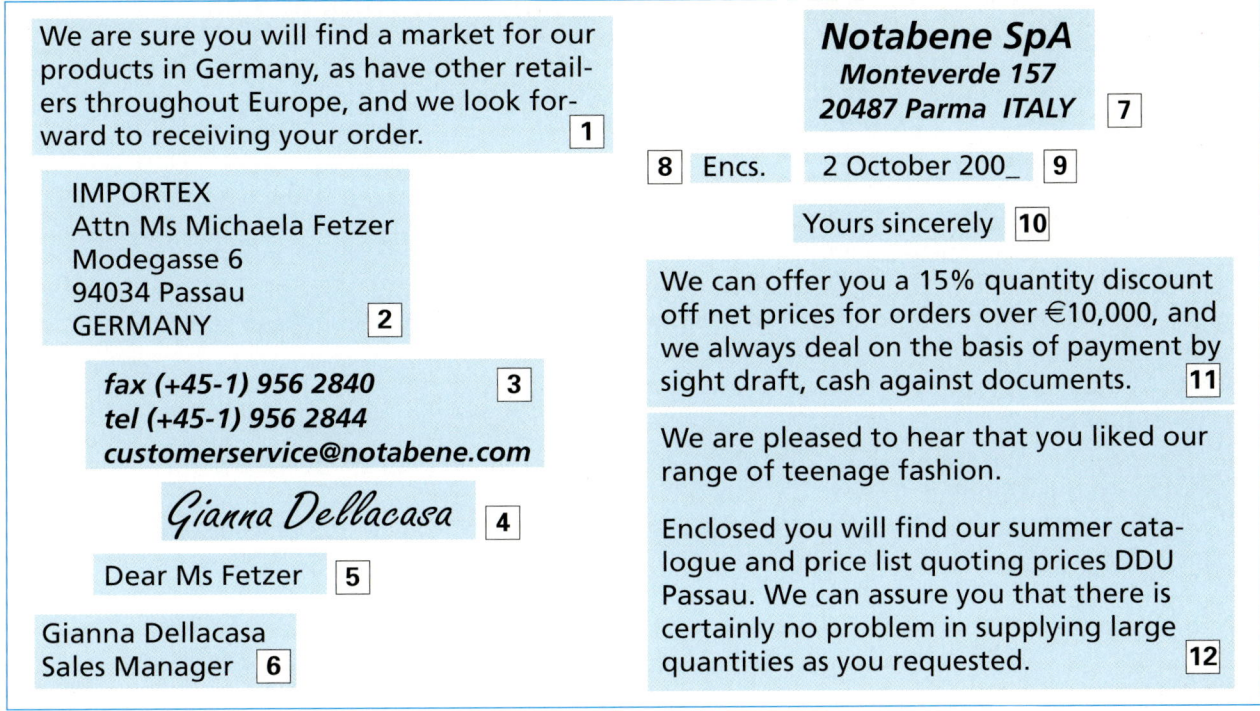

D Background information

D 1 Pricing policy

In many fields of business it is advisable to grant **discounts** off the list prices in order to attract or retain customers. The most common forms of discounts are:

- **trade discounts**, granted to retailers and intermediaries;
- **introductory discounts**, granted with a view to facilitating the introduction of a new product on the market;
- **cash discounts**, granted for payment within a short period, e.g. under the following terms of payment: 10 days 2 per cent, 30 days net;
- **quantity discounts**, granted for large orders. Offering **staggered prices** may serve the same purpose as granting quantity discounts.

Rebates differ from discounts in that they may be granted by suppliers to volume buyers or loyal customers (in this case they are called fidelity discounts) after the order has been executed, for example at the end of the year. Subsequent price reductions must sometimes be granted to settle justified complaints about the goods or services.

D 2 Risks in foreign trade

An exporter must carefully choose the appropriate terms of sale so as to avoid as far as possible the risks inherent in foreign trade. Major risks are:

- the customer might refuse to accept the goods. As a result the supplier would not make any profit and would even incur losses through extra costs, e.g. for the transportation of the goods back to his premises;
- the customer might refuse to pay the invoice amount or be unable to do so;
- fluctuations in the exchange rates of the exporter's own currency and the currency of the foreign country to which he is exporting might have a negative impact on profit margins or wipe out profits entirely. Financial provisions taken against such currency fluctuations are called hedging (see unit 10).

E IHK-Prüfungsvorbereitung

1. **Zusatzqualifikation Englisch für kaufmännische Auszubildende Fremdsprache im Beruf I***

Vermerk in Deutsch über ein englisches Telefongespräch (Bearbeitungszeit 20 Minuten)	Hilfsmittel: zweisprachiges Wörterbuch

Situation

Sie sind Anna Dell, Assistentin von Frau Schmale, der Leiterin des Einkaufs der Bekleidungskette *Große Mode*. Ihrer Chefin ist ein Prospekt des schottischen Herstellers von Strickwaren *Glencastle Woollens* in die Hände gefallen. Sie hat Sie gebeten, dort anzurufen.

Aufgabe

Fassen Sie den Inhalt Ihres Gesprächs für Frau Schmale in einer Gesprächsnotiz in Deutsch zusammen.
(Sie werden das Gespräch zweimal hören. Was Sie selbst sagen, haben Sie schriftlich vorliegen.)

A. Dell: Good morning. This is Anna Dell from Große Mode in Munich. We are a fashion retail chain with 24 shops all over Germany, specialising in large sizes.
...

A. Dell: We have a leaflet here showing some of your products and would like to have more information about your products and your firm.
...

A. Dell: That sounds very interesting. What precisely does your range of products include?
...

A. Dell: Große Mode, 25 Karlstraße, 89407 Munich. Have you got that?
...

A. Dell: Große Mode, 25 Karlstraße, 89407 Munich, Germany. Your leaflet says that you only use pure new wool. Do you manufacture cashmere garments as well?
...

A. Dell: Some of your competitors provide a guarantee of 12 months that covers faulty material or workmanship.
...

A. Dell: One last question. Have you got a distribution base in Germany?
...

A. Dell: Well, that seems to be all for the time being. We'll be waiting for your brochure and price list and you may then be hearing from us again Mr ... Sorry, what was your name?
...

A. Dell: Thank you very much. Goodbye.
...

* Die Bearbeitungszeit beträgt bei Fremdsprache im Beruf 30 Minuten, die Dialoge sind dementsprechend etwas länger.

2. Zusatzqualifikation Englisch für kaufmännische Auszubildende
Fremdsprache im Beruf I

Geschäftsbrief nach Stichwortangaben (Bearbeitungszeit 45 Minuten)	Hilfsmittel: zweisprachiges Wörterbuch

Situation

→ 30   Sie machen ein Praktikum in Großbritannien beim *Simple Trade Procedures Board (SITPRO)*, 151 Buckingham Palace Rd, London SW1 9SS, einer Institution, die Handbücher und Formulare für den Export herausbringt.
Pete O'Brien, Export Sales Manager von *Hyflyer plc*, 338 Weltmore Industrial Park, Warwick, CV43 6TS, hat SITPRO am 23. September 200_ eine Anfrage bezüglich der beiden Publikationen *New Export Guide* und *Top Form 2* geschickt. Heute ist der 25. September 200_.

Aufgabe

Bitte beantworten Sie diese Anfrage für Ihren Chef, Mr. John Dashwood, der den Brief auch unterschreiben wird, und berücksichtigen Sie dabei folgende Punkte:

- Dank für die Anfrage
- Beide Publikationen kosten je £20,-, einschließlich VAT, Porto und Verpackung
- Zahlung entweder per Kreditkarte oder per Scheck (zahlbar an SITPRO)
- Lieferung bei Zahlung mit Kreditkarte sofort, bei Zahlung per Scheck innerhalb einer Woche
- Standardformulare für den Export können auch bei den Vertragshändlern von SITPRO bestellt werden
- Liste der Vertragshändler in Großbritannien liegt bei
- Freundlicher Schlusssatz

3. Fremdsprachenkorrespondent/in

Geschäftsbrief nach Angaben in Deutsch (Bearbeitungszeit 45 Minuten)	Hilfsmittel: zweisprachige Wörterbücher

Situation

Sie arbeiten in der Exportabteilung der Firma Feinmechanik Krengel, Einsteinstr. 74, 70771 Leinfelden. Ihre Firma hat von Notabene SpA, Monteverde 157, 20487 Parma, eine Anfrage über zwei Prüfgeräte (test instruments) für Textilien erhalten. Heute ist der 13.06.200_

Aufgabe

Bitte unterbreiten Sie der italienischen Firma ein Angebot und berücksichtigen Sie dabei Folgendes:

- Bezug auf die von Gina Mastroiani unterschriebene Anfrage vom 08.06.200_
- Krengel-Prüfgeräte für Textilien aller Art geeignet, höchste Zuverlässigkeit
- Gegenstand des Angebots: Prüfgerät für Textilien, Art. No. T/Inst. 27
- Preis pro Stück: Euro 8700,-
- Lieferbedingungen: FCA Stuttgart Airport
- Zahlungsbedingungen: ein Drittel bei Auftragserteilung, ein Drittel bei Lieferung, ein Drittel 30 Tage nach Lieferung
- Lieferzeit: zwei Wochen nach Auftragseingang
- Lange Garantiezeit von zwei Jahren
- Für technische Fragen: Hotline des Kundendienstes in Italien (03 71) 42 61 38

4. Fremdsprachenkorrespondent/in

Zusammenfassung (in Deutsch) einer englischen mündlichen Nachricht (Bearbeitungszeit 30 Minuten)	Hilfsmittel: zweisprachige Wörterbücher

Situation

Sie sind Angestellte/r des Maklerbüros Immobilien-Maier-Darfeld. Herr Maier hat eine Nachricht in Englisch auf seinem Anrufbeantworter vorgefunden. Da er Englisch nicht sehr gut versteht, bittet er Sie, die Nachricht auf Deutsch zusammenzufassen.

Aufgabe

Fassen Sie die Nachricht in einem Vermerk für Herrn Maier schriftlich zusammen. (Sie werden die Nachricht zweimal hören.)

IMMOBILIEN MAIER-DARFELD

Telefonvermerk   Datum:

Für:

Verfasser:

Anrufer: Firma:

Betreff:

5. Fremdsprachenkorrespondent/in

Beantwortung einer englischen Korrespondenz nach Angaben in Deutsch (Bearbeitungszeit 60 Minuten)	Hilfsmittel: zweisprachige Wörterbücher

Situation

Sie sind Beate Kaiser und arbeiten bei einem Hamburger Handelshaus, das auf den Import und Export von Geschenkartikeln für den gehobenen Geschmack spezialisiert ist. Sie haben soeben die auf der nächsten Seite abgedruckte Anfrage per E-Mail erhalten.

Aufgabe

Bitte schicken Sie Mr. Elliot eine e-Mail in Beantwortung seiner Anfrage. Folgende Fakten sind dabei zu berücksichtigen:

- Sortiment gegenüber dem letzten Jahr leicht verändert: 1930er Aschenbecher nicht mehr im Angebot, Nachfrage dramatisch zurückgegangen
- Manschettenknöpfe und Ohrringe größer als früher
- Armbanduhr jetzt mit Armband aus echtem Leder
- Preise im Durchschnitt nur um 2% angehoben
- Angebot auf der Grundlage des neuen Katalogs und der gültigen Preisliste *(Auszug nachstehend)*

- Lieferung ab Lager möglich
- Mengenrabatte: ab 100 Stück 3%, ab 500 Stück 7%, ab 1000 Stück 10%
- Liefer- und Zahlungsbedingungen unverändert
- Aktueller Katalog und neueste Preisliste sowie Muster der Schmuckartikel per Post

Bezeichnung	Artikel-Nr. (neu)	Preis in Euro
Manschettenknöpfe, Silber	78833	48.95
Art Deco Ohrringe, Silber	78955	29.95
Art Deco Haarspange, Kristall	76944	19.95
Art Deco Damenarmbanduhr	79333	69.95

INCOMING MAIL

From: w.elliot@comlink.uk Walter Elliot, Fine Gifts Ltd.
Date: 17 August 200_
To: Beate Kaiser, Präsent-Import/Export, e-Mail: präsent.impex@firmlink.de
Subject: Art Deco articles

Dear Beate

I am delighted to say that our sales are ahead of expectations and so we are planning to stock up in preparation for Christmas. Demand has been particularly high for everything Art Deco and that is why we need information and – if possible – a quotation regarding the following items:

	Article No.
1930s silver-plated ashtray	67894
silver cuff-links	78953
art deco earrings	78941
art deco crystal hair clip	78936
art deco wrist watch	78920

The article numbers have been taken from last year's catalogue.

We may be ordering quantities between 100 and 1000 items, each, and would therefore expect generous discounts on your current list prices.

I trust you are still able to deliver ex stock as we need the articles urgently.

Thanks a lot.
Kind regards
Walter

6. Fremdsprachenkorrespondent/in

Übersetzung Deutsch/Englisch
(Bearbeitungszeit 60 Minuten)

Hilfsmittel:
zweisprachige Wörterbücher

Die Anziehungskraft von Sonne, Strand und Meer bleibt unverändert bestehen. Diese Tatsache hat zum kräftigen Wachstum des Umsatzes der deutschen Reiseveranstalter beigetragen. Laut einer Untersuchung der Zeitschrift "fvw International" haben die 52 größten Unternehmen ihren Umsatz im vergangenen Tourismusjahr um 8,9 Prozent auf 28,3 Mrd. DM gesteigert. Sie transportierten rund 27,4 Millionen Urlauber zu ihren Ferienzielen. Das ist fast zehn Prozent mehr als im Vorjahr.

Der Trend zur organisierten Reise hält an und alle großen Unternehmen profitieren davon. Die sieben größten deutschen Veranstalter konnten ihren Marktanteil auf 83 Prozent steigern. Aber auch einige kleine Reiseveranstalter waren sehr erfolgreich.

In diesem Jahr haben sich die Urlauber relativ früh für einen Urlaubsort entschieden. Nach Ansicht von Fachleuten lag das vor allem an den günstigen Angeboten der Veranstalter für Frühbuchungen. Das Last-Minute-Geschäft hat an Bedeutung verloren. Neben den Reiseveranstaltern profitieren auch die Fluggesellschaften und das Hotel- und Gaststättengewerbe von dem Wachstum der Tourismusbranche.

Auch der Trend zum Kurzurlaub in Deutschland hält an, was sich in der Zahl der Hotelbuchungen widerspiegelt.

7. Fremdsprachenkorrespondent/in

Übersetzung Englisch/Deutsch
(Bearbeitungszeit 60 Minuten)

Hilfsmittel:
zweisprachige Wörterbücher

More than half of all children now use the internet. The findings of a recent study paint a picture of an emerging generation of internet users whose skills are better than their parents' and who understand how the internet can help them in their education.

The opinion poll – the third in a series – indicates that 3.6m children aged between 7 and 16 surf the internet in the UK compared with 3.1m just six months ago, with under sixteens using the internet more than adults.

The fact that learning has turned out to be one of the prime drivers of internet use among the young will be welcomed by the government, which hopes that it can establish the UK as a world leader in developing interactive educational material for the internet.

However, the attractions of the internet are not limited to education – about five percent of children have already bought something online, usually using their parents' credit cards. 43 percent said that they used the internet to chat to friends.

The survey also revealed that boys were more likely to click on advertisements – 27 percent compared with 15 percent for the girls.

Both boys and girls said that well-designed advertisements did influence them when they were deciding which product to buy.

Unit 4 Comparing options

Introduction

■ Read the following information and complete the text using words from the box.

> how ∗ what ∗ where ∗ whether ∗ which

> When a number of offers have been obtained, it is necessary to compare them carefully to decide which is the most advantageous. Obviously price is important, but it is not the only consideration. ❶ favourable are the stipulated conditions of payment? ❷ discounts do the various companies offer on what order volumes?
> Different terms of delivery for the various offers also affect the actual end price.
> A further point to consider is ❸ the companies can supply when you need the products. Finally, ❹ relevant, depending on the type of product, guarantees and the availability of after-sales service will be important factors determining ❺ option you choose.

A Activities

A 1 Comparing written information

a Study the following three offers.

1

Dear Mr Murphy,

In answer to your telephone enquiry of this morning, I am pleased to quote you the following prices:

		unit	amount
4	HocusPocus LaserBolt 1200 incl. one 800-page feeder and a toner cartridge for 6,000 pgs	£445	£1,780
4	LB network adapters	£14.50	£58
1	HocusPocus 1200 Duplex Feeder for 50 double-sided prints complete installation incl. cables	£99.50 £44.50	£99.50 £44.50
	total		**£2,182**

Extra toner cartridges for ca. 6,000 pages are £45 per unit.

All HocusPocus products carry a one-year warranty, which can be extended for £25 per year. On-site repair is also available.

Our latest catalogue is enclosed. If you have any further questions, please do not hesitate to contact me.

Yours sincerely,

Terry Long

2

Dear Mr Murphy

Thank you for your interest in Necson printers. I am happy to enclose the latest catalogue and quote you the following prices excluding VAT:

QTY	Item	Unit Price	Total
4	**Necson 1612** with two standard sheet feeders and a toner cartridge for 10,000 pages	£774.50	£3,098
4	**Necson network adapters & cables**	£14.50	£58
1	**Necson DU 1612** (duplex unit holding 100 pages)	£124.50	£124.50
		TOTAL	£3,280.50

optional:
1	toner cartridge for 10,000 pages	£60

All Necson hardware comes with a three-year warranty including repair or replacement within 24 hours. The prices quoted above include delivery and set-up on your premises. Payment is to be made within 30 days net.

I will contact you shortly to discuss our quotation. If you have any further questions in the meantime, please do not hesitate to contact me.

Yours sincerely

Sean Fletcher

3

15 November 200_

Dear Ms Jones,

We would like to thank you for your interest in PowerComp printers.

We enclose a detailed brochure featuring the latest models and have pleasure in detailing our quotation, which we trust meets your requirements.

QTY	ITEM	UNIT PRICE	TOTAL
4	**PowerComp 8000** (incl. two 500-page sheet feeders and one toner cartridge for approx. 5,000 pages)	£705	£2,820
4	**Network adapters & cables**	£12	£48
1	**PowerComp 8000 DU** (duplex unit for 70 pages)	£78.50	£78.50
		TOTAL	£2,946.50

	additional toner cartridges for PC-8000 (approx. 5,000 standard pages)	£35

Please note that all hardware carries a two-year warranty with 24 hour on-site repair/replacement service. Our prices also include delivery and installation on your premises, but exclude VAT. Payment is to be made within 15 days after date of invoice.

If you have any further questions, please do not hesitate to call us on 019603 61572. We are available between 9.30 a.m. and 7 p.m.

Yours sincerely,

Alan Hughes

21 **b Get together in groups of four and compare the offers on the previous pages and the advertisements on page 21. Then discuss which of the printers you would buy at first glance. Use the phrases below.**

Phrases: Comparing printers			
If I had to buy a new printer, I'd	choose / pick / go for	the ... because	it offers the best value for money. / of its high printing speed. / it is cheaper than ...

You're right, the ... is cheaper than the ..., but it is more expensive in the long run because ...

When it comes to the	warranty / printing costs	the ... is	(far) better / (much) cheaper	than the ...

All in all, I think the ... is the best offer because ...

c Draw a table (see below) on a separate sheet of paper and list the specifications under the corresponding printers.

1. The HocusPocus LaserBolt 1200 is the first 1200 dpi colour network printer for £445.
2. The Necson 1612 prints 30 pages per minute at a cost of 0.6p per page.
3. The PowerComp 8000 has the same resolution as the HocusPocus, but prints 40 per cent faster.
4. The HocusPocus comes with a one-year warranty which can be extended for £25 per year.
5. The Necson is designed to print 6,000 colour pages a month, twice as many as the HocusPocus.
6. The PowerComp costs £260 more than the HocusPocus, but £69.50 less than the Necson.
7. The HocusPocus prints only 20 pages per minute, but the costs per page are 25 per cent higher than the Necson's.
8. The PowerComp's monthly output is 1,000 pages less than the Necson's, but the cost per page is 1/20 p cheaper than for the HocusPocus.
9. The Necson 1612 has the same resolution as the PowerComp and the HocusPocus, and it comes with a three-year warranty.
10. The PowerComp's warranty period is 365 days longer than that for the HocusPocus, but one year shorter than the Necson guarantee.

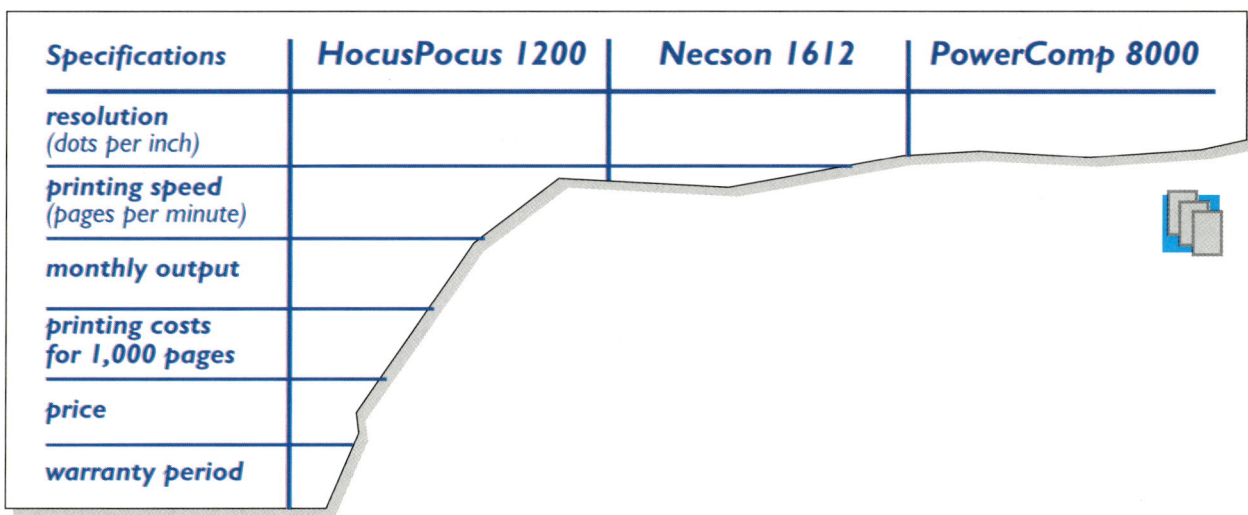

Specifications	HocusPocus 1200	Necson 1612	PowerComp 8000
resolution (dots per inch)			
printing speed (pages per minute)			
monthly output			
printing costs for 1,000 pages			
price			
warranty period			

Activities · Unit 4   61

A 2 Comparing information obtained by telephone → 59/60

a Listen to Amanda Jones and Fred Murphy discussing the printers and say which statements are correct.

1. The HocusPocus does not meet the requirements because
   a. it is designed to print 4,000 pages only.
   b. they print about 5,000 pages a month.
   c. of its slow printing speed and high costs.

2. In terms of the monthly printing costs
   a. the Necson 1612 is the most economical.
   b. the HocusPocus is cheaper than the Necson.
   c. the Necson will make up for its higher price within a year.

3. As to warranty and service, the Necson is best because
   a. PowerComp does not offer on-site repair or replacement service.
   b. the HocusPocus offer is very specific.
   c. it has a three-year warranty, with repair or replacement within 24 hours.

4. Fred Murphy recommends the Necson
   a. because there are no problems with the printer drivers.
   b. although it is more expensive than the others.
   c. because it is the fastest printer that you can get.

b Amanda Jones agrees with Fred, but the Finance Department questions why they should buy the Necson printers as they are £334 more than the PowerComps. So Fred writes a memo to the Finance Department to explain his point of view.

Read the memo, copy it and fill in the appropriate words from the list. Discuss Fred's opinion with a partner.

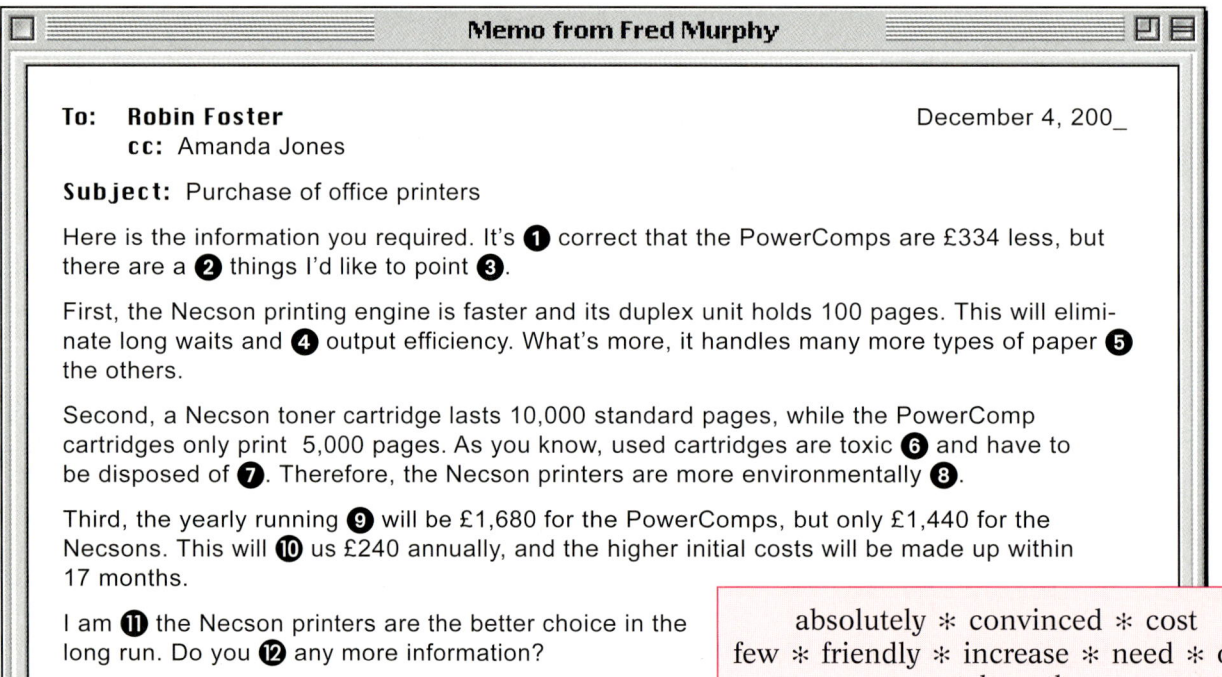

Memo from Fred Murphy

To: Robin Foster   December 4, 200_
  cc: Amanda Jones

Subject: Purchase of office printers

Here is the information you required. It's ❶ correct that the PowerComps are £334 less, but there are a ❷ things I'd like to point ❸.

First, the Necson printing engine is faster and its duplex unit holds 100 pages. This will eliminate long waits and ❹ output efficiency. What's more, it handles many more types of paper ❺ the others.

Second, a Necson toner cartridge lasts 10,000 standard pages, while the PowerComp cartridges only print 5,000 pages. As you know, used cartridges are toxic ❻ and have to be disposed of ❼. Therefore, the Necson printers are more environmentally ❽.

Third, the yearly running ❾ will be £1,680 for the PowerComps, but only £1,440 for the Necsons. This will ❿ us £240 annually, and the higher initial costs will be made up within 17 months.

I am ⓫ the Necson printers are the better choice in the long run. Do you ⓬ any more information?

absolutely ∗ convinced ∗ cost
few ∗ friendly ∗ increase ∗ need ∗ out
save ∗ separately ∗ than ∗ waste

c Study the following two offers.
The first one is a written offer, the second one an offer over the phone.

1. Written offer

In view of the coming summer season, Kate Paxton from Sports Unlimited has requested offers for swimwear from OSPEE, a well-known Korean manufacturer. **Study this list of price quotations, including delivery to three different places.**

OSPEE "FEMALE PERFORMANCE"
Price list as of December 200_

Quantity & models:
2000 Splashback two piece assorted sizes
3000 Olympia one piece assorted sizes
2000 Aquablade striped assorted sizes

Terms for 7,000 units:
FOB* Pusan: £69,800
CIF* Southampton: £75,450
DDU* Stratford: £76,750

* See Incoterms on page 72

2. Offer over the phone

Kate called Integrated Carriers to get an offer for transport from Pusan to Southampton or Stratford, and their representative promised to call back. **Listen to the telephone conversation, copy the following form and fill it in.**

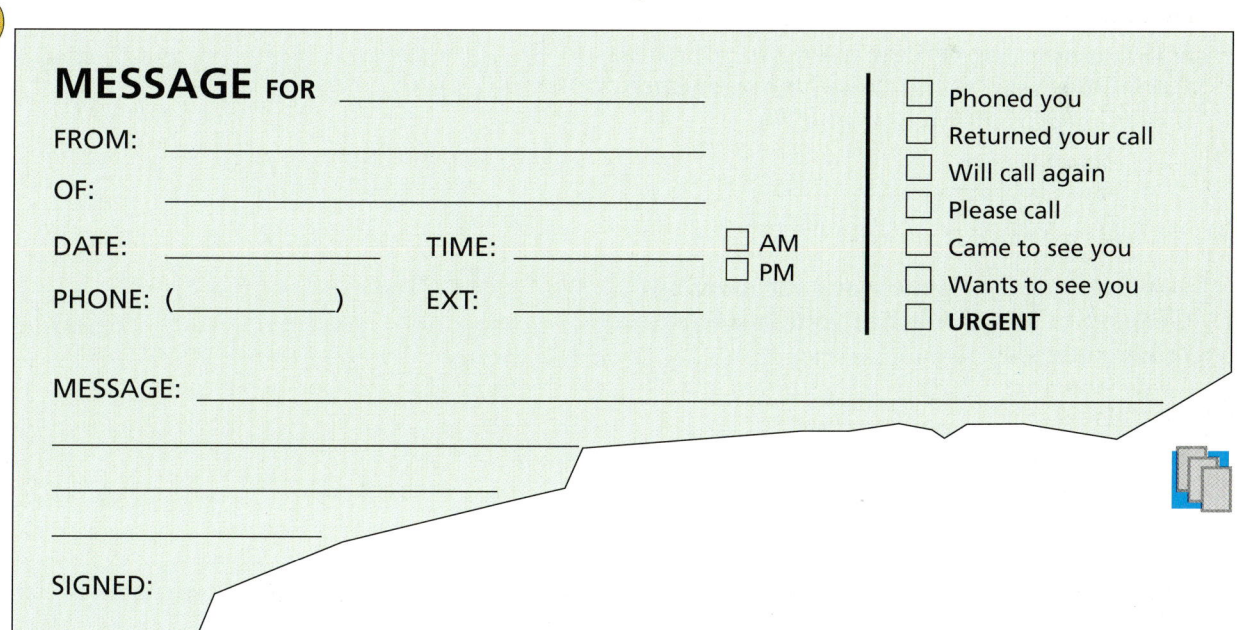

MESSAGE FOR _____

FROM: _____
OF: _____
DATE: _____   TIME: _____ ☐ AM
                               ☐ PM
PHONE: (_____)   EXT: _____

☐ Phoned you
☐ Returned your call
☐ Will call again
☐ Please call
☐ Came to see you
☐ Wants to see you
☐ **URGENT**

MESSAGE: _____
_____
_____
_____

SIGNED: _____

d Work with a partner. Compare the freight rates given by Integrated Carriers with OSPEE's offer and discuss the most favourable way of receiving the merchandise.

A3 Making comparisons in memos

a Use the table below to compare the mobile phones as in this example:

The NOSY is £5 more than the IKONA, and £7 more than the TOM O'ROLA.

Specifications	IKONA	NOSY	SANOPANIC	TOM O'ROLA
standby (without recharging)	(400 hrs)	350 hrs	300 hrs	350 hrs
talktime (without recharging)	25 hrs	(30 hrs)	25 hrs	25 hrs
number memory	250	250	(300)	250
weight (incl. batteries)	130g	170g	135g	(120g)
dimensions mm (width × height × depth)	55 × 100 × 20	40 × 75 × 15	50 × 90 × 17	50 × 120 × 20
price (£)	44.99	49.99	46.99	42.99

b You work with a British company which needs to equip its sales representatives with mobile phones.
Use Example 1 to write a memo to your boss, Brian Southam, about the advantages and disadvantages of the four models.

Example 1:

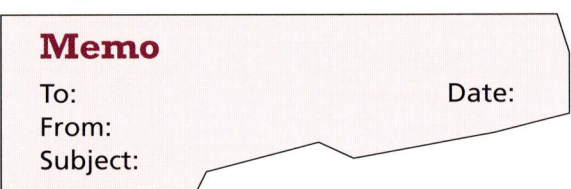

c Now you work with the London branch office of a German firm.
Use Example 2 to write a similar memo in German to Mrs Gruber at your headquarters in Duisburg.

Example 2:

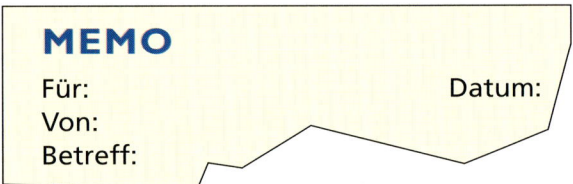

A4 Making comparisons in reports

a Snoozers Ltd has received detailed offers for the installation of a company-wide network. Jo Wheeler has asked Jerry Debug, her head technician, to examine the offers and to draft a report.

➡ 39/40 **Read his report on the next page and look up the words you don't know in a dictionary.**

TO: Ms Jo Wheeler
FROM: Jerry Debug
DATE: 18 December 200_
SUBJECT: Offers for setting up a company network

As you requested, I have examined and compared the offers for the installation of a company-wide network from various perspectives, viz performance, price, ease of maintenance and future expandability to protect the company's investments.

While BritComp, Brumshaw & Co. and Bell Networking offer TN-based Hexium IV or GAMMA server solutions, ComputerClinic and IntelliNet recommend PowerPC or Sparc solutions. The total costs of the complete installation including palmtop organizers are in the following range:

Bell Networking	Hexium IV, TN server software	£24,875.00
Brumshaw & Co	Hexium IV, TN server software	£25,632.12
ComputerClinic	PowerPC, OrangeServe server software	£27,490.00
IntelliNet	Sparc, Lunaris server software	£35,678.25
BritComp	GAMMA, TN server software	£38,498.70

In terms of performance, the pricy Sparc or GAMMA solutions would be the clear first choices. However, the Orange Workgroup server comes in third, and costs much less than the others. Hexium IV servers using TN software are even lower in price, but they are considerably slower than their competitors.

If we consider performance for money, the Orange Workgroup Server 9600 has a slight edge. In addition to its favourable price, its server software offers the highest level of security, and is easy to set up and manage.

Therefore, I would recommend ComputerClinic's solution, but suggest that we discuss the following points before signing the contract:

- Can Orange support 20 simultaneous log-ins at maximum speed? (I doubt it.)
- What upgrade options will protect our investment?
- Server price (comparable models cost £1,000 less, and the Orange server is now £7,800)
- Can we expect a discount on the palmtop organizers? (competitor's model is 10% cheaper)

b Now say whether the following statements are true or false.

1. Price is the only important thing when you choose a computer.
2. SNOOZERS Ltd. has received five offers that suggest four different server solutions.
3. GAMMA and Sparc are faster than the others, but not as expensive.
4. TN software is the easiest to operate networking software that money can buy.
5. Jerry wants an Orange because it supports 20 log-ins at the same time.
6. ComputerClinic charges 20% more for its organizers than other firms.

A 5 Giving presentations

39 In exercise **b** you are going to hear a presentation that Mrs Strand is giving for the members of the Wanstead Club of the British Food and Wine Society.

a First, match the words on the left with the explanations on the right.

1. to present somebody with something
2. complimentary
3. you will have ample opportunity
4. the wines are unrivalled
5. medieval castles
6. half-timbered cottages
7. rustic fare
8. gentle slopes
9. hospitality
10. vintners

a. free of charge
b. wine producers
c. small houses with a wooden frame
d. looking after guests
e. to hand something to somebody as a gift
f. there will be plenty of chances
g. other wines cannot compete
h. castles from the Middle Ages
i. country-style cooking
j. hills that rise and fall gradually

b Now listen to Mrs Strand's presentation. It will be in two parts with a break in the middle. While listening to the first part, make notes in order to answer the following questions:

1. Which wine-growing regions does she mention?
2. Why are the vineyards usually to be found in the river valleys?
3. Who originally introduced wine-growing to Germany?

c Listen to the second part of the presentation and make a brief summary in German of the main points.
Use the information on summaries on page 68.

d Work in groups and gather information on various tourist attractions, as shown below. Then present your findings to the class. Use the sample presentation on the cassette and the information on page 68 to prepare your presentation.

B Tool kit

B1 Memos and reports

Memos

You write a memo to someone who works in the same company. In large organizations, memos are no longer written on paper; they are e-mail messages that are distributed via the company network.

Many companies use their own preprinted memo forms. The arrangement of the heading may differ from form to form and company to company, but essentially, it contains the names of the sender and the recipient(s), the date (and time) and the subject of the memo.

If you do not use a preprinted memo form, you can use any standard paper format, from full-size (A4) to quarter-size (A6).

The key difference between a letter and a memo is the format. The memo, both traditional and e-mail, uses a simple two-part format:

1. The **heading**, which contains these guidewords:
   From indicates the name of the writer.
   To identifies the recipient(s).
   Date (**Time**) show when the memo was written.
   Subject gives a summary of the contents.

2. The **body**, which contains the message: Begin with the main idea or with the reason(s) why you are writing, and support or explain them in the following paragraphs. In many firms memos are initialled at the end.

Remember:
A memo has to be brief, clear and to the point.

Reports

While a memo is used to transmit smaller amounts of information, a report gives more details and larger amounts of information. There are several types of reports in use:

- An **informal report** is generally no longer than 2 – 3 pages and uses the memo format if it is distributed within the organization, or the letter format if it is used for distribution outside the company.

- A **business report** uses more formal formatting techniques and includes a title page containing:
  1. The title of the report.
  2. The name, title and address of the person for whom the report is intended.
  3. The name, title and address of the sender.
  4. The date of the report.

Business reports must be clearly structured. They should have headings and subheadings to highlight particularly important information:

RECENT TRENDS IN INTRA-NETWORKING

Prepared for Jo Wheeler, Manager
jwheeler@snoozers.co.uk

Prepared by Michael Lewis; CIO
mlewis@network.co.uk

Thursday, 20 December 200_

B 2 Summaries in German

In German companies, translations into German are sometimes replaced by a summary of the original text in German. Such summaries may take the form of memos (see B1).

If you are asked to summarise a text, first read the text through carefully several times, looking up any words or expressions you do not know in the dictionary. Give an overall idea of what the text is about in the form of a headline or subject line or in the first sentence. Be aware of the recipient's requirements, but do not take too much inside knowledge for granted. It may well happen that third parties, who are not familiar with this particular transaction, will need the information contained in your summary as a basis for their decisions later on. Repeat every bit of useful information, especially names, dates, figures, etc. but leave out any repetitive or less relevant remarks. A summary should at the same time be both as informative and as concise as possible.

If you are expressly required to write a summary of, say, one third the length of the original, you will, of course, have to restrict yourself to the essential information provided and make an effort to reduce the length of the German text by expressing yourself briefly and concisely.

B 3 Presentations

1. Giving a presentation

The success of a presentation depends on the following factors:

- Prepare your presentation carefully. Think of who you will be talking to and what you want to achieve. Brainstorm your ideas using mind maps, and use suitable examples and audiovisual aids whenever possible.
- Organize the contents of your presentation. A clear structure helps your audience to follow easily. Start by telling your audience what you are going to talk about, then talk about it. Finally, summarize the main points of your presentation in the conclusion.
- Use short and simple language. There is no point in using difficult words and structures. Too much information is difficult to absorb. Decide what is essential and leave out the rest. Also signal to your audience when you are moving to the next item on the agenda.
- When delivering your presentation, do not speak too fast, look around your audience to establish rapport and to get feedback. Watch your voice level and body language. Also vary your intonation to make your points more effectively.
- Use interesting examples, anecdotes and some humour to break the ice.
- Use your visual aids confidently and give your audience time to study them.
- Be prepared to deal with questions and give polite and diplomatic answers. If there are too many questions, suggest waiting until the end of the presentation.

2. Phrases: Presentations

- **To introduce the topic:**
  First of all, I'll …
  Let me start by …
  I'd like to begin by …

- **To move on to the next item:**
  Now let me turn to …
  Let's move on now to …
  Next, I'd like to …

- **To develop a point:**
  Let's look at … in more detail.
  What does this mean for …?
  I should like to expand on that, if I may.

- **To give an example:**
  For example/For instance, …
  To illustrate this point, let me say …
  A good example of … is …

- **When you have reached the end of a point:**
  We've looked at …
  Right. I've told you about …

- **To put off questions:**
  I'll deal with this question in more detail later.
  I won't comment on this now.
  I'll come back to this question later in my talk.

- **To summarize the main points:**
  I'd like to sum up now …
  Let me summarize the main points briefly.
  In conclusion …

- **To sequence your presentation:**
  First(ly) – Second(ly) – Third(ly) – Last(ly)
  First of all – Then – Next – After that – Finally
  To start with – Later – To finish with

C Additional practice

a GAMETOYS, Glückstraße 57, 93449 Spielberg, Germany, tel (09972) 738 287, fax (09972) 738288, www.gametoys.co.de, has just received this fax.
Study the fax and use your boss's notes to reply appropriately.

TELEFAX TRANSMISSION

To: GAMETOYs   Attention: Manager
From: Jiři Novotny   Subject: Enquiry
Date: 10/12/200_   Pages: 1 (incl. this one)

SUPERNOVA
Karlův most 26
Praha 1 CSR
Tel+Fax +42-1 648-7392

Your firm has been recommended to me by Ms Jana Marčik, with whom we have been doing business for many years.   *Gute Empfehlung!*

My firm has been specializing in toys and games for more than ten years. As demand for card and table-top games is growing rapidly, I would be interested in importing and adapting some of your games to suit the Czech market.   *Klingt vielversprechend!*

I would therefore appreciate it if you could send me your latest catalogues and price lists.

Best wishes
Jiři Novotny
Proprietor

Sofort faxen, sämtliche Prospekte und Kataloge noch heute express abschicken!

---

b IMPORTEX, 94034 Passau, Germany, Modegasse 6, tel (0851) 370301, fax (0851) 370312, www.importex.co.de, has just received the enquiry on the right from MAGYARMODA, Ady Endre utca 31, 1014 Budapest, Hungary.

Unfortunately, the new summer catalogue is not yet completed, but it will be available in three weeks.
Write a stopgap letter promising that you will mail your catalogue and price list as soon as they are available.

We have been given your address by the German Trade Delegate in Budapest.

We are a well-established firm which specializes in importing young fashion. Therefore, we would like to receive your summer catalogues and price lists including your terms of payment.

We look forward to hearing from you soon.

Béla Kovacs

Béla Kovacs
Manager

c ZISCHFRISCH Durststrecke 8, 73033 Göppingen, Germany, tel (07161) 73110, fax (07161) 73120, e-Mail durst@zischfrisch.de, has just received a phone call from a prospective customer.

Your boss took the call and made the notes on the right.
Use them to draft a reply.

> Tel. 14.d.M., 11:35
>
> <u>Angebot:</u> 25000 Dosen REDOX Energy Drink
>
> <u>Pawel Brzinsky</u>
> **POLARDRINK**
> Zgoda 35, 31-120 Krakow, Polen
> Tel 0048-12 22-06-63
> Fax 0048-12 22-67-83
> pbrzinsky@krakownet.com.pl
>
> <u>Preis:</u> FCA € 0,25/Dose, abzüglich 10% Mengenrabatt
>
> Zahlung netto 14 Tage nach Rechnungsdatum lieferbar am 17.d.M.

d WEDLER & Co produces and exports different kinds of sports equipment. It is based in Steilhang 45, 87527 Sonthofen, telephone 08321 38793, fax 08321 38795, www.wedler.co.de
Read this e-mail message from a prospective customer and use the price list to make an offer.

Best.Nr.	Artikel	Länge	Preis
452-81	Winner blue	165 / 175 / 185 / 195	€ 129
452-82	Winner red	165 / 175 / 185 / 195	€ 129
452-83	Winner silver	165 / 175 / 185 / 195	€ 149
452-84	Winner gold	165 / 175 / 185 / 195	€ 159
487-96	SuperStar	175 / 185 / 195	€ 199
487-97	UltraStar	175 / 185 / 195	€ 219

Preise FOB Rotterdam per 1. 1. 200_
Rabattstaffel: 10% ab Wert € 10.000
15% ab Wert € 20.000
Zahlung per Akkreditiv
Lieferung 3 Wochen ab Bestelleingang

Subject: Request for offer
Date: 200_/01/28
From: Elsa Griffith, Head
Organization: Mountaineer
To: sales@wedler.co.d

Mountaineer is New Zealand's leading retailer of winter sports equipment. The ski market is picking up again, and we would like to take the opportunity to introduce your new models to our customers.

As we usually place large orders, we would expect a substantial discount off net list prices, and our terms of payment are normally 30-day bill of exchange, documents against acceptance.

If you are interested in this market opportunity, and you can meet orders of over 500 pairs at one time, please send us your most favourable terms. We hope to hear from you soon.

Elsa Griffith, Head Buyer

e Sie arbeiten bei der Großhandelsfirma Sportwelt Fan-Artikel, Augsburg, E-Mail sportwelt@comlink.de. Sie haben gestern von Gino Giacomelli, Manager von Eurosport, Via dei Banchi 45, 78038 Firenze, E-Mail-Adresse giacomelli.eurosport@italink.com, eine Anfrage über Liverpoool Fan Club Sportbekleidung erhalten.

Die Leiterin der Exportabteilung, Denise Springer, hat Ihnen die englische Preisliste und die folgende Notiz auf den Schreibtisch gelegt. Erledigen Sie diesen Auftrag. Heute ist der 4. Dezember 200_

Bitte schicken Sie für mich Herrn Giacomelli noch heute eine E-Mail.

- *Unsere Angebotsnr. SB/It.247*
- *Danken Sie für Anfrage*
- *Machen Sie ein Angebot für die Artikel Nr. 961632, 973094, 961635 und 961580 unserer Preisliste*
- *Alle Artikel sofort lieferbar*
- *Preise verstehen sich CPT* Florenz (Firenze)*
- *Mengenrabatt: 5 % bei Abnahme von mehr als 50 Stück eines Artikels, 10% für Bestellungen von über 100 Stück*
- *Zahlung: bei Erhalt der Rechnung per Bankscheck, zahlbar an Sportwelt, Augsburg*
- *Schließen Sie mit einem freundlichen Satz.*

D. Sp.

CODE No.	ITEM	SIZES available	PRICE EXW*
961631	LFC Crew neck sweatshirt black	S M L XL	€9.99
961632	LFC Crew neck sweatshirt red	S M L XL	€9.99
973094	LFC Football T-shirt white	M L XL	€8.99
973095	LFC Football T-shirt teal	M L XL	€8.99
961634	LFC Jog pant adult black	32" 34" 36" 38"	€8.49
961635	LFC Jog pant adult red	32" 34" 36" 38"	€8.49
961580	LFC Warm-up suit navy adult	S M L XL	€21.99
961450	LFC Warm-up suit navy junior	28" 30" 32" 34"	€21.99

* see page 72 (Incoterms)

f Comparing options involves a lot of adjectives and if-clauses.
   Find the appropriate form of the adjective or verb in brackets.

1. If LeisureCorp (buy) the (new) printers before the end of the year, their tax bill will be (low) than last year.
2. If the HocusPocus 1200 had a (fast) printer engine and (low) operating costs, it (be) ideal for their purposes.
3. If Fred (not compare) the operating costs, LeisureCorp would have bought a (slow) and (expensive) printer.
4. The Necson 1612 is the (expensive) printer, but if you consider all aspects, it (turn out) to be the (economical).

D Background information: Incoterms 2000

The purpose of the Incoterms is to provide a set of international rules for the interpretation of the most commonly used delivery terms in foreign trade. It should be stressed that the scope of Incoterms is limited to matters relating to the rights and obligations of the parties to the contract of sale with respect to the delivery of goods sold.

The rules were developed by the International Chamber of Commerce in Paris and are recognised in most countries, although they do not take precedence over national law.

In 1990, for ease of understanding, the 13 terms were grouped in four categories which have been retained in the revised Incoterms 2000.

Group E comprises the most favourable term from the exporter's point of view, EXW, whereby the seller only makes the goods available to the buyer at the seller's own premises. It is followed by Group F (FCA, FAS and FOB) whereby the seller is called upon to deliver the goods to a carrier appointed by the buyer. Under Group C terms (CFR, CIF, CPT and CIP) the seller has to contract for carriage, but without assuming the risk of loss or of damage to the goods due to events occurring after shipment or dispatch. Group D, finally, comprises terms (DAF, DES, DEQ, DDU and DDP) whereby the seller has to bear all costs and risks involved in bringing the goods to the place of destination.

There are three changes compared with previous Incoterms versions in Incoterms 2000: the new FAS term requires the seller to clear the goods for export while the new DEQ term requires the buyer to clear the goods for import and pay for all formalities, duties, taxes and charges upon import. Under the new FCA term changes have been made concerning loading and unloading obligations. If delivery is to take place at the seller's premises, loading will be the seller's obligation.

(Adapted from ICC Incoterms 2000)

INCOTERMS 2000

Group E Departure	EXW	Ex Works * (... named place)
Group F Main carriage unpaid	FCA FAS FOB	Free Carrier* (... named place) Free Alongside Ship** (... named port of shipment) Free On Board** (... named port of shipment)
Group C Main carriage paid	CFR CIF CPT CIP	Cost and Freight** (... named port of destination) Cost, Insurance and freight** (... named port of destination) Carriage Paid To* (... named place of destination) Carriage and Insurance Paid To* (... named place of destination)
Group D Arrival	DAF DES DEQ DDU DDP	Delivered At Frontier* (... named place) Delivered Ex Ship** (... named port of destination) Delivered Ex Quay** (... named port of destination) Delivered Duty Unpaid* (... named place of destination) Delivered Duty Paid* (... named place of destination)

* Any mode of transport
** Maritime and inland waterway transport only

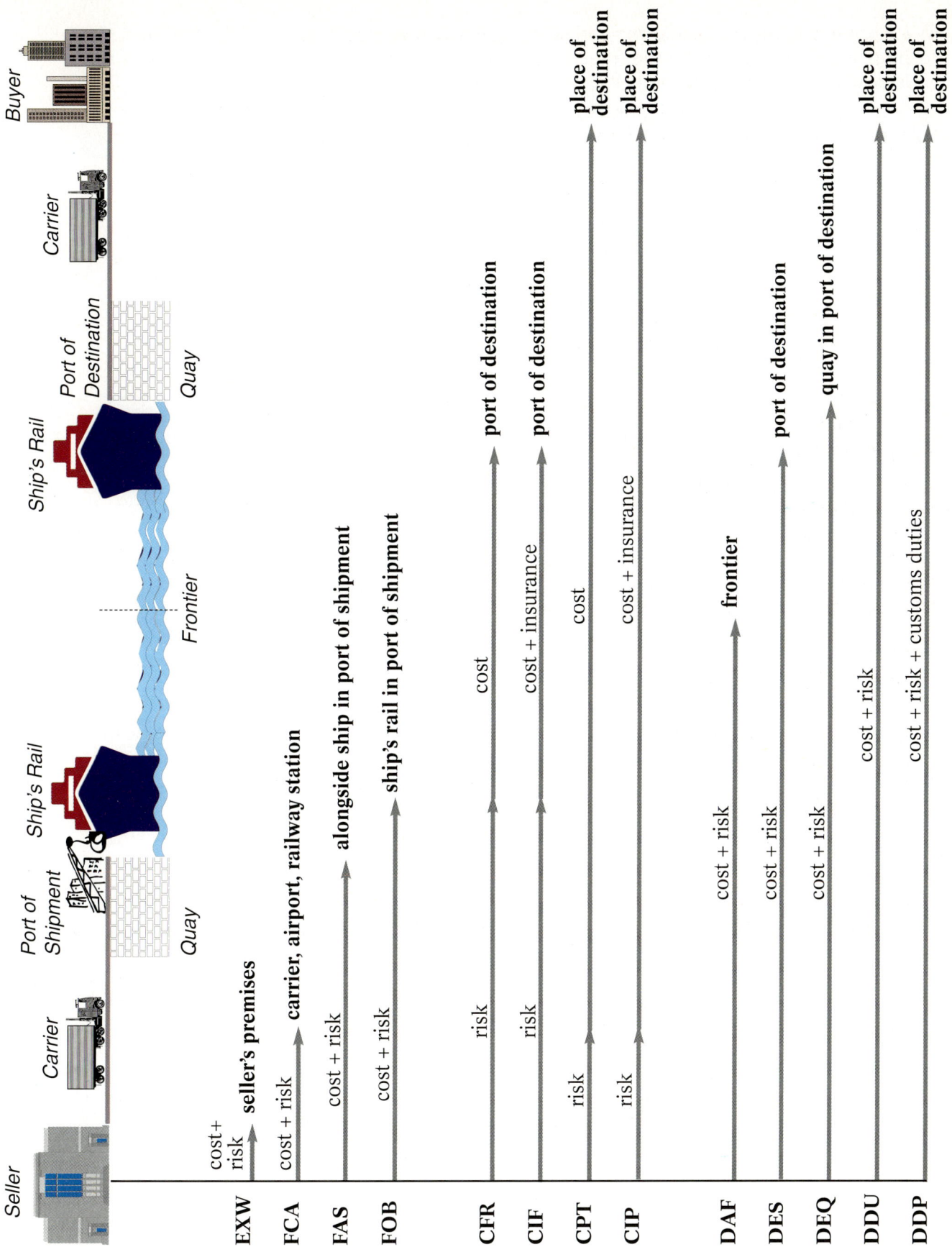

Background information · Unit 4

a Read the text on the Incoterms and study the charts on pages 72 and 73. Then find the information missing from the following table. Match the numbers in the table with the information given under points a. -n. on the next page.

Group	Incoterm	full designation	exporter's obligations	passing of risk
E	EXW	1	2	seller's premises
F	FCA	free carrier (named place)	all costs and risks until the goods have been handed over to the first carrier.	at the first carrier's
	FAS	free alongside ship (named port of shipment)	all costs and risks until the goods are on the quay in the port of shipment	3
	FOB	4	all costs and risks until the goods are on board ship in the port of shipment	ship's rail in the port of shipment
C	CFR	cost and freight (named port of destination)	5	ship's rail in the port of shipment
	CIF	6	7	ship's rail in the port of shipment
	CPT	8	all costs up to the named place of destination	at the first carrier's
	CIP	carriage and insurance paid to (named place of destination)	all costs and insurance up to the place of destination	at the first carrier's
D	DAF	9	all costs and risks up to the place of destination at the frontier	place of destination at frontier
	DES	delivered ex ship (named port of destination)	all costs and risks until the ship has reached the port of destination	on board ship in the port of destination
	DEQ	10	all costs and risks until the goods are on the quay in the port of destination	11
	DDU	12	all costs and risks up to the place of destination, excluding customs duties	place of destination
	DDP	delivered duty paid (named place of destination)	13	14

74 Unit 4 · Background information

a. carriage paid to (named place of destination)
b. delivered ex quay (named port of destination)
c. quay in the port of destination
d. ex works (named place)
e. placing the goods at buyer's disposal
f. delivered at frontier (named place)
g. free on board (named port of shipment)
h. quay in the port of shipment
i. all costs up to the port of destination
j. delivered duty unpaid (named place of destination)
k. place of destination
l. all costs and insurance up to the port of destination
m. all costs and risks including customs duties up to the place of destination
n. cost, insurance and freight (named port of destination)

b You work in the export department of a supplier of automotive components, based in Ludwigsburg near Stuttgart and you have customers in many parts of the world.
Match the Incoterms from box 1 with the places of delivery from box 2 stipulated by your customers.

Example:
Our terms of delivery are:
DAF Frankfurt an der Oder.

Box 1	Box 2
EXW	Bremerhaven
FCA	Frankfurt an der Oder
FOB	Ludwigsburg
CIF	Manchester
DAF	Singapore
DDU	Stuttgart Airport

c Now read these business transactions and match them with the right Incoterm.

1. DigiCorp arranges and pays for the transportation and loading of its brand-new UltraSpeed drives on board a cargo plane at Narita airport.

   DigiCorp sells ❓ Narita.

2. Hyflyer exports its mountain bikes by lorry and bears the costs of transportation to the border station at Hegyeshalom, Hungary.

   Their terms are ❓ Hegyeshalom.

3. Sally Cosmetics is a very powerful manufacturer and refuses to bear any risk, so the wholesalers have to pick up the goods at the factory.

   Sally Cosmetics sells ❓.

4. Cumbria steel plc has agreed to pay the costs of transport by road – excluding insurance – for a consignment of steel plates from its mill to Magdeburg, the place of delivery named by the buyer.

   The terms of delivery are ❓.

5. Sports Unlimited imports sportswear from South Korea by ship. The manufacturer of the sportswear pays for transportation to the South Korean port of Pusan, loading charges, and freight and insurance to Southampton, the English port of destination.

   Their terms are ❓.

6. Hyflyer imports Shimada components from Japan. Shimada arranges and pays for transportation to Yokohama, the port of shipment. Hyflyer has to pay the loading costs, freight, insurance and all other costs from Yokohama to Warwick.

   Shimada sells ❓.

7. When Computer Clinic orders components from Taiwan, the Taiwanese manufacturer bears all risks and costs, including U.K. customs duty, until the components have been delivered to Will Duncan's premises in Pembroke.

   Their terms are ❓.

E IHK-Prüfungsvorbereitung

1. Zusatzqualifikation Englisch für kaufmännische Auszubildende

Vermerk in Deutsch über einen Geschäftsbrief (Bearbeitungszeit 30 Minuten)	**Hilfsmittel:** zweisprachiges Wörterbuch

Situation

Sie arbeiten als Auszubildende(r) in der Exportabteilung des Unternehmens Computex GmbH in Münster. Sie haben heute, am 24. Juni … das beigefügte Schreiben der englischen Firma Palm Top Ltd, in Rawdon (Leeds), Großbritannien, erhalten.

Aufgabe

Bitte fassen Sie für Herrn Wildenbruch, den Leiter der Exportabteilung, den Inhalt des Briefes in einem Vermerk in deutscher Sprache zusammen (vollständige Sätze, keine Übersetzung). Verwenden Sie das für den Briefvermerk vorgesehene Formblatt.

PALM TOP LTD

46 Windsor Drive · Rawdon · LS1R 6L9 · UK

Computex GmbH
Pictorius Platz 15
48143 Münster
Germany

24 June …

Dear Sirs

Your palm-held computer Xion2K

I recently visited the Office Equipment Fair in Birmingham and picked up some of the sales literature on your stand. Unfortunately, I did not have time to take a closer look at the products you were exhibiting or discuss them with your representative. However, to judge from your sales literature, your palm-held notebook looks extremely interesting.

We are a wholesale company based in Yorkshire distributing to over five hundred retail outlets in the North of England. Your Xion2K would fit in very well with the rest of our range. There is considerable demand on the British market for this type of product not only from private individuals but also from corporate customers.

Assuming that prices and conditions are right we would place an initial order for 500 notebooks. Subsequent orders would be more substantial and we would expect favourable prices and open account terms on the basis of quarterly settlement by bank transfer within 30 days of your statement of account.

We should be grateful if you would let us know whether you are interested in doing business on this basis. Please let us have your offer for an initial order of 500. Could you also let us have a supply of your sales literature in English, which we would distribute to our customers.

We look forward to hearing from you.

Kind regards*

David Macmillan

David Macmillan
Managing Director

Computex GmbH Pictorius Platz 15, 48143 Münster

MEMO

Für: Datum:
Von:
Betreff:

---

* Eigentlich "Yours faithfully", aber diese Floskel wird oft als zu förmlich erachtet.

2. Fremdsprachenkorrespondent/in

Übersetzung Deutsch / Englisch (Bearbeitungszeit 60 Minuten)	Hilfsmittel: zweisprachige Wörterbücher

Die Incoterms sind für den weltweiten Außenhandel von besonderer Bedeutung. Durch Bezugnahme auf diese Klauseln können Verkäufer und Käufer unter anderem festlegen, welche Transportkosten und -risiken jeder Partner übernimmt.

1999 hat die Internationale Handelskammer, ICC, in Paris die Arbeiten an den neuen „Incoterms 2000" abgeschlossen. Die neuen Regeln gelten seit dem 1. Januar 2000 und bauen auf den „Incoterms 1990" auf.

Wie bisher gibt es 13 Klauseln, deren Bezeichnungen und Abkürzungen nicht geändert wurden. Allerdings ist es der ICC gelungen, neueste Entwicklungen der allgemeinen Handelspraxis zu berücksichtigen. Dies zeigt sich vor allem in zwei Änderungen bei den Klauseln FAS und DEQ sowie bei der Neudefinition des Lieferortes in der Klausel FCA.

Nach der neuen FAS-Klausel ist nun der Verkäufer (bisher der Käufer) verpflichtet, die Ware zur Ausfuhr freizumachen. Nach der neuen DEQ-Klausel erledigt jetzt der Käufer (bisher der Verkäufer) die Einfuhrformalitäten sowie die Zahlung der Zölle und anderer Kosten. Die neu formulierte FCA-Klausel ermöglicht es den Parteien, den Ort präzise zu bestimmen, an dem der Verkäufer seine Verpflichtungen erfüllt hat.

Keine Änderung hat es bei dem Übergang von Gefahren und Kosten bei FOB-Geschäften gegeben. Es bleibt bei der Schiffsreling. Zeitweise war diskutiert worden, ob dies in Anbetracht eines zunehmenden Containerverkehrs sinnvoll ist.

3. Fremdsprachenkorrespondent/in

Übersetzung Englisch / Deutsch (Bearbeitungszeit 60 Minuten)	Hilfsmittel: zweisprachige Wörterbücher

More and more organisations in many sectors of the economy are setting up their own operations in electronic trading.

In the rush towards using e-commerce in everything from car sales to banking, the problem of delivery is getting more and more important.

Although a great deal of attention goes into organising the electronic side of things and far more money is spent on marketing than in traditional operations, getting the product or service to the customer lags behind. A number of vital questions such as which delivery service to use or how to deliver at times convenient to the customer have to be addressed. As one industry analyst put it: "Logistics will become the one area in which a business can truly distinguish itself." As more and more homes have high-speed internet access the range of products that can be sold this way will surge.

Books4U.com has continued to dominate book retailing as a result of its excellent postal delivery service.

But even everyday products may pose complex delivery problems. The home delivery services being developed by major supermarkets are simple in theory, but someone has to be at home to receive the delivery. At the moment, it may be easier for the short-of-time executive to pop into the supermarket on the way home from work.

4. Fremdsprachenkorrespondent/in

| Geschäftsbrief nach Angaben (Bearbeitungszeit 45 Minuten) | Hilfsmittel: zweisprachige Wörterbücher |

Situation

Sie sind in der Importabteilung der Ultrabüro GmbH, Gewerbestr. 127, 07552 Gera, eines Großhändlers für Büromöbel, beschäftigt. Ein Hersteller aus Kanada, Ergofurniture Inc., 214 King St. West, Toronto, Ontario M5H 3S6, hat Ihnen gestern ein Angebot für ergonomische Bürostühle für PC-Arbeitsplätze gefaxt, das stellenweise nicht gut zu lesen war. Unterzeichnet war das Fax vom Exportleiter Edward Gardiner. Heute ist der 27. Mai 200_

Aufgabe

Bitte verfassen Sie in Ihrem eigenen Namen ein Schreiben an Ergofurniture Inc. Berücksichtigen Sie dabei folgende Einzelheiten:
- Einleitung
- Angebot interessant, besonders wegen der zahlreichen Möglichkeiten Sitz und Rückenlehne der Stühle individuell einzustellen.
- Mengenrabatte leider nicht vollständig lesbar. Bitte um erneute Angabe. Bestellungen von jeweils 500 Stück eines Modells möglich.
- Lieferzeit von 10 – 12 Wochen erscheint sehr lang. Kein anderer Lieferant benötigt mehr als 6 Wochen.
- Bitte um Zusendung von Mustern der Bezugstoffe. Für den deutschen Markt mehr als nur die drei angebotenen Farben erforderlich.
- Bei regelmäßigen Bestellungen günstigere Zahlungsbedingungen als Kasse gegen Dokumente erforderlich. *(Schlagen Sie eine andere Zahlungsbedingung vor)*.
- Schluss

5. Fremdsprachenkorrespondent/in

| Zusammenfassung in Deutsch einer englischen mündlichen Nachricht (Bearbeitungszeit 30 Minuten) | Hilfsmittel: zweisprachige Wörterbücher |

Situation

Sie (eigener Name) sind Assistent/in von Peter Lange, dem Verkaufsleiter einer Lederwarenfabrik. Herr Lange hat eine Nachricht in Englisch auf seinem Anrufbeantworter vorgefunden, die er nicht ganz versteht. Er bittet Sie, die Nachricht für ihn auf Deutsch zusammenzufassen.

Aufgabe

Fassen Sie die Nachricht in einem Vermerk für Herrn Lange schriftlich auf Deutsch zusammen. Der Vermerk soll alle wichtigen Einzelheiten enthalten. (Sie werden die Nachricht zweimal hören).

 Entwerfen Sie einen einfachen Vordruck für Ihren Vermerk.

Unit 5 Orders

Introduction

Under English law an offer is binding on the supplier as soon as the buyer accepts it. Under German law an order placed in reply to a firm offer results in a contract. Accordingly, the seller must deliver the goods at the place agreed upon within the period agreed upon, whereas the buyer must accept the goods and pay the price agreed upon within the period agreed upon.

A *trial order* is placed for a small quantity to test the merchandise or service. *Repeat orders* cover the goods or services ordered before. *Standing orders* ensure that identical quantities are supplied at regular intervals. *Orders on call,* i.e. orders placed for large quantities, called for at irregular intervals, play an important role within the concept of just-in-time delivery.

Many companies use special forms for ordering goods or services. They may use their own, called purchase order, or one provided by the seller, called order form. These forms have blank spaces to make sure that all the necessary information is provided. Nevertheless, there are times when a form is neither available nor appropriate. In this case, you must be sure to include complete, accurate information because incomplete orders can result in delayed deliveries or even deliveries of the wrong merchandise. Therefore, an order should include:

- date
- item number (catalogue number, style number, model number, etc.)
- quantity desired (often in large units such as dozens, cases, etc.)
- name of the item being ordered
- description (size, colour, extra features, etc.)
- unit price
- discounts
- total amount
- terms of payment and delivery
- delivery address
- delivery time/date
- signature

■ Translate the first two paragraphs into German.

A Activities

A 1 Order by letter with order form

■ Study the letter and the order form on the next page and check whether any important information is missing. Use the information from the introduction.

Dear Mrs Springer   10 December 200_

Order No. 3529

Thank you for your quotation of December 4.

Please send the items on the enclosed order form to the above address.

Enclosed is my banker's draft for €1905.93 made payable to Sportwelt, Augsburg.

Yours sincerely

Gino Giacomelli

Gino Giacomelli
Manager

Encs.

YOUR ORDER

CODE No.	ITEM	SIZE	QTY	PRICE	AMOUNT
961632	LFC Crew-neck sweatshirt red	S	50	9.99	499.50
961632	LFC Crew-neck sweatshirt red	M	50	9.99	499.50
973094	LFC Football T-shirt white	M	30	8.99	269.70
961635	LFC Jog pant adult red	32"	50	8.49	424.50
961635	LFC Jog pant adult red	34"	50	8.49	424.50

POSTAGE AND PACKING
€ 2.50 PER ITEM
€ 5.00 FOR THREE ITEMS OR MORE
FREE OVER € 100 ORDER VALUE

AIR MAIL CHARGES
ADD ON € 7.50 PER ORDER
FREE OVER € 500 ORDER VALUE

SUBTOTAL	2117.70
LESS 10% DISCOUNT IF APPLICABLE	211.77
PLUS POSTAGE & PACKING COSTS	--.--
PLUS VAT IF APPLICABLE	--.--
TOTAL €	1905.93

PAYMENT DETAILS

I enclose a ☐ CHEQUE ☐ EURO POSTAL ORDER ☒ EURO BANKERS DRAFT FOR: € 1905.93

SIGNED *Gino Giacomelli*   DATE 10 Dec 200..

A 2 Orders by letter

a Study these advertisements and write an order for one of the items.

Nail Polish @ £4.99
Order from:
GAROS MAIL ORDER
P.O. Box 398
St. Helier, Jersey JE8 4RQ
Add £1.50 for shipping and handling

Sweet Georgia Brown
#628 COTTON CANDY
#629 GOLDEN RUST
#630 JELLY BEAN
#631 VIRUS

YOUR PERSONAL T-SHIRT

Have you ever wanted a T-shirt with your own personal style?
Yes?
Give us your design, indicate size and colour, and we'll do the rest.

black & white   £19.99
one colour   £21.99
full colour   £24.99

Enclose cheque payable to:
TEEN WISH CO.
P.O. Box 472 · Peterborough
Cambridgeshire · PE2 3YB

from £19.99

ALIENS AND OTHER FUN FASHION ACCESSORIES

No. 3516
£3.99
Eyes glow in the dark

No. 3837
£2.99

No. 3594
£3.99
Wiggly eyes and legs

Call 0800-478270 for free brochure!
To order, make cheque payable to:
FUN FASHION
PO Box 2175
Tarbet   EN4 9BB

b Fred Murphy has convinced the Financial Director of LeisureCorp that the Necson printers are the best long-term choice for their office. Now the order has to be placed with Fletcher's Business Systems, 68 Woodstock Road, Belfast BT3 6OF.

→ 62

→ 60 **Refer to Fletcher's offer on page 60 and draft the complete order as suggested here.**

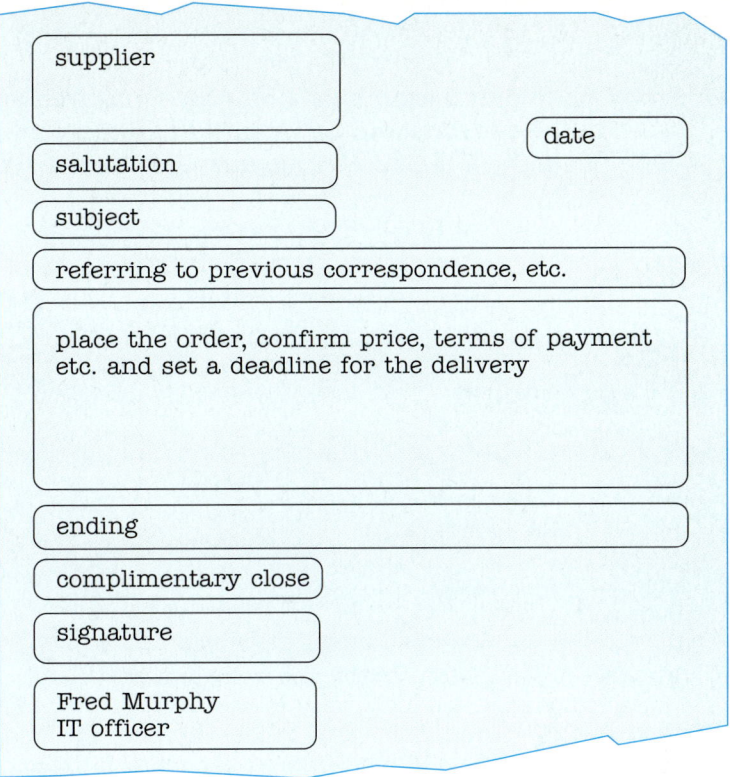

supplier

date

salutation

subject

referring to previous correspondence, etc.

place the order, confirm price, terms of payment etc. and set a deadline for the delivery

ending

complimentary close

signature

Fred Murphy
IT officer

c Study the building blocks on page 86 and 87 and choose the appropriate phrases to complete the order.

C 5062

C 3781

Dear Ms Dellacasa

❶ for your offer of 12 October.

❷ your catalogue and have chosen 2 models.

❸ the following items:
C 5062 Softly Tailored Top, size 14
C 3781 Jeans, size L, colour blue

❹ to stress that this is a trial order and if we are satisfied with your garments you may expect regular repeat orders.

❺ by cheque on receipt of your invoice.

❻ receiving the goods as soon as possible and doing further business with you.

❼

GlobalStores plc

Jane Fairfax

Purchasing Manager

Activities · Unit 5   81

A 3 Order by fax   ➡ 24 ➡ 43

■ Study again unit 2 exercise A4 on page 24 as well as unit 3 exercise A4 a on page 43. Next, listen to the conversation between Will Duncan and his partner Helen Webster. Then complete the body of the fax by choosing the correct alternatives from the box below.

COMPUTER CLINIC
12 Bedford Street   Pembroke SA62 6YE
Tel 01646 873894   Fax 01646 873894
www.compclinic.co.uk

FAX TRANSMISSION

from Helen Webster

To: DigiCorp K.K.
Attn: Kenichi Takano
Subject: Order
Date: 5 Jan 200_
# of pages: 1

Thank you for the brochures and your offer.
Your documentation and a very favourable review in ❶ magazine have convinced us that your UltraSpeed 1280 drives will meet ❷. Also, the quantity discount and the shipping rates you have offered are quite satisfactory.

We ❸ the following order:

100 UltraSpeed 1280 internal including NT and Mac compatible drivers	¥	1,950,000
❹ discount	¥	195,000
subtotal	¥	1,755,000
DDP Pembroke ❺	¥	185,000
total	¥	1,940,000

As agreed, please fax us ❻. On receipt, we ❼ the amount of invoice to your account no. 4829-12754 at Dai-Ichi Kangyo Bank, Takada Branch.

Delivery by 15 February is ❽ as we have very strict deadlines ourselves.

We look forward to receiving the shipment very soon and doing ❾ business with you ❿.

⓫

Helen Webster
Helen Webster

---

① The New Yorker/The Internet/The Networker
② our personal friends/our customer's requirements/all needs
③ place with you/send to you/are therefore placing
④ plus 10 %/less 10 % quantity/less 5% trade
⑤ including insurance/and handling/exclusive of VAT
⑥ back/your pro forma invoice/a written confirmation
⑦ will ship/shall be sending/will remit
⑧ quite normal/absolutely essential/quite desirable
⑨ further/another/more
⑩ currently/in the past/in future
⑪ Keep in touch/Best regards/Love

A 4 Order by telephone

➡ 52

a First copy the form below. Then listen to the telephone conversation between Walter McAdam and Jane Miller, who works at LeisureCorp's telephone booking service. While listening, fill in your form.

Name _____
Address _____
Postcode _____
Home telephone _____
Business telephone _____

Holiday code ☐ ☐☐☐☐

Hotel/Apt/Chalet name _____
No. of nights _____
Resort name _____

Meal requirements

Full board ☐   Half board ☐   Bed & breakfast ☐   Room only ☐

Transfer

Rail ☐   First class ☐   Second class ☐
Air ☐   Business class ☐   Economy class ☐

Departure from _____   Destination _____
Departure date _____   Return date _____

Private transfer ☐

Insurance

Not required ☐   14 days cover ☐   Extended cover ☐

Payment

VISA ☐   MASTERCARD ☐   AMERICAN EXPRESS ☐

No. ☐☐☐☐ ☐☐☐☐ ☐☐☐☐ ☐☐☐☐

Expiry date: _____

Accommodation

	Room/Apartment details					Mr/Mrs/Ms	First Name	Surname	Age
Room 1	PB	PS	WC	BAL	OTHER				
Room 2	PB	PS	WC	BAL	OTHER				

Special requests

b Now work with a partner and make up a similar telephone conversation using these details.

Patricia Carrington	Holiday code G 5467	Jan 15 – 22
167 South Street	Hotel Post	Extended insurance
Birmingham	Freudenstadt	AMEX 7433 2473 0187 2648
B9 3GR	Half board	Double with bath
Home: 0121 849153	Economy class	2 persons, husband Gary
Business: 0121 746357	Birmingham – Stuttgart	Ages 29 and 32

c Read Jerry Debug's report for Jo Wheeler again, page 65. ➡ 65
Listen to Will Duncan and Jo Wheeler, who are finalising a deal.
Take notes and first answer the following questions. Finally use your notes to complete this letter.

1. What were Will Duncan's objectives?
2. What were Jo Wheeler's main objectives?
3. Is there a clear winner or loser? Why (not)?
4. What were the main concessions made in the negotiation?
5. What would happen if Computer Clinic did not finish installation by March 15?
6. What would happen if the system broke down on August 25?

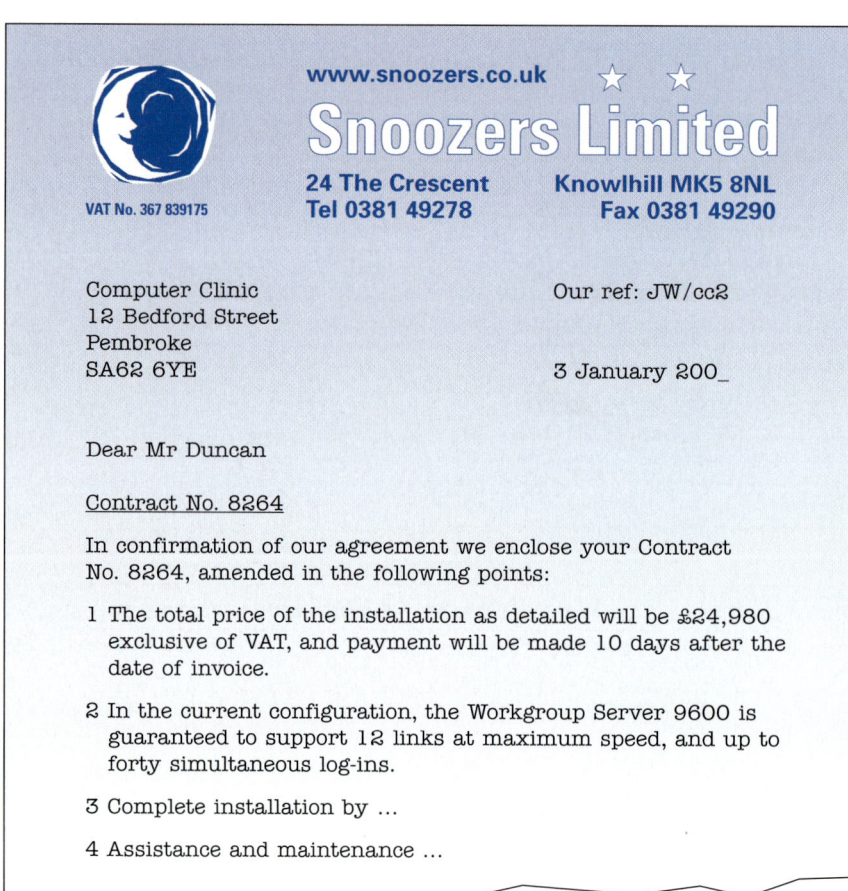

Snoozers Limited
www.snoozers.co.uk
24 The Crescent   Knowlhill MK5 8NL
Tel 0381 49278   Fax 0381 49290
VAT No. 367 839175

Computer Clinic
12 Bedford Street
Pembroke
SA62 6YE

Our ref: JW/cc2

3 January 200_

Dear Mr Duncan

Contract No. 8264

In confirmation of our agreement we enclose your Contract No. 8264, amended in the following points:

1 The total price of the installation as detailed will be £24,980 exclusive of VAT, and payment will be made 10 days after the date of invoice.

2 In the current configuration, the Workgroup Server 9600 is guaranteed to support 12 links at maximum speed, and up to forty simultaneous log-ins.

3 Complete installation by …

4 Assistance and maintenance …

B Tool kit

B1 Structure of business communications: Orders

Detailed orders should be structured like this:

Structure	Language to use
1. appropriate salutation	Dear Mrs/Ms/Mr Smith
2. reference to previous correspondence, quotation, samples etc.	Thank you for your letter **of** ..., in which you offered us ...
3. order (refer to the enclosed order form if necessary)	We enclose our order no. ... **for** ...
4. prices and discounts	... **at** the price **of** ..., less 15% trade discount.
5. terms of delivery	Delivery is to be effected CPT Potsdam.
6. terms of payment	We would like to confirm that payment is to be made **by** cheque **on** receipt of the goods.
7. deadline for delivery	The goods must reach us **by** ... **at** the latest, and we reserve the right to cancel the order after that date.
8. instructions as to packing and transport, if applicable	Please ensure that the goods are packed **in** sturdy crates.
9. request for confirmation, if necessary	Please acknowledge this order **at** your earliest convenience.
10. appropriate ending	If this order is executed **to** our full satisfaction, you may expect further substantial orders from us.
11. appropriate complimentary close	Yours sincerely
12. enclosure, if applicable	Enc. Order Form

■ What is the purpose of these sentences?
Find the appropriate numbers in *structure of business communications* on page 85.

1. We are therefore placing a trial order for 600 units as specified on the enclosed order form.
2. As agreed, payment is to be made within 30 days after date of invoice.
3. Thank you for your offer of 2 December 200_.
4. Prices include VAT and delivery.
5. We have thoroughly tested the samples and are satisfied with their performance.
6. We look forward to receiving the goods and doing further business with you in future.
7. Thank you for your letter of 20 November, in which you enclosed your catalogue and price list.
8. Please supply the following goods:
9. We enclose our Purchase Order No. 3290 for 200 mountain bikes.
10. Delivery by 20 December is essential, and we reserve the right to return the goods at your risk and expense should we receive them after that date.
11. We suggest payment by bill of exchange at 60 days after sight.
12. Thank you for your letter of 9 December quoting prices and delivery terms for removable media.
13. Complete delivery by 31 January 200_ is a firm condition of this order.
14. Our usual method of payment is by cheque, and we trust that this will be acceptable to you.

B 2 Building blocks for business communications: Orders

1 To refer to previous contacts and place an order

We have studied your	catalogue quotation	and	have found your products and terms satisfactory. enclose our Purchase Order No. … ask you to supply the following goods CIP Berlin.
We confirm our order by telephone this morning as follows: …			

Please	deliver send us supply	the following	items goods articles	**on** the	terms conditions	given stated mentioned	in your offer. below. in your brochure.
Thank you for your cost estimate for the repairs.							

2 To specify articles and price if you do not use a preprinted form

Quantity	Product name	Product code	Specifications	Unit price	Total
200	UltraStar	487-97	185cm	@ € 219	€ 4,180
60	Crew-neck shirts	CS-23470	XL, red	@ € 14.99	€ 899.40
50 NOSY GameGear US 64, incl. joypad at € 149 less 10% quantity discount, net 20 days.					

3 To confirm prices and discounts

We wish to place an order **for** model AC/7	**at** the price **of** priced **at**	€ 115.00, less 5%	quantity discount. introductory discount. trade discount.

Unit 5 · Tool kit

We would like to confirm that the prices are	taken **from** your price list. as follows: as per your price list **of** 1 September.
We are pleased to note that you will grant us an initial order discount **of** 3% **on** your list prices.	

4 To confirm method of payment

As agreed, we will effect payment by	SWIFT transfer banker's draft cheque	**on** receipt of	invoice. the goods.
		within ... days	**after** date of invoice. from inspection.

Payment will be	made effected	**by** irrevocable and confirmed letter of credit, to be opened **in** your favour, payable **at** a major London bank and valid **until** 31 March. **by** bill of exchange 60 days **after** sight. **on** the basis of documents against payment. one third **with** order, one third **on** delivery, one third 30 days **after** delivery.

5 To confirm terms of delivery

As agreed, delivery will be made DDU Leipzig.
Your above-mentioned prices are quoted CFR Hamburg.

6 To confirm delivery date and reservations

Please note that	delivery must be made the goods must be delivered the goods must reach us	**in** the course of next week. **before** the end of this month. **within** two weeks. **by** 1 November at the latest.

Complete delivery **by** ... is	absolutely essential. a firm condition of this order.

We reserve the right to return the goods **at** your risk and expense should we receive them **after** ...

7 To give instructions

Please	ensure make sure arrange	that	the sets are the articles are the merchandise is	not exposed **to** heat **during** transport. transported **by** air. packed **with** the utmost care.

We would appreciate **it** if the consultant would send us his manuscript two weeks in advance.

Tool kit · Unit 5

8 To close the letter

We look forward to	your confirmation of our order.
	receiv**ing** the goods in time and doing further business with you.
	plac**ing** further orders with you.

■ Use these building blocks to find equivalents for the following German sentences.

1. Wir danken Ihnen für Ihr Angebot vom 12. März und legen unsere Bestellung Nr. 5983 bei.
2. Wie vereinbart erfolgt die Zahlung per SWIFT-Überweisung innerhalb von 2 Wochen ab Rechnungsdatum.
3. Vollständige Lieferung der Waren bis Ende des Monats ist unbedingt erforderlich.
4. Wir behalten uns das Recht vor, danach die Waren auf Ihre Kosten und Ihr Risiko zurückzuschicken.
5. Wir freuen uns darauf, die Waren rechtzeitig zu erhalten und weitere Geschäfte mit Ihnen zu tätigen.
6. Wir bestätigen unsere telefonische Bestellung von heute morgen wie folgt:
7. 200 STELLA X4 Snowboards blau/gelb, Art.Nr. SX4-13 zum Einzelpreis von € 149, Gesamtwert € 2980.
8. Wie vereinbart wird die Bezahlung innerhalb von 30 Tagen ab Rechnungsdatum erfolgen.
9. Bitte liefern Sie uns nachstehende Artikel CIP Wiesbaden:
10. Wir erwarten die Bestätigung unserer Bestellung und Konditionen bis Ende dieser Woche.
11. Bitte sorgen Sie dafür, dass die Teetassen besonders sorgfältig verpackt werden.
12. Die Zahlungsbedingungen lauten: Unwiderrufliches und bestätigtes Akkreditiv zu Ihren Gunsten, zahlbar bei einer Londoner Großbank, gültig bis 31. Juli 200_.
13. Die Preise sind Ihrer neuesten Preisliste entnommen und verstehen sich EXW Glasgow.
14. Wir bitten Sie, uns 700 Stück zu den nachfolgend genannten Bedingungen zu liefern.
15. Wir freuen uns, dass Sie sich bereit erklärt haben, uns einen Einführungsrabatt von 20% zu gewähren.

B 3 Negotiations

In private life and business, we negotiate constantly. Negotiation is the art of persuading others to give you what you want. The success of a business depends to a large extent on the negotiating skills of its owners or representatives.

Successful negotiation depends just as much on the skills of the negotiator as on thorough preparation, which is essential for getting what you want. Here are some basic principles:

- Good negotiators consider many different things before starting to negotiate. They take time to study the other side, which is essential when dealing with people from another culture.
- Good negotiators research, prepare and organize all the material that will back up their position before they begin to negotiate. If they are dealing with more than one issue, they usually concentrate on the most important one.
- Good negotiators set themselves reasonable goals which can be achieved without detriment to the interests of the other side. Their focus is not on immediate gains, but rather on long-term benefits.
- Good negotiators always take their files with them, even during short breaks. Leaving files unattended could allow the other side to gain access to their plans and work out a counter-strategy.

- Good negotiators try to create a good rapport with the other party. This means that the atmosphere at the beginning is friendly and harmonious, which may make it easier to make concessions in the course of negotiations.
- Good negotiators are flexible. They develop fallback positions or even alternative goals, thus allowing for concessions without appearing to lose. This means that they aim to get what they want, but do not lock themselves into a position where they must get what they want.
- Good negotiators are good listeners as well. They check frequently to make sure that everything has been understood by both parties, which is essential when dealing with people whose mother tongue is not English.
- Good negotiators are tenacious. They often select only a few key arguments and repeat them in the course of the negotiation.
- Good negotiators will carry on negotiations even if a major problem arises. They are flexible enough to suggest solutions and/or alternatives that they have worked out in the course of their preparation.
- Good negotiators always point out what the benefits are to the other side, and try to make them feel good about any agreement reached.

B 4 Phrases for negotiations

To state your position:
We think …
We'd like to …
What we're looking for …
We were hoping for …
We can guarantee …
I'm afraid we can't …
We wouldn't want to …
There's no way …

To make suggestions:
We could …
How about …?
I'd like to suggest that …
Let's agree …, shall we?
Don't you think we should …?
I strongly recommend that …

To add information:
I'd like to add that …
Did you know that …?
Let me add a few things. First, …
Let me explain this in greater detail.
Let's look at it from another perspective.

To ask for further information:
Can you give me further details of …?
Could you expand on this point?
Could you explain this in a little more detail?
Now, could you be more precise on …?

To interrupt:
Sorry to interrupt you, but …
I've got to stop you there, because …

To ask for clarification:
What is the reason for this?
What do you have in mind?
Are you saying that …?
Could we go through that again?
What do you mean when you say …?
If I've understood you correctly, you're suggesting …
Am I correct in saying that …?

To rephrase a point:
What I'm trying to say is …
Maybe I haven't made myself clear.
Let me put it another way.
To be more specific, let me …

To ask for a reaction:
What do you think about this?
How does that sound …?
What do you say …?
How do you feel about …?

To correct misunderstandings:
No, I didn't say that …
I didn't quite say that.
No, I'm sorry. That's not what I said.
I'm afraid you've misunderstood me.

To express partial agreement:
I take your point, but …
Well, I agree in principle, but …
You certainly have a point there, but …
I can go along with most of what you've said, but …
I can accept your proposal by and large, but …

To express full agreement:
Yes, of course.
Perfect.
I fully agree to …
That's a deal.

To disagree with a proposal:
Do you really think so?
I'm not totally convinced.
I wouldn't say that.
I'm not entirely happy with this proposal.
I can't accept your position on that point.

To reject a proposal:
We just can't agree to …
I'm sorry, I can't go along with that.
No, I don't think I can accept that proposal.
I'm afraid, that is out of the question.

To bargain:
We're prepared to …, if you …
We'll …, providing you …
If you accept …, we could …
We could make an exception if you …

To buy time:
I'm glad you asked this question.
Now that's a very interesting question.
You've raised an important question there.
Well, it's rather difficult to answer this question now.
I'm afraid I can't answer this question at present.

C Additional practice

a Read this letter and choose the correct alternative from the box.

➡ 53

❶ Attn./Dear/To the order of
❷ expect/except/accept
❸ repeating/repeat/continuous
❹ agent/documents/instructions
❺ supply/shipments/delivery
❻ heading/first/chief

Notabene SpA
❶ Ms Gianna Dellacasa
Monteverde 157
20487 Parma
Italy

7 March 200_

Dear Ms Dellacasa,

Our order No. NB 001/03

Please find enclosed our purchase order for teenage garments in assorted sizes, colours, and designs.

We ❷ your 15% quantity discount and terms of payment, but would like to negotiate new terms for ❸ orders.

Please send the shipping ❹ and your sight draft to Sparkasse Passau, Donauplatz 2, 94032 Passau.

We expect ❺ within the next four weeks, and look forward to your confirmation.

Yours sincerely,

Michaela Fetzer

Michaela Fetzer
❻ Buyer

b Match the parts of these sentences and draft a complete letter.

Dear Ms Wilkins,

1. Thank you for your letter of 24 April and	a. and have found them satisfactory.
2. We have studied your products and terms	b. as per your quotation.
3. We would therefore like to place a trial order	c. as we require the goods very urgently.
4. List price €16.90 less 15% & 2%	d. the enclosed samples and price list.
5. Delivery must be made by 30 April by Parcel Express,	e. for 2000 Queenston 32MB SDRAM chips on the following terms:

Yours sincerely,

c GAMETOYS, Glückstraße 57, 93449 Spielberg, Tel (09972) 738287, Fax (09972) 738 288, *www. gametoys.co.de*, has received a catalogue, prices and terms from TINDONET Europe.
At a meeting, it was decided to place a trial order for 200 GameGear 256 consoles and assorted games.

Use the notes on the right to draft an order to:

TINDONET EUROPE
345 King Street
Oxford OX1 7HF
Tel (01865) 589 243
Fax (01865) 589 263
www.tindonet.com

Bestellung

200 Stk Tindonet 256 inkl.: Joypad
                                220 V Stromkabel
                                Euro-AV Kabel
                                Demo DVD deutsch

Spiele: 40 NBA 200_ à € 14,90
         50 Gran Turismo à € 16,90
         80 World Cup Soccer à € 19,90
         100 Tomb Raider 6 à € 21,90
         30 Final Fantasy 10 à € 12,90

Konditionen: 20% Großhandelsrabatt
              Wechsel auf 60 Tage Sicht
              Lieferung innerh. 6 Wochen komplett!

d Study this offer ZISCHFRISCH (Durststrecke 8, 73033 Göppingen, Tel (07161) 73110, Fax (07161) 73120, E-mail: *durst@zischfrisch.de*, **has just received from Clearly Canadian Beverages** (1700 Water St, Victoria, B.C. V8C R356, Canada, Fax 001-604 689-5366).

Place a trial order for 2,500 bottles of each flavour and accept terms and delivery date.

We appreciate your interest in Orbitz, the world's first texturally enhanced beverage offering the consumer two taste sensations. Orbitz is available in a distinctive 10oz glass bottle in four unique flavor combinations, including Pineapple•Banana•Coconut, Raspberry•Citrus, Blueberry•Melon•Strawberry, and Vanilla•Orange.

We are delighted to make this special introductory offer:

10,000 bottles in assorted flavors CIF Rotterdam Can$ 6,199.00

The drinks will be dispatched within three working days from receipt of your bank transfer to our account #2356 8973 1203 3469 at the Vancouver branch of First Canadian Bank.

We are confident that consumer response to Orbitz will be overwhelming, and look forward to receiving your order soon.

e IMPORTEX, 94034 Passau, Modegasse 6, Tel (0851) 370301, Fax (0851) 370312,
31 www.importex.co.de, has received catalogues, price lists and a few samples from
   headTOtoe, 200 Kilroy Street, Dublin 4, Ireland, Fax (+3531) 956 2840,
   e-mail: mulligan@head-to-toe.co.ri.

Read your boss's notes and study the price list, then write an order by e-mail.

ausgezeichnete Qualität, ansprechende Muster!

je 100 Stk

Schlagen Sie vor:
10% Mengenrabatt,
Zahlung per Wechsel 60 Tage,
Lieferung bis Ende Monat,
sonst Ware zurück!

je 50 Stk

CODE No.	ITEM	SIZES available	PRICE exw
(C-12671)	Ski cap red/yellow	one size fits all	€ 11.99
(C-12672)	Ski cap blue/yellow	one size fits all	€ 11.99
C-12673	Ski cap red/white	one size fits all	€ 12.99
C-12674	Ski cap blue/white	one size fits all	€ 12.99
S-17094	Aran sweater teal	S M L XL	€ 28.99
(S-17095)	zip sweater red	S M L XL	€ 28.99

D Background information

D 1 Cheques and banker's drafts

a Read this information about cheques and banker's drafts, and translate it into German.

For many decades the cheque has been a popular means of payment in domestic trade. It is an order in writing from an account holder to his bank ordering the latter to pay a certain
5 sum of money to the beneficiary and it may be transferred from one person to another by endorsement and delivery. **Open cheques** are paid out in currency over the bank counter whereas **crossed cheques** must be credited to
10 a bank account, which is a safer method of payment as it permits the flow of money to be traced. **Order cheques** are payable to a specified person or to his or her order, they are transferable by endorsement. **Bearer cheques**
15 are payable to any bearer. It should be noted that bearer cheques, such as Eurocheques, while known in Britain, are not popular, and some British banks no longer issue them to their customers at all. Despite the increasing
20 popularity of credit cards, personal cheques are still widely used in the UK and the cheque-book is a convenient way of keeping track of your expenditure. Cheque books normally contain crossed cheques.
Eurocheques are guaranteed by the respective 25 banks up to a certain amount by means of cheque cards. **Cheque cards** also serve as cash cards, enabling their holders to pay with them at points of sale and to withdraw money or receive statements of account at cashpoints or 30 automated teller machines (ATMs).
If a merchant like Mr Giacomelli (see page 79) wishes to buy goods from a supplier for the first time, a cheque for almost 2,000 euros would not be acceptable because the merchant 35 is not known to the supplier. This is why Mr Giacomelli asked his bank to issue a **banker's draft** – a cheque drawn by one bank on another - made out to Sportwelt for the sum required and marked A/c payee. This means that 40 the amount may only be credited to the bank account of Sportwelt and that Sportwelt can be sure of getting their money because the bank guarantees payment.

92   Unit 5 · Background information

b Study this cheque and note what is different compared to a Eurocheque. Then read the following instructions and check whether it has been made out correctly.

Instructions:
1. Enter the current date.
2. Enter the payee's name (i.e. the person or company to whom the money is to be paid) alongside the word 'Pay' on the cheque.
3. On the next two lines write the amount of the cheque in words starting on the left, beginning immediately under the word 'Pay' and leave the minimum space between the words. You may write the number of pence in figures instead of words.
4. Write the amount in figures in the box provided.
5. Sign the cheque on the line in the lower right-hand corner.
6. Record the details of the cheque on the cheque counterfoil provided in your cheque book.
7. Cheques should be written out in ink as carefully and clearly as possible. If you make a mistake, you must place your signature beside each correction. If there is additional space, you should draw a horizontal line.

D 2 Bills of Exchange

According to the Bill of Exchange Act 1882, a bill of exchange is "an unconditional order in writing, addressed by one person to another, signed by the person giving it, requiring the person to whom it is addressed to pay on demand or at a fixed or determinable future time a certain sum in money to, or to the order of, a specified person or to bearer."

There are three parties to a B/E: the drawer who makes out the B/E, the drawee who is required to pay and the payee to whom the money is to be paid. Frequently, the payee is identical with the drawer. At its initial stage the B/E is called a draft.

A B/E has to be paid (honoured) either immediately, i.e. at sight – then it is called a sight draft – or at a fixed or determinable future date, called the date of maturity. In this case it is called a time bill.

A time bill must be accepted by the drawee with his own signature on the face of the B/E and returned to the drawer/payee. The B/E may then be referred to as an acceptance. The payee now has three options: he may

- keep the B/E until maturity
- pass it on to a creditor of his in payment
- have it discounted by a bank, which means that the bank will pay him the face value of the B/E less a certain discount.

In the two latter cases the payee must endorse the B/E, i.e. sign it on the back in order to transfer ownership of the B/E. Every holder of the B/E may, however, be held liable for payment if the B/E is not honoured at maturity. The B/E is of particular importance for business as it is both a means of payment and a means of credit. By drawing a time bill on him, the drawer grants the drawee credit for the period until maturity while he himself may have the B/E discounted as soon as it has been accepted by the drawee. Thus the drawer (payee) may obtain the sum in question long before the date of maturity.

Who benefits from the B/E?

1. the *buyer*, e.g. retailers such as Sports Unlimited, who are granted credit until the date of maturity if they accept a B/E. This enables Sports Unlimited to sell the goods first and to honour the B/E afterwards out of the proceeds from the sale.
2. the *seller*, e.g. suppliers such as Hyflyer plc, who are enabled to grant their customers credit by drawing a bill of exchange on them which is due at a later date. But Hyflyer plc need not wait for the money until then. Once the B/E has been accepted by Sports Unlimited, Hyflyer plc can have it discounted by a bank, e.g. MetroBank. That means Hyflyer plc receive the invoice amount (less the discount) long before the B/E is due for payment.
3. the *bank*, e.g. MetroBank, which is enabled to advance money and earns a certain percentage of the invoice amount by discounting the B/E.

How does the B/E work?

1. Hyflyer draws a B/E at 60 days on Sports Unlimited. That means Hyflyer requires Sports Unlimited to pay the amount of the B/E in 60 days and sends Sports Unlimited the B/E for acceptance.
2. Sports Unlimited accepts the B/E by signing it on the face. Thus Sports Unlimited confirms its obligation to pay. Sports Unlimited then returns the accepted B/E to Hyflyer.
3. On receipt of the accepted B/E Hyflyer forwards the bicycles to Sports Unlimited.
4. Sports Unlimited sells the bicycles to its customers.
5. Hyflyer endorses the B/E, i.e. signs it on the back, in order to have it discounted by MetroBank. The bank pays Hyflyer the amount of the B/E less a small discount.
6. Two months later, MetroBank presents the B/E to Sports Unlimited, and Sports Unlimited pays the full amount of the B/E to MetroBank.

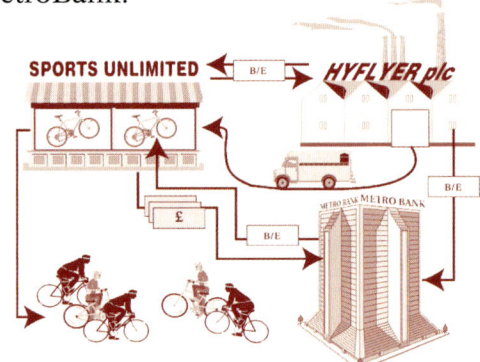

a Study the text on the B/E on page 93 and decide who is who in the above transaction:

- MetroBank
- Hyflyer plc
- Sports Unlimited

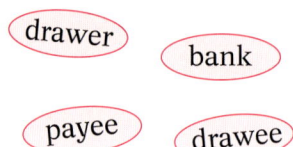

drawer — bank — payee — drawee

b Choose the right verbs from the box for the gaps.

The seller ❶ a B/E on the buyer. The buyer must ❷ the B/E and ❸ it to the seller. The bank ❹ the B/E. Before that the seller must ❺ the B/E.

accept ∗ discounts ∗ draws
endorse ∗ return

c Read this excerpt from a letter and find the appropriate prepositions.

We suggest that the total sum (❶ of / from) £ 4,620 should be paid (❷ with/ by) bill of exchange drawn (❸ up / on) us (❹ in / at) 30 days (❺ before / after) sight. Please confirm.

Yours sincerely

d This excerpt is from a letter that Hyflyer received from Badenbike, a German wholesaler who wants to import 20 Hyflyer DX-2000 bicycles to Germany at a unit price of £231.00 DDU Karlsruhe. **Write a full order using the excerpt you have just completed.** (Addresses see below)

e Hyflyer has decided to accept Badenbike's proposal and will draw a bill of exchange on them. **Study the information on the bill of exchange. Then decide where these parts belong in the bill of exchange below.**

ⓐ *30 days after sight* ⓑ *17 January*

ⓒ *Four thousand six hundred and twenty pounds sterling*

ⓓ *Signed: Peter Hamilton*

ⓔ *Badenbike*
Draisstraße 342
76189 Karlsruhe
Germany

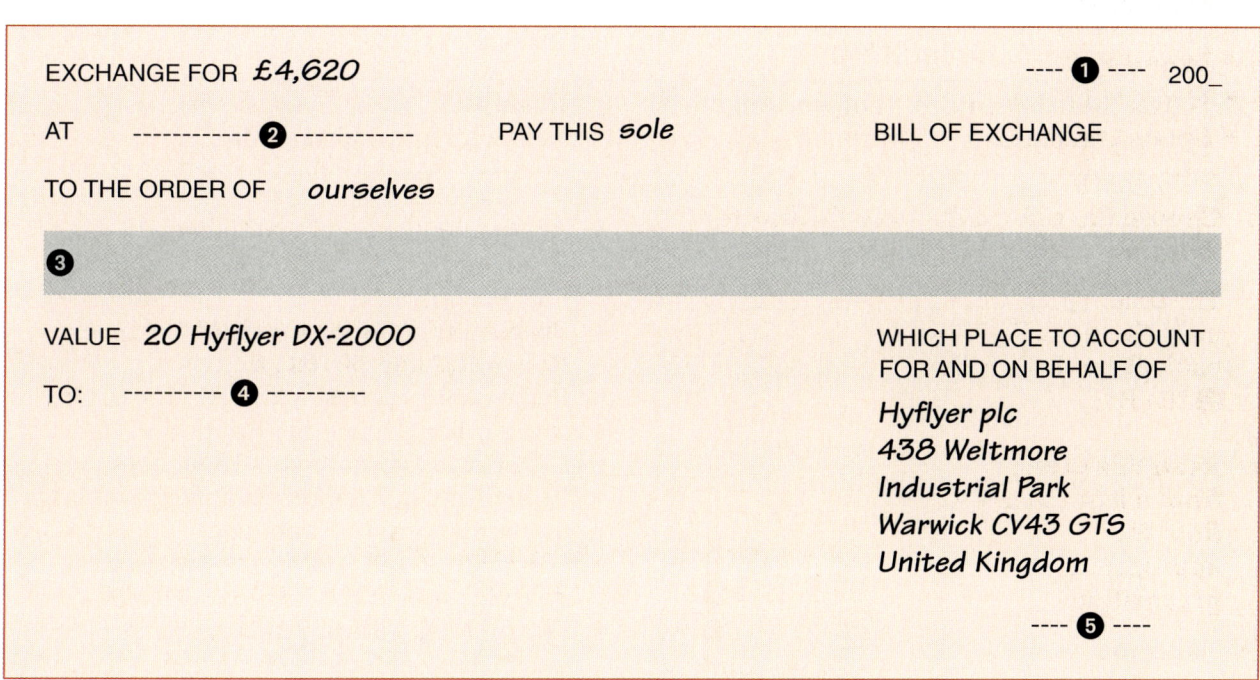

f Listen to Diana Ellington, who is a specialist in commercial banking, and take notes. Then match the words in the box and their translations, and decide whether the following statements are true or false.

1. drawer	a. Bezogener
2. drawee	b. Begünstigter
3. payee	c. Aussteller

1. Arab merchants used the bill of exchange as early as the 8th century BC.
2. The modern draft came into wide use during the 13th century in Italy.
3. The seller signs a draft, and the buyer receives payment by presenting it to the bank.
4. A bill of exchange can be issued either at sight, or at a number of days after sight.
5. If the seller needed the gold, he could sell the bill at a discount from its full amount.
6. The banker could debit the buyer's account before the bill became due.
7. There are more than two parties to a bill of exchange.
8. The drawer draws a bill of exchange on the payee.
9. The buyer accepts the draft by signing it and then returns it to the bank.
10. The payee is the person who must pay when the bill is due.
11. The drawer can also use the bill to pay debts of his own by endorsing it.
12. To endorse a B/E means to sign it on the back.

E IHK-Prüfungsvorbereitung

1.

Zusatzqualifikation Englisch für kaufmännische Auszubildende Fremdsprache im Beruf I	
Geschäftsbrief nach Stichwortangaben (Bearbeitungszeit 45 Minuten)	**Hilfsmittel:** zweisprachiges Wörterbuch

Situation

Sie arbeiten in der Einkaufsabteilung von Badenbike, Draisstr. 342, in 76189 Karlsruhe. Ihrer Firma liegt ein Angebot der italienischen Firma Eurosport, Via dei Banchi 45, 78038 Firenze, über einen zusammenlegbaren Motorroller (foldable motor scooter) vor, der mühelos im Kofferraum oder auf dem Rücksitz eines Autos transportiert werden kann. Heute ist der 14. Juni 200_

Aufgabe

Bitte verfassen Sie für Ihre Chefin, Frau Susanne Berger, ein Bestellschreiben und berücksichtigen Sie dabei folgende Punkte:

- Ansprechpartner: Gino Giacomelli
- Bezug auf Brief vom 4. Juni, mit Katalog und Preisliste
- Probeauftrag für 20 zusammenlegbare Roller, Katalog-Nr. 64145
- Preis € 799.- pro Stück, DDU Karlsruhe, zahlbar per Scheck bei Erhalt der Ware
- Lieferung innerhalb von 2 Wochen
- Einhaltung der Lieferfrist äußerst wichtig, momentan große Nachfrage
- Wenn Tests und Absatz positiv, größere Aufträge möglich
- Für größere Aufträge Mengenrabatte und günstigere Zahlungsbedingungen erforderlich
- Erwartung baldiger Lieferung und regelmäßiger Geschäftsbeziehungen bei Zufriedenheit mit dem Probeauftrag

2. Zusatzqualifikation Englisch für kaufmännische Auszubildende
Fremdsprache im Beruf I*

Vermerk in Deutsch über ein Telefongespräch (Bearbeitungszeit 20 Minuten)	Hilfsmittel: zweisprachiges Wörterbuch

Situation

Sie sind Jochen Speck und vertreten Frau Sabine Sängerlein, eine Sachbearbeiterin in der Exportabteilung der Firma Schwarzwald-Uhren in Villingen. Sie erhalten einen Anruf aus USA wegen Taucheruhren.

Aufgabe

Fassen Sie die Nachricht in einem Vermerk in Deutsch für Frau Sängerlein zusammen. (Sie werden das Gespräch zweimal hören. Was Sie selbst sagen, haben sie schriftlich vorliegen)

Vokabelangabe: *face* – Zifferblatt

Switchboard:
    Schwarzwald-Uhren. Guten Tag.

Caller: –

Switchboard:
    I'm afraid, she's not in today.
    I'll put you through to the export department.

Speck: Export department, Speck.
    How can I help you?

Caller: –

Speck: On Monday. Perhaps I can help you?

Caller: –

Speck: My name is Jochen Speck, S-P-E-C-K

Caller: –

Speck: I've got that. Anything else I can do for you?

Caller: –

Speck: O.K., 1000 Pacific ... The list price is $129.45 per unit.

Caller: –

Speck: Thank you very much. I've taken down your order for Mrs. Sängerlein. I'm sure, she will have your order dispatched first thing on Monday. And I'll fax you a confirmation right now.

Caller: –

Speck: Goodbye. Have a nice day.

3. Fremdsprache im Beruf I

Gelenkte Zusammenfassung (in Deutsch) eines Textes Schwerpunkte: Handel, Industrie (Bearbeitungszeit 45 Minuten)	Hilfsmittel: zweisprachiges Wörterbuch

Situation

Sie sind als Assistent/in der Geschäftsleitung eines deutschen Vertriebshauses für Designerbekleidung für die Auswertung der englischsprachigen Presse zuständig.

Aufgabe

Bitte fassen Sie für Ihre Chefin nachstehenden Artikel aus der Fachzeitschrift Fashion News vom 4. November 200_ (219 Wörter) in Deutsch auf ungefähr ein Drittel der Länge zusammen. Gehen Sie dabei auf folgende Fragen ein:
- Wer ist Bernard Artois?
- Worin bestand sein neues Konzept und wozu führte es?
- Position von LWAG in der Branche?
- Warum lernt Bernard Artois Italienisch?

* Die Bearbeitungszeit beträgt bei Fremdsprache im Beruf 30 Min., die Dialoge sind dementsprechend etwas länger.

Bernard Artois is the head of LWAG, the world's biggest luxury-goods group, an $8.5 billion empire that includes Henri Vason, the luggage maker, and Dom Château champagne, and he is also France's richest businessman. His mix of aggression and American-style commercialism has gained him the nickname "wolf in cashmere clothing" but he is exactly what the French luxury goods industry needed.

Behind the scenes he introduced a new concept, selling through directly owned shops rather than through licensees. This has helped LWAG to increase profits and to improve control over brand image and quality. Profit margins at Henri Vason, which earns half of LWAG's profits, have risen to 45%, twice as high as those of its biggest competitor, Leone.

Although LWAG is facing strong competition from companies such as Leone, it remains the biggest group in the luxury goods industry with a market share of 15% of the $68 billion global luxury-goods market.

Now Mr Artois is learning Italian, not because he is off on holiday or accompanying his pianist wife on a concert tour but because he wants to talk to Sergio Accardi, a famous Italian designer. "I want to ask him to work with me," laughs Mr Artois. He is learning Italian because his sworn enemy, Domenico Stella, the boss of Leone, is also interested in Mr Accardi.

4. Fremdsprachenkorrespondent/in

Übersetzung Englisch/Deutsch (Bearbeitungszeit 60 Minuten)	Hilfsmittel: zweisprachige Wörterbücher

The value of the global internet economy will reach $2,800bn in 2003 which is roughly 7% of world gross domestic product. A recent study emphasises that spending on upgrading the internet will have to reach $1,500bn a year in order to support the expected growth in communications traffic.

Today's internet is neither reliable nor fast enough for the smooth functioning of commercial transactions. E-commerce is expected to grow by 86% to reach $1,300bn annually by 2003. According to the study, E-business will grow fastest in Europe, with a 118% annual growth rate. Thousands of companies will move billions of dollars of commerce from traditional distribution channels to the web. This study questions the view that there will be excess internet transmission capacity as operators expand broadband networks using the latest technology.

It argues that there will be a shortage of capacity in both the US and Europe as use of the internet increases. The study also suggests that business to business e-business will grow much more quickly than business to consumer transactions and that revenues will be several times greater.

Despite recent setbacks the internet economy is expected to continue to grow strongly in the next few years.

5. Fremdsprachenkorrespondent/in

Übersetzung Deutsch/Englisch (Bearbeitungszeit 60 Minuten)	Hilfsmittel: zweisprachige Wörterbücher

Wenn jemand eine kreative Geschäftsidee mit Erfolg in die Tat umsetzen will, kann er die Hilfe von Experten der Industrie- und Handelskammern nutzen. Die Kammern geben Broschüren zur Existenzgründung heraus und bieten intensive Einzelberatung und Seminare an.
Finanzierung, Versicherung, Buchführung, Steuern, Rechtsformen von Unternehmen, Verträge – die Liste der Dinge, an welche die zukünftigen Unternehmer denken müssen, ist fast endlos. Gemeinsam mit den Beratern von der Industrie- und Handelskammer können die Gründer ihre persönlichen Checklisten durcharbeiten und die Chancen und Risiken ihrer Projekte abschätzen.

Mit ihren Gründerseminaren speziell für Arbeitslose haben die Kammern auch im vergangenen Jahr zahlreichen Menschen wieder neue berufliche Perspektiven gegeben. Rund ein Drittel der Teilnehmer hat es gewagt, sich selbständig zu machen – mit guten Aussichten auf Erfolg.
Ein Unternehmen muss nicht immer aus dem Nichts entstehen. Rund 300 000 Inhaber kleiner und mittlerer Unternehmen suchen in Deutschland einen Nachfolger. Die Industrie- und Handelskammern helfen auch in diesem Zusammenhang, kostenlos und über die Grenzen von Branchen hinweg, durch Veröffentlichungen in der IHK-Zeitschrift, im Internet und in einer regelmäßig auf den neuesten Stand gebrachten Broschüre.

Vokabelangabe: Existenzgründung – *founding of a new company*

6. Fremdsprachenkorrespondent/in

Beantwortung einer Korrespondenz (Bearbeitungszeit 60 Minuten)	Hilfsmittel: zweisprachige Wörterbücher

→ 41 **Situation**

Sie sind
Frau Rita Spielvogel von der
Firma GAMETOYS, Glückstr. 57,
93449 Spielberg,
Tel. +49 9972 738287,
Fax +49 9972 738288,
www.gametoys.co.de,
E-Mail: spielvogel@gametoys.de

Sie haben von der US-amerikanischen Firma Delta Games das in Unit 3, S.41, abgedruckte briefliche Angebot erhalten. Inzwischen sind auch die Muster des neuen Spiels "Hit and Run" eingetroffen. Heute ist der 2. August.

Aufgabe
Studieren Sie das Angebot und schicken Sie Mr. Wallis eine E-Mail. Gehen Sie dabei auf Folgendes ein:

- Muster von Mitarbeitern mit guten Englischkenntnissen getestet. Ergebnis positiv
- Strategiespiele im deutschsprachigen Raum sehr beliebt
- Spiel müsste für den deutschen Verbraucher sprachlich überarbeitet werden. GAMETOYS wäre dazu sofort in der Lage
- Könnte Delta Games anschließend die deutsche Version kurzfristig produzieren?
- Mögliche Größenordnung: 2500 Stück
- Lieferung bis Mitte September unerlässlich: Weihnachtsgeschäft!
- Höherer Sonderrabatt als Ausgleich für die Kosten der Überarbeitung durch GAMETOYS gewünscht
- Für Folgeaufträge günstigere Zahlungsbedingungen erforderlich *(Beispiel angeben)*

7. Fremdsprachenkorrespondent/in

Zusammenfassung (in Deutsch) einer englischen mündlichen Nachricht (Bearbeitungszeit 30 Minuten)	Hilfsmittel: zweisprachige Wörterbücher

76 Situation

Sie arbeiten in der Exportabteilung des Unternehmens Computex GmbH in Münster. Das Großhandelshaus Palm Top Ltd., in Rawdon (Leeds), Großbritannien hatte Ihnen ein Auftrag über das Palmtop-Modell Xion2K erteilt. (Vgl. Brief von Palm Top Ltd. an Computex, Unit 4 Seite 76)

Aufgabe:

Ihr Chef, Herr Wildenbruch, versteht wenig Englisch. Er bittet Sie daher einen Vermerk in Deutsch über eine Nachricht zu verfassen, die er auf seinem Anrufbeantworter erhalten hat. Ihr Vermerk muss alle wichtigen Einzelheiten enthalten. (Sie werden die Nachricht zweimal hören.)

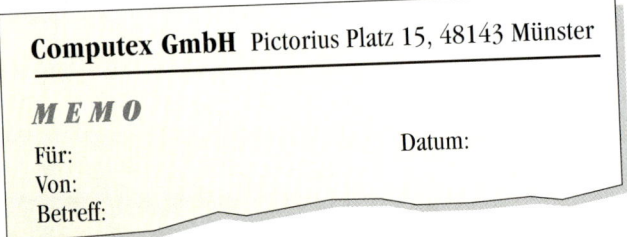

8. Fremdsprachenkorrespondent/in

Geschäftsbrief nach Angaben in Deutsch (Bearbeitungszeit 30 Minuten)	Hilfsmittel: zweisprachige Wörterbücher

Situation

Sie (eigener Name) sind bei der Großhandelsfirma Sportwelt Fan-Artikel, Wertachring 93, 86153 Augsburg, Tel. 0821 720473, Fax 0821 720659, für das Marketing zuständig. Die britische Firma Elton Business Accessories Ltd, 17 Highbury Road, Duffield, Derbyshire DE55 9BR, Tel. 01773 836100, Fax 01773 836200, hatte Ihnen am 18. August 200_ ein Angebot über ein als Werbegeschenk geeignetes Visitenkartenalbum gemacht, wobei die Frachtkosten zu Lasten des Empfängers gehen sollten und Zahlung bei Lieferung vorgesehen war. Das Angebot war von Augusta Hawkins unterschrieben.

Aufgabe

Formulieren Sie einen Brief, den Sie per Fax übermitteln, als Reaktion.
Berücksichtigen Sie folgende Einzelheiten:
- Interesse an Visitenkartenalbum "Business Class", Wildleder, bordeauxrot, 57 x 90 mm, Stückpreis £3.75
- voraussichtliche Bestellmenge: 500 Stück
- Bedingungen für Auftragserteilung:
    1. Mengenrabatt
       (Machen Sie einen Vorschlag)
    2. günstigere Lieferbedingungen
       (Machen Sie einen Vorschlag)
    3. Lieferzeit höchstens drei Wochen
    4. Zahlung 30 Tage nach Rechnungserhalt
- Name und Logo Ihrer Firma (siehe Briefkopf) in Goldprägung auf der Innenseite des Buchdeckels
- Alben einzeln in Seidenpapier eingeschlagen in Geschenkkartons

Unit 6 Order confirmation and cancellation, dispatch advice

Introduction

■ **Read this information and make a short summary in German of the most important points.**

Many companies today no longer acknowledge orders, particularly if the order is dealt with promptly. Some companies respond to orders by immediately sending invoices, and some use printed acknowledgement forms. Confirming an order helps to establish goodwill because the customer can be sure that his/her order has been received.

First orders should always be confirmed in order to welcome the new customer and encourage further business. Also, an unusually large order from a regular customer deserves a note of appreciation.

Orders placed on the basis of an offer without engagement or an offer with some reservation or other, for instance concerning prices or quantities available, must in any case be confirmed by the supplier.

Sometimes the confirmation of order contains particulars of the impending or effected dispatch of the goods. In some instances a separate advice of dispatch may have to be sent to the customer.

The confirmation of an order should let the customer know what is being done about his/her order and should contain the following information:

- date and number of the order
- reference to the invoice
- date and method of dispatch
- terms of payment and delivery

A confirmation can also be an opportunity for further sales. Clever salespeople often enclose information about related products that may spark the customer's interest and encourage future orders.

A Activities

A 1 Accepting orders by phone

a **Listen to the telephone conversation between Anthony Rattle, who attended Evelyn Strand's presentation, and Yvonne Gore, who works for Weinbauer Ltd., 105 Deansgate, Manchester M60 21R. Take notes of important points.**

b Yvonne Gore fills in the order form as follows while she takes Mr. Rattle's order over the telephone. **Listen to the telephone conversation again and check if Yvonne Gore has filled out the order form correctly.**

FIRST NAME	SURNAME	DELIVER TO
Anthony	Rattle	Angela Rattle
Address 167 Wanstead Road Wanstead London		Address 57a Wanstead Common Wanstead London
POSTCODE E11 6ST		POSTCODE E11 3LQ

QTY	ITEM	VINTAGE	PRICE PER BOTTLE	TOTAL
50	Ahr red "Sonnentröpfchen"	97	GBP 4.99	GBP 249.50
50	Franconian Riesling "Pfaffenlust"	95	GBP 5.99	GBP 299.50
			TOTAL	GBP 549.00
DATE OF ORDER 8 December 200_			DATE OF DISPATCH 2 January 200_	

c   Work with a partner. Student A works with Wedler & Co, manufacturers of sports equipment based in Sonthofen, Germany. Student B is head buyer with McPherson Sports, Aviemore, Scotland. He rings Wedler & Co as he wishes to include a further article in the order he placed with Wedler two days ago. Begin and close the conversation on a friendly note.

70 Student A: Study the price list on page 70. Then use the information below.
Student B: Study the price list on page 70. Then use the information on page 107.

Informationen für Student A, der/die bei Wedler & Co. beschäftigt ist

1. Herr Hintermooser ist auf Geschäftsreise, er kommt erst in zwei Wochen zurück.

2. Auftrag von McPherson Sports datiert 20.08, Nr. JY-1289 über 50 Winner gold Ski und 20 SuperStar erhalten. Auftragsbestätigung folgt heute Nachmittag.

3. Für Anfänger Winner blue oder Winner red geeignet.

4. Winner red ist schmaler und schneller als Winner blue. Winner blue speziell für Anfänger geeignet.

5. Winner red im Moment nicht lieferbar, Produktionsprobleme werden in ca. 3 Wochen behoben sein.

6. Bestellung vom 20. August schon in Bearbeitung, wird erweitert um Auftrag von heute.
   Lieferzeit wie versprochen (siehe Preisliste). Auftrag über 15 Winner blue wird zusammen mit dem Auftrag vom 20. 08. noch heute per Fax bestätigt.

7. Wedler dankbar für Auftrag, Kunde wird zufrieden sein.

A2 Order confirmation by letter

a Read this confirmation of Mr Rattle's order and decide which of the alternatives in brackets is correct.

Mr Anthony Rattle
167 Wanstead Road
Wanstead
London E11 6ST

December 8, 200_

Dear Mr Rattle

We are (**1** happy/lucky/pleased) to have received your order today and would like to welcome you as a new (**2** customer/guest/patron).

Your order for 50 bottles of red Ahr wine "Sonnentröpfchen" and 50 bottles of Franconian Riesling "Pfaffenlust" will be (**3** dispatched/worked/done) today. It will be (**4** deliver/delivered/delivering) to your address by Parcel Express, and payment will be made by (**5** letter of credit/bill of exchange/cheque).

We are confident that you will (**6** taste/have/enjoy) the excellent taste of these vintages. "Sonnentröpfchen" goes especially well with red meats, while Riesling is best enjoyed with poultry, fish and seafood. For further details, please (**7** look/refer/see) to the enclosed Wine Guide.

Yours (**8** truly/sincerely/faithfully)

b First, rewrite the following letter using the correct spacing, punctuation and capitalization as in the letters in the previous units. Next, study the excerpts from Sports Unlimited's purchase order on the next page. Then write a confirmation thanking them for their first order and confirming the order and terms.

sports unlimited 76 the mall stratford e15 1xd tel 020 8226 3112 fax 020 8226 3112 rob sullivan sales manager hyflyer plc 438 weltmore industrial park warwick cv43 6ts 8 january 200_ dear mr sullivan order for DX-2000 thank you for your letter of 20 december in which you enclosed your quotation and catalogue for the coming season we have studied your offer thoroughly and have found that your new dx-2000 line is very competitive both in specifications and price your terms are also quite satisfactory we are therefore placing an initial order for 1200 bikes as detailed on the enclosed purchase order bk 32984 payment is to be made by b/e at 60 days after sight please note that delivery by 15 february is essential and we reserve the right to return the goods at your risk and expense should we receive them after that date we look forward to receiving your consignment before 15 february and to doing further business with you in future yours sincerely kate paxton head buyer enc purchase order bk 32984

PURCHASE ORDER   BK 32984

QTY	DESCRIPTION	UNIT PRICE	TOTAL
500	HYFLYER DX-2000 model E Titanium fork and frame Shimada XT 12-speed gears, shifters, brakes, levers, rims and hubs 26" tyres	169.00	84,500.00
400	HYFLYER DX-2000 model F Titanium fork and frame Shimada XT 24-speed gears, Rapidfire S shifters, V-brakes, levers, rims and hubs Ritchey Alfabite 26" tyres	199.00	79,600.00

TERMS

DELIVERY: by 15 February, 200_

CARRIAGE: CPT Warehouse Stratford

PAYMENT: B/E at 60 days after sight

INVOICE: in duplicate

INSURANCE: none

MKS & NOS: BK 32984 E1–5, F1–4, L1–3

SIGNED: *Kate Paxton*   **DATE:** 8 January 200_

PLEASE QUOTE OUR ORDER NUMBER BK 32984 ON ALL RELEVANT CORRESPONDENCE

---

c Study the notes you took in Unit 5 (page 83) and use them to draft a confirmation of Walter McAdam's reservation. Use the following checklist to make sure that everything is included in your letter.

CHECKLIST:

1. Mr McAdam's name and address
2. enter today's date
3. start with a personal salutation
4. open the letter by thanking Mr McAdam for the reservation
5. confirm all the details of the reservation as on the form in unit 5 (page 83)
6. say that you have charged £45 to Mr McAdam's credit card account to pay for the insurance premium
7. let Mr McAdam know that he will receive the airline tickets and the vouchers 10 days prior to departure
8. close the letter with a standard phrase
9. use an appropriate complimentary close
10. prepare the letter for signature by Amanda Jones, Manager

A3 Order confirmation by fax

■ Fletcher's has just received LeisureCorp's order for office printers (see unit 4, p.60, unit 5, p.81). Sean Fletcher immediately confirms the order by fax. **Restore the correct order of the jumbled elements and rewrite the fax.**

TELEFAX TRANSMISSION

Fletcher's Business Systems

68 Woodstock Road, Belfast BT3 6OF
Telephone (01232) 846879   Fax (01232) 846888

To: Fred Murphy, IT Manager ①

Attention: Sean Fletcher ②

From: one ③

Subject: 14 December 200_ ④

Date: Your order no. 7497/06 ⑤

Pages incl. this one: LeisureCorp ⑥

Best wishes ⑦

As agreed, the equipment will be delivered to your premises on Monday, 18 December at 9.00 am. Network installation will take approximately two hours, so that office routine can be resumed by noon. ⑧

4	**Necson 1612** with two standard sheet feeders and a toner cartridge for 10,000 pages	£774.50	£3,098
4	**Necson ENA-6** Ethernet adapters & wiring	£14.50	£58
1	**Necson DU-1612** duplex unit holding 100 pages	£124.50	

⑨

If you do not receive all the pages, please advise us as soon as possible. ⑩

TOTAL £3,280.50 ⑪

Sean Fletcher ⑫

Thank you very much for your order no. 7497/06, which we received this morning and confirm as follows: ⑬

We are confident that our printers will meet all the requirements of a busy office environment. ⑭

A 4 Sales confirmation and proforma invoice

■ The German exporter Drescher AG sends the following sales confirmation in duplicate to a customer in Tanzania. **Study the sales confirmation, look up the words you don't know in a dictionary and find out with a partner what the transaction is about.**

SALES CONFIRMATION and PROFORMA INVOICE Ref. 200/236533112

Quantity 11 x 20 ft FCL containers, each containing 437 bags à 50 kilos net or 21,850 metric tons net per container, total 240,350 metric tons net

Commodity WHEAT FLOUR

Origin Federal Republic of Germany

Type Soft White Breadmaking Flour Type 550

Specifications

Ash (Minerals)	max. 0.60% on dry matter
Protein	min. 13.00% on dry matter
Moisture	max. 14.00%

Freshly milled wheat flour, quality sound and suitable for human consumption.

Packing In 50 kilos net, new, white, woven export polypropylene bags, marked on two sides in two colours with buyer's logo.

Shipment From Hamburg to destination Dar-es-Salaam, Tanzania, in July 200_

Price US Dollars 255.00 per metric ton net, CFR Dar-es-Salaam.

Payment By draft payable at 90 days, draft to be guaranteed by your bank Banque Bruxelles Lambert (BBL), Bruxelles.

Shipping documents
  Commercial Invoice, 3-fold
  Certificate of Origin issued by the Chamber of Commerce
  Packing List
  Certificate of Analysis issued by the producing mill
  3/3 Original Bill of Lading marked "freight prepaid"

Other conditions
  Maritime insurance to be covered by buyers at their own expense.

Please return to us a copy of this contract duly signed and stamped by you. Thank you.

Buyers: **Sellers:** Drescher AG
                                                                  Michelsen

A5 Cancellation of order by letter

■ A few weeks later, Mr Rattle is obliged to cancel his order for German wines. **Copy his letter and fill in the gaps using the appropriate expressions from the box.**

> I regret to say ✻ my sincere apologies ✻ confirm cancellation ✻ short notice ✻
> no intention of ✻ any inconvenience ✻ readily appreciate ✻ at regular intervals ✻ to ask you

Anthony Rattle

167 Wanstead Road
Wanstead
London
E11 6ST

Weinbauer Ltd.
105 Deansgate
Manchester
M60 21R

Dear Ms Gore   26 December, 200_

Re: My order of 8th December for 50 bottles of Franconian Riesling (Pfaffenlust) and 50 bottles of red Ahr wine (Sonnentröpfchen), and your confirmation of the same date.

❶ that I have no alternative but ❷ to cancel the order. I realise this is very ❸. My daughter informs me now that she has ❹ getting married either on the date planned or in the foreseeable future. Naturally, she has cancelled the reception, to which she had invited a large number of guests.

As I am sure you will ❺, I cannot possibly consume such a large quantity of the same wine. I should, however, be happy to commute my order to five bottles of each wine.

Please accept ❻ for ❼ this may cause. I should be grateful if you would ❽ of my order. I fully expect to place smaller orders ❾ in the future.

With kind regards
Anthony Rattle

Information for Student B, head buyer with McPherson Sports, see page 102.

1. You ring because of your order of 20 August, No. JY-1289, for 50 Winner gold skis and 20 SuperStar skis. Contact person: Josef Hintermooser.

2. Order was sent by fax. No confirmation yet.

3. A basic, inexpensive ski for beginners is also to be included in McPherson's range. Which article would be suitable?

4. Difference between Winner blue and Winner red?

5. Additional order for 10 each of Winner blue and Winner red will be placed if available from stock.

6. As winner red is not available, you place an order for 15 winner blue. The additional order must not delay the delivery of the original Order no. JY-1289. Confirmation by fax requested.

7. Further major orders possible. Winter sports a growth industry in Scotland.

A6 Informing of delay in execution

➡ 30
➡ 55 ■ Study again the SITPRO advertisement in Unit 2 (page 30). Then read this excerpt from the letter from SITPRO and complete it using the appropriate words from the box below.

> ❶ Mr O'Brien,
>
> In response to your ❷, please find enclosed *Top Form 2* as requested. ❸, we are ❹ not in a position to include the *New Export Guide*, as demand for this new edition has been ❺.
>
> However, a reprint is ❻ being prepared, and you will receive the *New Export Guide* as soon as it is ❼. ❽, we have, for the present, charged only £20 to your VISA account for *Top Form 2*.
>
> Please accept my apologies for the inconvenience.
> Yours ❾,

> accordingly ✳ available ✳ currently
> dear ✳ overwhelming ✳ order
> sincerely ✳ temporarily ✳ unfortunately

A7 Dispatch advice by letter*

➡ 71/79 ■ In this dispatch advice for Mr Giacomelli's order (see units 4, p.71 and 5, p.79), there are four errors. Find these errors.

**Sportwelt
Fan-Artikel**

Wertachring 93
86153 Augsburg
Tel +49 821 720473, Fax +49 821 720659
E-Mail sportwelt@comlink.de

Reference No: SB/lt.247   19 December 200_

Mr Gino Giacomelli
Via dei Banchi 45
78038 Firenze
Italy

Dear Mr Gino,

Your order dated 10 February
I am pleased to inform you that the garments you ordered are now ready for dispatch.
We are using United Parcel Force standard delivery service for the delivery of 5 parcels.
They will be collected on 21 December 200_ from our warehouse and the delivery will be made 12 working days from the date of dispatch.
Your estimated delivery date will be 5 February 200_.
If you have any problems, please call me on the above number or send me a fax or an e-mail and I will be happy to assist you.
I would be grateful if you could fax or post me the slip at the end of the letter, so that I can be assured that you have received your goods and everything is in order.

Yours sincerely,
Denise Springer
Denise Springer
Personnel Manager

Reference No: SB/lt.247,
Mr. Gino Giacomelli, Firenze

Yes, I have received all of my parcels ❑   No, I did not receive the goods on the estimated delivery date. ❑
I have waited an extra week and nothing has been delivered. ❑
Please contact me on: Signature:

108   Unit 6 · Activities   * see also p. 159

B Tool kit

B 1 Structure of business communications: Confirmation of orders

Confirmations should be structured like this:

Structure	Language to use
1. personal salutation	Dear Mrs Cole
2. reference to order	Thank you for your order **for** …
3. acknowledgement of order, repeating particulars of the offer, if necessary • nature and quality of the product • quantity • price(s) and possible discount(s) • terms of payment and delivery	… which we confirm as follows: Colour measurement instruments ZR20 15 pcs. unit price €145.00 cash **on** delivery; DDU Plymouth
4. information on what has been or will be done concerning delivery	We have contacted World Cargo to arrange **for** transport **to** Plymouth next week.
5. acknowledgement of instructions	We are confident that we can meet the delivery deadline **of** 14 June.
6. goodwill phrase	We are convinced that the instruments will give you many years' reliable service.
7. complimentary close	Yours sincerely

a What is the purpose of these sentences? Find the appropriate numbers in *structure of business communications* above.

1. We are pleased to confirm that the goods will reach you by February 28.
2. We have already dispatched our pro forma invoice no. 23756.
3. Thank you for your order no. 3476 for 600 units of …, which we received today.
4. The goods will be shipped as soon as we have received your payment.
5. We look forward to receiving further orders.
6. As requested, delivery will be made CPT MERYTON.
7. We are pleased to inform you that you will be granted 10% introductory discount.
8. Your order will be dispatched immediately upon receipt of your SWIFT transfer as per enclosed pro forma invoice.
9. Your order no…, for which we thank you, arrived this morning.
10. We are confident that the goods will reach you in time and in good condition.
11. Thank you very much for your trial order for Shimada gears and levers.
12. We have already made arrangements for the goods to be shipped upon notification of the opening of your documentary credit.

consignment ✻ delivery ✻ supply

b Match the appropriate words from the box with the numbers.
We assure you that ❶ will be effected before the end of the month.
You will be pleased to hear that we can ❷ the entire order from stock.
As requested, the ❸ will be dispatched upon confirmation of your bank guarantee.

B 2 Building blocks for business communications: Confirmation of orders

1 To refer to the order

Thank you for We have received	your order No. RF/62	of dated	23 May,

2 To confirm the order

which we now	confirm acknowledge	as follows:

We are pleased to We herewith	confirm acknowledge	your order **for** brass tacks.
Our order confirmation is enclosed.		

3 To refer to particulars of your offer

As stated in our offer As agreed	our prices are quoted **for** delivery CPT Sunderland.
We are pleased to confirm that you will be granted a quantity discount of 15%.	

4 To say what you have done or are going to do about the delivery

	delivery will be made		in the course of next week. before the end of this month. **by** Friday at the latest.
As requested,	the goods will be	delivered dispatched	
The order The consignment	will be	dispatched shipped	as soon as we have received your instructions. immediately (up)on receipt of your bank transfer.

We have already	made arrangements arranged	**for**	immediate shipment. the goods to be shipped next … dispatch within …

We have already contacted	our forwarding agent our shipping agents Eurotrans	to	ensure arrange **for**	prompt delivery. dispatch within … shipment by air.

5 To acknowledge instructions

Your instructions	concerning **as to** regarding	packing documentation just-in-time delivery	will be strictly	observed. adhered **to**.

6 To close the letter

Thank you for placing this order **with** us. We assure you that it will be	given priority. dealt with promptly and carefully.
We trust that the consignment will reach you **in** time and in good condition.	
We are confident that we can meet the delivery deadline **of** 31 August.	
We look forward to	doing further business with you. receiving further orders from you.

7 To refuse an order

Much as we should like to do business with you, we fear that we cannot economically manufacture such small quantities.	
As we only sell **through** our agents Since we only supply to authorised dealers	we have no alternative **but** to decline the order.
We regret that as a result of the shortage of skilled programmers we are unable to accept your order.	

8 To apologise and suggest alternatives

Unfortunately, We are sorry that	the goods the model	you require you ordered	are is	temporarily out of stock. no longer available.
Nevertheless, we could supply		model … a suitable substitute		from stock. within a week.

9 To cancel an order

We	are very sorry but we must deeply regret having to are much to our regret compelled to	cancel our order

	due to owing to as a result of	an unexpected tightening of import regulations. the sudden bankruptcy of our customer. the severe recession following the earthquake.

We hope We assure you	that we will soon be able	to place to give you to make up for the loss by placing	another order.

Tool kit · Unit 6   111

■ Use the building blocks on the previous pages to find equivalents for the following German sentences.

1. Wir danken Ihnen für Ihre Bestellung vom 18. April, die wir heute erhalten haben.
2. Leider ist Modell 433, das Sie bestellt haben, nicht vorrätig und erst in vier Wochen erhältlich.
3. Wir können jedoch einen geeigneten Ersatz, Modell 443, innerhalb einer Woche liefern.
4. Bitte teilen Sie uns mit, ob Sie Modell 443 bestellen oder vier Wochen warten möchten.
5. Wir freuen uns darauf, bald von Ihnen zu hören.
6. Wir bedanken uns für Ihre telefonische Bestellung von heute und bestätigen wie folgt: 200 STELLA X4 Snowboards blau/gelb, Art.Nr. SX4-13 zum Stückpreis von € 149,00 Gesamtwert € 2980,00.
7. Die Lieferung erfolgt innerhalb einer Woche nach Eingang Ihrer Banküberweisung.
8. Hiermit bestätigen wir Ihre Bestellung vom 30. Juli und weisen darauf hin, daß die Lieferung DDU Edinburgh erfolgt.
9. Leider können wir diesen Auftrag nicht annehmen, da wir ausschließlich den Großhandel beliefern.
10. Wir sehen uns zu unserem Bedauern gezwungen, die oben angegebene Bestellung zu widerrufen, da unser Hauptabnehmer in Konkurs gegangen ist.
11. Wir hoffen allerdings, Ihnen in Kürze wieder größere Aufträge erteilen zu können.
12. Besten Dank für diesen Auftrag, den wir mit größter Sorgfalt erledigen werden.

B 3 Structure of business communications: Advice of dispatch

An advice of dispatch should be structured like this:

Structure	Language to use
1. personal salutation	Dear Mr Fitzwilliam
2. reference to the order	Re: Your order No.. **for** ..., dated ...
3. information that the goods are ready for collection or have been dispatched	We are pleased to inform you that the goods have today been shipped as air freight.
4. particulars about the transport	Air Canada Flight No. AC704 leaves Munich Airport **on** 3 May **at** 21:30 and arrives **at** Montreal Airport on... at..
5. details of packing, if applicable	The goods are packed **in** 2 LDC containers.
6. reference to terms of payment and invoice	Our invoice No... is enclosed **for** settlement.
7. reference to documents enclosed or handed over to bank, as appropriate	As per your instructions we are enclosing the following documents: ...
8. goodwill phrase	We hope that the goods will arrive punctually and look forward **to** serving you again.
9. complimentary close	Yours sincerely

■ What is the purpose of these sentences? Find the appropriate numbers in *structure of business communications* on page 112.

1. All delicate parts are wrapped in soft material and packed in sturdy wooden boxes.
2. Thank you once again for your order for micro floppy disks of 1 June.
3. As agreed we have drawn on you at 30 days' sight. Please accept the enclosed draft and return it to us.
4. We are convinced that the equipment will give you reliable service and thank you for placing the order with us.
5. MS "Summer Wind" will be leaving the port of Pusan on 29 March and is due to dock at Antwerp by the end of April.
6. We are now pleased to inform you that the goods are ready for collection at our Portsmouth plant.
7. A full set of clean bills of lading, commercial invoice, marine insurance policy and certificate of origin, all in triplicate, are being forwarded to your bank.

B 4 Building blocks for business communications: Advice of dispatch

1 To say that the goods are ready for collection

We are pleased	to inform you to advise to let you know	that the consignment	is ready for collection. can be collected **at** our Derby works.

2 To say that the goods have been dispatched

The consignment has The merchandise has The machines have	now today this morning	been handed over to the freight forwarder. been sent **by** courier. left our premises **for** Budapest **by** lorry.

The goods have now been	dispatched shipped forwarded	by	air freight. inland waterway vessel. refrigerated truck.

Yesterday the goods were loaded **on** board MS Seagull in Bremerhaven.

3 To give particulars about the transport

The consignment	will arrive **at** your warehouse is expected to reach you is scheduled to be delivered	tomorrow afternoon. **on** Wednesday. **by** 17 January.

MS Island Queen is	due to leave Antwerp on... and	dock **at** arrive in/at	Singapore on ...

Estimated time of arrival: **on or about** 29 December.	
Flight No. SA6941 will depart **from** Johannesburg International Airport **at** 20:35 (local time) **on** Monday and land **at** Frankfurt Airport at 6:10 on Tuesday.	

4 To give particulars about packing

As requested According **to** your instructions As usual	the goods are packed **in**	strong solid sturdy	seaworthy containers. wooden crates. cardboard boxes with steel bands. metal drums. polythene bags.

5 To refer to payment

Our	statement for the first quarter invoice No. A/17, dated 2 March,	is enclosed **for** settlement.

We enclose invoice No. A/17 of 2 March **in** duplicate and would ask you to transfer the amount in question to	the account given below. our account **with** MetroBank.

We have drawn **on** you **for** the invoice amount at **60** days and enclose the draft for your acceptance.

6 To refer to documents

The documents required **under** the letter of credit have been handed over to our bank.
We are sending you enclosed copies of the following documents: …. The originals will be released **to** you by your bank **against** payment.

7 To close the letter

We hope the consignment will arrive	punctually. safely and in good condition. in good time.

Thank you once again for this order. We should be very pleased if you would contact us again in case of further requirements.
Please do not hesitate to contact us should you have any further requirements in the future.

■ **Use the patterns above and find the equivalents for these sentences:**

1. Die Sendung wurde der Spedition Eurotrans bereits übergeben.
2. Die 15 Kartons stehen ab Dienstag zur Abholung vor unserem Lager in Ulm bereit.
3. Die Kisten sind entsprechend Ihren Anweisungen markiert.
4. Die Maschine wurde gestern von der MS Poseidon in Hamburg an Bord genommen.
5. Die bestellten Ersatzteile sind heute früh per Luftfracht an Sie abgegangen
6. Voraussichtliche Ankunftszeit: 20:45 Ortszeit, Flughafen Sao Paulo.
7. Anbei erhalten Sie Kopien der Versanddokumente.

B 5 Telephoning

■ **Study the telephone phrases on the following pages. Then find the English equivalents of the following German telephone phrases.**

1. Ach, wie nett, dass ich Sie erreicht habe. Wie geht's Ihnen denn?
2. Wie ist denn das Wetter bei Ihnen? Hier regnet es seit Wochen.
3. Könnten Sie mich mit Mrs. Bennet aus der Exportabteilung verbinden?
4. Soll ich ihm etwas ausrichten oder soll er Sie zurückrufen?
5. Ich bin da nicht zuständig. Soll ich Sie zu Frau Neff durchstellen?
6. Würden Sie mich bitte benachrichtigen, wenn ...
7. Bitte kümmern Sie sich darum, dass ...
8. Damit können wir uns leider nicht einverstanden erklären.
9. So hatten wir uns das nicht gedacht.
10. Bitte entschuldigen Sie die Verzögerung.
11. Es tut mir schrecklich Leid, aber ...
12. Kann ich Sie zurückrufen, ich muss erst in den Unterlagen nachsehen?
13. Wir wollen doch nichts überstürzen.
14. Eins nach dem andern.
15. Das sollten wir erst einmal überschlafen.
16. Könnten wir uns nicht auf der Buchmesse treffen?
17. Mir wäre es lieb, wenn wir den Termin um eine Woche verschieben könnten.
18. Der Bericht muss spätestens Donnerstag vorliegen.
19. Vielen Dank für Ihren Anruf.
20. Auf Wiederhören.

Useful telephone phrases

To make friendly remarks at the beginning of a telephone conversation Oh, hello Sarah. Nice to hear from you. How are things over there? Good morning Mrs Weston. I hope you enjoyed your holiday. Good afternoon Mr Fraser. How is the weather in Scotland?	**Reactions** Just fine, thank you. Thank you, it was very relaxing. We've had a lot of snow recently. And you?

To ask for somebody Could I speak to Mrs Foster? Could you put me through to Ms King? I'd like to speak to someone from the sales department.	**To say that somebody isn't available** I'm afraid Mrs Foster isn't in. ... is in a meeting. ... has a visitor. ... is in the USA on a business trip. ... is out at lunch. ... is no longer with our company.

To offer to ring back or take a message I'm afraid Mrs Foster is speaking on the other line. Would you prefer to wait or shall I ask her to ring you back? Can she call you back this afternoon? Can I give her a message? Would you like to leave a message?	**Reactions** Thank you, I'll ring back later. I'm afraid I won't be in this afternoon. Tomorrow morning would be better. Yes, please. Could you take the following message: ... Yes, that would be best. Could you tell her that ...

To refer somebody to someone else I'm afraid I'm not | familiar with that order. in charge of this transaction. I'll put you through to Mr Croft. Shall I put you through to Mrs Lucas? Perhaps she can help you. Would you like to speak to somebody from the accounts department?	**Reactions** Thank you. No, thanks. I really need to speak to the export manager.

To ask for something Would you please let me know if ... ? I'd like to ask you whether it would be possible to ... You'd be doing us a great favour if you could ... Please make sure that ... We must ask you to remit the invoice amount by Friday at the latest.	**Reactions** Certainly. Yes, of course. We'll do our best, but ... You may depend on it.

To refuse something I'm afraid I cannot agree to that proposal. I'm afraid that sounds quite/totally unacceptable to us.	**Reactions** That's too bad. I'm sorry to hear that.

Much as I regret it, I have to say no. I'm terribly sorry, but I simply can't see any way of making this concession. Unfortunately, this is not what we had in mind.	Well, I'm afraid there's nothing to be done. Is there nothing you can do?
To apologise I'm terribly sorry but ... I'd like to apologise for the trouble you've been having. Please accept our apologies. I can only repeat that I am extremely sorry for what has happened.	**Reactions** Alright, don't mention it. Well, please try to avoid this happening in the future. It has caused us a lot of problems.
To play for time Can I ring you back? I need to study our files first. I must discuss the matter with the head of department. I'm afraid I can't access the file on my monitor right now. I'll call you back in half an hour. I'd rather not rush things. I'll get back to you after 5 p.m. if that's alright. I'll have more time then to discuss the matter. Let's deal with one point at a time. I suggest we think the problem over for a few more days.	**Reactions** I'm afraid I am not prepared to be put off again. I insist on speaking to the person responsible. That's a good idea. I totally agree with you.
To make an appointment Would it be possible for you to meet me at the Boat Fair? Would Tuesday suit you? I'm free on 22 May all afternoon. Couldn't we switch the appointment to the next morning, say at 10:30? What about postponing the meeting to the last week in May? On 22 May at 3 p.m. then.	**Reactions** Certainly. I'll be there on Wednesday. I'm afraid Tuesday is full. I'm afraid I've got an appointment at that time. That would be alright with me. Yes, Wednesday would be fine.
To request that something is done by a certain date We need the goods by Wednesday at the very latest. I repeat, we require the documents by 3 May. Please make sure that it arrives no later than the end of April. Monday, 31 July is the final deadline.	**To promise something** We promise you that ... You have my word, the documents will reach you on Monday. We will certainly see to it that ... You may rely on it, the goods will be dispatched tomorrow.
To end the telephone conversation Goodbye Mrs Benwick. Thanks for calling. Goodbye Mr Hayter. Have a nice weekend.	**Reactions** You're welcome. Goodbye. You too, Mrs Dalrymple.

C Additional practice

90 a Read this letter and supply the missing words and phrases.

15 March 200_

Dear Ms Fetzer,

Your ❶ No. NB 001/03

❷ you for your order for teenage garments in assorted sizes, colours, and designs.

We ❸ you that all the items can be supplied from stock. We have already ❹ arrangements with our shipping agent, and are ❺ that the consignment will arrive at your premises before 15 April.

The shipping documents and the sight draft will be sent to Sparkasse Passau in due course.

Yours sincerely,

Gianna Dellacasa

Gianna Dellacasa
❻ Manager

b Match the parts of these sentences and draft a complete letter.

1. Thank you for your order	a. we will contact you immediately.
2. We are sorry to inform you that we have run out of these chips	b. before offering them to our customers.
3. At present we are testing 32MB SDRAMs which we have imported from South Korea,	c. and do not expect another delivery before the end of next month.
4. Therefore, we would like to test them thoroughly	d. for 2000 Queenston 32MB SDRAM chips.
5. However, if we find them satisfactory,	e. but these do not yet have the official approval of the National Standards Committee.

c Wedler& Co. (Steilhang 45, 87527 Sonthofen, Tel 08321 – 38790, Fax 08321 – 38814, www.wedler.co.de) has received this order from McDermot Bros. (35 Redwood Crescent, East Kilbride G74 5PR, Scotland, Fax 01387 – 85621). **Study the order and the notes, then draft an appropriate reply.**

> Demand for your Victor snowboard (art. no. 974-23) has been higher than anticipated, and we urgently require another consignment of 100 boards before the end of the month.
>
> Please confirm delivery date.
>
> Sincerely

O.K., sind versandbereit, werden Montag von Eurotrans abgeholt, Lieferzeit ca. 10 Tage. Bitte um Rückmeldung bei Erhalt!

d ZISCHFRISCH (Durststrecke 8, 73033 Göppingen, Tel (07161) 73110, Fax (07161) 73120, durst@zischfrisch.de has just received another order from POLARDRINK (Zgoda 3, 31-120 Krakow, Poland, Tel 0048-12 22-06-63, Fax 0048-12 22-67-83, pbrzinsky@krakownet.com.pl).

> Please supply by the end of next week:
>
> 100,000 cans of REDOX energy drink @ € 0.25 per can
> less 15% quantity discount, net 14, FCA.
>
> Sincerely

Unfortunately, ZISCHFRISCH cannot supply from stock because demand for REDOX has been very high lately. **Therefore, send Mr Brzinsky an e-mail to inform him that you are currently out of stock, and that you will be able to supply the quantity required in four weeks. Ask him to send you further instructions.**

e GAMETOYS (Glückstraße 57, D-93449 Spielberg, Tel (09972) 738 287, Fax (09972) 738288, www.gametoys.co.de) has just received this order from a private individual. **Draft a reply using the notes on the letter.**

> *Wir sind kein Einzelhandel! Legen Sie Liste der Einzelhändler in Ungarn bei!*
>
> Szabadság körút 34
> 2400 Kapuvár
> Hungary
>
> 1 April 200_
>
> Dear Sir or Madam,
>
> Please supply C.O.D. to the above address:
>
> 1 64-bit NOSY GameStation
> 1 Tomb Raider 5
> 1 NASCAR Racing
>
> I look forward to receiving these products as soon as possible.
>
> Yours faithfully,
>
> Imre Hegedüs

D Background information: Trade Unions

The trade union movement began in the UK in the 18th century among skilled craftsmen. Trade unions (US: labor unions) are associations of employees who have organised themselves on a permanent basis with the aim of improving their wages, working hours, conditions of employment, training, benefits, etc. in negotiations with
5 their employers.

Unlike employees in all major German firms, in the UK employees do not generally participate in the management's decision-making process neither at board level (co-determination) nor through works councils. In Britain, trade unions are represented in factories by shop stewards, elected by their fellow workers, to negotiate with the tier of management
10 responsible.

Negotiations between unions and employers' associations take the form of free collective bargaining. If the negotiators fail to reach an agreement, the dispute may be referred to arbitration. Should this be unsuccessful, the unions will resort to industrial action, for example, call a strike, once their members have signalled agreement in a secret ballot.
15 In very rare cases the employers may resort to a lock-out, i.e., prevent all the employees from entering the premises.

■ Study the text on trade unions and look up the words you don't know in a dictionary. Then decide whether the following statements are true or false.

1. The trade union movement began among farmers.
2. All British firms have works councils.
3. Trade Unions must first hold a secret ballot before calling a strike.
4. A lock-out means that the employees prevent the directors from entering the building.

E IHK-Prüfungsvorbereitung

1.	Zusatzqualifikation Englisch für kaufmännische Auszubildende Fremdsprache im Beruf I	
	Kurzgefasste/Informelle Mitteilung (Bearbeitungszeit 30 Minuten)	Hilfsmittel: zweisprachiges Wörterbuch

Situation

Sie (eigener Name) arbeiten bei der Firma Präsent-Import/Export in Hamburg, die nur Einzelhändler beliefert. Ihre Chefin hat Ihnen nebenstehende E-Mail aus Polen mit ihren Anweisungen auf den Schreibtisch gelegt (siehe nächste Seite).

Aufgabe

Schreiben Sie die entsprechende E-Mail als Antwort auf die Anfrage.

Netscape Messenger

Inbox ▾ 1 messages, 0 unread

From: a.cebulla@comlink.pl **Date:** 24 Feb 200_

To: praesent.impex@firmlink.de **Cc:**

Re: Travel bag and shoulder bag **Attachment:**

Dear Sirs
I've seen your catalogue and think that your travel goods are very attractive.
Please send me one Roadster Travel Bag C317J at € 165 and one Roadster Shoulder Bag TD80J at € 85, as per your catalogue.
How do you wish payment to be made? Would a cheque drawn on a Polish bank be alright?

My address is
Anna Cebulla, Wilcza 20, OO-679 Warszawa, Poland

Regards
Anna Cebulla

You are offline.

Auftrag bitte ablehnen, Lieferung nur an den Handel.
Bedauern ausdrücken, für Interesse danken, auf Einzelhändler verweisen, in Warschau:
Polska Globetrotter
Ul. Rynek 22
00-029 Warszawa
Tel. (022) 826 1504
Preise im Katalog gelten nur für Wiederverkäufer.

Unterschreiben Sie selbst.
Danke! Kaiser

2. Zusatzqualifikation Englisch für kaufmännische Auszubildende Fremdsprache im Beruf I*

Vermerk in Deutsch über ein Gespräch (Bearbeitungszeit 20 Minuten)	**Hilfsmittel:** zweisprachiges Wörterbuch

Situation
Peter Schröder, Exportleiter Ihrer Firma, hat mit Pamela Brown von der britischen Firma Technoline Ltd auf der Messe für Büroeinrichtungen ein Gespräch geführt. Das Gespräch wurde aufgezeichnet.

Aufgabe:
Herr Schröder hat Sie nun gebeten, den Inhalt dieses Gesprächs in einem Aktenvermerk in deutscher Sprache zusammenzufassen. Sie werden das Gespräch zweimal hören. Was Herr Schröder sagte, haben Sie vorliegen.

* Die Bearbeitungszeit beträgt bei Fremdsprache im Beruf 30 Minuten, die Dialoge sind dementsprechend etwas länger

Schröder:	Guten Morgen. Schröder. Kann ich Ihnen helfen?
Schröder:	Please take a seat, Mrs. Brown. What are you interested in specifically?
Schröder:	The retail price of the basic model is about DM 1,600. You can add more features such as sliding shelves which can push up the price to about DM 2,000. It is expensive, but as you say it is beautifully made and highly functional.
Schröder:	The trade price is DM 1,150 ex works. We also grant quantity discounts on orders for more than 20 units.
Schröder:	I think we could supply this quantity from stock. I'll just check on my monitor. Yes, we could do that in two weeks' time.
Schröder:	No problem. We would also grant you a 10% introductory discount.
Schröder:	I will send you a supply of brochures in English together with your order. Could you give me your firm's address?
Schröder:	Thank you, Miss Brown. I look forward to doing business with you.

3. Zusatzqualifikation Englisch für kaufmännische Auszubildende

Spracherergänzungstest Text 1
(Bearbeitungszeit für beide Texte zusammen: 20 Minuten) | Wörterbücher **nicht** gestattet

Bitte setzen Sie 20 der 23 angegebenen Wörter in die Lücken des Textes ein.

according · back · considerable · dispatch · few · give · high · letter · low · moment
obligations · over · overtime · parcels · position · promise · provided · result · soon · stocks
understand · utmost · within

E-Mail

Dear Ms Denham
Thank you for your letter of 6 June enclosing your order No. 875. Concerning the date of delivery we regret to say that as a ❶ of the lorry driver's strike which has now lasted for a week, we are unable to ❷ all the instruments ❸ the time stated in your letter. We have been trying our ❹ to fulfil our ❺ promptly but our attempts have been fruitless.
Our ❻ are running ❼ but we are in a ❽ to dispatch two ❾ by rail, ❿ to your instructions, ⓫ that you ⓬ us the go-ahead by e-mail within the next ⓭ days. As ⓮ as the strike is ⓯ we will work ⓰ and do everything we can to execute ⓱ orders. The best we can ⓲ at the ⓳ is to deliver the goods by the beginning of July.
We hope you will ⓴ our difficult situation.

Best regards

Spracherganzungstest Text 2

In diesem Text ist jeweils nur eine der drei nachstehend vorgeschlagenen Formen korrekt. Bitte setzen Sie die richtige Lösung ein.

It is the ❶ responsibility ❷ the customs authorities of the country of importation that the goods are ❸ imported and to ❹ the ❺ information. Goods will be ❻ up in customs ❼ the duty on ❽ has ❾, unless they ❿ to a bonded warehouse or free zone.

"Entry forms" must ⓫ informing customs of the quantity, type, value and destination ⓬ the consignment. Customs ⓭ have the right to ⓮ goods and ⓯ documents and, ⓰ they inspect, the cost of ⓱ damage to packing cases, etc. ⓲ to be ⓳ by the importer. Entry forms ⓴ lodged a few ㉑ prior to importation in order to speed up processing. Otherwise, they must ㉒ ㉓ within 14 days of arrival or the goods ㉔ to a ㉕ warehouse and storage charges ㉖ .

If the customs authorities of the ㉗ country believe that you are "dumping" goods in ㉘ nation, that means selling them ㉙ a price below the price charged in the UK, ㉚ are allowed to impose special import taxes.

Auswahlliste für Spracherganzungstest Text 2

1.	importer importing importer's	2.	to tell to be telling telling	3.	be been being
4.	presenting have presented present	5.	correctly correcting correct	6.	hold held holding
7.	until when by	8.	they their them	9.	be paid been paid paid
10.	go has gone going	11.	be completing been completed be completed	12.	of from by
13.	officer officer's officers	14.	inspecting inspection inspect	15.	accompany accompanying accompanied
16.	if whether why	17.	result resulted resulting	18.	has have had
19.	borne bear bearing	20.	may may be may have	21.	day daily days
22.	normal normally normality	23.	been deposited being deposited be deposited	24.	will be sending will be sent will send
25.	specialize special specially	26.	have imposed had been imposed will be imposed	27.	imported imports importing
28.	those these that	29.	to by at	30.	they them this

4. Zusatzqualifikation Englisch für kaufmännische Auszubildende
Fremdsprache im Beruf I

Mündliche Prüfung: Telefongespräch (Vorbereitungszeit ca. 5 Min.)

Angaben für den Prüfling

Situation

Sie (eigener Name) arbeiten bei Badenbike, Draisstr. 342, 76189 Karlsruhe, Tel. (0721) 4670975. Die Leiterin der Einkaufsabteilung, Frau Berger, hat Ihnen nachstehenden Auftrag an die Firma Hyflyer plc, Tel. 01926 439523, Fax 01926 451427, zusammen mit der beiliegenden Notiz auf den Schreibtisch gelegt. Heute ist der 20. April.

MEMO

Liebe/r
Frau/Herr (Ihr eigener Name)

würden Sie sich bitte bei Herrn Rob Sullivan von Hyflyer plc nach unserer Bestellung erkundigen? Wir haben bis jetzt weder eine Auftragsbestätigung noch eine Versandanzeige erhalten.

Wir benötigen vor allem die 24-Zoll-Reifen für das DX 2500 ganz dringend. Im Katalog von Hyflyer ist eine Lieferzeit von 3 Wochen angegeben, da müssten die Reifen eigentlich schon da sein. Wenn sie nicht bis Ende nächster Woche geliefert werden, müssen wir den Auftrag für diesen Posten annullieren.

Die 26-Zoll-Reifen für das DX 2000 brauchen wir auch baldmöglichst für den Beginn der Saison.

Wenn es Rückfragen gibt, ich bin morgen früh bis 11 Uhr telefonisch zu erreichen.

BADENBIKE

76189 Karlsruhe, Draisstr. 342
Tel. (0721) 4670975
Fax (0721) 4670979
E-Mail badenbike@aol.com

Hyflyer plc
438 Weltmore Industrial Park
Warwick
CV43 6TS
U.K.

20 March 200_

OUR ORDER NO. MB 474-3

Quantity	Description	Unit Price	Total
200	Ritchey Alfabite 26" tyres for DX-2000 mountain bikes	€ 13.00	€ 2,600.00
150	Ritchey Alfabite 24" tyres for DX-2500 mountain bikes	€ 11.50	€ 1,725.00

Terms of delivery and payment as stipulated in your quotation.

Angaben für den Prüfenden

You are Rob Sullivan from Hyflyer plc. The German firm Badenbike from Karlsruhe has placed the order on page 124 with you.

Your firm's software program has undergone major changes and you're afraid that there have been some hitches. That is why the order has not yet been confirmed. Apologize.

The tyres for the DX 2500 will be shipped tomorrow morning by lorry by Eurocargo Hauliers and are due to arrive at Badenbike's premises the day after tomorrow late in the afternoon.

The 26" tyres have been recalled by the manufacturers. So you are currently unable to deliver. But the manufacturers have meanwhile sorted out their problems and will be sending you a large consignment by the end of the week. Consequently you can promise delivery by the end of the month.

Have the caller spell his/her name and ask for his/her boss's name and telephone number as you wish to inform him/her of the delivery date for the DX 2000 tyres as soon as possible.

5. Fremdsprachenkorrespondent/in

Übersetzung Englisch/Deutsch (Bearbeitungszeit 60 Minuten)	Hilfsmittel: zweisprachige Wörterbücher

A major disagreement has developed between the British government and industry over the proposed energy tax. Important trade bodies are refusing to sign agreements until the EU has said whether it will approve British government policy. The government plans to offer tax reductions to companies signing voluntary agreements to increase investment with the aim of reducing industrial pollution.

The EU must decide whether these reductions could be seen as subsidies which are illegal under EU law. The Ministry of the Environment would like to sign agreements with energy-intensive industries from papermakers to steelmakers as soon as possible. The ministry is confident that the EU commissioner responsible will declare the tax rebates are not state aid.

However, a decision is likely to take some time and companies will find it difficult to meet the government's deadline for signing the agreements. Companies are worried that the EU Commissioner will decide that the agreements are more likely to encourage them to try to avoid tax than to improve energy efficiency.

At the same time major manufacturing companies are fighting the energy tax which they claim would threaten jobs, investment and the future of their plants.

6. Fremdsprachenkorrespondent/in

Übersetzung Deutsch/Englisch (Bearbeitungszeit 60 Minuten)	Hilfsmittel: zweisprachige Wörterbücher

Eine neue Studie zeigt, dass in den USA die E-Mail die traditionelle Schneckenpost allmählich ersetzt. Das Versenden von E-Mails hat in großen Teilen der amerikanischen Gesellschaft die alten Formen der Kommunikation – Brief, Fax und das Telefongespräch – verdrängt.

Nach Angaben der befragten Unternehmen wird 80% der Geschäftskorrespondenz heutzutage per E-Mail erledigt. In 72% aller Fälle habe die E-Mail auch das Fax ersetzt. Noch wird jedoch das persönliche Telefongespräch der E-Mail vorgezogen, aber der Abstand ist klein – nur 55% der Befragten bevorzugen das Telefon.

Schneckenpost = snail mail

Die Hochkonjunktur der E-Mail-Technologie könnte in naher Zukunft erhebliche Folgen für die Post haben. Bislang habe die elektronische Post noch nicht zu einem Rückgang des Postvolumens geführt, sagte ein Sprecher der amerikanischen Post.
Die privaten Paketdienste verzeichnen allerdings einen starken Rückgang des Transports von Geschäftsdokumenten – früher ein wichtiges Geschäft. Stattdessen wächst der Bereich des Übernacht-Transports von Päckchen. Die meisten kleinen Pakete enthalten Produkte – Bücher, Arzneimittel oder CDs – die online bestellt wurden.

7. Fremdsprachenkorrespondent/in

Geschäftsbrief nach Angaben (Bearbeitungszeit 45 Minuten)	Hilfsmittel: zweisprachige Wörterbücher

Situation

Sie (eigener Name) sind bei der Firma Sportwelt Fan-Artikel,
Wertachring 93, 86153 Augsburg,
Tel. (0821) 720473, Fax (0821) 720659,
E-Mail sportwelt@comlink.de, für den Import von Textilien zuständig. Sie hatten vorgestern bei einem langjährigen Lieferanten, der indischen Textilfabrik Taj Mahal Garments, Vth Cross, Industrial Estate Peenya, Mumbai 400 099, Tel 009122 8 32 27 21, Fax 009122 8 34 55 16, 500 Stück grünweiße Baumwollschals mit dem eingewebten Namen "SV Mittelstadt" bestellt, Auftragsnummer: SI/12-23. Gerade haben Sie erfahren, dass der Kunde, für den die Schals bestimmt waren, überraschend Konkurs angemeldet hat. Heute ist der 18. August 200_. Ihr Ansprechpartner ist Mr Saddhu Patel.

Aufgabe

Bitte annullieren Sie den Auftrag in einem Brief, den Sie vorab per Fax übermitteln. Berücksichtigen Sie dabei folgende Punkte
- Einleitung
- Bedauern
- Gründe für die Annullierung
- Schals anderweitig nicht absetzbar, Interesse an diesem Verein örtlich eng begrenzt
- Bitte um Verständnis, Verweis auf langjährige Geschäftsbeziehungen
- Neuer Auftrag über 2500 T-Shirts mit Aufdruck vermutlich nächste Woche. Verkaufsverhandlungen mit einem dänischen Kunden abgeschlossen, Unterzeichnung des Vertrags erst Montag wegen Auslandsreise des Geschäftsführers
- Bitte um Bestätigung der Annullierung
- Schlusssatz

Unit 7 Payment

Introduction

Invoices

An invoice is a business document which is made out whenever one person or business sells goods or supplies services to another. The invoice is made out by the seller, and there are always at least two copies. In some business transactions, however, there are four or even more copies.

The invoice is used as evidence of a contract for the sale of goods or the provision of services. Therefore, an invoice must provide the following information:

1. The date and number of the invoice.
2. The name and address of the person or business that is selling the goods or supplying the services in question.
3. The name and address of the person or business that is buying the goods or the services.
4. The date and number of the order.
5. The date of sale of the goods or supply of the services.
6. An exact description of the goods or services, such as quantity, designation, item number, size, colour, etc.
7. Unit and quantity price.
8. Details of discount(s) (if granted).
9. Total amount of invoice.
10. The terms of payment on which the goods are sold or the services supplied, e.g. discount and credit period. (The words 'terms net' mean no discount is allowed. The words 'prompt settlement' mean no credit period is allowed.)

Commercial export invoices also include information on:

11. Terms of delivery.
12. Mode of transport.
13. Net weight and gross weight.
14. Details on packing, markings and dimensions of the package(s).
15. Transport costs.

It may happen that the seller has charged the buyer too much, for instance by not taking a discount into account that they had agreed on; in such cases the buyer will ask the seller for a **credit note** (see page 205). Similarly, **debit notes** are used to correct mistakes, such as an amount undercharged in an invoice.

In international trade prospective customers often require **pro forma invoices** to apply for an import licence, a letter of credit etc. Such a pro forma invoice contains all the details of the eventual commercial invoice. Pro forma invoices sometimes also serve as quotations.

■ Read the text several times. Then try to remember as many as possible of the 15 items of information that may be required in an export invoice.

A Activities

A1 Pro forma invoice

➡ 82 **a** Meanwhile, DigiCorp has responded to Computer Clinic's order. The sentences of this confirmation have been jumbled. **Put them into the correct order.**

1. According to our forwarding agent, the drives should reach you within five days.
2. Best wishes,
3. Kenichi Takano
4. Thank you for your order for 200 UltraSpeed 1280 magneto-optical drives.
5. The order will be shipped as soon as the total amount of invoice has been credited to our account.
6. Therefore, we are confident that we can meet your delivery deadline of 15 February.
7. We are happy to confirm that we can supply the drives from stock, and we attach a pro forma invoice DDP Pembroke, exclusive of VAT and/or taxes.
8. We look forward to receiving further orders from you.

➡ 82 **b** Study this pro forma invoice, then read the information on page 127 and decide which items are missing.

PRO FORMA INVOICE 94476441 GB

DigiCorp K.K.
4–9–37 Takada,
Shinjuku-ku
172 Tokyo
Japan

To: COMPUTER CLINIC
12 BEDFORD STREET
PEMBROKE
SA62 6YE
UNITED KINGDOM

January 9, 200_		Order # n/a	
100	DigiCorp UltraSpeed™ 1280 internal including driver software v1.02 for Windows NT and v1.01 for Macintosh DDP Pembroke exclusive of VAT and/or taxes less quantity discount	unit price JAP¥ 21,350	213,500 19,500
		AMOUNT DUE JAP¥	194,000

Please remit the net amount of invoice to our account no. 4829-12754 at Dai-Ichi Bank, Takada Branch, Tokyo, Japan.

A 2 Commercial invoice

■ Study the export invoice below and the Incoterms in unit 4. Then discuss with a partner the arrangements Cumbria Steel had to make and the costs and risks they had to bear in connection with this export shipment.

Cumbria Steel plc
Cumbria House
Dryslwyn Carmarthen, Dyfed SA32 7BY

Invoice

Shan Ling Machine Co. Ltd.
7 Ching-Chien 4th Road
Kuan-Yin Inc. Park
Kuan-Yin 382
Taiwan

Order No. 237543
Invoice No. 3006553
Date 31 Aug 200_

Your order: CST-4007010
Person in charge: Mrs R. Evans
Tel. extension: 01558 769 323
Telefax: 01558 769 325
E-mail: r.evans@cumbria.aol.uk

Material of UK origin for export to Taiwan

Shipment by MS "Lone Star" on/abt. 31/08/200_ from Milford Haven to Taipei Port, Taiwan

Commodity:
Hot rolled stainless steel AISI 304/No 1-ASTM A240
tolerance EN 10051/92
details as per contract 237543 shan-cumbria (June 14, 200_)

Item 1	4.00 mm x 1,500.00 mm x 6,000.00 mm	
	9,715 kgs USD/1,000 kgs 1,200.00	= USD 11,658.00
	12 packages 12,130 gross kgs 9,715 net kgs	
Item 2	5.00 mm x 1,500.00 mm x 6,000.00 mm	
	11,680 kgs USD/1,000 kgs 1,200.00	= USD 14,016.00
	13 packages 14,350 gross kgs 11,680 net kgs	

Packages 25
gross kgs 26,480
net kgs 21,395   Total Amount   USD 25,674.09

Prices   Trade terms: CIF Taipei Port, Taiwan
Packing: Export standard packing

Payment: Under irrevocable L/C no. 070082991LC2665 of the Taiwan Trade Bank, Taipei.

Marking: Stainless Steel
Contract Number
Net weight / gross weight
Number of sheets inside each bundle
Taipei Port
Shan Ling Machine
Made in the United Kingdom   **Cumbria Steel plc**

A 3 Payment by bank transfer

➡ 128 ■ As Will Duncan is keen on receiving the drives as soon as possible, he remits the money to DigiCorp's account the same day. **Copy the form and complete it on the basis of Digicorp's proforma invoice on page 128.**

Rural Bank International Payments Service
Customer Order Form
Please complete in BLACK INK using BLOCK CAPITALS

To: Rural Bank plc

Account Holding Branch Name: **PEMBROKE**

Sort Code: **2 2**

Please Send:

Name of Currency:
Currency Code: **J P Y**
Amount:
Decimal:

Amount in words:

In: Currency to be sent: **JAPANESE YEN**
Currency code:
Priority Service (At Extra Charge) 'X' Here

To: Beneficiary (Name): **D I G I C O R P   K. K.**

Account Number:

Address (If Acct No Not Known):

At: Beneficiary Bank Name & Address:

Bank Code:

Payment Details: (Information for Beneficiary) **1 0 0   U L T R A S P E E D   1 2 8 0   I N T E R N A L**
D D P   P E M B R O K E

By Order: (Your name or company name)

Please charge my/our account with: a) Amount of payment plus all charges   or b) Amount of payment plus UK charges only   or c) Amount of payment only (all charges to be deducted)

Account Number: **98 765432**

Currency of Account: **GBP**

Debit charges from account (if different from above)

Please make the above payment. I/We have read and agreed to be bound by the Terms and Conditions described overleaf.

Signature(s) ....

For and on behalf of **COMPUTER CLINIC**   Date **9 JAN 200_**

A4 Payment by cheque

■ Some time ago, Pete O'Brien from Hyflyer plc, Warwick, requested information about business opportunities in Canada. After a while, he receives an envelope from the Canadian Chamber of Commerce, which contains this letter. **Read the letter, copy the following forms and fill them in according to the instructions in the letter. See page 92 for the necessary information on cheques. See page 20 for Hyflyer's complete address.**

Dear Mr O'Brien,

Enclosed is the leaflet *Business Opportunities in Canada* as requested. I apologize for the delay in forwarding it to you; however, we have only just received the reprint here at the Chamber.

I am sure you will appreciate the work involved in creating *Business Opportunities in Canada* – both in terms of time and money – for the Canadian Chamber of Commerce. We would be most grateful to receive a modest contribution of £20.00 (cheque made out to CCC) together with the enclosed remittance slip to the Accounts Section.

I hope you will find *Business Opportunities in Canada* of interest. I look forward to hearing from you in due course.

Yours sincerely,

To: The Canadian Chamber of Commerce, Accounts Section
    143 Buckingham Palace Road, London SW1W 9SS

Business Opportunities in Canada

Please find enclosed my cheque for £20.00

Name: ....

Company: ....

Address: ....

.... Postcode: ....

Telephone No: .... Facsimile No: ....

A 5 Payment by letter of credit

63 a Listen to Kate Paxton and Harry Newton, a trainee, discussing the details of their order for swimwear. Check if the following form has been filled out correctly.

PURCHASE ORDER SW 6827

QTY	DESCRIPTION	UNIT PRICE	TOTAL
300	23 8013 Splashback two piece, medium leg, 6	GBP 10.95	GBP 4,380.00
600	23 8014 Splashback two piece, medium leg, 8	GBP 10.95	GBP 6,570.00
700	23 8015 Splashback two piece, medium leg, 10	GBP 10.95	GBP 7,665.00
200	23 8016 Splashback two piece, medium leg, 12	GBP 10.95	GBP 3,285.00
600	23 8496 Olympia one piece, high leg, 6	GBP 9.75	GBP 4,875.00
800	23 8497 Olympia one piece, high leg, 8	GBP 9.75	GBP 7,800.00
900	23 8498 Olympia one piece, high leg, 10	GBP 9.75	GBP 9,750.00
700	23 8499 Olympia one piece, high leg, 12	GBP 9.75	GBP 6,825.00
400	23 8809 Aquablade striped, medium leg, 6	GBP 12.15	GBP 4,860.00
800	23 8810 Aquablade striped, medium leg, 8	GBP 12.15	GBP 9,720.00
1000	23 8811 Aquablade striped, medium leg, 10	GBP 12.15	GBP 9,720.00

TERMS

DELIVERY:	by 31 March, 200_
CARRIAGE:	CIF Southampton
PAYMENT:	irrevocable letter of credit

INVOICE:	in quadruplicate
INSURANCE:	against marine and war risks, 110% of amount of invoice
MKS & NOS:	

SIGNED: *Kate Paxton*   DATE: 10 January 200_

PLEASE QUOTE OUR ORDER NUMBER SW 6827 ON ALL RELEVANT CORRESPONDENCE

63 b Study the letter and decide which of the alternatives in brackets is correct.

SPORTS UNLIMITED

76 The Mall   Stratford E15 1XD
Tel 020 8226 3112   Fax 020 8226 3112

Please visit our new website at
www.sportsul.co.uk

Mr Kim Chong Il
Sales Manager
OSPEE SPORTSWEAR INTERNATIONAL
134 Imun-Dong, Dong Dae Mun-Ku
123 Seoul
South Korea   10 January 200_

Dear Mr Kim

Order for swimwear

Thank you for your offer of 12 December and the samples (**1** what/which) we received by (**2** separate/separately) mail. Your samples have convinced us that your products will meet the tastes and demands of our exacting customers, and your prices and terms are also (**3** quiet/quite) satisfactory.

We are therefore placing an order for 7,000 units as specified on the enclosed Purchase Order SW 6827, CIF Southampton. We will instruct our bank to open a letter of credit (**4** to/in) your favour on receipt of your confirmation. You will be informed through your bank of the type and number of documents that are required for this transaction.

Please (**5** notice/note) that this order is subject to delivery (**6** until/by) 31 March, and that we reserve the right to cancel the order and to return the goods (**7** at/to) your risk and expense should we receive them after this date.

We look forward to receiving your shipment and doing further business with you in future.

Yours (**8** sincerely/faithfully)

Kate Paxton
Kate Paxton
Head Buyer

Enc: Purchase Order SW 6827

➡ 133 **c Answer the following questions about the letter.**

1. Where is the subject line and what does it say?
2. Why have Sports Unlimited decided to order from OSPEE?
3. What are OSPEE's obligations under the terms CIF Southampton?
4. How will Sports Unlimited pay for the goods?
5. What could happen if the swimwear arrives sometime in April?
6. Do Sports Unlimited see this transaction as a one-off order?
7. Why should the letter end with "Yours sincerely"?
8. What else goes into the same envelope? Why?

➡ 132
➡ 133 **d Read this part of the cover page of the OSPEE fax, and complete the fax by matching the numbers in the fax with the words in the box.**

> *advise * attached * delays * irrevocable * effect*
> *March 1 * notify * pro forma * terms * Woodae*

Please find ❶ the following two items:
- confirmation of your order SW 6827 of January 10
- ❷ invoice

Would you check the order confirmation and ❸ us immediately if there are any discrepancies.

To avoid any possible ❹ in shipment, please make arrangements to ❺ payment so that we receive it by **the end of this month.**

Please note the following ❻ in issuing the ❼ letter of credit:
- Partial shipments must be **ALLOWED**.
- Latest shipment date - February 15
- Expiry date - ❽
- Payment at sight by irrevocable letter of credit with ❾ Bank

Please ❿ us when the L/C has been issued.

Thank you & best regards

134 Unit 7 · Activities

e Read these excerpts from a fax from OSPEE.

Dear Ms Paxton

Thank you for your order for swimwear, which we received today.

We are pleased to inform you that we can supply all of the items from stock. We have already made arrangements with our shipping agent, and trust that the consignment will reach you before March 31. The order will be dispatched as soon as we have received notification of your irrevocable letter of credit.

Thank you & best regards

To: Sports Unlimited
76 The Mall
Stratford E15 1XD
United Kingdom

Ref: Your order SW6827

Date: January 15, 200_ 2:34 pm

OSPEE
SPORTSWEAR INTERNATIONAL
134 Imun-Dong, Dong Dae Mun-Ku
123 Seoul   South Korea
Tel (...+82-2) 430-3842
Fax (...+82-2) 430-3864

PRO FORMA INVOICE GB 3759

QTY	ITEM# AND DESCRIPTION	UNIT PRICE	AMOUNT
400	23 8013 Splashback two piece, medium leg, 6	£ 10.95	£ 4,380
600	23 8014 Splashback two piece, medium leg, 8	£ 10.95	£ 6,570
700	23 8015 Splashback two piece, medium leg, 10	£ 10.95	£ 7,665
300	23 8016 Splashback two piece, medium leg, 12	£ 10.95	£ 3,285
500	23 8496 Olympia one piece, high leg, 6	£ 9.75	£ 4,875
800	23 8497 Olympia one piece, high leg, 8	£ 9.75	£ 7,800
1,000	23 8498 Olympia one piece, high leg, 10	£ 9.75	£ 9,750
700	23 8499 Olympia one piece, high leg, 12	£ 9.75	£ 6,825
400	23 8809 Aquablade striped, medium leg, 6	£ 12.15	£ 4,860
800	23 8810 Aquablade striped, medium leg, 8	£ 12.15	£ 9,720
800	23 8811 Aquablade striped, medium leg, 10	£ 12.15	£ 9,720

total value of order CIF Southampton £ 75,450

f Now decide whether the statements below are true or false.

1. OSPEE is able to supply all the items immediately.
2. The prices include only the costs of packing and transport to Southampton.
3. Sports Unlimited must arrange for the insurance of the goods from the port to their warehouse.
4. OSPEE has already contacted a forwarding agent to be sure to meet the deadline.
5. OSPEE will send off the goods immediately after receiving payment.

A 5a Application for L/C

■ Use the information on pages 132-135 to complete the application form (copy the application form below) to open an irrevocable letter of credit in favour of OSPEE under the terms listed. Then write a fax cover letter to Claybars Bank, International Services Branch, 134 Brooke Street, London W3 8DE, mentioning that you are attaching the form and OSPEE's pro forma invoice.

PLEASE OPEN THE FOLLOWING ☐ REVOCABLE ☐ IRREVOCABLE DOCUMENTARY CREDIT:	
PLACE: **STRATFORD**	DATE: **day month 200_**
APPLICANT:	BENEFICIARY:
APPLICANT'S BANK: **Claybars Bank** **134 Brooke Street** **London W3 8DE**	BENEFICIARY'S BANK: **Woodae Bank, Mun-Ku Br.** **54 Chan Dong** **123 Seoul** **South Korea**
AMOUNT:	DATE AND PLACE OF EXPIRY: **Seoul, 200_**
	TERMS OF SHIPMENT
PARTIAL SHIPMENT ☐ ALLOWED ☐ NOT ALLOWED	GOODS INSURED BY ☐ BUYER ☒ SELLER
DISPATCH FROM **Pusan**	FOR TRANSPORTATION TO LATEST DATE OF SHIPMENT
DOCUMENTS MUST BE PRESENTED NO LATER THAN DAYS AFTER DATE OF SHIPMENT	
BENEFICIARY MAY DISPOSE OF THE CREDIT AMOUNT AS FOLLOWS: ☒ AT SIGHT UPON PRESENTATION OF DOCUMENTS ☐ AFTER DAYS FROM DATE OF PRESENTATION OF FULL SET OF DOCUMENTS ☐ BY DRAFT DUE _____ DRAWN ON THE ☐ APPLICANT'S BANK ☐ THE BENEFICIARY'S BANK WHICH THE ☐ APPLICANT'S BANK ☐ THE BENEFICIARY'S BANK WILL ACCEPT	
AGAINST PRESENTATION OF THE FOLLOWING DOCUMENTS:	
☐ INVOICE IN _____	☐ INSURANCE CERTIFICATE IN **duplicate**
☐ BILL OF LADING ☐ DUPLICATE WAYBILL ☐ AIR WAYBILL	COVERING ☒ OTHER: **certificate of origin**
NOTIFY ADDRESS IN BILL OF LADING: **Sports Unlimited plc** **76 The Mall** **Stratford, E 15 IXD** **U.K.**	GOODS: **Assorted swimwear** **2000 Splasback** **3000 Olympia** **2000 Aquablade**
THE BENEFICIARY'S BANK IS REQUESTED TO NOTIFY THE BENEFICIARY	
☐ ADDING THEIR CONFIRMATION	☒ WITHOUT ADDING THEIR CONFIRMATION
PAYMENT TO BE DEBITED TO OUR ACCOUNT NO. **SU 935 5354 7631**	SIGNATURE

Unit 7 · Activities

A 5b Notification of L/C

a Rocky Bike Ltd. in Vancouver, Canada has decided to import Hyflyer bicycles. They have therefore instructed their bank to open a letter of credit in favour of Hyflyer.
Read this notification from the English correspondent bank.

IRREVOCABLE LETTER OF CREDIT

DOYLES BANK plc
INTERNATIONAL SERVICES BRANCH
67 HIGH STREET, HOVE, BN3 2BE. UK. TEL: 0172 534934, FAX: 0172 534946

BENEFICIARY:
HYFLYER plc
438 WELTMORE INDUSTRIAL PARK
WARWICK CV43 6TS
UNITED KINGDOM

OPENING BANK:
FIRST METROPOLITAN BANK
348 FIRST STREET
VANCOUVER, BRITISH COLUMBIA
CANADA

ADVICE OF
IRREVOCABLE DOCUMENTARY CREDIT
NUMBER XUK 30259324/09
DATED 15 JANUARY 200_
DATE OF EXPIRY: 1 MARCH 200_
PLACE OF EXPIRY: UNITED KINGDOM
AMOUNT: UP TO GBP 40,000
UP TO FORTY THOUSAND
AND 00/100 POUNDS STERLING
OUR ADVICE NUMBER: DBIS8136629

APPLICANT
ROCKY BIKE LTD
8192 NINTH STREET
VANCOUVER, BRITISH COLUMBIA
CANADA

25 JANUARY 200_

DEAR SIRS

THIS LETTER OF CREDIT IS AVAILABLE WITH DOYLES BANK plc BY PAYMENT AGAINST PRESENTATION OF THE DOCUMENTS DETAILED HEREIN AND OF YOUR DRAFTS AT SIGHT DRAWN ON DOYLES BANK plc HOVE FOR ONE HUNDRED PER CENT OF INVOICE VALUE.

DOCUMENTS REQUIRED:

1. COMMERCIAL INVOICE IN TRIPLICATE
2. INSURANCE POLICY IN DUPLICATE COVERING MARINE RISKS FOR 110 PER CENT OF THE INVOICE VALUE
3. FULL SET OF CLEAN ON BOARD BLANK ENDORSED PORT TO PORT BILL OF LADING MARKED NOTIFY ROCKY BIKE LTD 8192 NINTH STREET VANCOUVER, BRITISH COLUMBIA.

COVERING THE FOLLOWING GOODS:

200 HYFLYER DX-2000 TITANIUM FRAME AND FORK, SHIMADA XTR 24-SPEED GEARS, SHIMADA XTR RAPIDFIRE SHIFTERS,
SHIMADA XTR V BRAKES, SHIMADA LEVERS, RIMS AND HUBS, RITCHEY ALFABITE 26" TYRES
COST, INSURANCE, FREIGHT VANCOUVER
SHIPMENT FROM SOUTHAMPTON
NO LATER THAN 15 FEBRUARY 200_
FOR TRANSPORTATION TO VANCOUVER

DOCUMENTS MUST BE PRESENTED AT PLACE OF EXPIRY WITHIN TWO WEEKS OF ISSUE DATE OF TRANSPORT DOCUMENT AND WITHIN THE L/C VALIDITY.

DOCUMENTS ARE TO BE ACCOMPANIED BY YOUR BILL OF EXCHANGE DRAWN ON DOYLES BANK plc AT SIGHT MARKED 'DRAWN UNDER IRREVOCABLE LETTER OF CREDIT NUMBER XUK 30259324/09 OF FIRST METROPOLITAN BANK VANCOUVER, CANADA AND QUOTING OUR REFERENCE NUMBER DBIS8136629.

IMPORTANT: PLEASE CAREFULLY CHECK THE DETAILS OF THE CREDIT AS IT IS ESSENTIAL THAT DOCUMENTS PRESENTED CONFORM IN EVERY RESPECT WITH THE CREDIT TERMS. SHOULD YOU BE UNABLE TO COMPLY, PLEASE COMMUNICATE WITH ROCKY BIKE LTD, VANCOUVER, CANADA IMMEDIATELY IN ORDER TO ARRANGE A SUITABLE AMENDMENT WITHOUT DELAY. IF DOCUMENTS ARE PRESENTED WHICH DIFFER FROM THE CREDIT TERMS, WE RESERVE THE RIGHT TO MAKE AN ADDITIONAL CHARGE.

WE ADD OUR CONFIRMATION TO THIS CREDIT AND UNDERTAKE THAT THE BILL OF EXCHANGE AND THE DOCUMENTS DRAWN UNDER AND IN STRICT CONFORMITY WITH THE TERMS THEREOF WILL BE HONOURED ON PRESENTATION.

THIS CREDIT IS SUBJECT TO THE UNIFORM CUSTOMS AND PRACTICE FOR DOCUMENTARY CREDITS, ICC PUBLICATION NUMBER 500 (REVISION 200_).

YOURS FAITHFULLY

Geoffrey Greenaway   *Richard Dixon*

GEOFFREY GREENAWAY, MANAGER   RICHARD DIXON, CHIEF CASHIER

→ 137 **b** Work with a partner. Partner A studies the notification on page 137.
Partner B asks partner A to get the information necessary to complete the sentences.

Example: 1. Question: "What are the terms of delivery?"
Answer: "The terms of delivery are CIF Vancouver."

1. *The terms of delivery are* ❓
2. The address of the importer is ❓
3. The address of the exporter is ❓
4. The bill of exchange is to be drawn on ❓ at ❓
5. Payment will be made against presentation of these documents: ❓
6. The documents must be presented within ❓
7. Shipment must be made from ❓ no later than ❓
8. The credit is available to Hyflyer until ❓

→ 137
→ 95 **c** Use the information on page 137 to make out this bill of exchange, which Peter Hamilton from Hyflyer plc draws on Rocky Bike Ltd. (copy the form below). Compare this bill with the one in unit 5 on page 95 and consider where you must add this phrase:
*Drawn under irrevocable documentary credit no. XUK 30259324/09 dated 15 January 200_*

```
                                                                    200_
EXCHANGE FOR
                                        PAY THIS ............ BILL OF EXCHANGE ..............
AT ...........................................
TO THE ORDER OF ..................................................................





............................................
                                                        WHICH PLACE TO ACCOUNT
VALUE ......................................            FOR AND ON BEHALF OF

TO:   ..................................
      ..................................
      ..................................
      ..................................
```

SPECIMEN

138 Unit 7 · Activities

A 6 Confirming payment

a When payment has been received, it is customary to send a receipt to confirm payment. Receipts are generally accompanied by a simple cover sheet like the one Pete O'Brien received from the Canadian Chamber of Commerce. **Complete the receipt matching the words and figures from the box below with the numbers.**

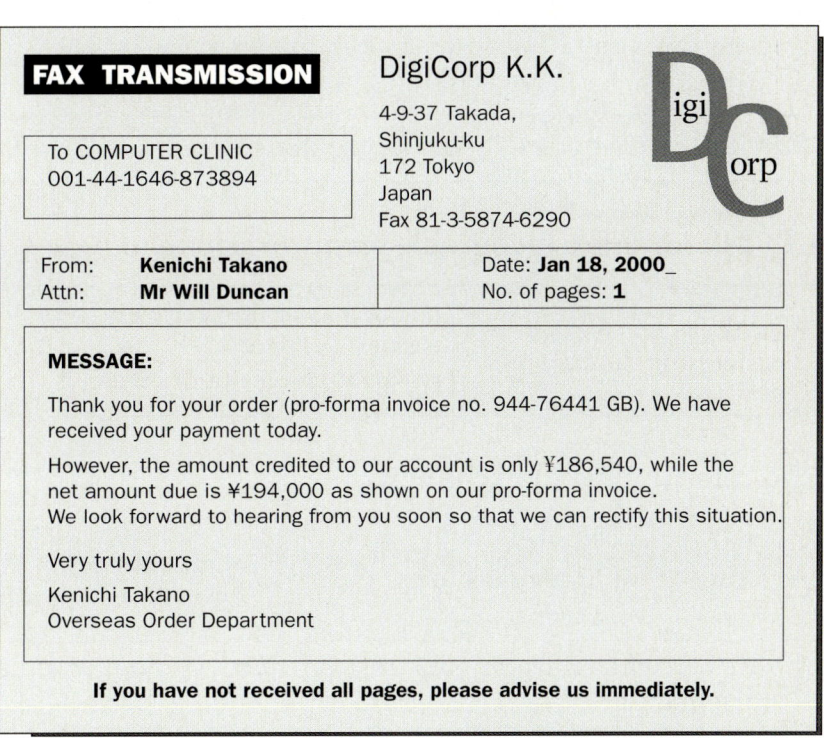

CCC
The Canadian Chamber of Commerce
143 Buckingham Palace Road, London SW1W 9SS

Direct Line 020 7687

With Compliments

Tel: +44(0) 20 7268 9837
Fax: +44(0) 20 7268 9839
E-mail: reference@ccc.org
Internet: www.ccc.org

RECEIPT

CCC
The Canadian Chamber of Commerce
143 Buckingham Palace Road,
London SW1W 9SS
Direct Line 0171 687

Receipt No **193298**
Date **20–2–200_**

Received from ___❺___   Company ___*Hyflyer plc*___

DESCRIPTION	CURRENCY	NET	VAT	TOTAL	A/C CODE
Business Opportunities in Canada	❶	*17.02*	❷	*20.00*	❸
TOTAL				❹	

Box:
2.98
20.00
GBP
Pete O'Brien
NMG

b In unit 5 (p.82) Will Duncan ordered UltraSpeed drives from DigiCorp K.K. and remitted ¥194,000 to their account. A few days later, however, he received this fax.

On checking the remittance form, he discovers that he forgot to instruct his bank to debit all the charges to his account.

Draft a fax on behalf of Will Duncan. First apologize for this error and then explain what happened and how you are going to adjust the mistake. Remember: You need the drives urgently!

FAX TRANSMISSION

To COMPUTER CLINIC
001-44-1646-873894

DigiCorp K.K.
4-9-37 Takada,
Shinjuku-ku
172 Tokyo
Japan
Fax 81-3-5874-6290

From: **Kenichi Takano**
Attn: **Mr Will Duncan**
Date: **Jan 18, 2000_**
No. of pages: **1**

MESSAGE:

Thank you for your order (pro-forma invoice no. 944-76441 GB). We have received your payment today.

However, the amount credited to our account is only ¥186,540, while the net amount due is ¥194,000 as shown on our pro-forma invoice. We look forward to hearing from you soon so that we can rectify this situation.

Very truly yours

Kenichi Takano
Overseas Order Department

If you have not received all pages, please advise us immediately.

B Tool kit

B 1 Building blocks for business communications: Payment

1 To refer to the invoice or statement of account

We are enclosing	our pro forma invoice as requested. our quarterly statement of account showing a balance of £437.50 **in** our favour. invoice no ... amounting to US$ ... and would appreciate early settlement.

2 To announce payment

We have instructed our bank to remit the invoice amount to your account **with** .... Bank.		
We are sending you enclosed our cheque for €245.00	in part payment in full settlement	of your invoice no ...
	as the first instalment under our agreement.	

3 To refer to discrepancies

When checking your invoice Comparing the statement with our own records	we noticed the following	error. omission. discrepancies.

It seems that you	forgot to deduct the quantity discount. made an error in totalling. omitted the amount of the credit note.
Please let us have a credit note for the difference.	

4 To ask for more favourable terms of payment

As we have now been doing business on the basis of	documents against payment cash on delivery payment on receipt of invoice	**for** two years	we would like to ask you to grant us open account terms.

5 To refer to bills of exchange

As arranged we have drawn **on** you	**at** 60 days' sight. **for** £1200.00 payable at sight.
We are herewith returning your draft provided with our acceptance and will duly honour the bill **at** maturity.	

The documents will be surrendered to you by the bank against	payment of the sight draft. acceptance of the bill of exchange.

6 To refer to payment by letter of credit

Payment is to be	made effected	by irrevocable (and confirmed) letter **of** credit **in** our favour, payable **at** a German bank and valid **until** 31 July.

We will instruct We have instructed	our bank to	open a series of monthly irrevocable letters of credit of US$21,730 each, **in** your favour.
		open an irrevocable letter of credit **in** your favour, valid **until** ...
		issue a letter of credit to cover the full amount of your invoice.
The letter of credit	will be confirmed by will be available through	First Metropolitan Bank, Vancouver.
The letter of credit will be available against presentation of the following documents:		

Please submit the following documents: The following documents are required:	invoice bill of lading air waybill insurance policy certificate of origin packing list inspection certificate	in duplicate. in triplicate. in quadruplicate. ,3-fold.

You will be informed through your bank of the type and number of documents required for this transaction.	
Please note the following terms in issuing the L/C:	expiry date 15 June. latest shipping date 1 June. payment at sight. partial shipments allowed. transshipments not allowed.

■ **Use the building blocks on the previous pages to find equivalents for the following German sentences.**

1. Wir fügen unsere Rechnung Nr. 328 über DM 42.764,50 bei und bitten Sie, diesen Betrag auf unsere Kontonummer ... bei der Stadtsparkasse Wuppertal zu überweisen.
2. Als Anlage erhalten Sie unseren Scheck über DM 463.- als zweite Rate.
3. Der Vergleich mit unseren Unterlagen hat eine Differenz von DM 8,37 zu Ihren Gunsten ergeben.
4. Nachdem Sie uns nun seit einem Jahr auf der Basis von Zahlung bei Rechnungserhalt beliefern, möchten wir Sie um offenes Zahlungsziel bitten.
5. Wie vereinbart, haben wir einen 90-Tage-Wechsel auf Sie gezogen. Wir bitten Sie, diesen mit Ihrem Akzept zu versehen und an uns zurückzuschicken.
6. Die Royal Trade Bank wird Ihnen die Dokumente gegen Einlösung unserer Sichttratte aushändigen.
7. Wir haben unsere Bank angewiesen ein unwiderrufliches Akkreditiv zu Ihren Gunsten zu eröffnen, das bei einer Bank in Toronto zahlbar und bis 15. Oktober gültig ist.
8. Das Akkreditiv ist benutzbar gegen Vorlage folgender Dokumente in vierfacher Ausfertigung:

B 2 Translation of business texts

Translation is a craft consisting in the attempt to replace a written message and/or statement in one language by the same message and/or statement in another language.
(Peter Newmark)

You should try to translate the contents, that is the meaning, of a text faithfully and completely. Every bit of information contained in the original text ought to appear in the translation as well. If, for instance, it says in the original "The management was very disappointed at the results", you must not forget to translate the "very" as it carries meaning in emphasising the degree of disappointment.

However, this does not mean that you ought to translate texts word for word. On the contrary, in most cases you will have to change the word order or the structure of the sentence in the original language so as to achieve a sentence that sounds natural in the target language. As English and German are closely related there is a lot of interference between the two languages and translations easily sound "translated". Translating German texts word by word will result in sentences like "Very cautiously react people in the 32-51 age group to this question", which sounds very strange to English ears, the correct word order being "People in the 31-51 age group react very cautiously to this question". The same is true, of course, of German structures when translating from English into German. It is, for example, perfectly alright to speak of the "Daimler-Benz Chrysler merger" in English, whereas no such short form is really possible in German. It should be "Die Fusion von Daimler-Benz und Chrysler".

Generally, a sound knowledge of the rules of grammar will greatly help you to improve your translations into English. Use an up-to-date grammar textbook and study texts in the business sections of English language newspapers and magazines.

Above all, you must learn to work with a dictionary. Study the signs, symbols and letters used to give additional information on the meaning and usage of the word you are looking up in the dictionary. Read the entire entry and choose the right word by careful consideration of the examples given. The first translation mentioned in the dictionary need not necessarily be the best translation in your particular case. Pay attention to the correct prepositions and collocations, i.e. which verb goes with which noun and vice versa.

Make sure that you complete the translation in time to enable you to check it carefully with the help of the following check list.

CHECKLIST: Translations

- Has all the information provided by the text been translated?
- Have I overlooked a word or a sentence?
- Are the tenses correct?
- Are there any discrepancies with singulars and plurals?
- Does the English / the German sound natural?
- Have I paid attention to the points of grammar which I am likely to get wrong?
- Have I checked the entire sentence when making changes in one word or structure?
- Is the punctuation correct?

account s 1. *econ* a) Berechnung f, Rechnung f, open ~ offenes Zahlungsziel n; b) pl Geschäftsbücher, pl, (Jahres)Abschluss m, c) **transaction for the ~** *(Börse)* Termingeschäft n; 2. *fin.* (Bank)Konto n; **statement of** ~ Kontoauszug m; 3. *mkt.* Kundenetat m, (Etat)Kunde m; 4. Rechenschaft f, Rechenschaftsbericht m, ~ sales Verkaufsabrechnung f *(Vertreter)*

■ **Find the correct translations for the word account with the help of the above excerpt from a dictionary.**

1. Please remit the amount due to our account with Bull's Bank mentioned below.
2. In recent months several major companies have been very slow in settling their accounts.
3. Before we enter into negotiations about a possible co-operation we must ask you to permit us to study your accounts for the last three years.
4. This advertising campaign must be given top priority as we do not wish to lose this key account.
5. As an attachment I am sending you my account sales for the second quarter.

C Additional practice

a Complete the following sentences choosing the correct prepositions from the box.

> after (2x) * against (2x) * at * by (2x) * in (2x) * of (2x) * on * to (2x) * until * up * with

- Payment is to be effected ❶ our account no. 17 345 87 ❷ ABCD Bank.
- Please transfer the amount ❸ DM 17,920.00 ❹ our account.
- Please remit the invoice amount 15 days ❺ delivery.
- The draft is payable 60 days ❻ the date ❼ the B/L.
- Payment is to be made ❽ bank transfer.
- Please send us a cheque ❾ payment.
- Please effect payment ❿ the 15th of the month following the month of delivery.
- Our terms of payment are cash ⓫ documents.
- If the customer fails to take ⓬ the documents please contact Mr Abdul Hafis.
- We will draw a 60 days' draft ⓭ you.
- Terms of payment: Letter of credit, to be opened ⓮ a London bank ⓯ our favour, valid ⓰ 31 May 200-, available ⓱ presentation of the following documents:

b Wedler & Co., Steilhang 45, 87527 Sonthofen, Tel. 08321 / 38790, Fax: 08321 / 38795, www.wedler.co.de, has received this message from Elsa Griffith, MOUNTAINEER's head buyer (108 Darlington Road, Miramar, Wellington 3):

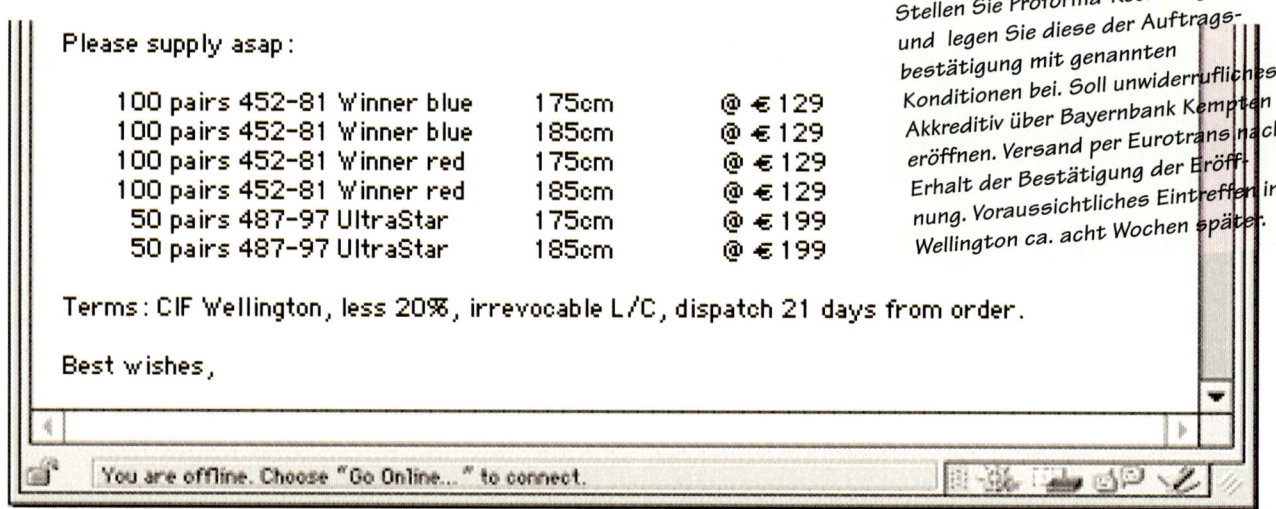

```
Please supply asap:

    100 pairs 452-81 Winner blue     175cm     @ €129
    100 pairs 452-81 Winner blue     185cm     @ €129
    100 pairs 452-81 Winner red      175cm     @ €129
    100 pairs 452-81 Winner red      185cm     @ €129
     50 pairs 487-97 UltraStar       175cm     @ €199
     50 pairs 487-97 UltraStar       185cm     @ €199

Terms: CIF Wellington, less 20%, irrevocable L/C, dispatch 21 days from order.

Best wishes,
```

Stellen Sie Proforma-Rechnung aus und legen Sie diese der Auftragsbestätigung mit genannten Konditionen bei. Soll unwiderrufliches Akkreditiv über Bayernbank Kempten eröffnen. Versand per Eurotrans nach Erhalt der Bestätigung der Eröffnung. Voraussichtliches Eintreffen in Wellington ca. acht Wochen später.

Carry out these instructions.

D Background information

D 1 Methods of payment in international trade

Payment can be effected by

- **Bank transfer**, with the buyer's bank transferring the invoice amount to the seller's bank account using the SWIFT (Society for Worldwide Interbank Financial Telecommunication) network for transfers worldwide or the TARGET system for express transfers within the EU via the European Central Bank.
- **Letter of credit** (see page 146)
- **Bill of exchange** (see unit 5 and page 148, documents for collection)
- **Cheque** (see unit 5)
- **Banker's draft** (see unit 5)
- **Credit card**

Credit cards are issued by credit card companies in order to give their customers credit when they purchase goods or services. When the cardholder buys something he or she shows the credit card to the salesperson and signs a transaction slip. The amount in question is advanced by the credit card company and the cardholder normally gets a monthly statement of account to be paid in full or by instalments. Some credit card companies charge membership fees. The advantages of credit cards are convenience and relative security.

Charge cards (or pay/debit cards) differ from credit cards in that the customer's account is immediately debited with the amount of the transaction.

D 2 Terms of payment in international trade

The terms of payment chosen in an international transaction will depend on the size of the order, the creditworthiness of the customer and the banking system and political situation in the customer's country. The following examples of terms are listed roughly in the order of the degree of security provided for the seller:

1. Cash with order
2. Payment in advance
3. Letter of Credit
4. Documents against payment (D/P)
5. Cash on delivery (COD)
6. Payment on receipt of invoice
7. Staggered payment (e.g. One third with order, one third on delivery, one third 30 days after delivery
8. Open credit (e.g. 30 days net, ten days 2%)
9. Documents against acceptance (D/A)
10. Bill of Exchange (B/E) at 60 days
11. Open account terms

D 2.1 Open account terms

In longstanding business relations, it is customary to trade on 'open account terms'. This means that the buyer of the goods does not pay individual invoices, but waits for the monthly statement of account.

The statement is a business document which shows the balance outstanding on a buyer's account requesting payment. Smaller firms usually send out statements on the last day of the month, while large companies spread out billing over the entire month. Thus, some customers get their statements on the 10th of each month, while others get their statements on the 20th, etc.

Having received the statement, the buyer pays for the goods according to the terms agreed, e.g. 10 days 2%, 30 days net..

■ Read the following text and decide which of the alternatives in brackets is correct.

Open account terms are (① granted / guaranteed) by a seller to a regular customer with (② who / whom) he has been doing business (③ since / for) some time and in whom he has complete confidence. Payment may (④ then / than) be made monthly or quarterly by bank transfer, cheque or bill of exchange.

D 2 II Letter of credit

There are a number of risks involved in international trade. On the one hand, the exporter may not get paid after all the effort of designing, manufacturing and shipping the goods abroad. On the other hand, the importer may never receive the goods if he/she pays in advance. Obviously, it is necessary to find some arrangement which safeguards the interests of both parties.

The letter of credit, in foreign trade also called documentary credit, provides security for both buyer and seller and has consequently become one of the most widely used methods of payment.

It is an undertaking by the importer's bank, the opening bank, to pay a certain sum to the exporter upon presentation of specified documents. Consequently, it is not just the importer who is obliged to pay. In addition, the exporter can rely on the promise to pay made by the importer's bank. In the case of a **confirmed** letter of credit a second bank, this time the advising bank in the exporter's country, also assumes responsibility for payment under the letter of credit.

Nowadays letters of credit are almost always **irrevocable**, that is to say they can only be revoked with the consent of all the parties involved. Frequently, the shipping documents to be presented by the exporter are accompanied by a sight draft or time bill drawn by the exporter on the importer or his bank.

The basic procedure is as follows:
1. The importer negotiates the terms of the deal with the exporter and agrees to pay by letter of credit.
2. The importer instructs his/her bank to open a letter of credit in favour of the exporter.
3. The importer's bank issues an irrevocable letter of credit, and notifies the exporter's bank, the advising bank, which confirms the credit if a confirmed L/C has been agreed upon in the sales contract.
4. The exporter is notified that there is a letter of credit in his/her favour.
5. The exporter ships the goods as specified in the L/C and receives in return a bill of lading, which embodies the ownership of the goods.
6. The exporter presents the required documents, including the B/L, to his/her bank.
7. The exporter's bank verifies that the documents conform to the specifications of the L/C and pays the exporter.
8. The exporter's bank sends the documents to the importer's bank, which checks them again.
9. The importer's bank settles with the exporter's bank.
10. The importer's bank releases the documents to the exporter and debits his/her account with the amount of the L/C.
11. The goods arrive safely and the importer can collect them from the port area as he is now in possession of the bill of lading.

a Read the following information and check whether the numbers in the circles are correct.

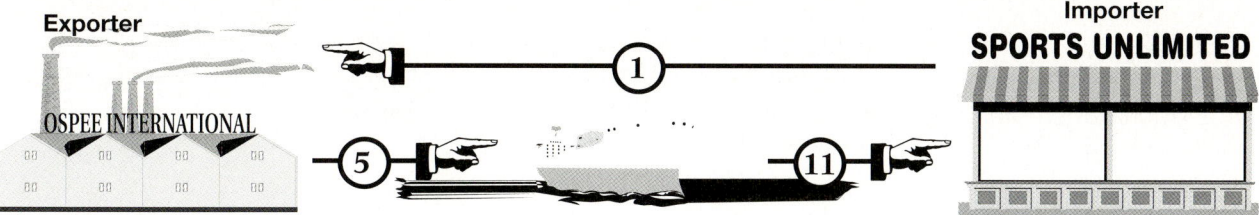

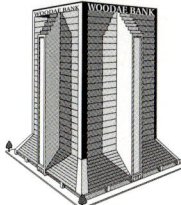
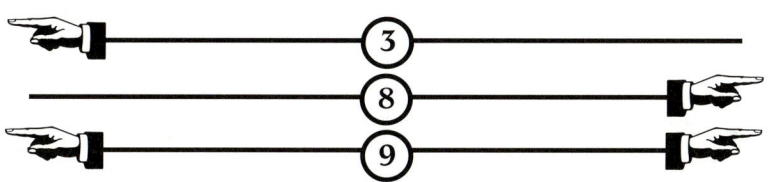

1. Sports Unlimited places an order for swimwear with OSPEE and agrees to pay by L/C.
2. Sports Unlimited instructs Claybars Bank to open a letter of credit in favour of OSPEE and to find out which documents are necessary for importing the goods to Britain.
3. Claybars Bank sets out all the terms and specifications in an irrevocable L/C, and sends full details of the L/C to Woodae Bank, which confirms the credit with Claybars Bank.
4. Woodae Bank notifies OSPEE that an irrevocable and confirmed letter of credit in their favour has been opened.
5. OSPEE ships the goods exactly as required in the L/C and receives in return a bill of lading.
6. The goods are on their way to Britain, and OSPEE presents the documents required to Woodae Bank.
7. Woodae Bank verifies that the documents conform to the requirements of the L/C and pays OSPEE.
8. Woodae Bank sends the documents to Claybars Bank, which checks them again.
9. Claybars Bank settles with Woodae Bank.
10. Claybars Bank passes the documents on to Sports Unlimited and debits their account.
11. The swimwear arrives safely at Southampton and Sports Unlimited can clear the goods through customs and transport them to their warehouse in Stratford.

b To understand why the documentary letter of credit is the safest method of payment for both the exporter and the importer study the procedure concerning the transaction between OPSEE and Sports Unlimited once more. **Read the following text and complete it using words from the box.**

> lading * letter * payment * released
> sell * shipping * submit

It has already been mentioned briefly that one of the ❶ documents involved in L/C transactions is the **bill of lading (B/L)** and that anybody in possession of the bill of lading is considered the rightful owner of the goods (see unit 8, p.171).

When OSPEE ship the goods they obtain the bill of ❷ and when they ❸ it to Woodae Bank, together with the other documents and once the bank has checked the documents, OSPEE receives ❹. For the periods that Woodae Bank and Claybars Bank are each advancing money under the ❺ of credit they are each in possession of the B/L and could ❻ the goods should Sports Unlimited suddenly be unable to pay. In the end, the shipping documents are ❼ to Sports Unlimited against payment. Possession of the B/L means ownership of the goods for Sports Unlimited and hence the right to claim them from the carriers.

D 2 III Documents for collection

Under the heading "documents for collection" two different terms of payment are grouped together as both involve the use of a bill of exchange (see unit 5). "Documents" here means shipping documents, the most important being the bill of lading as it embodies the ownership of the goods (see unit 8).

If payment by **documents against payment** (D/P) has been agreed upon (arrow 1), the procedure is as follows:
1. The exporter draws a sight draft on the importer and hands it over to his bank together with the shipping documents (arrow 2). The exporter's bank sends the documents together with the sight draft to a correspondent bank in the importer's country (arrow 3).
2. The correspondent bank notifies the importer and releases the documents to him against payment of the sight draft (arrow 4). Possession of the documents will entitle the importer to take possession of the goods.
3. The money is then remitted to the exporter via his bank (arrows 5 and 6).
   In this system, the sight draft is frequently omitted, as the bank will in any case only hand over the documents to the importer when payment is made.

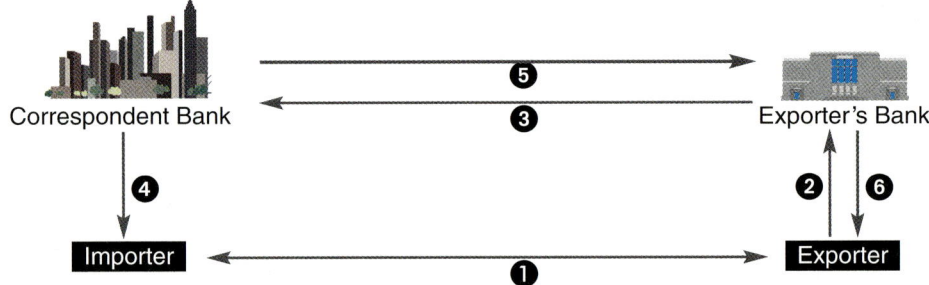

Payment by **documents against acceptance** (D/A) is agreed upon if the seller wishes to grant the buyer credit for a certain period (arrow 1). The procedure is as follows:
1. The exporter draws a time bill (e.g. a B/E at 90 days) on the importer and hands it over to his bank together with the shipping documents (arrow 2).
2. The bill of exchange and the documents are forwarded to a correspondent bank in the importer's country (arrow 3).
3. The correspondent bank notifies the importer and surrenders the documents to him when he accepts the bill of exchange (arrow 4).
4. The accepted bill of exchange is returned to the exporter's bank (arrow 5) for transmission to the exporter (arrow 6) who may have it discounted and thus receive the money (less the bank discount) before maturity.
5. At maturity the bill of exchange is presented to the importer for payment (arrow 7).

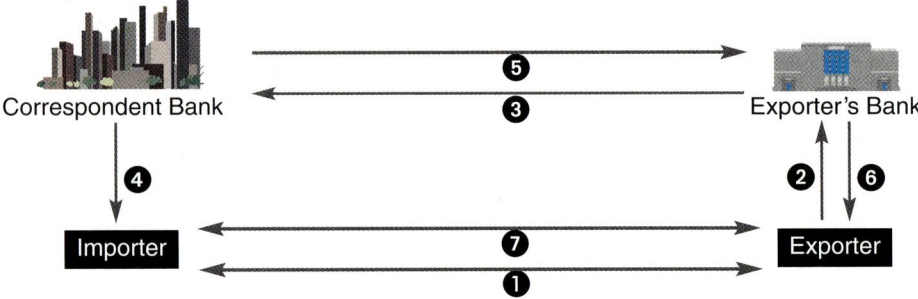

It should be noted that in both these cases the banks do not assume any responsibility for payment. For the exporter there is the risk that the importer will not "take up" the documents, i.e.

refuse to either pay the sight draft or accept the bill of exchange as the case may be. This risk can, however, be reduced by requiring the customer to furnish a **bank guarantee**. The terms D/P and D/A do not provide the same degree of security as the letter of credit but they are less expensive. They are used for transactions with reliable companies from the EU and from other major industrialised countries.

■ **Complete the following business transactions by matching the appropriate terms of payment in the box below with the numbers.**

> irrevocable and confirmed documentary letter of credit ✳ 30 days net, 10 days 2% ✳
> documents against acceptance ✳ open account ✳ one third with order,
> one third on delivery, one third after start-up of the machinery ✳ cash with order

- Cumbria Steel plc have received an enquiry for steel plates worth £85,000.00 from a firm in Colombia they do not know. In their quotation Cumbria Steel requests payment by ❶.

- Hyflyer gets a phone call from the wholesaler in Germany whom it has been supplying for 10 years, asking for another batch of spare parts. They will arrange for payment on ❷.

- Sally Cosmetics is anxious to win a large order from a well-known American cosmetics retail chain which insists on being granted credit for 90 days. Sally Cosmetics may decide on ❸.

- Austen Lifts and Escalators PLC are going to manufacture and install lifts in a large office complex in Berlin. Their terms of payment are most likely ❹.

- Computer Clinic has received another order from a firm which has never paid on time and had to be sent one or two reminders in every instance. The terms of payment Computer Clinic's chief accountant insists upon are ❺.

- Denise Springer from Sportwelt Fan-Artikel dispatches 400 fan scarves to Eurosport in Italy the manager of which, Mr Giacomelli, is personally known to her. The terms of payment mentioned on the invoice are ❻.

Background information · Unit 7

E IHK-Prüfungsvorbereitung

1. Zusatzqualifikation Englisch für kaufmännische Auszubildende
Fremdsprache im Beruf I

Kurzgefasste/Informelle Mitteilung (Bearbeitungszeit 30 Minuten)	Hilfsmittel: zweisprachiges Wörterbuch

Situation

Sie arbeiten bei der Kunststofftechnik AG, Fax (0551) 344 471, in der Finanzbuchhaltung. Heute ist der 7. April. Ihre Chefin, Frau Ruth Wolf, legt Ihnen nachstehende Rechnung auf den Schreibtisch, auf der sie Unstimmigkeiten vermerkt hat, und sagt zu Ihnen:

Aufgabe

„Leider muss ich sofort weg. Würden Sie für mich bitte ein Fax an Mr. Gardiner von Foster & Gardiner verfassen, das ich dann gleich unterschreiben kann, wenn ich wieder zurück bin.

Folgendes stimmt bei dieser Rechnung nicht:
1. Mr. Gardiner hatte uns in seinem Angebot vom 15. März einen Rabatt von 20 % versprochen.
2. Wir hatten von Position 2, PVC-Zylinder, zwei Stück bestellt und haben auch zwei erhalten.

Bitten Sie ihn um eine neue berichtigte Rechnung und Stornierung der vorliegenden. Außerdem soll er seine Bankverbindung mit der Bankleitzahl angeben. Bis später."

Foster & Gardiner

74, Maple Grove, Somercotes
Derbyshire, DE55 9BR
Tel. 01773 835794, Fax 01773 834790

Kunststofftechnik AG
Gottfried-Daimler-Ring 97
37075 Göttingen
Germany

3 April 200_

INVOICE NO. 147/G/29

Your Order No. 7004/G dated 27 March 200..

Pos.	Quantity	Description	Code Number	Unit Price £	Total £
1	5	PVC Tube	HDT 35X200	35.00	175.00
2	~~1~~ *2*	PVC Cylinder	HDC 20X400	42.00	~~42.00~~ *84.00*

~~217.00~~ *259,00*

less ~~15%~~ *20%* discount: ~~32.55~~ *51,80*

207,20
~~£184.45~~

Please remit the net invoice amount within two weeks.

gez. Wolf

2. Fremdsprachenkorrespondent/in

| Übersetzung Englisch /Deutsch (Bearbeitungszeit 60 Minuten) | Hilfsmittel: zweisprachige Wörterbücher |

Would you complete a credit card slip before deciding whether or not to buy anything? Probably not, but on the internet many sites ask for credit card details before giving access to even basic services. Recent surveys show that a large majority of people are concerned about revealing such information.

A widespread fear is that the details could get into the wrong hands. Fortunately this danger is reduced to a minimum on modern e-commerce sites by the use of the appropriate technology (SET). A private code makes information illegible for unauthorised persons. You can tell whether a retailer is using SET by the picture of a little key or padlock that appears when you are asked to give your details.

Another concern is that the retailer might not be reliable enough to be entrusted with your details. He may try to re-use the details at some time in the future. Of course, we are faced with this dilemma whenever we use our credit cards in person or on the phone. In online transactions customer rights are the same as in traditional shopping. You are not liable for unauthorised transactions should they occur in the future.

Eventually it will be possible to effect payment online through the online arm of your bank, which will remove the need for giving information directly to retailers; the retailer will simply receive confirmation that you have authorised payment.

3. Fremdsprachenkorrespondent/in Englisch

| Übersetzung Deutsch/Englisch (Bearbeitungszeit 60 Minuten) | Hilfsmittel: zweisprachige Wörterbücher |

Geschäfte, die auf Akkreditivbasis abgewickelt werden, bringen oftmals Schwierigkeiten aufgrund spezieller Akkreditivbedingungen mit sich. Den Banken wird in diesem Zusammenhang manchmal vorgeworfen, sie seien bei der Prüfung der Versanddokumente zu pedantisch. Es darf jedoch nicht vergessen werden, dass die Banken gerade in diesem Bereich sehr genau prüfen müssen, da die Dokumente die Grundlage für die Auszahlung bilden.

Es ist deshalb ratsam, bei der Ausstellung von Dokumenten mit größter Sorgfalt vorzugehen und die Spezifikationen der eröffnenden Bank sehr genau zu beachten. Es ist schon vorgekommen, dass die Zahlung verweigert werden musste, weil ein Komma übersehen worden war.

In diesem Zusammenhang sollte ausdrücklich darauf hingewiesen werden, dass eine Überprüfung der Akkreditivbedingungen bei Erhalt des Akkreditivs unbedingt erforderlich ist. Besser – und damit für beide Geschäftspartner eindeutig und bindend – ist es natürlich, die Akkreditivbedingungen im Kaufvertrag möglichst genau zu beschreiben. Der Exporteur sollte hinsichtlich der Formulierung des zu eröffnenden Dokumenten-Akkreditivs die Erfahrung seiner Bank in Anspruch nehmen. Damit können Probleme, die bei Vorlage der Dokumente auftreten könnten, bereits in der Anfangsphase eines Geschäfts vermieden werden.

4. Fremdsprachenkorrespondent/in

Geschäftsbrief nach Angaben
(Bearbeitungszeit 45 Minuten)

Hilfsmittel: zweisprachige Wörterbücher

Situation

Sie (eigener Name) arbeiten im Rechnungswesen des deutschen Herstellers von Wintersportausrüstung Wedler & Co., Steilhang 45, 87527 Sonthofen, Tel. 08321 38790, Fax 08321 38795, E-Mail accounts@wedler.co.de. Der norwegische Großhändler für Sportartikel, L. Svensson A/S, Nygaten 75, N-0155 Oslo, bezieht seit Jahren regelmäßig größere Mengen von Ihrer Firma. Der Inhaber, Lars Svensson, hat bei einer Besprechung am 2. Februar 200_ mit Ihrem Geschäftsführer, Toni Schäfer, für seine Firma offenes Zahlungsziel vereinbart.

Aufgabe

Bestätigen Sie dies in einem Schreiben an Herrn Svensson und berücksichtigen Sie dabei bitte folgende Punkte:

- Einleitung
- Konto jetzt eröffnet, Konto-Nr. 0137689
- vierteljährliches Kredit-Limit für das Konto €30,000
- eingeräumtes Zahlungsziel: 60 Tage
- Übersendung von Kontoauszügen erfolgt monatlich
- Bitte um Überprüfung der Richtigkeit der Anschrift
- Verweis auf allgemeine Geschäftsbedingungen (beiliegend)
- zuständiger Verkaufsleiter, Peter Strenkert, von der Kontoeröffnung informiert
- Bei Fragen: Ihre Durchwahl +49 8321 3879 321.

5. Fremdsprachenkorrespondent/in

Zusammenfassung in Deutsch einer englischen mündlichen Nachricht
(Bearbeitungszeit 30 Minuten)

Hilfsmittel: zweisprachige Wörterbücher

Situation

Sie sind Angestellte/r der Firma Solutor Systeme, Leipzig, die eine Niederlassung in London einrichten will.

Aufgabe

Ihr Chef, Heiko von Benzelsdorf, der wenig Englisch kann, bittet Sie, einen Vermerk über diese Nachricht, die er auf seinem Anrufbeantworter vorfindet, in deutscher Sprache zu verfassen. (Sie werden den Text zweimal hören.)

SOLUTOR-SYSTEME, LEIPZIG

Telefonvermerk   Datum:

Für:

Verfasser:

Anrufer: Firma:

Betreff:

Unit 8 Documents in foreign trade

Introduction

International trade

Compared with domestic trade or trade within the EU, international trade is far more complex for a number of reasons:

- There are often 10–15 participants involved in a transaction.
- There is a wide choice of trade terms.
- Detailed terms of payment have to be worked out to keep the currency risk to a minimum.
- There are more government controls before, during and after the movement of the goods.
- Long distances have to be covered, which increases the risk of damage or loss.
- The fact that the customer is overseas often creates language and/or cultural problems.

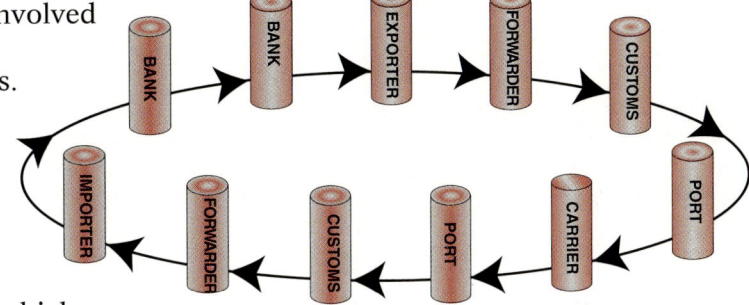

a Read this advice on export strategy and fill in the appropriate verbs from the box.

| choose * consider (2x) * cost * prepare * make sure * research * train |

❶ _____ the countries to which you may be interested in exporting. For the new exporter, it is essential to plan to export to only one country at a time.

❷ _____ the markets. Consider the foreign country's customs and culture and how your product and packaging may have to be changed. Make sure you know what is associated with certain colours in the host country. Don't forget that certain animal products may be offensive due to religious beliefs. Also investigate technical standards as your product may have to be adapted at the production stage. It is also important at this stage to begin to assess costs.

❸ _____ the presentation of your products and marketing materials. Make sure that any literature is translated into the language of the country. If this material includes pictures, be certain that potential customers can relate to them.

❹ _____ how you intend to get the goods to the market, whether you intend to organize everything yourself, including transport and documentation, or to use a freight forwarder.

❺ _____ what terms of payment you would like to use and how flexible you can be with the buyer.

❻ _____ staff who will be involved in the everyday export operations and, ideally, employ someone with a previous knowledge of export documentation and methods of payment. Documents in foreign trade must be processed with extreme care and accuracy. A research study carried out on behalf of the European Commission revealed that docu-

Introduction · Unit 8 153

mentation typically accounts for 4 to 7% of a business's export costs and may rise to as much as 15% if the documentation contains errors. Differences in goods descriptions, discrepancies in order numbers, uncompleted boxes on forms, absence of instructions, spelling errors in letter of credit documentation etc. may cause long delays and serious financial losses.

❼ that the export department works closely with sales and production to meet deadlines and ensure product quality. This is even more crucial in exporting than on the domestic market and should receive appropriate attention.

❽ all the above and any other expenses which may be incurred. These include bank charges, which, for certain methods of payment, can be quite high, transportation and shipping costs, credit insurance and insurance of the goods in transit. All these costs should not unexpectedly reduce an exporter's profits.

b Give a short summary of the text in German.

A Activities

A 1 Arranging for transport

→ 137 **a** Get together in groups of four.

First, study the notification that Doyles Bank sent to Hyflyer in unit 7, p.137, again.

Then discuss within your group which pieces of correspondence were necessary to initiate such a business transaction. When you have finished, compare your findings in class.

Next, each member of your group drafts one of the pieces of correspondence between Hyflyer plc and Rocky Bike Ltd. in the form of a fax.

→ 137 **b** Some time before Hyflyer plc received the notification of the documentary credit, Sales Manager Pete O'Brien started making arrangements for shipment. He called his shipping agent to arrange for the dispatch of the consignment. **Listen to his telephone conversation and take the message for Liz Martin from WorldCargo on a form like the following:**

MESSAGE FOR	FROM:	❏ Phoned you
OF:		❏ Returned your call
		❏ Will call again
DATE: ( )	TIME: ❏ AM	❏ Please call
☏ ( )	❏ PM	❏ Came to see you
	EXT:	❏ Wants to see you
MESSAGE:		❏ **URGENT**
....		
....		
....		
SIGNED:		

c Liz Martin checked the timetables of a few shipping lines, but could not find a suitable vessel for Hyflyer's consignment. So she contacted MyBonny Shipping Line's website, as shown on the right. **Copy the website and fill in all the information available to obtain a valid offer for the shipment, which is 200 packages in two 30ft containers, each package weighing 11.5 kilograms and measuring 1.7 metres in length, 0.9 metres in height and 0.15 metres in depth.**

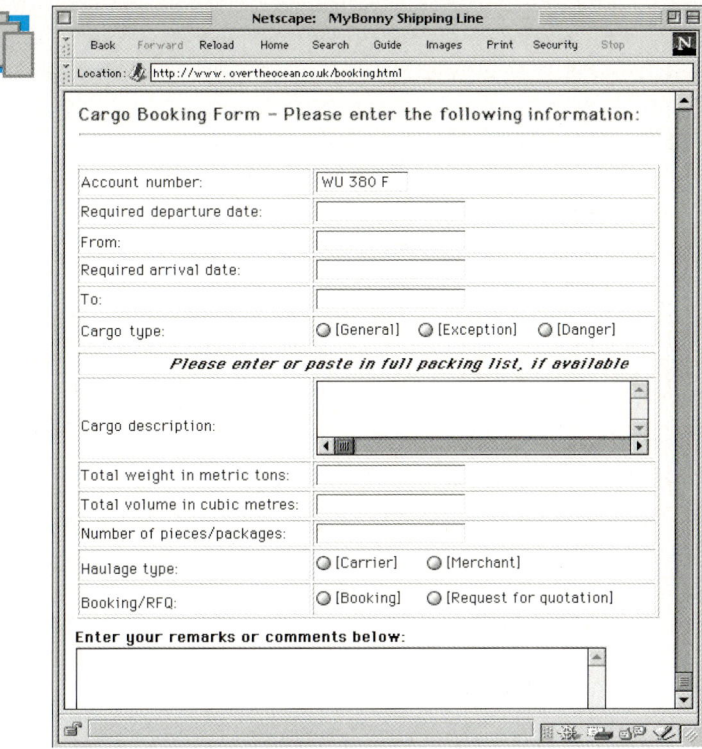

d On checking her e-mail some time later, Liz Martin finds this message from MyBonny Shipping Line. **Study it carefully.**

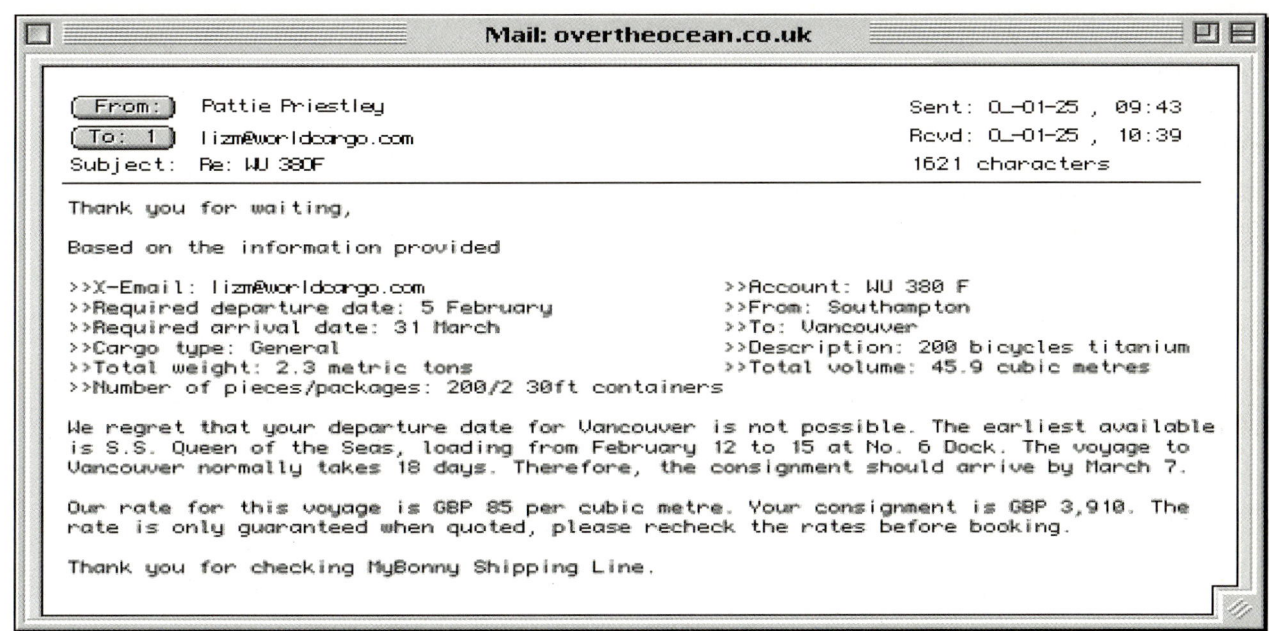

e Now decide whether these statements are true or false, or not in the text.

1. There is no vessel sailing from Southampton to Vancouver on February 5.
2. S.S. Queen of the Seas will be loading from 12 to 15 Feb. at No. 6 dock.
3. Goods are transported from Southampton to Vancouver within three weeks.
4. Unfortunately, the departure date is too late for the goods to arrive on time.
5. Sea cargo is generally charged by volume, not by weight.

Activities · Unit 8   155

A2 Taking out insurance

155 **a** Liz Martin contacted several insurance companies for the best policy for Hyflyer's consignment, and she received this fax from Elmans Insurance Brokers. **Study the body of the fax and answer the questions below.**

> Based on the information provided:
>
> Consignment: **200 bicycles**   From: **Warwick, U.K.**   Shipment date: **5 February 200_**
> Value: **GBP 39,800**   To: **Vancouver, Canada**   Vessel: **not known**
>   Coverage: **All risks excluding war risk**
>
> Your rate is 30p for £100 of value, amounting to a premium of **GBP 119.40** for the consignment.
>
> The rate is only guaranteed if the goods are packed according to the usual standards and shipped by any of the approved lines detailed on the attached list.
>
> Please let us know as soon as possible whether you want us to cover your consignment. We will then make out the policy accordingly.

1. What risks does the insurance cover? See the background information on insurance, page 169, and use your dictionary to make a list of possible risks.
2. What percentage of the value is the insurance premium?
3. Is seaworthy packing essential to insure the goods at the rate offered? Why? Why not?
4. What is the second condition mentioned? Think of reasons why the insurer stipulates such a condition.
5. What will the broker do if Pete O'Brien accepts their offer?

b Meanwhile, Liz has arranged for an open insurance policy to be made out by London Fire and Marine Insurance. **Study this document and find the words you don't know in the dictionary.**

LONDON FIRE AND MARINE INSURANCE
Certificate of Insurance No. C3984457

THIS IS TO CERTIFY THAT THERE HAS BEEN DEPOSITED AN OPEN COVER EFFECTED BY ELMANS INSURANCE BROKERS, ACTING ON BEHALF OF HYFLYER plc, DATED 1 FEBRUARY 200_, WITH LONDON FIRE AND MARINE INSURANCE IN THE PROPORTIONS SHOWN ON THE BACK HEREOF.
THE SAID COMPANY HAS UNDERTAKEN TO ISSUE TO HYFLYER plc POLICIES OF TRANSPORT INSURANCE TO COVER UP TO £200,000 (TWO HUNDRED THOUSAND POUNDS STERLING) IN ALL BY ANY ONE VESSEL, OR SENDING BY AIR OR PARCEL POST BICYCLES OR PARTS THEREOF, TO BE SHIPPED ON OR BEFORE TENTH FEBRUARY 200_ FROM ANY PORT OR PLACE IN THE UNITED KINGDOM TO ANY PORT OR PLACE IN THE UNITED STATES OF AMERICA AND CANADA; AND THAT HYFLYER plc ARE ENTITLED TO DECLARE AGAINST THE SAID OPEN COVER THE SHIPMENTS ATTACHING THERETO.

Lester Spears
DATED AT LFM HEADQUARTERS, LONDON, 1 FEBRUARY 200_

£ 39,800 Stg

WE HEREBY DECLARE FOR INSURANCE UNDER THE SAID COVER **THIRTY-NINE THOUSAND EIGHT HUNDRED POUNDS STERLING** ON INTEREST AS SPECIFIED HEREON SO VALUED PER S.S. QUEEN OF THE SEAS FROM WORKS WARWICK U.K. TO PORT OF VANCOUVER SUBJECT TO THE TERMS OF THE STANDARD FORM OF LONDON FIRE AND MARINE POLICY PROVIDING FOR THE SETTLEMENT ABROAD AND TO THE SPECIAL CONDITIONS STATED BELOW AND ON THE BACK HEREOF.
THIS CERTIFICATE IS NOT VALID UNLESS THE DECLARATION IS SIGNED BY HYFLYER plc.

INTEREST, MARKS AND NUMBERS
200 HYFLYER DX-2000 TITANIUM FRAME AND FORK, SHIMADA XTR 24-SPEED GEARS, SHIMADA XTR RAPID-FIRE SHIFTERS, SHIMADA XTR V BRAKES, SHIMADA LEVERS, RIMS AND HUBS, RITCHEY ALFABITE 26" TYRES
TWO CONTAINERS MARKED ROCKY BIKE LTD
                           VANCOUVER, CANADA
                           1 AND 2
P.P. HYFLYER plc
SIGNED
Carey Dumont
DATED AT WARWICK, 1 FEBRUARY 200_

UNDERWRITERS AGREE THAT LOSSES, IF ANY, SHALL BE PAYABLE TO THE ORDER OF HYFLYER plc ON SURRENDER OF THIS CERTIFICATE. IN THE EVENT OF LOSS OR DAMAGE WHICH MAY RESULT IN A CLAIM UNDER THIS INSURANCE, IMMEDIATE NOTICE SHOULD BE GIVEN TO THE AGENT OF LONDON FIRE AND MARINE INSURANCE AT THE PORT OR PLACE WHERE THE LOSS OR DAMAGE IS DISCOVERED IN ORDER THAT HE MAY EXAMINE THE GOODS AND ISSUE A SURVEY REPORT.

A 3 Packagings

a Are you familiar with these words? Match the English terms with their German equivalents. Use a dictionary, if necessary.

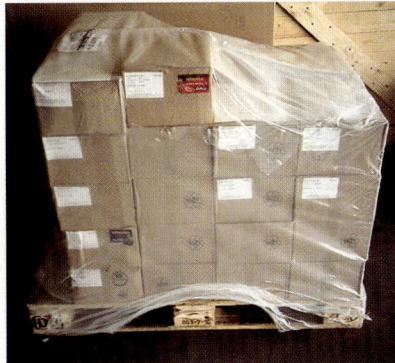

1. bale
2. barrel
3. bundle
4. carboy
5. cardboard box
6. case
7. coil
8. container
9. crate
10. drum
11. jiffy bag
12. keg
13. packages
14. padding material
15. parcel
16. polystyrene mould
17. pallet
18. sack
19. skid
20. steel strapping
21. plastic foil
22. shrunk-wrapped
23. 4-ply paper bag

a. Ballen
b. Bündel
c. Container
d. Fass
e. Füllmaterial
f. (Holz-) Fässchen
g. Karton
h. Kiste
i. Kolli (Plural)
j. Korbflasche, Glasballon
k. Kunststoff-Folie
l. Lattenkiste, -verschlag
m. Paket
n. Palette
o. Rolle, Coil
p. Sack
q. Schlitten
r. Stahlbandumreifung
s. Styroporform
t. Trommel, Eisenfass
u. vakuumverpackt
v. vierfacher Papiersack
w. wattierter Umschlag

b Which of the types of packaging named in exercise a are shown in the illustrations below?

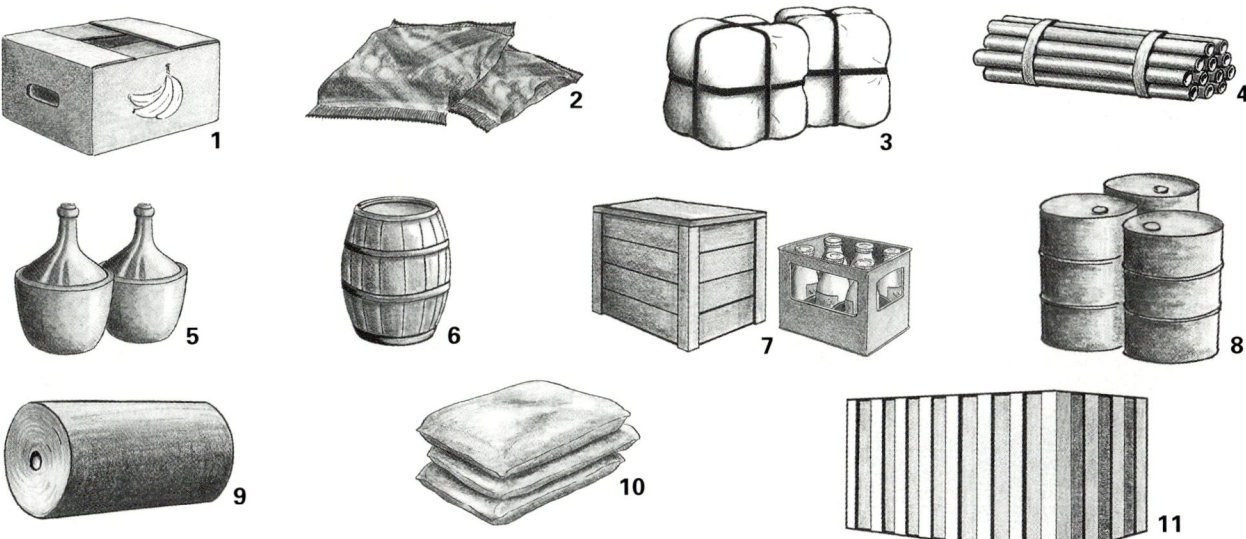

c Now discuss with your partner what kind of packaging is generally used for the following goods: cotton, machines, sherry, cement, petrol, shoes.

d Work in groups and find other goods and typical packagings for them.

A 4 Shipping and caution marks

Shipping marks stencilled on the outside of packages may show the consignee's logo (1.), the port of destination (2.), the number of the particular package and the total number of packages (3.), weights (4.) and dimensions (5.) as well as a mark of origin (6.).

1. IUBras
2. Santos
3. 3/5
4. GROSS WEIGHT 1235 kg
   NET WEIGHT 1194kg
5. 1200 x 800 x 800mm
6. MADE IN GERMANY

To ensure adequate handling of packages in international transport, also in parts of the world where English is not universally understood, pictograms like the following are used as **caution marks** which speak for themselves.

■ Match the caution marks with the instructions.

1. sling here
2. centre of gravity
3. use no hooks
4. this side up
5. handle with care
6. store in cool place
7. store inside
8. radioactive
9. inflammable

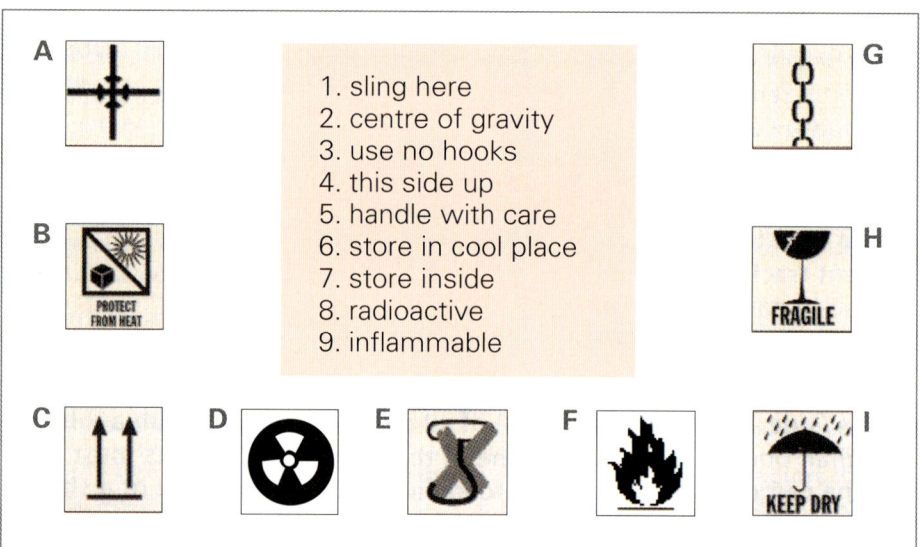

A5 Shipping documents

■ Hyflyer have ordered a consignment of gears and brakes for their mountain bikes from Shimada Engineering, their Japanese suppliers. **Study Shimada's advice of dispatch and discuss with a partner which terms of payment and delivery may have been agreed upon for this transaction.**

Faxed and posted

Shimada Engineering Ltd
3-5, 2-chome Jonan-jima
Ohta-ku
Tokyo 143
Tel. (03) 3799-40-11, Fax 3790-80-44

Hyflyer plc
438 Weltmore Industrial Park
Warwick
CV43 6TS
U.K.

Ref. File No. 4154-612.01   23 March 200_

Your order No. BG145, dated 3 March 200_
for 6,500 Shimada XTR 24-speed gears and 3,000 Shimada XTR "V" brakes
Letter of Credit No. 324/LC 9500016

Dear Mrs Middleton

We are pleased to inform you that the consignment has now been loaded on board MV "Fujiyama Maru", which is due to leave the port of Yokohama tomorrow. The vessel is expected to arrive at Southampton on or about 1 May.

The goods are packed in one 20 ft container, marked: HFL BG 145 Southampton.

The original shipping documents (3/3 original clean Bills of Lading, 3 copies each of Commercial Invoice, Insurance Certificate, Certificate of Origin and Packing List) have been handed over to our bank, NIPPON CREDIT, which will pass them on to DOYLES BANK in Warwick. The invoice amount has already been credited to our account. Copies of the documents are enclosed for your reference.

Thank you once more for the confidence you have shown in our products. We hope that the goods will arrive safely and give you satisfaction.

Yours sincerely

Keizo Harajuku

Keizo Harajuku
Export Department

Enclosures

A 5 I Export Invoice

■ Meanwhile the bicycles are ready for dispatch and Hyflyer makes out the invoice in triplicate.
Match the letters of the items with the appropriate figures in the invoice. (Note that there are four items that do not fit!)

- **A** HYFLYER DX-2000 TITANIUM FRAME AND FORK, SHIMADA XTR 24-SPEED GEARS, SHIMADA XTR RAPIDFIRE SHIFTERS, SHIMADA XTR V BRAKES, SHIMADA LEVERS, RIMS AND HUBS, RITCHEY ALFABITE 26" TYRES
- **B** S.S. QUEEN OF THE SEAS
- **C** GBP 35,820.00
- **D** 10
- **E** 30 January 200_
- **F** PREPAID
- **G** COST, INSURANCE, FREIGHT VANCOUVER IRREVOCABLE LETTER OF CREDIT NUMBER XUK 30259324/09 OF FIRST METROPOLITAN BANK
- **H** GBP 3,980.00
- **I** SOUTHAMPTON
- **J** 200
- **K** GBP 199.00
- **L** DOYLES BANK plc 67 HIGH STREET HOVE, BN3 2BE UNITED KINGDOM
- **M** CANADA
- **N** LONDON MARINE AND FIRE INSURANCE
- **O** GBP 39,800.00
- **P** 9 February 200_
- **Q** VANCOUVER
- **R** SAME AS CONSIGNEE
- **S** DBIS8136629
- **T** ROCKY BIKE LTD 8192 NINTH STREET VANCOUVER, B.C. CANADA
- **U** UNITED KINGDOM
- **V** VANCOUVER

HYFLYER plc
88 Weltmore Industrial Park, Warwick, CV43 6TS
tel: 01926 439523   Fax: 01926 451427
V.A.T. reg. no. GB 234 9376 51

INVOICE 23472573

| DATE OF INVOICE ❶ | YOUR REFERENCE NO. ❷ |

| CONSIGNEE ❸ | BUYER (if not consignee) ❹ |

COUNTRY OF ORIGIN OF GOODS ❺	COUNTRY OF DESTINATION ❻	TERMS OF DELIVERY AND PAYMENT ⓫
PORT OF LOADING ❼	PORT OF DISCHARGE ❽	
VESSEL/FLIGHT NO. ❾	PLACE OF DELIVERY ❿	

| QUANTITY ⓬ | DESCRIPTION ⓭ | UNIT PRICE ⓮ | TOTAL ⓯ |

DISCOUNT % ⓰   ⓱
VAT %   not applicable
AMOUNT DUE £ ⓲

TITLE IN THE GOODS DESCRIBED ON THIS INVOICE DOES NOT PASS TO THE BUYER UNTIL THE INVOICE IS PAID IN FULL.

Unit 8 · Activities

A 5 II Bill of Lading

■ Using all you know about the Hyflyer/Rocky Bike transaction, complete this Bill of Lading. (Copy the form on the right). See the background information on the bill of lading on page 171.

SHIPPER Hyflyer plc 438 Weltmore Industrial Park Warwick CV43 &TS	CUSTOMER NO. WU 380 F	REF. NO. WOC 3029	B/L NO. 247156812390
CONSIGNEE	LINER BILL OF LADING		
NOTIFY Rocky Bike Ltd. 8192 NINTH STREET VANCOUVER, BC	**MBSL** MyBonny Shipping Line 568 HARBOUR STREET, SOUTHAMPTON, SO4 3DL UNITED KINGDOM		
LOCAL VESSEL Lorry	FROM Warwick	GENERAL AGENTS WORLD WIDE WORLDCARGO	
OCEAN VESSEL	PORT OF LOADING			
PORT OF DISCHARGE	FINAL DESTINATION Vancouver	FREIGHT PAYABLE AT Southampton	NUMBER OF ORIGINAL B/L three
MARKS & NUMBERS	NUMBER OF PACKAGES/DESCRIPTION OF GOODS	GROSS WEIGHT Kos.	MEASUREMENT Cbm.
Rocky Bike Ltd. Vancouver Nos 1 & 2	COPY NON NEGOTIABLE	2,300 kg	
FREIGHT AND CHARGES GPB 3,910.00	Shipped on board in apparent good order and condition...		

PLACE AND DATE OF ISSUE
SOUTHAMPTON
SIGNED FOR THE MASTER BY:
Francis Drake

A 5 III Air Waybill

■ Work with a partner. Partner A turns to the information on page 173. Partner B studies the excerpt from an air waybill below. Ask your partner questions to get the information necessary to fill in the white spaces. Then answer your partner's questions. When you have finished, compare your information and figures.

Partner B

Handling information	NITTSU AWB 845-25745747			NOTIFY: COMPUTER CLINIC 12 BEDFORD STREET PEMBROKE SA62 6YE	
No. of Pieces	Gross Weight kgs.	Chargeable Weight	Rate Charge	Total	Nature and Quantity of Goods
	24.80		1,600		NECSON PHOTOGRADE PRINTER
1		12.30		19,680	
	9.80		1,600		TANQUM SCSI CONTROLLERS
2		13.50		21,600	
6				112,320	

A5 IV Forwarding Agent's Certificate of Receipt

■ Study the document on page 285. Compare the translation of the conditions with the original German text of the form and find the two mistakes and the two superfluous hyphens.

A5 V Certificate of Origin

■ Study the certificate of origin and find out whether the following statements are true or false.
1. The consignee is based in Düsseldorf.
2. Shan Ling Machine Co. Ltd. is a Taiwanese company.
3. The consignment consists of 42 packages of cold rolled steel.
4. The consignment has a net weight of 49,270 kgs.

1 Absender · Consignor · Expéditeur · Expedidor EISEN-STAHL EXPORT GMBH MICHEL-MÜLLER-STR. 125 40235 DÜSSELDORF Tel. 211/671-1, Fax 211/671-2364	T 389841 L 652368	ORIGINAL
2 Empfänger · Consignee · Destinataire · Destinatario SHAN LING MACHINE CO. LTD 7 CHING-CHIEN 4th ROAD KUAN-YIN INC. PARK KUAN-YIN 382, TAIWAN	EUROPÄISCHE GEMEINSCHAFT EUROPEAN COMMUNITY · COMMUNAUTE EUROPEENNE · COMUNIDAD EUROPEA URSPRUNGSZEUGNIS CERTIFICATE OF ORIGIN · CERTIFICAT D'ORIGINE · CERTIFICADO DE ORIGEN	
	3 Ursprungsland · Country of origin · Pays d'origine · País de origen GERMANY	
4 Angaben über die Beförderung · means of transport · expédition · expedición BY VESSEL	5 Bemerkungen · remarks · observations · observaciones	
6 Laufende Nummer; Zeichen, Nummern, Anzahl und Art der Packstücke, Warenbezeichnung		7 Menge
42 PACKAGES HOT ROLLED STAINLESS STEEL MARKING: STAINLESS STEEL CONTRACT NUMBER NET WEIGHT/GROSS WEIGHT NUMBER OF SHEETS INSIDE EACH BUNDLE TAIPEI PORT SHAN LING MACHINE MADE IN GERMANY		GROSS: 49,270 KGS

8 DIE UNTERZEICHNENDE STELLE BESCHEINIGT, DASS DIE OBEN BEZEICHNETEN WAREN IHREN URSPRUNG IN DEM IN FELD 3 GENANNTEN LAND HABEN
The undersigned authority certifies that the goods described above originate in the country shown in box 3.
L'autorité soussignée certifie que les marchandises désignées ci-dessus sont originaires du pays figurant dans la case No. 3
La autoridad infrascrita certifica que las mercancías abajo mencionadas son originarias del país que figura en la casilla no. 3

B Tool kit: Describing graphs and diagrams

Statistics are easier to read if they are presented in the form of graphs or diagrams, the most widely used being line graphs, bar charts and pie charts.

Such graphic representations must sometimes be described in words, for example as part of a presentation. If you are asked to describe a graph in writing, first say what the graph is about. Where graphs contain a lot of individual data you may have to summarise the information provided. Describe the main developments or facts and quote important figures, such as highs, lows and figures which remain the same over a period of time. Try to avoid monotony by varying expressions and sentence structures. Any explanatory remarks contained in the graph should also be incorporated in your description.

B1 Line graphs

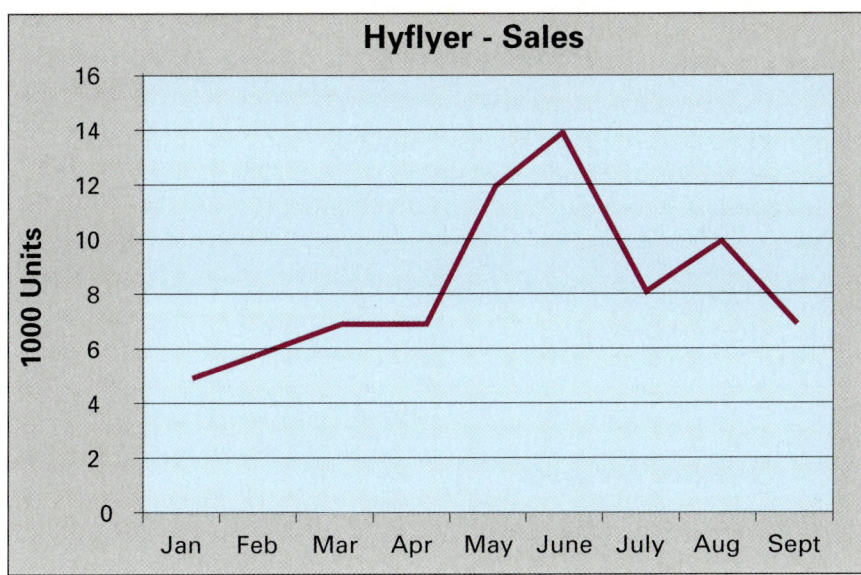

In line graphs solid (_____), broken (- - - - - -) or dotted (............) lines serve to represent developments (vertical axis) within a certain period of time (horizontal axis).

The following verbs, nouns, adjectives and adverbs may be used to describe the developments represented in line graphs. Note the prepositions.

Phrases: Line charts

upwards ↑

to rise/increase/go up/surge/ **by ... from ... to ...**
*In December exports rose **to** around $12m.*
*Between March and May sales went up **by** 10% **from** 1000 units **to** 1100 units.*

to reach a peak/high/maximum/ **of** ...
*In 1999 the price reached a peak **of** $9.25.*

to recover/pick up/rally
Exports recovered in the first quarter.

an increase / a rise/jump/ **in ... of ... to ...**
*There was an increase **in** prices **of** 20 % **to** £7,400.*

Tool kit · Unit 8   163

unchanged →

to remain/stay unchanged/stable/flat/ at ...
Imports remained unchanged at around 120,000 units.

to fluctuate **between ... and ...**
*In recent months prices have been fluctuating **between** $290 **and** $295.*

downwards ↓

to fall/decline/go down/slump/drop/ **by ... from ... to ...**
*In October sales fell **to** their lowest level.*
*In the course of the second quarter the price declined **by** 2% **from** €100 **to** €98.*

to reach a low/minimum/ **of** ... , to reach a trough/the lowest point/ **at** ...
*In the nineties the crime rate reached a low **of** 23,000.*
*In February the lowest point was reached **at** a growth rate of 0.75 per cent.*

a decrease/decline/fall/slowdown/drop/ **in ... of ... to ...**
*In July there was a fall **in** turnover **of** 40% **to** $780,000.*

Degree of change

Adjectives and adverbs help to describe the speed or degree of the change in movement.

dramatic(ally)
rapid(ly)
sudden(ly)
steep(ly)
sharp(ly)
substantial(ly)
significant(ly)
marked(ly)
steady/steadily
gradual(ly)
moderate(ly)
noticeable/noticeably
slow(ly)
slight(ly)

164 Unit 8 · Tool kit

a **Find the correct preposition.**

> at * by * between * from * of * to * to

In January prices fell ❶ 1.4% ❷ the lowest level in three years. This followed an increase ❸ 4 % in December. ❹ March and May sales surged ❺ $7m ❻ $9.5m. They are generally expected to remain ❼ this level in June.

b **Find the correct adjective or adverb:**

1. In the second quarter imports rose (sharp / sharply).
2. There was a (considerable /considerably) increase in turnover.
3. Prices remained (constant / constantly).
4. Fees have been going down (gradual / gradually).
5. A (slight / slightly) fall in sales had to be expected.
6. Contributions fell (noticeable / noticeably).

> **Note: Graphs and Tenses**
> Past developments are described using the simple past *(In January prices fell by 17%.)*. When the period of time described is not completed, the present perfect must be used *(This year we have so far seen a marked increase in sales.)*. What is going on at present should be described using the present continuous *(Prices are fluctuating at the moment)*. Whenever a graph becomes a projection into the future, the will-future or another appropriate verb form must be used for the description *(During the next few months prices are expected to rise to last year's levels.)*.

c At a board meeting in October Hyflyer's export manager presents the company's sales figures for Germany for the first nine months of the year. In Germany spring had been rather late and four weeks of dismal weather in June and July had badly affected sales of outdoor sports equipment in general.
Study the line graph on page 163 and find the missing expressions in the export manager's description of the graph:

> decline from * fall to * increase of * peak of * recovered
> remained * rise * stood at * went up

"The line graph describes the development of Hyflyer's exports to Germany in the first nine months of the year.
In January sales ❶ 5,000 units. Until March there was a steady ❷ 20% to 7,000 units. For four weeks sales ❸ flat but when spring came at last exports ❹ sharply until May to 12,000 units and continued to ❺ steadily reaching a ❻ 14,000 units in June. From June to July there was a steep ❼ 8,000 units as a result of four weeks of dismal weather. Sales then ❽. Between August and September sales figures showed a substantial ❾ 10,000 to 7,000 units. Apparently, the autumn slowdown is setting in rather early this year."

B2 Bar charts

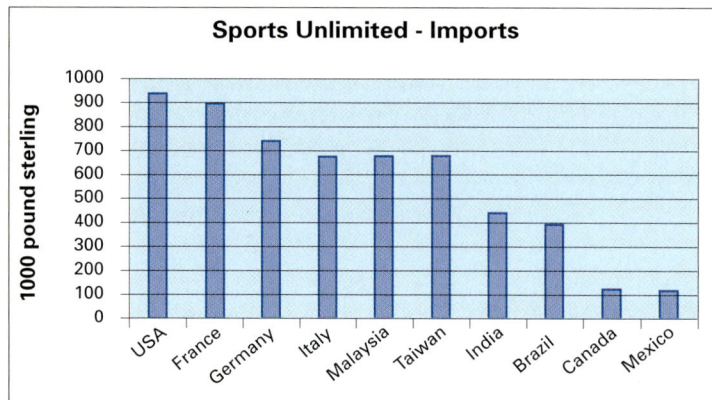

Bar charts are the most effective way of making comparisons, e.g. of a company's imports from different countries, with the help of bars varying in height or length.

To describe the comparisons and rankings which are graphically shown in bar charts, use the following expressions:

Phrases: Bar charts

| to be high**er**/lower/bigger/smaller/**more** expensive/**more** developed etc./ **than** ...
Car prices in the UK are high**er than** in Germany. |

| to be **as** high/low/big/small/expensive etc./ **as** ...
Earnings are just **as** poor in this industry **as** in the construction industry. |

| to be the bigg**est**/smallest/**most** expensive etc. / ... **of** ...
Boots and Belts Ltd. is the bigg**est** producer **of** all. |

| to be/come first/second/last/next/ **with** ...
Spain comes first **with** 30m tourists a year. |

| to be/follow/ **in** first/tenth/last/ place
Brighton and Ramsgate are **in** second and third place. |

| to be followed **by** ...
Italy is followed **by** Portugal and Greece which both import around 350,000 litres per month. |

| to be **at** the top/bottom of the list/table/league
The USA is **at** the top of the list. |

| to bring **up** the rear
Germany brings **up** the rear with just 17 per cent. |

■ Sports Unlimited imports sportswear from all over the world. A bar chart in the import manager's office shows where the garments come from and the respective import volumes for the previous year in £1000s.
Study the bar chart on page 166 and then find the prepositions missing in the description below:

> about ❋ at ❋ by ❋ for ❋ from (2x) ❋ of ❋ to (3x) ❋ under ❋ up ❋ with (3x)

The bar chart shows the countries Sports Unlimited imports sportswear from and the respective volumes in £1000s.
❶ the top of the list is the USA. ❷ this country Sports Unlimited imports goods worth £950,000. The USA is closely followed ❸ France ❹ £900,000. Germany is number three, ❺ imports amounting ❻ £750,000 and Malaysia, Taiwan and Italy take ❼ places four ❽ six ❾ almost identical volumes ❿ just ⓫ £700,000. ⓬ the next countries in line, India and Brazil, Sports Unlimited imports goods worth ⓭ £450,000 and £400,000 respectively. Canada and Mexico are the least important countries ⓮ Sports Unlimited as regards imports, their total value amounting ⓯ only £120,000 each.

B3 Pie charts

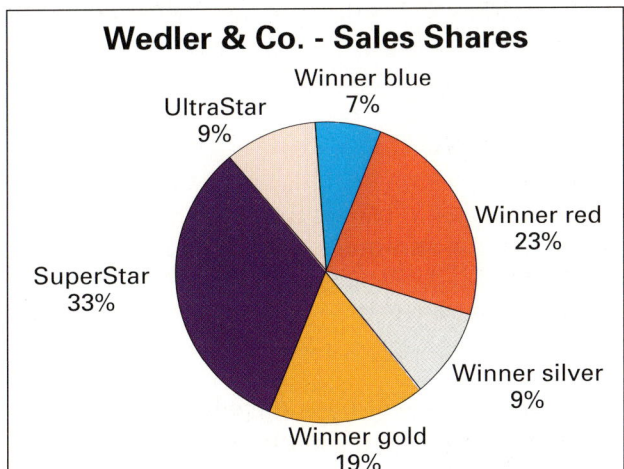

Pie charts are used to show percentages.

To describe pie charts you need the following expressions:

Phrases: Pie charts

> to make **up** ...
> Nail varnish makes up 15% of the total.
>
> to account **for** ...
> Lipsticks account **for** three quarters of the turnover of Sally Cosmetics.
>
> to have a share/percentage/slice **of** ...
> Hairspray has a share **of** only 10 per cent.

■ In their annual report Wedler & Co. have reproduced the above pie chart.
Study the pie chart above and the description below and complete the description as appropriate.

The pie chart shows the extent to which Wedler's six models contributed to its ski division's success last year.
❶ accounted for a third of sales, followed by ❷ with 23%. With 19% ❸ was next.
❹ and ❺ each made up 9% and ❻ contributed a share of 7%.

C Additional practice

a Complete this excerpt using the information from the box. Then find out who the sender and recipient are and rewrite the letter in full.

> - your pro-forma invoice no. MNZ 001/03
> - Bayernbank Kempten
> - First Wellington Bank

> We have instructed our bank, ❶, to open an irrevocable letter of credit for €57,200, valid until 21 April, on the basis of ❷.
> The L/C will be available to you through the ❸.
>
> The following documents are necessary for this transaction:
> – Invoice CIF Wellington, in triplicate
> – Insurance policy
> – Bill of lading in duplicate
>
> We usually ask our suppliers to pack each pair individually to ensure safe and easy handling and to inform us in writing about any possible alterations of the contract.

b You have just received these faxes from International Insurers Inc. and EuroSecure. **Read them and make a summary of their most important points in German.**

> Thank you for your interest in our services.
>
> Based on the information provided, viz 500 pairs of skis, value € 71,500, from Sonthofen to Wellington, N.Z., vessel and shipment date not known, we can quote you for all risks except war risk:
>
>   35¢ per € 100 value, total € 250.25
>
> Please note that the rate is only valid if the goods are shipped in seaworthy packing by any of the lines on the attached list.
>
> Please let us know by return whether you want us to cover your shipment, as time is rather short. We will then make out the policy accordingly.
>
> Sincerely

> We are pleased to inform you that our premium rates for your consignment of skis from your premises to your client's warehouse in Wellington, N.Z. would be 36¢ per € 100 of value if the goods are shipped by any of our approved lines.
>
> Kindly inform us on 0800-327-2347 extension 3275 if you would like us to cover your consignment, so that we can make out the policy in time.
>
> Kind regards,

D Background information

D1 Transport

■ Make a grid for yourself like the following with four vertical columns for transport by rail, road, air and sea or inland waterways. The grid's three horizontal columns should be as follows: *Advantages – Disadvantages – Suitable for*.
Now listen to the interview with Liz Martin, who works for WorldCargo, several times and fill in your grid, adding whatever other advantages, disadvantages and suitable cargoes you can think of. Compare the result with a partner's information in the grid.

Advantages				
Disadvantages				
Suitable for				

D2 Insurance

Consignments may be damaged, or even totally lost or stolen, when they are being transported from the exporter's premises to the importer's warehouse. Exporters/importers, therefore always take out insurance to protect themselves against heavy financial losses. When a consignment is damaged or lost in transit, the insurer will compensate the exporter/importer for the loss.

The insurance system originated at Edward Lloyd's coffee house in London in the 17th century. This was a popular gathering place for seamen, merchants and bankers, and soon became a place where merchants 'underwrote', i.e. signed, slips of paper describing the risks covered and promising compensation in the case of loss or damage. This early form of marine insurance was possible because those wealthy merchants were liable to the full extent of their personal property.

Modern insurance companies take on a risk against payment of a small percentage of the value of the cargo. This creates a pool of money much as in a lottery, but there is a difference: the money does not go to a lucky winner, but to somebody hit by bad luck.

To take out insurance, you must fill in a proposal form, which details what is insured, for how long it will be insured, and against what risks it is to be insured. The underwriter, who works for the insurance company, then assesses the risk and calculates the premium – the price of the insurance.

If the risk is too high, insurers may refuse to insure altogether; for example in Japan, property cannot be insured against earthquakes, because all insurance companies would go bankrupt if a major earthquake hit a big city. The client then receives the insurance policy – a written contract between the insurer and the insured which is issued on the basis of the underwriter's calculation.

Instead of dealing with an insurance company, it is advisable to go to an insurance broker, because the broker can choose among several offers and will find the most favourable policy for the client. The broker receives a commission from the insurance company whose policy is chosen.

Export shipments are usually covered by one of the following policies:

- **open policy**, also called open cover. This is a contract of insurance whereby an insurer undertakes to insure an exporter's consignments within a given period. Each consignment is declared to the insurer who issues an **insurance certificate** (see page 156). The premium is calculated after the consignment has been shipped. If Hyflyer regularly shipped bicycles to North America they might take out an open policy with a particular insurance company in order to simplify procedures and obtain more favourable insurance rates.
- **floating policy**. In this case a **lump sum** is insured in advance and the value of each individual shipment is set off against this total sum until the sum is exhausted. The premium is calculated in advance. For Hyflyer a floating policy might be interesting if they had to make several shipments of bicycles to Rocky Bike. They could then take out a floating policy for, say, £200,000. Each time they shipped a consignment for £40,000, Hyflyer would declare its value on a special form and the underwriter would issue an **insurance certificate**. After the fifth shipment the sum would be used up.
- **voyage policy**, which covers a consignment for the duration of a particular voyage only. If Hyflyer only shipped a single consignment of bicycles to Rocky Bike they might take out a voyage policy.

Policies are issued on a "valued" or on an "unvalued" basis.

- Under an **unvalued policy** the sum paid in the event of a loss is fixed according to the value of the goods at the time of the loss. Motor insurance, for instance, is provided on an unvalued basis; the owner of a motor car only gets what the vehicle was worth at the time of the accident.
- Under a **valued policy** the amount of compensation in case of loss is fixed in advance. Policies taken out for export shipments are valued policies, that is to say, insurance cover may be obtained for the total value of the goods plus 10% "**imaginary profit**", i.e. the profit the importer would have made by selling the goods if the loss or damage had not occurred. Obviously, Hyflyer's transport insurance for their consignment of bicycles to Canada will be issued on a valued basis.

The scope of the cover provided by an insurance policy has been defined by, among others, the Institute of London Underwriters in its **Institute Cargo Clauses**. To understand them, two definitions are required:

general average = deliberate loss, e.g. throwing cargo over board to get the ship afloat again. The loss has to be borne jointly by all owners of the cargo.

particular average = accidental loss, which has to be borne by the owner of the goods concerned.

Nowadays most consignments are insured **against all risks**. That would mean coverage on the basis of clause A of the Institute Cargo Clauses which covers general average (see above), particular average (damage or loss due to sinking, fire, sea water, wind etc.) plus damage from other causes (theft, rough handling etc.). Some risks, however, among them war, nuclear risks, strikes, riots and civil commotion, are not even covered by an all-risks policy. Consequently, additional insurance has to be taken out to obtain compensation should they cause loss or damage.

a Study the text on insurance and decide which of the following statements are true.
1. Marine insurance originated in a coffee house.
2. Insurance is exactly like a lottery.
3. An underwriter assesses risks and calculates premiums.
4. An insurance policy is a contract between the insurer and the insured.
5. With an open policy the premium is paid in advance.
6. A voyage policy covers a lump sum.
7. A motor insurance policy is a valued policy.
8. Export shipments may be insured for more than the total value of the goods.
9. Very few consignments are insured against all risks.

b Match these types of insurance with the risks they cover.

1. fire insurance
2. product liability insurance
3. export credit insurance
4. third-party insurance

a. liability for damage caused by the use of a firm's products
b. non-payment by overseas customers
c. liability for damage caused to third parties
d. loss or damage due to fire or explosion

> **Note:**
> **export credit insurance** is provided by private-sector insurance companies. However, in order to promote foreign trade the government may step in where insurance companies regard the political risks involved as too high. In Germany this is done via the Hermes export credit guarantees, in the UK it is the Export Credit Guarantee Department, under the direction of the Department of Trade, which provides such guarantees to exporters.

D 3 Documents in foreign trade

The **Bill of Lading** (B/L) (see pages 161 and 284) is the most important document for transport by sea and for transportation involving at least two modes of transport, so-called multimodal transport. It is at the same time
- evidence of the contract of carriage between the shipper (exporter) and the carrier (shipping company)
- proof that the goods have been handed over to the carrier, i.e. a receipt for the goods.
- a **document of title**. This means that anyone lawfully possessing the B/L is considered to be the rightful owner of the goods. Consequently, the ownership of the goods can be transferred by handing over the B/L, provided the B/L is made out "to order" (i.e. these two words appear in the box marked "consignee") and has been **endorsed** (signed on the back) by the person wishing to sell the goods. This makes it possible to sell goods while they are still at sea.

The B/L contains the names and addresses of the shipper and the consignee, a notify address if the B/L is made out to order, and details of the goods and of the transport (description, weights, measurements, number of packages, marks, mode and route of transport, name of the vessel, port of shipment, port of destination, freight and other charges as well as the date of issue and reference numbers). It is usually completed and signed by the carrier, e.g. the captain of the ship, or by the carrier's agent. Should the carrier discover any defects or damage as regards the external condition of the packages he will make a note to this effect on the B/L. As a result the B/L will not be "**clean**" but "dirty", "foul" or "claused". The carrier may be prevented from clausing a B/L by a **letter of indemnity** from the shipper, whereby the shipper assumes any obligations resulting from the external defect of or damage to the packages.

Whenever a bank advances money for a transaction under a letter of credit, it will insist on a clean, on-board B/L. **On board** means that the goods have actually been loaded on board ship. If no ship is available, the carrier issues a **received for shipment** B/L which can later be converted into an on-board B/L.

For multimodal transport, especially for container transport, the **FIATA Multimodal Transport Bill of Lading (FBL)** has replaced the combined transport B/L. FIATA is an international association of carriers.

Waybills, also called consignment notes, are used in road, rail or air transport. They provide similar information to bills of lading and are likewise
- evidence of the contract of carriage
- and proof of the receipt of the goods

but they do not represent the goods as they are not documents of title.

German exporters use the following waybills:
- for transport by rail the **International Rail Consignment Note** CIM
- for transport by road the **International Consignment Note** CMR and the FIATA FCR (**Forwarder's Certificate of Receipt**) (see page 285)
- for transport by air the **Air Waybill** (see page 287)

Shipping documents are made out in sets consisting of originals and copies for all parties involved. In the UK the Simple Trade Procedures Board (SITPRO Board) publishes samples of all the official export forms.

Commercial Invoice, see Unit 7, page 129.

Proforma Invoice, see Unit 7, page 128.

Consular Invoice. This is an export invoice which has been legalised by the consulate of the importing country. Such invoices are required by some South American countries as a true basis for charging import duty.

Customs Invoice. It is prepared and signed by the exporter and a witness on an official form issued by the importing country and gives information as to the domestic value of the goods and the country of origin. It is required by numerous Commonwealth countries for customs purposes.

Certificate of Origin (see pages 162 and 286). It shows the country of origin of the goods or the country in which they were mainly produced. EU countries use a common form certifying that the goods are of EU origin. Certificates of origin must be legalised, usually by a chamber of commerce. They may be required
- for political reasons (if, for instance, there are bans on imports from certain countries)
- if import quotas have been imposed on certain goods from certain countries
- if preferential duties have been agreed upon between the exporting and importing countries.

Movement Certificate. It is a declaration made by the exporter on the form EUR 1 and is attested by the customs authorities. It enables goods of EU origin to benefit from preferential rates of customs tariffs in Switzerland, Cyprus, Malta and certain East European countries.

Export Declaration. Exports must be declared to the exporter's national customs authority on the appropriate forms (INTRASTAT) for statistical purposes.

Export Permit. May be required by the exporting country if goods, such as arms and weapons, which are subject to export controls, are to be exported.

Test, Analysis or Weight Certificates and such like, issued by independent inspection authorities, provide some guarantee for the importer as to the quality and quantity of the goods.

Packing List. This is a detailed statement of the goods supplied in a particular consignment.

Insurance Policy/Certificate, (see pages 169/70).

■ Study the above information on shipping documents and the examples of documents on pages 160-162. Then complete the sentences with the words from the box, some of which must be capitalised.

> board * carriage * certificate * clean * consignment
> consulate * domestic * endorsed * lading * multimodal
> notify * origin * shipment * title

1. A bill of ? is a contract of ?, a receipt for the goods and a document of ?.
2. If goods are to be sold by handing over the B/L, the B/L must first be ?.
3. A B/L may contain a ? address.
4. If the consignment is in good condition from the outside, the B/L will be ?.
5. A received for ? B/L may later be converted into an on ? B/L.
6. For container transport the FIATA ? Transport Bill of Lading is used.
7. In road transport we find the International ? Note and the FIATA Forwarder's ? of Receipt.
8. A consular invoice must be legalised by the ? of the importing country.
9. Customs invoices give information on the ? value of the goods.
10. Certificates of ? may be required for political reasons.

➡ |6|

■ Study this excerpt from an air waybill. Answer your partner's questions first, then ask questions in turn to get the information missing in your copy.

Partner A

Handling information			HANDLE WITH CARE		
AWB 845-25745747			COMPUTER CLINIC		
LHR via NRT			12 BEDFORD STREET PEMBROKE SA62 6YE		

No. of Pieces	Gross Weight kgs.	Chargeable Weight	Rate / Charge	Total	Nature and Quantity of Goods
1		24.80		39,680	
	12.30		1,600		TANQUM DISK DRIVES LV8196
2		19.60		31,360	
	6.75		1,600		CONAN SL-35 SLIDE SCANNERS
	53.65				

Background information · Unit 8

E IHK-Prüfungsvorbereitung*

1. Fremdsprache im Beruf I
Gelenkte englische schriftliche Beschreibung einer Grafik

(Bearbeitungszeit 30 Minuten)
Schwerpunkte: Industrie, Handel

Hilfsmittel: Zweisprachiges Wörterbuch

Situation

Sie arbeiten bei der Rubin Kosmetik AG. Ihre Firma ist an einer Zusammenarbeit mit der amerikanischen Firma Sally Cosmetics interessiert. Sie sollen Ihre Firma bei Sally Cosmetics vorstellen und bereiten diese Präsentation in Englisch schriftlich vor. Wir befinden uns am Ende des Jahres 2003.

Aufgabe

Verfassen Sie als Teil Ihrer Vorbereitung eine schriftliche Beschreibung in Englisch der Umsatzentwicklung Ihrer Firma in den letzten zehn Jahren.

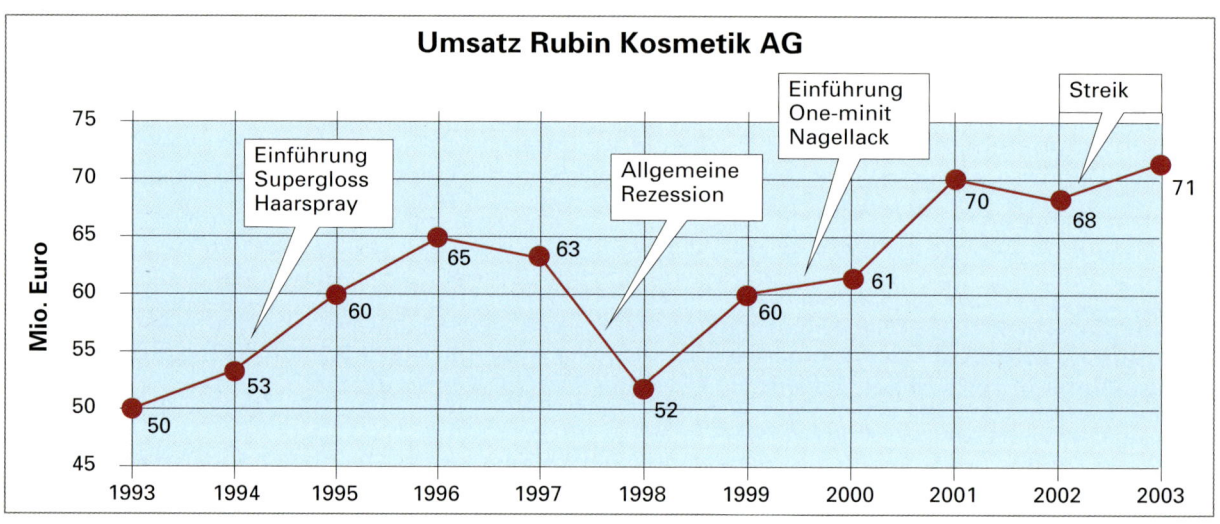

2. Fremdsprachenkorrespondent/in
Beantwortung einer Korrespondenz

(Bearbeitungszeit 60 Minuten.)

Hilfsmittel: Zweisprachige Wörterbücher

Situation

Sie (eigener Name) arbeiten bei DRESCHER Getreide-Import GmbH, Dortmund, als Assistent/in des Abteilungsleiters Markus Michelsen. Ihre Firma hatte bei Rob Martin Inc. in Rockford, Illinois, 1.000 to US-Gerste, lose, Verladung 1. – 31. August CIF Rotterdam, bestellt. Ihr Chef hat heute früh nachstehende E-Mail vorgefunden. Er legt Ihnen den Ausdruck mit seinen Anweisungen zur Beantwortung auf den Schreibtisch.

---

* Weitere Aufgaben (mit Lösungsvorschlägen) im Lehrerhandbuch

e - mail

From: cole.robmartin@aol.com
To: michelsen.drescher@firmlink.de
Date: 27 June 200_

Attachments:

Subject: Letter of Credit No. DC134086176, your order No. AG/17-a of 15 April 200_

Dear Mr Michelsen

Sorry but we need some alterations to the above L/C.

First, we must ask for an extension of the validity of the L/C of at least 5 days as it will be impossible for us to get the consular invoice legalized within 10 days of the date of the B/L. The nearest consulate is in Chicago and it takes some time to get the invoice legalized.

Second, in their L/C conditions the Handelskredit-Bank requires an insurance policy to be submitted together with the shipping documents. However, we intend to insure the consignment under our open policy with Suncommerce Insurance Corp. and can only get an insurance certificate for this particular shipment.

Finally, a weight certificate by a sworn weigher is required under the letter of credit. Unfortunately there is no sworn weigher located in our area. We can only submit a weight note signed by the sworn weigher of the export silo. Will that be o.k.?

We intend to book freight space on the MV "American Dream", due to leave the port of Duluth/Lake Superior around 15 August and we'll keep you informed of the vessel's position. If you prefer shipment by the end of August, please let us know.

Best regards
Ross T. Cole

Ich muss jetzt unbedingt losfahren. Beantworten Sie das bitte gleich für mich.
Unterschreiben Sie als mein/e Assistent/in
Geben Sie der Bank in meinem Namen sofort Anweisung:
1. Gültigkeit des L/C auf 15 Tage nach B/L Datum verlängern,
2. Bedingungen für das Akkreditiv so ändern, dass Versicherungsschein statt Versicherungspolice, und Gewichtsnota statt Gewichtszertifikat zulässig.
Wäger muss aber tatsächlich vereidigt sein!
Bestätigen Sie Mr Cole dies alles ausdrücklich.
Verschiffung auf der „American Dream" o.k. Erwarte baldmöglichst nähere Angaben dazu.
Danke. Michelsen

Unit 9 Complaints

Introduction

1 Making complaints

When transactions go wrong, the customer must promptly notify the seller of the problem in writing. The customer, therefore, drafts a **letter of complaint**, and the seller will respond with a **letter of adjustment**.
A letter of complaint is written to inform the seller of the nature of the problem and to suggest fair compensation.
In some cases legal implications will have to be mentioned, for instance when the contract provides for damages to be paid in case of non-performance or delayed performance by one of the parties to the contract. No matter how great the inconvenience, a complaint should not be written to express anger, but to get results. A complaint should, therefore, be calm and polite, but also firm. A complaint should begin with the facts, first explaining all the necessary details of the problem. These details should include the order and/or invoice number and the nature of the problem, such as delivery of incorrect or damaged merchandise, etc.
The second part of the complaint should emphasize the inconvenience or loss that has been suffered. Again, the account should be factual and unemotional.
Finally, the complaint should suggest a reasonable adjustment which encourages the seller to take immediate steps to compensate the buyer.

a Read this information and translate it into German in two groups. Compare the two translations.

b Complete the following text by deciding which of the alternatives in brackets is correct.

People all over the world (❶ *do/commit/make*) mistakes, at least sometimes. However, the way people deal with mistakes differs (❷ *strongly/strictly*) from culture to culture. When Europeans discover a mistake, more often (❸ *as/is/than*) not they try to find somebody to blame for it. Some Asian cultures, (❹ *particular/particularly/special*) the Japanese, do not blame others, but immediately set (❺ *about/on/to*) fixing the mistake.

Also, the style of complaining is (❻ *different/diverse/several*) in other cultures, and therefore it is important to (❼ *avoid/prevent/dodge*) harsh, direct criticism. Even cool, direct criticism may be interpreted as overly aggressive, and may often not (❽ *guide/lead/transport*) to the solution of the problem.

II Adjusting complaints

a Complete the following text using the correct alternative (adjective or adverb).

Complaints should be answered (❶ prompt/promptly) with a letter that will restore the customer's goodwill and confidence in your business. A letter of adjustment should be written in a positive tone, emphasizing the solutions you offer rather than the error. It should also convince your customer that you understand his/her situation and that you want to be (❷ fair / fairly).
If the complaint is not wholly unfounded, one of two solutions is possible:
1. you grant the adjustment as suggested.
2. you suggest a compromise.

While it is fairly easy to grant full adjustment, suggesting a compromise or even saying *no* to a customer's unreasonable suggestions, is a most delicate matter.
Such a letter must let your customer know that you have considered his/her position very (❸ careful / carefully) and that you want to be fair. It should be based on facts, and make a counter-offer that meets your customer's suggestions halfway. If you refuse any adjustment, explain the reasons (❹ clear / clearly) **before** you say no, and always suggest an alternative course of action your customer could take to resolve the problem.

Referring the case to arbitration is an option if you cannot reach an amicable settlement with your customer. Arbitration is the settlement of disputes out of court by expert arbitrators who have been appointed by the parties to the contract in question. This is (❺ great / greatly) to be preferred to litigation as court actions, especially in foreign countries with different legal systems, tend to be both lengthy and expensive and the outcome may often be uncertain.
Whether or not you are at fault, even the (❻ suspicious / suspiciously) complaint should be answered positively. A letter of adjustment should never be unfriendly or negative; it must never blame the customer for the problem.

Remember: Dissatisfied customers will take their business elsewhere, and it is much harder to win new customers than to lose old ones!

b Here are some common reasons used to apologize for mistakes. Choose the correct prepositions to complete the sentences.

1. Please accept our apologies ❶ this mistake, which was made ❷ one of our trainees.
2. The reason ❸ the delay is a fire ❹ our main supplier's factory, which has brought production ❺ a complete standstill.
3. The delay ❻ sending the goods is due ❼ extremely bad weather conditions.
4. We apologize for the mistake ❽ the packing list. Pressure ❾ work is extremely high ❿ the summer season.
5. The problem ⓫ delivery was caused ⓬ temporary staff that we have to hire ⓭ the holiday season.

Introduction · Unit 9   177

A Activities

A1 Complaints on the telephone (making and dealing with complaints)

a   You work with Netzwerk-Lösungen GmbH in Weimar. A few days ago you sent Will Duncan of Computer Clinic in Pembroke, UK, twelve SCICO MR-36 routers. **Listen to Will Duncan's message on your answering machine, take notes and write a memo in German for your boss, Petra Spreng. Copy the model memo below.**

```
Netzwerk-Lösungen GmbH           MEMO
Schillerpromenade 35
99423 Weimar

Von: _____   Datum: _____

Für: _____

Betreff: _____
        _____
```

b   Restore the correct order of this jumbled dialogue between Fred Murphy and Sean Fletcher.

SEAN FLETCHER

1. Fletcher's Business Systems. Good morning. Sean Fletcher speaking. How can I help you?
2. Oh yes, I remember. Four Necson 1612 …
3. Oh dear. That's really bad. May I ask what paper you're using?
4. Hmmm, strange. Did anyone change the printer settings after installation?
5. Could we go through the settings now?
6. Is duplex printing enabled?
7. Is there an alert message on your screen?
8. Hmmm, I don't think we can fix the problem over the phone.
9. Well, I'll try to get a new duplex unit for you. Tony, my technician, will call on you first thing tomorrow morning.
10. I'm sorry that this has happened, Fred.

FRED MURPHY

a. Yes. It says 'default settings'. I'll start it … Now, it's printing … Oh, it's jammed again.
b. So what are you suggesting, Sean?
c. Standard 80 gram. But I don't think the paper is the problem. I rather suspect that the duplex unit is defective.
d. Right. They're fine, but the duplex unit is giving us a hard time. The paper gets jammed very easily, and each time I remove the paper jam, the printer brings down the network.
e. Fred Murphy here. I'm calling about the printers you installed at LeisureCorp.
f. Just a second. I need to open the driver … Here we go.
g. No. Just the jam alert on the printer.
h. Not that I know of …
i. That sounds good.

178   Unit 9 · Activities

c Listen to the 3 conversations, copy the following grid on a separate piece of paper, and fill it in.

	problem	action to be taken
1		
2		

d Now discuss these points in class:
- Was the complaint properly dealt with?
- How would you act if you were the buyer/seller?
- Have you ever been in a similar situation?

e Work with a partner. Student A is Walter Elliot, managing director of Fine Gifts Ltd. in Bath, a British mail-order house specializing in upmarket giftware. Student B is assistant to Ms Beate Kaiser, export manager with the Hamburg import/export company Präsent-Import/Export. Mr Elliot rings Präsent-Import/Export because he is not satisfied with the execution of his order. Act out the telephone conversation, then change roles. Don't forget to be polite and helpful.

Information for Walter Elliot

- You wish to speak to Ms Kaiser without delay.

- Have the assistant spell his/her name. You are disappointed with Order No. PE/14, dated 20 August.

- 25 earrings, article No. 78955, are missing, which is very inconvenient as orders for them are coming in very fast.

- 12 out of the 150 hair clips, article No. 78944, do not close properly. You have no use for them. All the others are o.k. and you are quite pleased with them.

- It's the first time you've had cause for complaint. Up to now business relations have always been pleasant.

- You hope the replacements will arrive in the next few days.

Informationen für den/die Assistent/in von Frau Kaiser

- Frau Kaiser ist auf Geschäftsreise in Indonesien. Kommt in 10 Tagen zurück.

- Sie haben den Auftrag im Computer und sind mit dem Vorgang vertraut.

- Offenbar Versehen der Versandabteilung, Aushilfskräfte wegen Ferienzeit. Lieferschein und Rechnung über korrekte Anzahl ausgestellt. Fehlende Stücke werden noch heute per Luftpost nachgeschickt.

- Sie haben die Haarspangen schon zwei Jahre im Sortiment und bisher hat es noch nie Beanstandungen gegeben. Bitten Sie um Rücksendung zwecks Untersuchung. Ersatzlieferung geht ebenfalls heute per Luftpost ab.

- Entschuldigen Sie sich für die Unannehmlichkeiten.

- In einigen Tagen Spezialkatalog „Gifts for business people" versandbereit. Viele interessante Angebote.

Activities · Unit 9   179

A 2 Making complaints in writing

→ 108 **a** This is an excerpt from Mr Giacomelli's e-mail in response to the shipment he has received from Sportwelt, Augsburg (see unit 6, page 108). **Study the e-mail and translate it into German.**

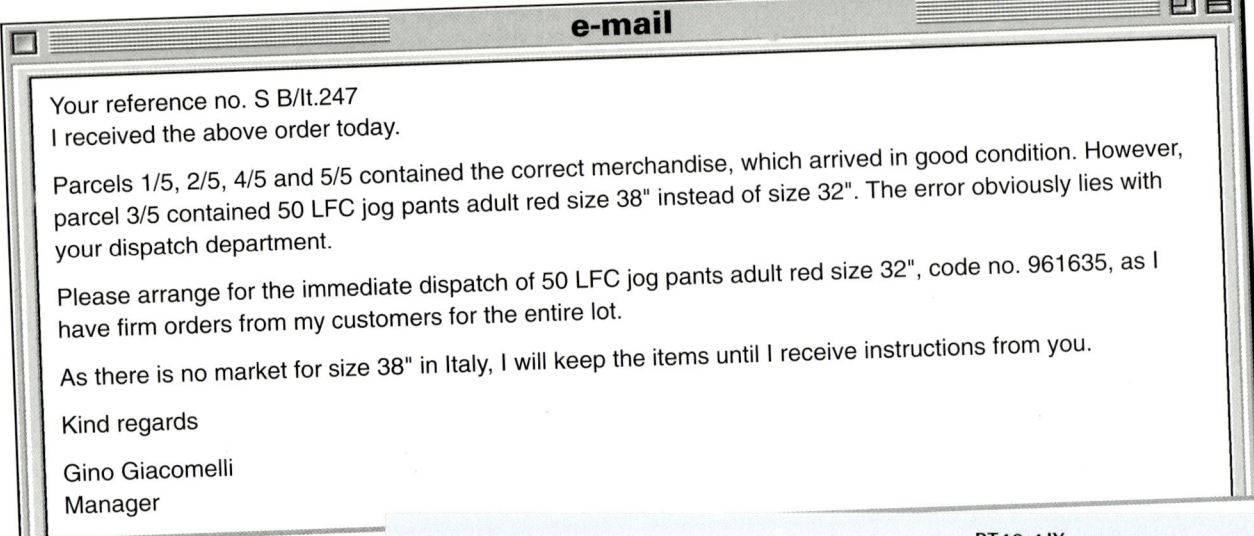

e-mail

Your reference no. S B/lt.247

I received the above order today.

Parcels 1/5, 2/5, 4/5 and 5/5 contained the correct merchandise, which arrived in good condition. However, parcel 3/5 contained 50 LFC jog pants adult red size 38" instead of size 32". The error obviously lies with your dispatch department.

Please arrange for the immediate dispatch of 50 LFC jog pants adult red size 32", code no. 961635, as I have firm orders from my customers for the entire lot.

As there is no market for size 38" in Italy, I will keep the items until I receive instructions from you.

Kind regards

Gino Giacomelli
Manager

b Some elements of this letter are not in the right places. **Put them where they belong.**

→ 17
→ 40

BT40 4JX
34 Harcourt Parkway
Larne, County Antrim

LeisureCorp
36 Kerr Street
Limavady
BT49 0HA
The Manager

26 January 200_

Dear Sir or Madam,

Firstly, we had booked a tour to the mountains surrounding Kuantan, but to our surprise, we were told at very short notice that the tour had been cancelled because there were not enough participants. Instead, we spent the whole day in the steamy city.

We had the misfortune to book our trip to Malaysia, Singapore and Thailand from 12 January to 2 February with you. There were several major problems.

Secondly, on our River Kwai tour, our guide's command of English was quite unacceptable, and we had to ask local people in order to obtain the basic information he was expected to have provided.

We were quite prepared to put up with a little inconvenience, but this was too much for us. If we do not receive appropriate compensation, we will be forced to place the matter in the hands of our solicitor.

Thirdly, on arrival at the Orchid Resort in Pattaya, we were told that there was no reservation in our name. We spent the better part of the evening plus £65 in taxi fares looking for a place to stay the night.

Yours faithfully,

Ellen Woodford

Ellen Woodford

A 3 Adjusting complaints by letter

a Match the complaints on the left with the appropriate explanations on the right.

1 Although we received your shipping advice more than two weeks ago, our order no. 592 has not yet arrived. Could you please look into this matter?

2 According to your packing list, each container holds 80 items. In fact, they contain only 75 items. Will you please arrange for the missing 20 items to be shipped to us immediately?

3 As we have not received any acknowledgement of our order no. 92374 of June 30, we are concerned that it may not have reached you. Could you please let us know if you have received our order?

4 We regret to inform you that the fuse of your new model blows frequently, because of the inadequacy of the transformer. This renders the machines useless, and we cannot pass them on to our customers. Therefore we ask you to send us replacements that feature a stronger transformer.

a Please accept our apologies for not having confirmed your order. The reason is that two of our secretaries have been ill for the past two weeks. Your order has been received and is on its way to you now.

b Please accept our apologies for supplying you with faulty goods. The transformers are indeed inadequate and have been replaced by heavy-duty models. We are glad to inform you that replacements were sent off by courier service this morning.

c We wish to apologize for this mistake. At the last moment, we discovered a technical problem, and had to delay shipping. Unfortunately, the advice had already been mailed, and we failed to inform you of the delay. We are pleased to say that the problem has been solved and your order will be shipped by Friday.

d We are very sorry that this mistake should have occurred. Lately, we have begun using smaller and sturdier packing to provide extra safety. Unfortunately, an error was made in adjusting the packing instructions, and as a result, your order was short by 20 items, which will be dispatched this afternoon.

b Choose the correct alternatives for the excerpt from the letter accompanying the express shipment to Mr Rattle.

Dear Mr Rattle,

Thank you for your telephone call (**1** of / from) this morning.

Please (**2** except / accept) my sincere (**3** excuses / apologies) for the delay in delivery. The only explanation I can offer is pressure of work, as we were (**4** extreme / extremely) busy before the holiday season.
As a small compensation for the inconvenience you have been caused, I enclose a copy of the (**5** last / latest) edition of the lavishly (**6** illustrating / illustrated) German Wine and Food Guide, value £15.
I am confident that you (**7** will appreciate / will be appreciated) the light and fruity taste of our vintages. Sonnentröpfchen goes especially well with red meats, while Pfaffenlust is best enjoyed with fish and seafood. For further details please (**8** referring / refer) to the enclosed guide.

Yours sincerely,
Yvonne Gore
Yvonne Gore
Sales Manager

Enc. German Wine and Food Guide

▶ 179 c Study this reply to the complaint concerning A1c conversation 3.

I am sorry to hear that the OLYMPUS jogging shoes you purchased have not lived up to your expectations and that our assistant was not as helpful as she should have been.

I am indeed surprised that there is a problem with the new OLYMPUS TW line. I appreciate your returning them to us, and I will be happy to reimburse you for the postage.

Instead of a refund, may I suggest that you apply the price of the OLYMPUS TW plus a 30 per cent discount to the cost of a pair of EKIN jogging shoes of your choice. Your own experience will bear out their quality, and I am convinced that you will be very pleased with the EKIN brand.

If you would like to take advantage of this offer, please call me on 0181 226 3112 to arrange a date and time for your visit. I will be more than happy to assist you in finding a pair of EKIN shoes that meets your requirements perfectly.

Yours sincerely,

A 4 Adjusting complaints by e-mail

▶ 180 a Read Denise Springer's e-mail in response to Gino Giacomelli's e-mail in activities 2 and choose the appropriate alternatives.

Absender: sportwelt@comlink.de (Denise Springer)
Datum: 6 Jan 200_
Empfänger: giacomelli.eurosport@italink.com
Kopieempfänger:
Anlagen:
Betreff: Reference No.SB/It.247

Dear Mr Giacomelli,

Thank you for your (**❶ e-mail/fax**) of today, in which you informed us that parcel 3/5 of our (**❷ consignment/supply**) no. 394848-32 contained the wrong merchandise.

I have looked into this (**❸ affairs/matter**), and indeed, the dispatch department packed jog pants size 38" instead of 32". The confusion was due to our merchandise coding system, which will be reviewed to (**❹ repeat/avoid**) similar mistakes in future.

I have already dispatched 50 LFC jog pants adult red size 32" by United Parcel Force express delivery. The (**❺ replacements/substitute**) should reach you by Friday morning. At the same time, please (**❻ hand over/send**) parcel 3/5 to the United Parcel Force delivery person.

I would like to apologize for the inconvenience you have (**❼ caused/suffered**) and to thank you for your patience.

I look forward to receiving confirmation of the (**❽ safe/secure**) arrival of the goods and to doing further business with you.

Kind regards,

Denise Springer
Export Manager

b You work with Importex, Passau. Your boss, Mrs Michaela Fetzer, has received the following e-mail from a British manufacturer of photocopiers. **Study the e-mail and summarise its contents in German in a memo for Mrs Fetzer.**

IMPORTEX

MEMO

Von:

Für:

Betreff:

Datum:

Kopie:

Subject: Your ZERO copier
Date: 10 Feb 200_
From: knight@zerocopiers.uk
Organization: ZERO COPIERS (UK) LTD
To: m.fetzer@importex.de

Dear Mrs Fetzer,

Thank you for your comments and for giving us the opportunity to inspect your malfunctioning ZERO photocopier.

I am extremely sorry that you are not completely satisfied with your copier. You are entirely justified in expecting more than 22 months of reliable performance from a ZERO office machine, and my staff and I are always eager to service any product that does not for some reason meet our standards.

The damaged copier was thoroughly inspected by Tim Janssen, my head technician and ZERO service representative in Germany. According to his findings, two problems have caused the breakdown of the unit. Firstly, it has been used for a significantly higher volume of copying than it was built for (as is clearly indicated in the user's manual). Secondly, there are indications that the cover has not always been properly closed before copying. These "sky-shots" have burned out a number of electronic components.

Therefore, I regret that I cannot offer you a replacement copier as you suggest, as the warranty period expired ten months ago. Nevertheless, I would be happy to trade in the damaged copier for another, higher-capacity ZERO copier.

This arrangement would meet your firm's needs better and be more economical than further repairs. Please contact me to discuss the terms of a trade-in.

Kind regards,

Edward Knight

B Tool kit

B1 Structure of business communications: Complaints

Complaints should be structured like this:

Structure	Language to use
1. appropriate salutation	Dear Mr Crawford
2. reference to goods supplied or services rendered (date and no. of order, date of delivery etc.)	We have received the consignment of ... under our order No. ..., dated ...
3. detailed description of the problem	Seventeen out of twenty trays are in perfect condition. However, three trays are badly dented and cannot be repaired.
4. likely reasons for the problem	In our opinion, the damage is due to faulty packing.
5. solution suggested	Please arrange for the immediate shipment of replacements at your expense.
6. action already taken or to be taken by the customer, if appropriate	We are holding the faulty material pending your instructions.
7. request for prompt adjustment	We trust you will ensure that the missing items are dispatched without further delay.
8. appropriate close	Yours sincerely

■ What is the purpose of these sentences? Find the appropriate numbers from *structure of business communications* above.

1. Will you please send us a replacement as soon as possible?
2. We will keep the damaged items until we receive instructions from you.
3. I am writing with reference to your last delivery of ...
4. The goods you promised to supply by ... have still not arrived at our warehouse.
5. We look forward to receiving replacements which will meet the requirements of our customers.
6. I regret to inform you that my customers have complained repeatedly about the quality of your products.
7. On January 16, we received one case of ....
8. On unpacking the goods, we found that the housing was badly scratched and dented.
9. Items 205 and 208 are seriously damaged because they were packed without any padding.
10. Your sales representative had assured us that the new boards would be 100 per cent compatible.
11. We received our order no ... for hard disk drives today.
12. We look forward to hearing from you in this matter.
13. However, we have had many complaints about incompatibilities, and six have been returned by dissatisfied customers.

B2 Building blocks for business communications: Complaints

1 To start a complaint

| I am writing
We are writing | about
with reference to | our order no. | , which | has reached us
we received
arrived | today.
yesterday.
on … |

| We are sorry
Much to our regret we have | | to inform you that | the units have not yet reached us.
we are still waiting for the consignment.
the parcel has not yet arrived. |

2 To point out positive aspects

| Two cases
Container no. 2
Parcels 2 and 3 | contained | the correct merchandise
the goods ordered
the articles required | , which | arrived
reached us
we received | in good condition. |

3 To give reasons for your complaint

| However, | | one article
item no. … | is | badly
seriously
completely
partly
slightly | damaged.
defective.
bent.
dented.
scratched.
broken.
stained.
cracked. |
| We are afraid
We regret to inform you | that | some units | are | | |

| When we examined the
On inspecting the | goods,
crates,
containers, | we | found
discovered | that | one box was missing.
they contained the wrong goods.
the quality was not up to sample.
there was a shortage **in** weight of 7 kgs.
You have delivered more units than we ordered. |

To our surprise, Unfortunately	the machines the items the products	proved turned out to be	extremely very quite	unsafe. unreliable. difficult to use.

We are afraid We must point out	that	the work performed is **below** standard. your services have been rather unsatisfactory. the repair work has been poorly executed.

4 To provide evidence

As evidence To illustrate our claim	we are enclosing	samples of ... the survey report **by** Messrs. ... photographs of the faulty items.

5 To mention likely reasons for the problem

We	believe think are sure	that the	delay damage breakage	is due to was caused **by** occurred **through**	inadequate storage. rough handling **in** transit. faulty packing. an error **in** packing. careless execution of the order.
There is little doubt It is quite obvious					
Apparently, our order was mixed up with another customer's order.					

6 To inform the seller what you expect them to do and what steps you are taking

Please arrange for the immediate dispatch of	the missing items. suitable substitutes which will meet our requirements.

We would ask you to	compensate us for the loss by granting us a discount of 20%. release us from the contract.		
	replace	the faulty goods	**by** faultless ones **at** your expense.
	have		repaired as soon as possible. collected **at** our warehouse.

We are keeping	the faulty products the defective machines	**in** our warehouse **at** your disposal	until	we receive instructions from you. we hear from you.
The defective items will be returned to you **at** your risk and expense.				

We are prepared to keep the	soiled damaged wrongly delivered	articles if you	grant us a price reduction **of** 5%. indemnify us **for** the loss. cut the price **to** £560.00.

7 To demand prompt adjustment

Please look **into** this matter immediately and make suggestions **as to how to** settle it.			
We	are convinced expect trust	that you will	settle this matter speedily and **to** our entire satisfaction. adjust this business without further delay. send the replacements **by** the next available flight.

■ Use the building blocks to find the equivalents of these German sentences.

1. Wir nehmen Bezug auf unseren Auftrag Nr. AB4 vom 27.11.200_, den wir heute morgen erhalten haben.
2. Pakete 1 und 3 enthielten die richtigen Waren, die in gutem Zustand ankamen.
3. Beim Auspacken von Paket 2 entdeckten wir jedoch, dass 24 Artikel fehlten.
4. Wir bedauern Ihnen mitteilen zu müssen, dass die Sendung noch nicht angekommen ist.
5. Leider müssen wir Ihnen mitteilen, dass 24 Teile stark zerkratzt sind.
6. Wir müssen Sie darauf aufmerksam machen, dass wir mit der Ausführung der Reparatur nicht zufrieden sind.
7. Zum Beweis fügen wir diesem Schreiben das Schadensgutachten bei.
8. Höchstwahrscheinlich ist der Schaden auf unsachgemäße Behandlung beim Transport zurückzuführen.
9. Wir bitten Sie die schadhaften Teile abholen zu lassen und uns unverzüglich Ersatz zu senden.
10. Wir sind bereit die mangelhafte Ware zu behalten, sofern Sie uns einen Preisnachlass von 50% gewähren.
11. Wir behalten die Teile hier, bis Sie uns weitere Anweisung erteilen.
12. Bitte kümmern Sie sich sofort um diese Angelegenheit und lassen Sie uns wissen, wie Sie sie zu regeln gedenken.
13. Wir hoffen, dass Sie die Sache zu unserer Zufriedenheit und ohne jede weitere Verzögerung bereinigen werden.
14. Anscheinend wurden zwei Bestellungen verwechselt und wir haben die für einen anderen Kunden bestimmten Bücher erhalten.
15. Insgesamt beträgt das Fehlgewicht 23,5 kg.

B3 Structure of business communications: Replies to complaints

Replies to complaints should be structured like this:

Structure	Language to use
1. personalised salutation	Dear Mrs Dashwood
2. reference to the communication and thanks for the information	We have just received your fax and thank you for drawing the shortcomings of our service to our attention.
3. apologies	Please accept our apologies for the inconvenience caused.
4. explanation of the problem / promise to investigate the problem	We have looked into the matter and found that the problem was caused by a misleading expression in our operation manual.
5. suggestions for adjustment	We are pleased to inform you that our service engineer will be arriving tomorrow morning.
6. conditions / action to be taken by the customer	Would you be so kind as to instruct your technical staff accordingly.
7. promise of improvement	You may rest assured that similar occurrences will be avoided in future.
8. polite ending	We hope that this unfortunate incident will not affect our cordial business relations.
9. appropriate close	Yours sincerely

■ **What is the purpose of these sentences? Find the appropriate numbers from *structure of business communications* above.**

1. We are pleased to inform you that the reason for the software failure has now been found.
2. Thank you for your e-mail informing us about the delay in delivery.
3. We would like to apologize for the delay.
4. We are sure you will understand that we cannot accommodate you any further as we are only partly to blame for the failure. We look forward to serving you again in the near future.
5. Please excuse this error.
6. We are doing our utmost to bring our after-sales service in line with our foreign customers' requirements.
7. We are extremely sorry that you had to wait four days.
8. We would suggest that you dispose of the excess quantity at your end. To facilitate sales we will grant you a price reduction of 35%.
9. The problem is that the two systems are not wholly compatible.

188 Unit 9 · Tool kit

B 4 Building blocks for business communications: Replies to complaints

1 To refer to the complaint

| We | acknowledge receipt of / have received | your letter **of** ... concerning your order No. 324. your fax and thank you for the information **about** ... |

| Thank you for your e-mail drawing a serious problem to our attention. We refer to your telephone call informing us **about** the breakdown of the conveyor belt. |

2 To apologise

| Please accept our apologies We wish to apologize We are very/extremely sorry | **for** | this mistake / error / oversight. the inconvenience you have been caused. the poor service. |

3 To explain the problem or promise to investigate it

| We have looked **into** the matter and found that the problem | lies **with** the dispatch department. was caused **by** inadequate packing. |

| The reason is that | we are extremely busy during this time of the year. we discovered a technical problem and had to delay shipment. the goods have not been packed **to** the usual standards. |

| As a result of | the holiday season a software problem an error **by** our supplier | your order could not be executed | as usual. **in** time. as stipulated. |

| We will investigate the matter thoroughly and inform you **of** our findings and the remedies taken. |

4 To suggest a solution

| We are pleased to say We are glad to inform you | that | your order replacements the missing items | will be shipped tomorrow. was / were sent off this morning. is / are now on their way to you. |

Tool kit · Unit 9   189

| To | retain your custom
make **up for** the inconvenience caused
compensate you for the loss | we are willing | to undertake the repairs free of charge.
to grant you a price reduction of 20%. |

| Although we are not | **at** fault
to blame
responsible for the delay | we are prepared to release you **from** the contract. |

| As an agreement seems difficult to reach, we would suggest referring the matter to arbitration. |

5 To inform the buyer what you expect him to do

| Please | keep the goods refrigerated **until** the arrival of our representative.
return the faulty items carriage forward.
send us all the evidence you have. |

| We will make this concession if you are prepared to keep the goods. |

6 To promise that things will improve

| We | promise
assure you | that we will | make every effort to guarantee
make sure
do our utmost to ensure | that | your orders are given priority.
this does not happen again.
similar occurrences are rendered impossible. |

7 To close on a note promoting good will

| We hope that | the matter can be settled amicably.
the solution suggested will find your approval.
this proposal will help to satisfy all parties concerned. |

| We regret that we cannot meet your wishes **in** full and hope this will not impair our business relations. |

| We hope you will understand our situation and thank you for your patience **in** this matter. |

8 To reject a claim

| We note with regret that you | feel obliged
find it necessary | to complain **about** the | execution of the maintenance work.
quality of the equipment. |

| After | careful
thorough | examination
investigation | of | the case
your complaint
the matter | we must | say
point out
inform you | that | the responsibility **for** this unfortunate affair does not lie **with** us.
your order was carried out in accordance **with** the contract.
we cannot be held liable **for** the damage. |

| As
Since | we | are **in** no way to blame
are not **at** fault
have fulfilled the contract down **to** the dot | we | have no alternative **but** to refuse
have to reject
are afraid we cannot accept | your claim. |

■ Use these building blocks to find equivalents for the following German sentences.

1. Wir bestätigen den Eingang Ihres Schreibens vom 09.12.200_ und danken Ihnen dafür, dass Sie uns auf dieses Problem aufmerksam gemacht haben.
2. Wir möchten uns für dieses Versehen vielmals entschuldigen.
3. Wir haben den Fall untersucht und festgestellt, dass die Schwierigkeiten auf ein Softwareproblem bei unserem Lieferanten zurückzuführen sind.
4. Wir freuen uns Ihnen mitteilen zu können, dass die Ersatzlieferung noch heute an Sie abgehen wird.
5. Da wir Sie für die Ihnen entstandenen Unannehmlichkeiten entschädigen möchten, sind wir bereit Ihnen einen Preisnachlass von 15 % zu gewähren.
6. Wenn Sie sich entschließen die Teile zu behalten, werden wir den Preis auf €27,50 pro Stück ermäßigen.
7. Wir versichern Ihnen, dass wir alles daran setzen werden, unseren Service zu verbessern.
8. Bitte haben Sie Verständnis dafür, dass wir Ihre Beschwerde zurückweisen müssen, da uns keinerlei Schuld an diesem Transportschaden trifft.
9. Wir hoffen, dass diese Angelegenheit damit zu Ihrer Zufriedenheit erledigt worden ist und würden gerne wieder für Sie tätig werden.

B5 *Phrases: Complaining and apologizing in person or on the phone*

To mention the problem indirectly:
Excuse me... I bought this device yesterday, but it ...
I'm sorry to bother you, but there's a problem with this unit. It ...
I'm sorry but the unit you delivered yesterday...

To say what the problem is:
It's not the right size/colour/kind...
It's not working properly.
I unpacked it and found that it was damaged/dented/ scratched ...
I've had it for only two weeks, and it has already started giving me problems. It ...

To clear up errors or misunderstandings:
I think you may have forgotten to deduct the 20 per cent discount we agreed on.
There may have been a misunderstanding about the delivery date.
It may have slipped your mind, but you said you were going to send off the consignment before Friday.

Sometimes it is necessary to be more direct: I'm not at all happy/satisfied with this machine. It … What are you going to do about the malfunctioning unit? Will you repair it or exchange it?	**To ask for the reason for the complaint:** What exactly is the problem? I'm sorry to hear that. What is wrong with it?
	To apologize and to explain: I'm sorry. – I'm very/extremely sorry. Sorry, my fault. I didn't realize that … There's been a problem in our accounting department.
If polite methods do not work: If you don't exchange the unit by Friday, I'll cancel my next order. What do you mean, you can't give me my money back? I want to speak to the manager.	**To accept someone's apology:** That's all right. – It's quite/perfectly all right. That's okay. It really doesn't matter.

■ Work with a partner. Think of at least three different situations in which you can use these phrases, and make up short dialogues. Also note that in Britain, complaints are generally made in a polite, tentative tone!

C Additional practice

a Complete the body of this letter using the words from the box. Then draft a full complaint, supplying all necessary particulars (names, dates etc.) from your own imagination.

Boxes No. 1, 3 and 4 reached us in perfect condition. ❶, box No. 4, ❷ contained the T-shirts, was badly damaged, ❸ looked as if it had been broken open.

❹ we examined the enclosed packing list, we found that 125 shirts were missing, and ❺ the rummaging in the boxes, quite a few other shirts were torn and ❻ cannot be sold.

❼ the transaction was on a DDU basis, we would ask you to contact your forwarding agent with regard to compensation.

❽ you will find a list of the damaged and missing shirts, and we would ask you to send us replacements as soon as possible. The damaged articles will be kept at our warehouse ❾ we hear from you.

*and * As * because of*
*Enclosed * However * therefore*
*until * When * which*

b Match the parts of this e-mail by Wedler & Co., (e-mail exports@wedler.co.de). Then draft a complete e-mail to LOAMSON S.A., 57 rue de Fixation, 69400 Tremplin, France, (e-mail loamson@aol.com)

1	We are writing with reference to our order no. SM 873/04,	a as this is their first order and it would give us an opportunity to open up the New Zealand market.
2	We tried to contact you by telephone yesterday,	b but you were unavailable and unfortunately have not returned our call.
3	Our deadline is 7 April, and the skis are now ready for dispatch,	c except for the bindings that need to be fitted.
4	It is absolutely essential for us to deliver this consignment on time to our customer,	d in which we asked you to supply 500 SM-300 bindings by 24 March for an export order to New Zealand.
5	If we do not receive the bindings within the next three days,	e we will have to cancel the order and find a more reliable supplier elsewhere.

c **Importex**, (Modegasse 6, 94034 Passau, e-mail: m.fetzer@importex.de) ordered 200 ski caps and 200 zip sweaters from **HEADTOTOE** (200 Kilroy Street, Dublin 4, Ireland, e-mail mulligan@head-to-toe.co.ri). A firm condition of the order was delivery by the end of the month, but the deadline has expired, and Importex have still not received their order. **Read your boss's notes and draft an e-mail complaining about the delay.**

> *Lieferung HT/043 schon 5 Tage überfällig!*
> *Was ist passiert? Abmachungen müssen eingehalten werden!!!*
> *Storno, wenn Best. nicht bis Ende Woche eintrifft.*

d **Wedler & Co**, (Steilhang 45, 87527 Sonthofen, e-mail exports@wedler.co.de) has just received this e-mail from McDermot Bros. (35 Redwood Crescent, East Kilbride G74 5PR, UK, e-mail McDermot@sportslink.uk). **Study their correspondence and draft an appropriate e-mail using the notes.**

```
Dear Mr Wedler,
We are writing to you concerning our order for 100 Victor snowboards,
art. no. 974-23, which we placed with you on 15th February 200_.

We received your consignment this morning, and on examining the contain-
ers, we discovered that they contained 85 UltraStar boards instead of 100
Victor as ordered. We can only assume that your dispatch department has
made a mistake, and that these boards were intended for another customer.
```
Verwechslung! UltraStar waren für Sports Unlimited bestimmt, Victor für McDermot!
```
As demand is very strong, we must ask you to arrange for the immediate
dispatch of the correct merchandise, viz article number 974-23.
```
Eurotrans holt Victor von Sports Unl. morgen, schickt sie direkt an McDermot weiter, in drei Tagen in Schottland!
```
We will keep your consignment in our warehouse until we receive further
instructions from you.
```
Eurotrans holt UltraStar morgen ab.
```
Yours sincerely,
```

D Background information: International Organisations

D 1 The European Union (EU)

History
The history of the EU began in 1951 with the establishment of the European Coal and Steel Community. The European Economic Community was founded in 1957 by the Treaties of Rome. The Single Market, which removed the last barriers to the free movement of people, goods, services and capital, came into force on 1 January 1993. This created a single market of more that 340m consumers. The Maastricht Treaty came into force on 1 November 1993 and created the European Union. This provides for far-reaching political and economic integration with common policies on defence, foreign affairs, social and economic affairs. The treaty also provided for monetary union and the introduction of a common currency (euro). The euro was launched on 1 January, 1999 and became legal tender on 1 January 2002 with the issuing of coins and notes.

Member States
The founding members were France, Italy, Belgium, the Netherlands, Luxemburg and West Germany. The United Kingdom, Ireland and Denmark joined in 1973 and Greece in 1981. Spain and Portugal became members in 1986 and Austria, Sweden and Finland in 1995. A number of countries in Eastern and Southern Europe have now applied to join.

Institutions

Commission
The Commission is the executive organ of the EU. It makes proposals and implements legislation by means of directives. It also ensures that European legislation is implemented in the member countries. There are at present 20 Commissioners, each responsible for a certain field such as competition, agriculture, foreign affairs, finance, transport etc. They act independently of the country that seconds them.

Council of Ministers
The Council of Ministers takes major policy decisions. It consists (at present) of 15 ministers responsible for the respective area of policy in the country they represent. Thus the agricultural ministers meet to decide on agricultural policy, transport ministers to decide on transport issues etc. Decisions may require unanimity or may be taken by a qualified majority, where votes are weighted to take account of the size of the country. In preparation for the admission of new members the areas where majority decisions can be taken have been extended. However, the summit in Nice in 2000 agreed new rules: in order to be adopted a measure must command a threefold majority: a majority of member states, a majority of the votes in the council of ministers and a majority of at least 62% of the population of the EU (demographic factor).

The European Parliament
Members of the European Parliament are elected directly in the member countries.
An important role is to monitor the work of the Commission and to approve the EU budget.

European Central Bank (ECB)
The ECB is politically independent. Its main aim is to safeguard internal price stability within the Eurozone, which generally means keeping inflation under control. Since 1 January 1999 it has had sole responsibility for monetary policy.

D 2 Other international organisations

OECD
The Organisation for Economic Co-operation and Development (OECD) is based in Paris. The 29 wealthiest countries are members. Originally founded after the second world war to administer American aid to Europe, it now produces statistics and economic analyses and makes recommendations to governments and industry.

WTO
The World Trade Organisation continues the work of Gatt (General Agreement on Tariffs and Trade), based on a treaty signed in 1947 with the aim of reducing or removing barriers to trade. 133 countries are now members of the WTO, which has powers to enforce agreements.

World Bank
The World Bank is an international organisation which was founded in 1944 to finance post-war reconstruction and projects in developing countries. It lends and guarantees loans to governments.

International Monetary Fund (IMF)
The IMF was founded in 1944 to encourage monetary co-operation and stabilise currencies. The organisation provides loans to countries which are having difficulties re-paying or servicing debt.

D 3 Customs Unions and Free Trade Areas

The **European Economic Area (EEA)** embraces all the EU member countries plus Norway and Iceland and provides for the free movement of people, goods, services and capital between the 17 countries.

The **North American Free Trade Area (NAFTA)** came into being in 1994 and includes the United States of America, Canada and Mexico. The term "free trade area" implies that impediments to trade (particularly tariffs) are gradually phased out to facilitate the exchange of goods and services without any commitment to political union. Talks have begun to include other Latin American countries.

ASEAN (Association of South East Asian Nations) was founded in 1967 by Indonesia, Malaysia, Philippines, Singapore and Thailand. Brunei joined later.

MERCOSUR (Southern Cone Common Market) was founded in 1995 and comprises Argentina, Brazil, Paraguay and Uruguay, with Bolivia as an observer.

Other free trade areas are being established in South America and Asia.

- Work in pairs. Ask your partner for information on the EU and other international organisations and free trade areas. Then change roles.

D 4 Economic Indicators

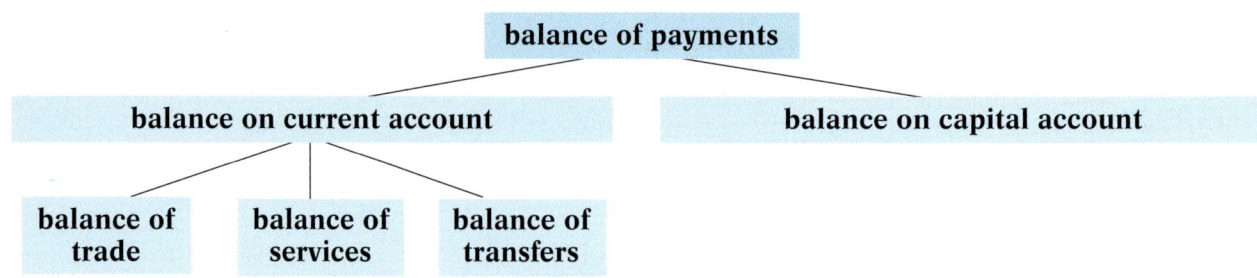

The **balance of payments** (Zahlungsbilanz) covers the total economic transactions of a country with the rest of the world. It includes the following two balances:

The **balance on capital account** (Kapitalverkehrsbilanz) records inflows and outflows of capital, e.g. for investment purposes.

The **balance on current account** (Leistungsbilanz) covers exports and imports of goods and services (without capital movements). It is made up of three balances:

1. The **balance of trade** (Handelsbilanz) covers trade in visible goods by value. If the value of goods exported is greater than that of imports the balance is in surplus. If the value of imports is greater than that of exports the balance is in deficit. As Germany is one of the world's leading exporters of visible goods, its balance of trade has always been positive.

2. The **balance of invisible trade** (Dienstleistungsbilanz) (also called balance of services): this is the balance of payments for services rendered or received and includes such areas as transport, tourism, banking, insurance, legal services, accountancy, advertising and marketing, royalties etc. In Britain where this is the most dynamic and rapidly growing sector of the economy these products may be referred to as "invisibles".

3. The **balance of transfers** (Übertragungsbilanz) records a country's contributions to international organisations like the EU or the United Nations, remittances by foreign workers to their relatives in their home countries, development aid and other transfers not made in connection with trade.

Gross Domestic Product (GDP) is the total value in money terms of all the goods produced and services rendered in a given country. It does not include income from abroad, for example profits made by a company's subsidiary based in a foreign country.

Gross National Product (GNP) is the same as GDP plus income from abroad.

Inflation basically arises when the demand for goods and services is greater than the supply. The inflation rate, which measures how fast prices are rising, is expressed as a percentage. Central banks like the Bank of England and the European Central Bank (ECB) are charged with keeping inflation under control. They set a target – say 2% - which they try to achieve by raising or lowering interest rates in order to influence the level of demand by making credit cheaper or more expensive.

E IHK-Prüfungsvorbereitung*

1. | **Zusatzqualifikation Englisch für kaufmännische Auszubildende**

Vermerk in Deutsch über einen Geschäftsbrief (Bearbeitungszeit 30 Minuten)	**Hilfsmittel:** zweisprachiges Wörterbuch

Situation
Sie arbeiten als Auszubildende(r) in der Exportabteilung des Unternehmens Computex GmbH in Münster. Sie haben heute, am 15 Dezember 200_, das beigefügte Schreiben der englischen Firma Palm Top Ltd, in Rawdon (Leeds), Großbritannien erhalten.

Aufgabe
Bitte fassen Sie für Herrn Wildenbruch, den Leiter der Exportabteilung, den Inhalt des Briefes in einem Vermerk in deutscher Sprache zusammen (vollständige Sätze, keine Übersetzung).

PALM TOP LTD
46 Windsor Drive · Rawdon · LS1R 6L9 · UK

Computex GmbH
Pictorius Platz 15
48143 Münster
Germany

11 Dec. 200_

Dear Mr Wildenbruch

Your palm-held computer Xion2K

We received a consignment of 1000 Xion2K palm-held computers on 1 November 200_ as per our order of 2 October 200_.

Unfortunately this consignment is giving us a great deal of trouble. We have delivered 600 to the retail outlets we supply and have already received a large number of complaints. As far as we can ascertain, the general standard of workmanship is not as satisfactory as it was with the first 500 we ordered. Roughly 50 cannot be closed properly as the catch is defective. In a further 50 or so the plastic casing is severely discoloured. We have examined the 400 still in our stocks and find that 70 are affected. We have asked all our customers to check their consignments and let us know as soon as possible how many items are defective.

This is a considerable disappointment to us as our trial order gave absolutely no cause for complaint. It is causing great inconvenience both to us and our customers. What are your procedures for monitoring quality before products leave your factory? We propose to recall all the defective items and send them back to you immediately at your expense. Of course, we shall need replacements within two weeks.

I am sure that you will appreciate that this is a highly competitive market where a reputation for reliability can be very easily lost. We must insist that any products you supply to us should be carefully monitored for quality and finish before dispatch.

I look forward to receiving your comments by return.

David Macmillan
David Macmillan
Managing Director

Computex GmbH Pictorius Platz 15, 48143 Münster

MEMO

Für: Datum:

Von:

Betreff:

---

* weitere Aufgaben (mit Lösungsvorschlägen) im Lehrerhandbuch

2. Fremdsprachenkorrespondent/in

Übersetzung Englisch/Deutsch (Bearbeitungszeit 60 Minuten)	Hilfsmittel: Zweisprachige Wörterbücher

The basis of the Total Quality Management (TQM) philosophy in business is that a company must satisfy all the groups it deals with. Generally speaking, a company deals with three different groups of people – customers, users and suppliers. There are differences between these groups and it is important to deal with each in an appropriate manner in order to ensure the continued success of the business.

Seeking to achieve customer satisfaction is one of the main ideas of TQM. Successful companies emphasise the importance of providing products and services which satisfy their customers. A customer in a business transaction is the person who pays for the product or service. According to the TQM philosophy it is possible to regard your boss as your customer because he pays you for your services.

The customer is not always identical with the user. There may be a difference between the person who pays for a product or service and the person that ultimately uses it. A mother buying a toy for a child is the customer but the child is the user. Obviously, it is essential that both should be satisfied with the purchase.

It is a supplier's job to keep you, his customer, happy. However, it is also in your interest to maintain a good relationship as reliable and helpful suppliers are essential to the success of your business.

3. Fremdsprachenkorrespondent/in Englisch

Beantwortung einer Korrespondenz (Bearbeitungszeit: 60 Minuten)	Hilfsmittel: Zweisprachige Wörterbücher

Sie arbeiten bei der TESTCO GmbH, einem Hersteller elektronischer Prüfanlagen. Diese Anlagen müssen zweimal jährlich von Ihren Kundendienst-Ingenieuren gewartet und justiert werden. Ihr Chef, der Geschäftsführer, Herr Christian Kleine, hat heute folgende E-Mail von einem Kunden in Irland, Clare Laboratories, Shannon Free Zone, IRL-Shannon Co. Clare, erhalten:

---

e-mail

From: clarelab@eirelink.ri
To: kleine@testco.de   Cc:
Date: 29 Mar 200_   Attachments:
Subject: Testing System

Dear Mr Kleine

I'm writing to you personally to express my growing dissatisfaction with TESTCO's services. You will remember that two years ago you supplied us with an electronic testing system under our order number AB-7, dated 17 January 199_ and that we commissioned you with the semi-annual servicing of the system under our order number WV-204 of 15 June 199_.

For the first year the service you gave us was impeccable. Since then, though, we've noticed a gradual deterioration. Twice your service engineers postponed their visits at very short notice, which badly upset our laboratory's work schedule. Yesterday things came to a head when your service engineer, Herr Heinz Schnacke, arrived a day later than announced and – to make things worse – failed to bring along some of the documentation required. It took some time for these documents to be faxed from Germany, which resulted in further downtime for our laboratory equipment. In addition to all that, I've just noticed that Herr Schnacke forgot to sign the test certificate which we will have to submit to the inspection authority within the next few days.

I must now urgently request you to contact Herr Schnacke immediately and instruct him to call on us as soon as possible before returning to Germany. I believe he is still in Ireland, servicing other TESTCO equipment.

Whereas your testing plants do give us reliable service, your customer service does not, I'm afraid. Please ensure that in future your service engineers arrive fully prepared and on the day agreed upon. I'm sure you do not wish to jeopardise our business relations.

Regards
Richard Walls
Plant Manager

Aufgabe
Antworten Sie Mr Walls per E-Mail unter dem Namen von Herrn Kleine und berücksichtigen Sie dabei unter anderem folgende Punkte:

- Verzögerungen bei der Wartung (servicing) gelegentlich unvermeidlich, wenn unvorhergesehene Probleme auftauchen
- Herr Schnacke erfahrener, erstklassiger, zuverlässiger Kundendiensttechniker, gestern trotz Fieber und beginnender Grippe zu Clare Laboratories gefahren
- Mit Herrn Schnacke gesprochen, wird morgen gegen 9.30 Uhr bei Clare Laboratories vorbeikommen und Unterschrift anbringen

4. Fremdsprachenkorrespondent/in

Zusammenfassung in Deutsch einer mündlichen Nachricht (Bearbeitungszeit: 30 Minuten)	Hilfsmittel: Zweisprachige Wörterbücher

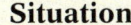

Situation
Ihr Chef hat folgende Nachricht auf seinem Anrufbeantworter vorgefunden. Er bittet Sie einen Vermerk in deutscher Sprache anzufertigen, den er dem Exportleiter geben kann.

Aufgabe
Bitte fassen Sie (unter Ihrem eigenen Namen) die Nachricht in deutscher Sprache für den Exportleiter Claus Sonntag zusammen. (Sie werden die Nachricht zweimal hören.)

Unit 10 Reminders

Introduction

Reminders

There are times when a bill goes unpaid, and steps must be taken to collect the invoice amount. The problem in this case is that the supplier wants to obtain his/her money *and* maintain the customer's goodwill. Reminders should, therefore, be persuasive, tactful, and like all other business communications, you-oriented. Sometimes several reminders have to be sent to achieve the desired result. The tone of the correspondence will gradually become more insistent, depending on the past payment record of the customer. The interval between the reminders may vary from ten days to a month, and each should contain this information:

- date and number of invoice
- amount owed
- how long the bill is overdue
- request for payment

The **first** reminder usually includes a copy of the invoice or statement of account. As non-payment is not always the customer's fault, the first reminder should be positive and understanding and not embarrass the customer. First reminders may also be included in other correspondence addressed to the customer (hidden reminders).

If the first reminder fails to get results, the **second** will be more insistent, but still friendly, asking for an explanation and perhaps offering help while at the same time requesting payment.

The **final** reminder will appeal to the customer's fairness and desire to maintain his/her reputation by stressing the consequences of non-payment. A final deadline for payment is set and the customer is warned that should he/she fail to meet this deadline, the supplier will turn the matter over either to his solicitors or to a collection agency. Even at this stage it may be appropriate to express regret at having to take such steps.

Replies to reminders

Ideally the customer should inform the supplier in good time about any difficulties he may be having in meeting his obligations and ask for a respite. Consequently there should be no occasion for the supplier to remind the customer. In reality, however, many firms will receive reminders at one time or other and will have to react to them.

If payment has already been made or will be effected immediately and in full, it will be sufficient to inform the supplier at once and to apologize for the delay.

Should your company be unable to make payment in full, you will have to negotiate a new payment plan with the supplier. In the end each side will have to make concessions. What you could ask for is one, or a combination, of the following options:

- a respite, i.e. an extension of the due date for payment
- making a down payment and paying the rest at a later date
- payment by instalments

Giving reasons for the delay and offering apologies is essential in order to retain the supplier's goodwill.

■ **Get together in groups of two or more. Study the above text. Divide the text into several parts, with each student translating a part in writing. Then read out your translations to the other students.**

A Activities

A1 Standardised collection series

■ Many firms use a standardised series of collection letters. Study the letters below, then decide in which order you would send these letters if one of your customers failed to settle your invoice.

1

Dear <title> <surname>,

Your order <order #> of <date>

I am writing to inform you that I have not yet received payment of my invoice no. <invoice #> for <total>.

You will understand that it is not possible for me to supply goods on such favourable terms unless my customers clear their balances as agreed.

Despite my previous reminder, you have not given me any explanation concerning the delay in settling my invoice. Therefore, please let me know as soon as possible what arrangements you are making for payment.

Yours sincerely,

2

Dear <title> <surname>,

Your order <order #> of <date>

You have been a reliable customer for many years, and I am truly at a loss to understand why you still have not cleared the balance of <total>, which is now two months overdue.

I am afraid you are placing your credit rating in danger, and only by settling the invoice by the end of this week can you secure the continued convenience of buying on credit.

I would be extremely sorry to lose a long-standing customer. Please allow me to continue to serve you.

Yours sincerely,

3

Dear <title> <surname>,

Your order <order #> of <date>

To date, you have failed to answer any of my requests to settle my invoice no. <invoice #>. You will understand that it is not possible for me to wait any longer, and I am planning to place the matter in the hands of my solicitor.

Before taking this action, however, I would like to appeal to your sound business judgement. I am sure that, if you telephone me, we can find ways and means of settling this matter without the need for court proceedings.

Therefore, I would ask you to contact me by the end of this week, so that we can avoid an unpleasant situation.

Yours sincerely,

4

Dear <title> <surname>,

Your order <order #> of <date>

I am writing to inform you that the balance of <total> in respect of the above order is now overdue.

According to the terms agreed, settlement of this balance was to be made <terms>. However, I have not yet received payment from you.

I enclose a copy of invoice no. <invoice #> in case the original has been lost in the mail.

I would be grateful for an early settlement.

Yours sincerely,

A 2 First reminder

a Study this statement first. Then read the lines below and find the correct text for the accompanying letter. Reformat the text so that it becomes the body of the letter accompanying the statement.

HYFLYER plc
438 Weltmore Industrial Park, Warwick, CV43 6TS
Tel: 01926 439523   Fax: 01926 451427
V.A.T. reg. no. GB 234 9376 51

STATEMENT as per   31 Jan 200_

DATE	INVOICE	DEBIT	CREDIT	BALANCE
BALANCE FORWARDED				
01-Jan-200_				27,750.00
03-Jan-200_	634203-UK	13,875.00		41,625.00
09-Jan-200_	CR 14875		27,750.00	13,875.00
20-Jan-200_	634508-UK	29,600.00		43,475.00

1. dear ms paxton enclosed please find our statement of your account for January, which shows a balance of £43,475.00 in our favour please transfer the amount due to our account yours faithfully

2. dear ms paxton enclosed please find our statement of your account for January, which shows a balance of £43,475.00 in our favour please transfer the amount due to our account yours sincerely

3. dear ms paxton enclosed please find our statement of your account for January, which shows a balance of £43,475.00 in your favour please transfer the amount due to our account yours sincerely

b Fletcher's supplied office printers to LeisureCorp (Invoice No. N14/12 of 14 December, amounting to £3,280.50), and payment was due on January 18. However, when Sean Fletcher checked his records at the end of January, he realized that he had not yet received payment from LeisureCorp. **Write a first reminder**.

68 Woodstock Road, Belfast BT3 6OF
Telephone (01232) 846879   Fax (01232) 846888
E-mail accounts@fletchers.uk

Fletcher's Business Systems

LeisureCorp
36 Kerr Street
Limavady
BT49 0HA

1 February 200_

c Listen to the conversation in Hyflyer's accounting department and draft a fax to Badenbike to remind them that payment is overdue.

(Fax numbers:
Hyflyer: 01926 451427
Badenbike: 0721 4012021)

```
EXCHANGE FOR  £4,620
AT  30 days after sight   PAY THIS  sole      17 January  200_
TO THE ORDER OF  ourselves              BILL OF EXCHANGE
Four thousand six hundred and twenty pounds sterling
VALUE  20 Hyflyer DX-2000
TO:   Badenbike                          WHICH PLACE TO AC-
      Draisstraße 342                    COUNT
                                         FOR AND ON BEHALF OF
      76189 Karlsruhe                    Hyflyer plc
      Germany                            438 Weltmore
                                         Industrial Park
        Günther Radler                   Warwick CV43 6TS
                                         United Kingdom
                                  Signed:  Peter Hamilton
```

A 3 Second reminder

a One of Snoozers' long-standing customers has not answered Snoozers' previous reminder. They therefore send this letter. **Study the letter and decide which of the alternatives in brackets is correct.**

Snoozers Limited
www.snoozers.co.uk
VAT No. 367 839175
24 The Crescent   Knowlhill MK5 8NL
Tel 0381 49287   Fax 0381 49290

Sleepwell Bros.
28 Farringdon Road
Elswick
Newcastle-upon-Tyne
NE5 7RD

23 January 200_

Dear Mr Sleepwell,

Our invoice no. 34287 of 23 October 200_

You (**1** are/have been/was) a reliable customer for many years, and we (**2** are able to/cannot/could not) understand why you still (**3** settle/have not settled/did not settle) the balance of £3,489.20 in respect of the above invoice, which (**4** has been/is/was) now three months overdue.

We are afraid that you (**5** were placing/has placed/will place) your credit rating in danger. It is only by (**6** have paid/pay/paying) our invoice by the end of this month that you can secure the continued convenience of (**7** bought/buy/buying) on credit.

We (**8** are/should be/have been) extremely sorry to lose a long-standing customer. Please allow us to continue (**9** serve/serving/to have served) you.

Yours sincerely,

Jo Wheeler

Jo Wheeler
Manager

A 4 Final reminder

➡ 203 a Read the letter and choose the appropriate words for the gaps from the box.

Sleepwell Bros.
28 Farringdon Road
Elswick
Newcastle-upon-Tyne
NE5 7RD

5 February 200_

Dear Mr Sleepwell,

Our invoice no 34287 of 23 October 200_

I regret to note that you appear to have ignored my letter of 23 January just as you ignored my previous ❶.

Your failure to communicate with me and to settle this long overdue ❷ leaves me with no alternative but to demand payment by 8 February 200_ . If the invoice is not settled by this date, we will have to take legal steps to ❸ payment.

In view of our long-standing business relations I very much hope that such ❹ will not be necessary.

Yours sincerely,

Jo Wheeler

Jo Wheeler
Manager

*account * enforce * measures * reminder*

b A few days later, Jo Wheeler sees this article in a trade magazine. **Read it and discuss in class what Snoozers could do to recover the outstanding money.**

Bankruptcies in quick succession?

Sleepwell Bros. has collapsed under the burden of liabilities of £840,000 accumulated over the past two years. The market is nervously watching other distributors. According to industry analyst Gary Baker, "the Sleepwell failure may only be the first of a series of major breakdowns in the furniture business."

A 5 Replies to reminders

a In unit 9 Rob Sullivan agreed to grant a 20 per cent discount for having supplied faulty bicycles. However, Kate Paxton discovered that this discount is not shown on the statement she received. **Complete her reply to Hyflyer choosing the appropriate prepositions from the box.**

Dear Mrs Tyler,

We have received your statement ❶ January showing a balance ❷ £43,475.00 ❸ your favour.

❹ verification, however, we noticed that you have failed to include the 20 per cent discount which Rob Sullivan granted when I telephoned him to discuss the problem ❺ your last delivery.

We have therefore deducted £5,920 ❻ your balance and will transfer the sum ❼ £37,555, which we believe to be the correct amount.

We would ask you to look ❽ this matter and send us a credit note.

Yours sincerely,

> for ∗ from ∗ in ∗ into ∗ of (2x) ∗ on ∗ with

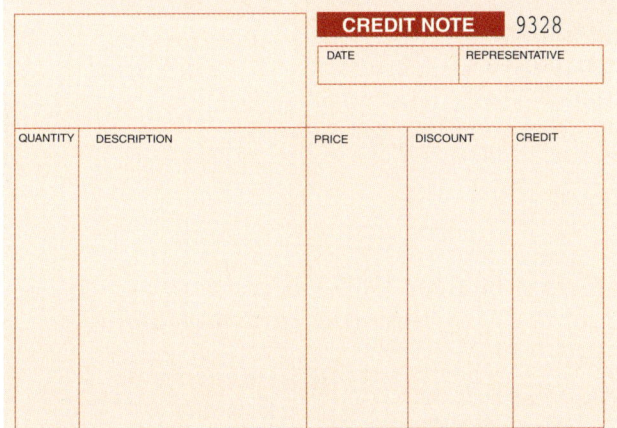

b Use these jumbled elements to write a reply to the letter above, copy the credit note on the left and fill it in.

Please accept my apologies for this error and my thanks for your patience.
We are currently adjusting our accounting system in order to prevent similar mistakes in the future.
Thank you for your letter of 9 February 200_ concerning our statement for January.
I have looked into this matter and found that the error is due to a wrong entry having been made.
I have credited £5,920 to your account and enclose credit note no. 9328.

LeisureCorp Memo

FROM: Amanda
TO: Tracy
DATE: 5/2

for ACTION 3
COMMENT
INFORMATION
DISCUSSION

please DISPLAY
FILE
RETURN

SUBJECT: Fletcher's invoice

I've just received Fletcher's reminder. Please look into the matter and send him a cheque today. Tell him oversight is due to computer problems in accounting department.

c Use the memo on the left and the information on page 202 (A2b) to draft a letter.

d Badenbike are in arrears in paying Hyflyer's invoice. **Read Mr Radler's fax and answer the questions below.**

Dear Mr Hamilton

We have recently been experiencing major problems with one of our largest customers, which has resulted in an unfortunate delay in honouring your bill of exchange.

We are extremely sorry that this development has affected your company, and we would like to request a special payment plan to cope with this difficult situation.

We could remit 50 per cent of the outstanding amount in the near future and settle the remainder soon thereafter.

We would very much appreciate it if you could agree to our proposal, as liquidation on our part would not be in your own interest either.

Yours sincerely

Günther Radler
Manager

---

1. What is the reason for the delay in payment?
2. What does the manager suggest?
3. If you were Mr Hamilton, would you insist on immediate payment? Why? Why not?
4. What could happen if you insisted on immediate payment?
5. What are the risks if you agree to Mr Radler's proposal?
6. Would you write a further reminder threatening to take the matter to court?

A6 Reminder and reply to reminder by telephone

■ Work with a partner. Partner A is Mr Hamilton from Hyflyer, who has just received the above letter. Partner B is Mr Radler from Badenbike. Use these role cards to simulate a telephone conversation.

Mr Hamilton

1 You are quite worried about the outstanding account. Enquire what exactly has happened, so that you can assess the situation.

2 As Mr Radler's fax does not specify an exact date of payment, try to get a promise to pay by a specific date.

3 Suggest this payment plan:
50 per cent should be settled by the end of April, the remainder by 30 June.

Herr Radler

1 Erklären Sie, dass einer Ihrer wichtigsten Kunden, die Firma RADPROFI, seit Dezember keine Rechnungen mehr bezahlt hat. Vor zwei Wochen hat sie dann Konkurs angemeldet.

2 Legen Sie sich möglichst nicht auf irgendwelche Zeitpunkte fest. Wegen der schwierigen Situation können Sie nichts Genaues versprechen.

3 Machen Sie ein Gegenangebot, 30 Prozent bis Ende April, den Rest in vier Raten zum Ende jedes folgenden Monats.

B Tool kit

B1 Structure of business communications: Reminders

Reminders should be structured like this:

Structure	Language to use
1. personal salutation	Dear Mrs Clay
2. reference to invoice / statement of account date and number of invoice due date previous reminder(s), if applicable	We refer to our letter of 30 July asking for settlement of our invoice No. AB4/17 of 18 May, which is now five weeks overdue.
3. suggestion of oversight etc. on the debtor's part, if appropriate	Apparently the account has escaped your attention.
4. request for explanation, if appropriate	As you have so far always paid your bills promptly, we are at a loss to understand this delay in payment.
5. request for payment, setting a deadline in the case of 2nd or 3rd reminders	We must, therefore, ask you to remit the balance without delay.
6. steps that will be taken unless payment is made, if appropriate	Should you fail to settle our statement of account we shall unfortunately have to reconsider the terms of payment.
7. hope for settlement and continued business relations	We trust that you will remit the outstanding amount in the next few days and that our cordial business relations can be continued.
8. complimentary close	Yours sincerely
9. enclosure (invoice, statement), if applicable	Encl. September statement of account

■ **What is the purpose of these sentences? Find the appropriate numbers in *structure of business communications* above.**

1. We wish to point out that your account still shows an outstanding balance of $7,234.50 in our favour.

2. You have not yet replied to our reminder of 3 June. Should you have any particular reason for withholding payment, please let us know immediately.

3. Your arrears in payment constitute a breach of contract. We are considering breaking off business relations with you.

4. We would, therefore, ask you to remit the outstanding amount by the end of the week.

5. We hope that this matter will soon be settled to the satisfaction of both parties.

6. As we have now been waiting for settlement of our invoices Nos. 34 and 36 for three months, we regret that we will have no alternative but to institute legal proceedings against you unless the balance of £745.90 is remitted to our account by 31 July without fail.

7. Since you have always been a reliable customer we assume that this invoice must have been overlooked.

8. You will undoubtedly remember that we stipulated payment within 10 days after receipt of the goods.

B2 Building blocks for business communications: Reminders

1 To refer to the invoice / statement of account / previous reminder(s)

We refer to		our	statement of account for April.
We would like to	remind you **of** draw your attention **to**		invoice no. AB700 of 20 September. letter dated 14 June. reminders of 14 and 30 June.
The invoice The sum of €20,359.00 The balance of $720.75		was due **on** 31 July. is still outstanding. is now four weeks overdue.	
The account shows a balance of €7,390 **in** our favour.			

2 To suggest an oversight, request an explanation and/or express disappointment

As you have	never exceeded the credit period always paid punctually always been a reliable business partner	we think we assume we believe	that	there must have been some misunderstanding. you must have overlooked our invoice. you may have been prevented from paying by exceptional circumstances.

You have neither remitted the amount due nor given us any explanation for the delay in payment.
Given your previous excellent payment record we are wondering why you are withholding payment.

3 To demand payment and set a deadline

Please We would ask you to We must insist that you	clear the balance remit the amount settle the account make payment transfer the sum **of** € 4,220.00 send us a cheque **for** $375.50	without further delay. immediately. **by** the end of next week. **by** 7 May **at the latest.** **within** seven days. as agreed.

4 To point out the consequences of non-payment

Should you fail to If you do not Unless you	meet this deadline make payment **by** this date remit the amount **in** time	we	regret that we will have to are afraid we shall be forced to shall have no option but to

	change our terms of payment. supply you **on** "cash with order" terms in future. terminate our business relations. take legal steps. institute legal proceedings.	
	hand the matter over to	our legal department. our solicitors. a collection agency.

5 To close a reminder

In the event that payment has already been effected in the meantime, please disregard this letter.	
We would be grateful for We are looking forward to	an early settlement.
Please	let us know what arrangements you are making for payment. contact us immediately so that we can avoid an unpleasant situation.
We would be very sorry to lose a long-standing customer. So please make sure that the matter is settled to our mutual satisfaction.	

■ **Use the building blocks to find the equivalents of these German sentences.**

1. Mit Bezug auf unsere Rechnung Nr. XZ34 vom 29 Dezember 200_ müssen wir Sie leider darauf aufmerksam machen, dass der Rechnungsbetrag von $620,- noch immer nicht bei uns eingegangen ist.
2. Wir bedauern Ihnen mitteilen zu müssen, dass Ihr Konto inzwischen einen Saldo von €16.820,55 zu unseren Gunsten aufweist und bitten Sie das Konto unverzüglich auszugleichen.
3. Da die Zahlung nun seit acht Wochen überfällig ist, sehen wir uns gezwungen, ein Inkassobüro mit der Angelegenheit zu betrauen.
4. Sofern Sie die Rechnung nicht bis spätestens 31. Juli begleichen, werden wir gerichtliche Schritte in Erwägung ziehen müssen.
5. Es ist uns unverständlich, warum Sie uns keine Erklärung für das Ausbleiben der Zahlung gegeben haben.
6. Wir hoffen, die Angelegenheit kann zu unser aller Zufriedenheit erledigt werden.

B 3 Structure of business communications: Replies to reminders

Replies to reminders should be structured like this:

Structure	Language to use
1. personal salutation	Dear Mr Harville
2. reference to reminder(s)	We have received your letter of 2 April concerning your invoice No. 17/456
3. apologies	...and would like to offer our sincere apologies for the delay in payment.
4. explanation for the delay in payment	Unfortunately, one of our main customers went bankrupt last month, which has placed us in a difficult situation.
5. solution suggested, e.g. • extension of due date • down payment and payment of the balance at a later date • payment by instalments	That is why we have to ask you for a respite of three weeks. Alternatively, we could pay half of the sum now and the rest in four weeks' time.
6. request for understanding	I hope you will understand our predicament and see your way clear to granting us this concession considering our satisfactory business relations so far.
7. assurance that payment will be made	As we are expecting major payments by our customers in the next few weeks, you may be sure that we will be in a position to settle the invoice by the time suggested above.
8. appropriate ending	I am very sorry for the inconvenience caused and look forward to receiving your comments.
9. complimentary close	Yours sincerely

■ **What is the purpose of these sentences? Find the appropriate numbers in *structure of business communications* above.**

1. We are expecting a considerable tax refund in the near future and this will enable us to meet our obligations in full.
2. Business has been sluggish recently and our own customers have been very slow in paying their bills.
3. I am extremely sorry that the due date was overlooked by our accounts department.
4. Much to our regret we have to ask you for an extension of credit until 31 October.
5. We would suggest that we pay the invoice amount in three instalments of €7,500 each, due 10 June, 20 June and 30 June, respectively.
6. Having been your customer for so many years I feel sure that you will agree to my proposal.
7. We acknowledge receipt of your letter dated 3 January reminding us that your invoice was due on 15 December.

B4 Building blocks for business communications: Replies to reminders

1 To inform the supplier about payment

		€ …		**to** your account.		
We will	transfer / remit	the amount	due	**by**	SWIFT	transfer.
We have	transferred / remitted	the sum	in question		giro	

Enclosed you will find / We are enclosing / We are sending you	our cheque no. 3486 / our banker's draft	**for** € …	**in**	payment / settlement	**of**	your invoice No. … / your statement of …
	your bill of exchange at 60d/s, duly accepted.					

2 To refer to reminder(s)

We have received / We acknowledge receipt of	your	invoice / statement / letter	of 2 May and thank you for	drawing the account to our attention. / your patience.

3 To apologize

We sincerely apologise / We are very sorry / We offer our sincere apologies	**for** this	oversight. / delay in payment. / software failure.
	for the inconvenience caused by this state of affairs.	

We very much regret / We are deeply sorry	that	there has been a delay in settling the account. / you should have had to remind us of the due date. / the invoice has become past due.

4 To mention the reasons for the delay in payment

Your invoice has not yet been paid	as a result of / as a consequence of	a breakdown of our computer system. / an error **by** our bank. / an unexpected fall **in** demand. / the sharp downturn in our industry. / the unforeseen decline **in** e-commerce.

Payment has not been made	because	you charged us the wrong price.	
		a major customer of ours	has gone bankrupt. failed to meet his obligations. has gone into compulsory liquidation.
		you sent us the wrong goods.	
As we have As we are having	substantial outstanding accounts temporary difficulties problems in collecting our accounts	we are unfortunately unable	to settle our accounts. to meet our commitments. to pay our bills.

5 To ask for an extension and/or suggest an alternative

To our regret we are obliged to ask you	to grant us a respite of two months. for an extension of three weeks.	
	to extend	the deadline **by** 10 days. the date of maturity of the draft **by** one month. the credit **on** your March statement.

We would suggest **that**	we remit €10,000 now and the balance in three months. we pay in three identical instalments of $30,330. we send you a cheque **for** £5,000 now and that you draw **on** us **at** 60 days for the rest.

6 To give assurances that payment will be effected

We assure you You may rest assured	that	payment will be effected promptly there will be no further delay in payment your invoice will then be paid **in** full	as	we are expecting a considerable payment **from** one of our debtors. there are clear signs that our situation is likely to improve shortly. business is already picking up noticeably.

7 To ask for understanding

In view of our long-standing business relations we would be grateful if you could We trust that you will understand our difficult situation and	make this concession. grant the respite requested. agree **to** our suggestions. find our proposal acceptable.

8 To close the letter

| We hope that | future contacts will not be affected by this unfortunate affair
our business relations will not be impaired by this | and look forward to your | comments.
reply. |

9 To grant the request for extension

| Considering
In view of
Because of | our long-standing business relations
the exceptional circumstances
the guarantees you offered to provide | we are prepared to | agree to payment **by** instalments.
grant the extension of credit.
accept the solution suggested. |

10 To offer a compromise and mention conditions

| We have decided
We are prepared | to accept a down payment of €1,500
to agree to your proposal | if you | remit the balance no later than 31 August.
pay the remainder **by** 10 May.
accept a draft **at** 30 days' sight. |

11 To refuse the request for extension

| We understand
We are aware of | your difficulties but | are unfortunately not in **a** position to accommodate you
are unable to extend the credit any further
must to our regret insist **on** immediate payment |

| as
since | the account is already six months overdue.
we are obliged to meet our own commitments.
this is the third time you have failed to balance your account within the agreed period. |

■ **Use these building blocks to find equivalents for the following German sentences.**

1. Hiermit teilen wir Ihnen mit, dass wir unsere Bank angewiesen haben, den Restbetrag von €430,75 auf Ihr Konto bei der Hampshire Bank zu überweisen.

2. Da die Geschäfte zur Zeit sehr schlecht gehen, muss ich Sie um einen weiteren Zahlungsaufschub von vier Wochen bitten.

3. Zu meinem Bedauern muss ich Ihnen mitteilen, dass es mir momentan nicht möglich ist, Ihre Rechnung vom 30. Dezember in voller Höhe zu begleichen.

4. Wir bedauern die Verzögerung und bitten um Entschuldigung für die Ihnen hierdurch entstandenen Unannehmlichkeiten.

5. Die Zahlung konnte noch nicht vorgenommen werden, da unsere eigenen Kunden wegen der Rezession im Einzelhandel unsere Rechnungen nur sehr schleppend begleichen.

6. Ich hoffe, dass Sie sich angesichts unserer langjährigen Geschäftsbeziehungen in der Lage sehen, unserem Vorschlag zuzustimmen.

7. Wir wären Ihnen sehr verbunden, wenn Sie damit einverstanden wären, dass eine Teilzahlung von £6,500 sofort erfolgt und der Rest im Laufe des Monats beglichen wird.

8. Da wir in Kürze den Eingang größerer Zahlungen erwarten, können Sie sich darauf verlassen, dass die Überweisung pünktlich erfolgt.

9. In Anbetracht unserer bisher so erfreulichen Geschäftsbeziehungen sind wir bereit, Ihnen diesmal entgegenzukommen.

10. Wir können Ihre Schwierigkeiten durchaus nachvollziehen, dennoch ist es uns unmöglich, noch länger auf die Begleichung unserer Rechnung zu warten.

C Additional practice

a **Study the invoice from a previous transaction and the notes, then draft an appropriate piece of correspondence.**

→ 193

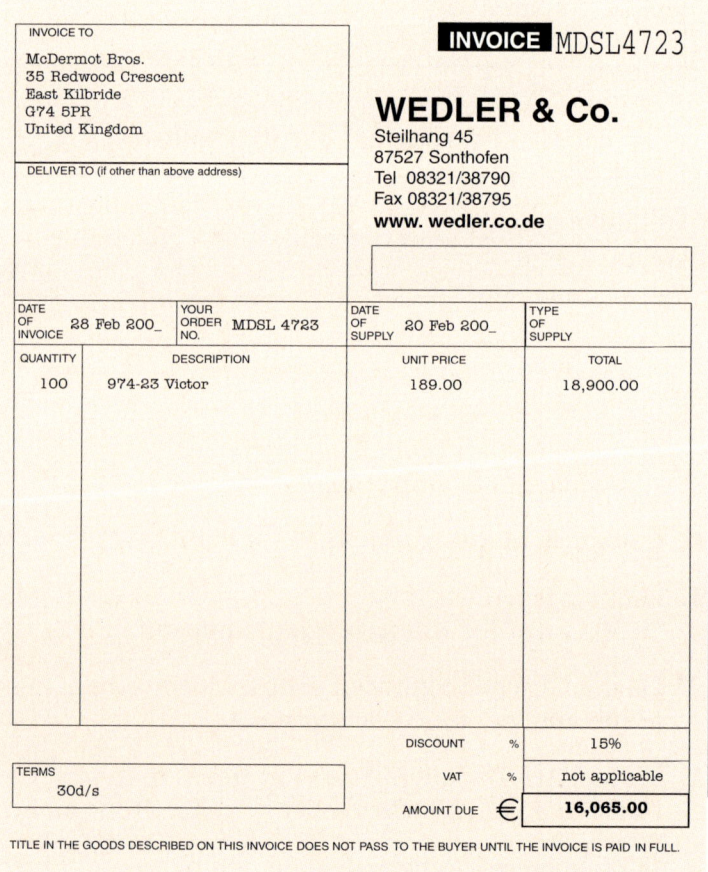

Normalerweise gute Zahler!?!

Rechnung ist schon mehr als einen Monat fällig!

Erinnern Sie McDermot und legen Sie Rechnungskopie bei!

b **Zischfrisch**, Durststrecke 8, 73033 Göppingen, Tel. +49 7161 73110, Fax +49 7161 73120, durst@zischfrisch.de, has just received this reminder from FIZZDRINK, Barrel Street, London EC4 4BY. **Study this piece of correspondence and the hand-written notes, and reply appropriately.**

> In our letter of 7 September we enclosed copies of all the invoices that made up your July statement.
>
> To date, however, we have not received payment of the outstanding amount of €8,973.87.
>
> As we have been dealing with you for almost ten years, we were quite disappointed that we have neither received your remittance nor any explanation as to why the balance has not been cleared.
>
> We therefore ask you urgently to either explain your reasons for non-payment or send us a cheque to clear the account within the next two weeks.

Einbrecher haben Buchhaltung verwüstet und Feuer gelegt, wodurch auch unsere Daten teilweise verloren gegangen sind.
Derzeit arbeiten wir an der Wiederherstellung der Daten und bitten noch um etwas Geduld. Wir werden den Betrag in Kürze überweisen.

c **Importex**, Modegasse 6, 94034 Passau, Tel. +49 851 370301, Fax +49 851 370312, www.importex.de, has already sent these two collection letters to MAGYARMODA; Ady Endre utca 31, 1014 Budapest, Hungary. Again, three weeks have elapsed, but there has been no response so far. **Draft an appropriate letter.**

> Dear Mr Kovacs,
> We are writing to inform you that the balance of €947.45 in respect of your recent order is now overdue.
> According to the terms agreed, settlement of this balance was to be made 30 days net. However, we have not yet received payment from you.
> We enclose a copy of invoice no. MM 004/03 in case the original has been lost in the mail.
> We would be grateful for an early settlement and look forward to obtaining further orders from you.
>
> Yours sincerely,

> Dear Mr Kovacs,
> We are writing to inform you that we have not yet received payment of our invoice no. MM 004/03 for €947.45.
> You will understand that it is not possible for us to supply goods on such favourable terms unless our customers clear their balances as agreed.
> Despite our previous reminder, you have not given us any explanation concerning the delay in settling our invoice. Therefore, we ask you to let us know as soon as possible what arrangements you are making for payment.
>
> Yours sincerely,

d A few days later **Importex**, Modegasse 6, 94034 Passau, Tel. +49 851 370301, Fax +49 851 370312, www.importex.de, receives this reply. **Work with a partner to find an appropriate way to deal with this situation.**

> I am sorry to inform you that I am not able to meet my obligations at present.
>
> Three months ago, Mr Nagy from Pecs, a major customer, declared insolvency. As a consequence, I have found myself in great difficulty, as I have outstanding balances of more than €50,000.
>
> However, I am presently discussing an extension of my credit line with my bank, and am certain that I will receive the money in the very near future.
>
> Therefore, I would ask you to allow me a further 30 days to clear my account.
>
> I would be most grateful if you could help me in this matter.

D Background information: Banking services

Current accounts are used for making payments by bank transfer (see unit 7) and receiving payments. Salaries, for example, are transferred to employees' current accounts. Money may be withdrawn from current accounts at any time but normally no interest is paid on the money deposited and handling fees are charged. If the account holder wishes to make regular payments he may
5 place a *standing order* with his bank instructing it to transfer a fixed amount at regular intervals to a specific account, for instance in order to pay rent or insurance premiums etc. For regular payments which vary in amount, like electricity or telephone bills, *direct debiting* is used, which means the account holder authorises a third party (e.g. the telephone company) to debit his or her account with the sum to be paid. Moreover, banks issue cheques and cheque cards to the
10 holders of current accounts. Cheques and cheque cards can both be used to make payment (see unit 5)

Money deposited in a **savings account** earns a modest rate of interest. But one has to give notice in advance if one wishes to withdraw larger amounts. Savings accounts cannot be used for remitting money by bank transfer.

15 **Fixed deposit accounts** are used to deposit major sums of money for a fixed period of time. They carry a higher rate of interest than ordinary savings accounts. Interest rates charged or granted by banks usually vary with the key interest rates set by the central bank.

Besides accepting and safeguarding deposits from their customers, banks lend money to private and corporate customers who wish to borrow.

20 Holders of current accounts are usually granted **overdraft credit** facilities, which means that they may overdraw their accounts up to a certain limit which depends on their monthly income. Banks normally charge a high rate of interest for this service. Overdraft credits are suitable for short-term borrowing to smooth out fluctuations between income and expenditure.

Taking out a personal **loan** is recommended for major purchases like a car or furniture, as the in-
25 terest rate charged is much lower than for overdrafts. Loans are repaid either by instalments or in one sum at the end of the credit period. Banks will ask for some sort of security when granting a loan. This may be a regular salary, shares or other assets. If a loan is to be used for buying real estate, like a house, a flat or business premises, the property itself will serve as collateral. Such a loan is commonly called a **mortgage**. When loans are granted to corporate customers the com-
30 pany's creditworthiness plays an important role, the **credit line** (or ceiling) being the limit of credit extended to a corporate customer.

In the UK there are usually no charges for ordinary transactions on current accounts. The interest paid on deposit accounts usually depends both on the period of notice required for withdrawals – normally 30 days, 60 days or 90 days – and the sum deposited. Instant access savings accounts
35 usually carry a lower rate of interest. Some online accounts allow instant access and pay higher rates of interest whatever the deposit.

Naturally there are many services in addition to those offered to private customers that banks can offer to businesses:

Factoring is a service whereby banks agree to buy outstanding invoices at a discount, i.e. less a
40 certain percentage. In this way suppliers do not have to wait a long time for payment.

Banks change money into **foreign currency** required for export or import transactions. As the rates of exchange of most other currencies against the euro tend to fluctuate, foreign trade involves considerable insecurity and risk. Banks help businesses to make provisions against such contingencies by facilitating **forward exchange dealings.** Forward exchange dealing means contracting to buy or sell a foreign currency at a previously agreed price at some fixed date in the future. This form of hedging (see unit 3) makes an exporter or importer to some extent independent of currency fluctuations for this particular period of time.

In foreign trade, **bank guarantees** are frequently required when as terms of payment either "documents against acceptance" or "documents against payment" have been agreed upon (see unit 7).

Moreover, banks provide **information** on companies and markets (see unit 11), open and confirm **letters of credit** (see unit 7) and discount **bills of exchange** (see unit 5).

■ Complete the following text using the appropriate words from the box below.

> **credit line** ✴ **direct debiting** ✴ **factoring** ✴ **overdraw**
> **personal loan** ✴ **savings account**
> **standing order** ✴ **fixed deposit account**

Louisa Hurst has inherited £5,000 from her grandmother. She would like to deposit the money for a year as she intends to set up as a translator by then and will be needing money for data processing equipment. She ought to open a ❶ rather than a ❷ as the latter would yield less interest.

Lately, most of the customers of Randalls Office Services Ltd. have been very slow in paying their bills and Randalls are getting into financial difficulties. The Managing Director discusses the situation with his bank manager. The bank manager tells him that the bank is unable to extend Randalls' ❸ and advises him to avail himself of the bank's ❹ services, instead.

Harriet Morland has just moved into a new flat. She now gives a ❺ to her bank to transfer the rent to her landlady on the 2nd of every month. In her arrangements for paying her telephone bills she makes use of the system of ❻.

Frank Weston loves fast cars. A friend has made him a favourable offer for a used sports car. But Frank's savings are not sufficient to pay for the car. The bank clerk advises Frank to apply for a ❼ rather than ❽ his current account.

E IHK-Prüfungsvorbereitung *

1. Fremdsprachenkorrespondent/in

Geschäftsbrief nach Angaben (Bearbeitungszeit 45 Minuten)

Hilfsmittel: Zweisprachige Wörterbücher

Situation

Sie (eigener Name) machen ein Praktikum bei der ungarischen Firma MAGYARMODA, Ady Endre utca 31, 1014 Budapest, Fax +36 1 267-5657. Diese Firma hatte bei der Firma Sportwelt Fan-Artikel, Wertachring 93, 86153 Augsburg, Fax +49 821 720659, Waren im Werte von € 947,45 bestellt. Die Rechnung vom 31. April 200_, Rechnungs-Nr. MM 004/03, war entsprechend den vereinbarten Zahlungsbedingungen 30 Tage nach Rechnungsdatum fällig. Am 15. Juni und 2. Juli hatte Sportwelt Ihrer Firma je eine Zahlungserinnerung geschickt. Ihr Chef, A. Kovacs, bittet Sie nun für ihn als Antwort ein Fax in Englisch an Sportwelt zu verfassen. Ihre Ansprechpartnerin ist Frau Nadine Gerstenberg aus der Rechnungsabteilung. Heute ist der 15. Juli 200_.

Aufgabe

Bitte verfassen Sie diese Antwort und berücksichtigen Sie dabei folgende Punkte:

- Bezug auf Sachverhalt
- Bedauern
- Schwierige finanzielle Lage: Absatzprobleme bei Bademode, ungewöhnlich kühles und regnerisches Wetter in den letzten Monaten
- Dadurch erhebliche Außenstände
- Verhandlungen über Partnerschaft mit Investor aus Österreich kurz vor dem Abschluss
- Bitte um weiteren Zahlungsaufschub von 30 Tagen
- Entsprechender Schlusssatz

2. Fremdsprachenkorrespondent/in

Mündliche Prüfung - Telefongespräch (Vorbereitungszeit ca. 5 Minuten)

Angaben für den Prüfling

Situation

→ 179

Sie (eigener Name) arbeiten bei dem Hamburger Handelshaus Präsent-Import/Export, das sich auf hochwertige Geschenkartikel spezialisiert hat. Ihre Chefin, Frau Beate Kaiser, ist zu einer Geschäftsreise gestartet. Vorher hat Sie Ihnen noch nebenstehende Rechnung gegeben und folgendes gesagt:

> „Bitte rufen Sie Mr. Elliot für mich an. Seine Nummer ist 0044 (12225) 466451. Die Rechnung ist nun drei Wochen überfällig. Sonst hat er immer pünktlich gezahlt. Fragen Sie ihn, was los ist. Ich kann mir nicht vorstellen, dass mit der Lieferung etwas nicht in Ordnung war. Sie ist pünktlich rausgegangen und – wie Sie wissen – jedes Stück wird vor Versand genau geprüft. Wir haben diesmal besonders aufgepasst, weil es bei seinem Auftrag vom August Grund zur Beanstandung gegeben hat. Sollte Mr. Elliot finanzielle Probleme haben, könnte man ihm vielleicht ein wenig entgegenkommen, er ist ein langjähriger Kunde. Sagen wir mal, einen Aufschub von höchstens drei Wochen gewähren oder zwei bis drei Teilzahlungen innerhalb von vier Wochen akzeptieren. Ich überlasse das Ihnen. Sie werden es schon richtig machen. Jedenfalls verärgern Sie ihn nur nicht. Wenn Sie mit ihm nicht zurechtkommen, muss die Sache halt warten, bis ich zurückkomme."

---

* Weitere Aufgaben (mit Lösungsvorschlägen) im Lehrerhandbuch

Präsent-Import/Export

Fahrenkrönstieg 124
22179 Hamburg
Tel.: 040 6434426, Fax: 040 6434427
E-mail: impex@firmlink.de

Invoice No. UK/374

Mr Walter Elliot
Fine Gifts Ltd
Laura Place
Bath
BA2 6LD
UK

26 November 200_

Order: AD/171 of 19 November 200_

Quantity	Description	Article No	Unit Price (euro)	Total Price (euro)
75 pairs	Art deco silver earrings	78955	29.95	2,246.25
50	Art deco crystal hair clip	76944	19.95	997.50
25	Art deco silver bracelet	79957	24.95	623.75
				3,867.50
	less 10% trade discount			- 386.75
			Amount due	**3,480.75**

Terms of payment: 10 days 2%, 30 days net.

Angaben für den Prüfenden

- You are Walter Elliot (or his wife and business partner Elizabeth), owners of the upmarket mail-order company Fine Gifts Ltd. in Bath.

- Somebody from Präsent-Import/Export in Hamburg rings you. Have the caller spell his/her name.

- Ask the caller to give you particulars about the invoice he/she is talking about (date and number, order no. etc.) while you are trying to access it on your monitor.

- Unlike your August order, this time the consignment has given no cause for complaint.

- You fully realise that the invoice was due on 27 December.

- On 17 December your premises were flooded knee-deep and your computer system broke down completely. The river Avon had burst its banks after three weeks of incessant rain. The caller may have seen the floods in the Bath and Bristol region on TV. You were unable to get hold of a software specialist before Christmas and the New Year. The situation was chaotic. You are only just beginning to cope again and it will take a few more weeks before things get back to normal.

➤

- Could they grant you four weeks' respite?

- You are afraid three weeks will not be enough. You won't have sorted out everything by then. Your firm is somewhat short of cash anyway until the insurance company has compensated you in full.

- Payment by instalments won't help you much. The first instalment could only be paid in three weeks' time at the earliest.

- What if you pay the entire sum in four weeks and pay interest for the fourth week?

- Try to persuade the caller to take a decision as that would help you a lot.

3.

Fremdsprachenkorrespondent/in	
Übersetzung Deutsch/Englisch (Bearbeitungszeit 60 Minuten)	Hilfsmittel: zweisprachige Wörterbücher

In allen größeren Städten gibt es inzwischen Trainer für interkulturelle Kommunikation. Ihre Kunden sind Geschäftsleute, die im Ausland, zumeist in Asien, Fuß fassen wollen. Ein Trainer, der im Fernen Osten gelebt hat, kann seine Kunden darauf vorbereiten, dass Absichtserklärungen in asiatischen Ländern nichts Definitives sind und dass Menschen dort über Stunden Gespräche führen, ohne sich in die Augen zu schauen.

In einer zunehmend vernetzten Welt, in der mehr und mehr Menschen in internationalen Teams arbeiten, wird der Bedarf an interkultureller Kompetenz immer größer. Ein Münchner Raumfahrtunternehmen musste einen Experten für interkulturelle Komunikation zu Hilfe rufen, weil deutsche und französische Ingenieure, die gemeinsam einen Hubschrauber entwickeln sollten, völlig unterschiedlich an die jeweils andere Gruppe herangingen. So kam es, dass die Gruppen monatelang nebeneinander her und nicht miteinander arbeiteten und es kaum privaten Kontakt gab. Erst nach der Analyse und Beratung durch den Experten gestaltete sich die Zusammenarbeit positiv.

Mangelnde interkulturelle Kompetenz ist die Ursache dafür, dass Auslandsaufenthalte für so manchen Mitarbeiter eine Enttäuschung sind. Oft bleiben sie ohne jeden privaten Kontakt zu Einheimischen und beschränken sich auf eigene Clubs und Restaurants.

4. Fremdsprache im Beruf I
Gelenkte Zusammenfassung (in Deutsch) eines englischen Textes

Schwerpunkt: Banken
(Bearbeitungszeit 45 Minuten)

Hilfsmittel:
zweisprachiges Wörterbuch

Situation
Sie sind bei einer Bank für die Betreuung von Kreditkarten-Kunden zuständig und haben im Internet nachstehenden interessanten Artikel gefunden.

Aufgabe
Bitte fassen Sie für Ihre Kollegen den Artikel (ca. 230 Wörter) in Deutsch auf ungefähr ein Drittel der ursprünglichen Länge zusammen. Berücksichtigen Sie dabei folgende Fragen:
- Worin besteht das Haupthindernis für die Ausbreitung des Internet-Handels?
- Wie verfahren die Banken gegenwärtig bei angeblich ungerechtfertigten Forderungen aus Online-Geschäften?
- Welche Lösung plant eine Kreditkarten-Gesellschaft?
- Was sind die Nachteile dieser Lösung?

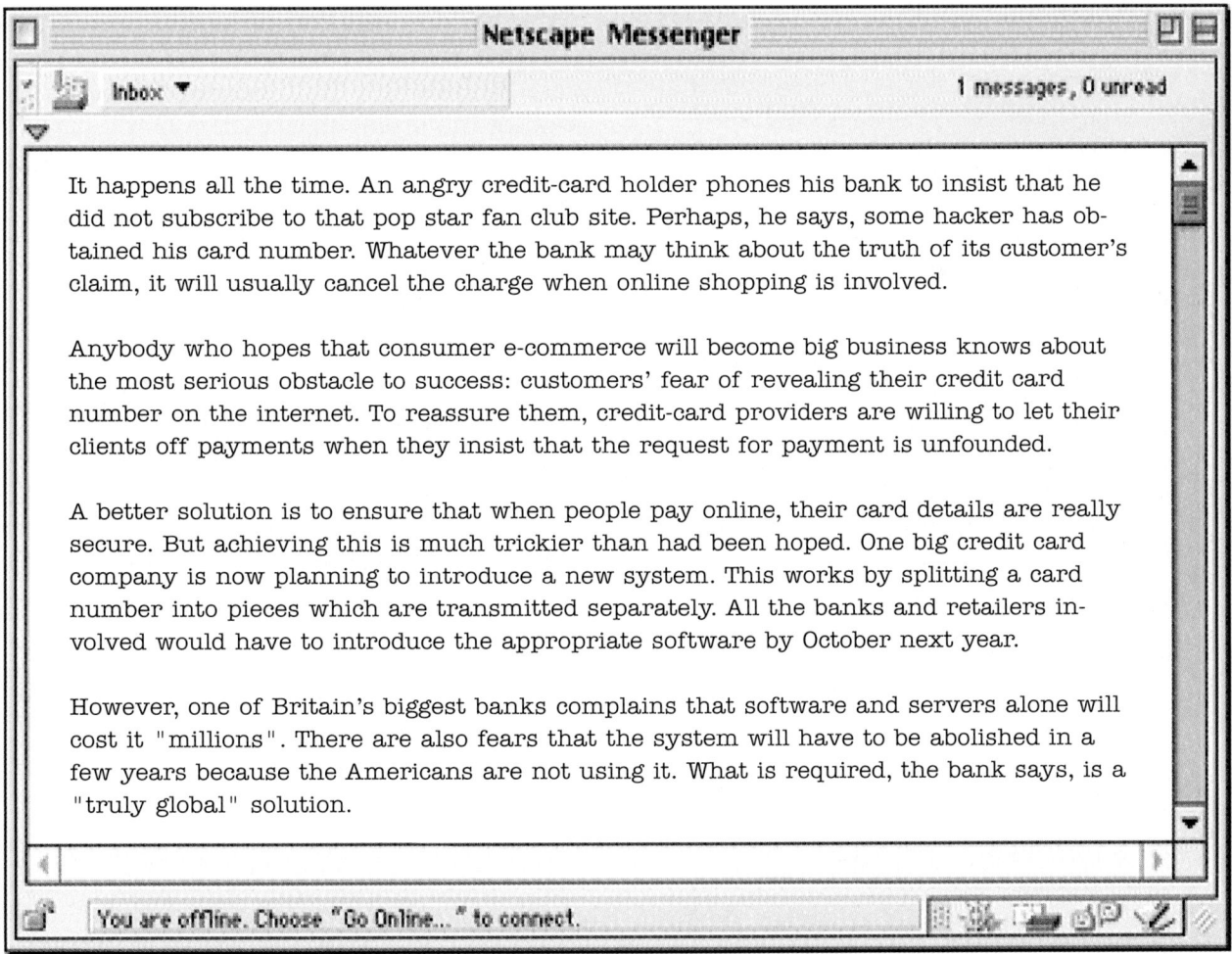

It happens all the time. An angry credit-card holder phones his bank to insist that he did not subscribe to that pop star fan club site. Perhaps, he says, some hacker has obtained his card number. Whatever the bank may think about the truth of its customer's claim, it will usually cancel the charge when online shopping is involved.

Anybody who hopes that consumer e-commerce will become big business knows about the most serious obstacle to success: customers' fear of revealing their credit card number on the internet. To reassure them, credit-card providers are willing to let their clients off payments when they insist that the request for payment is unfounded.

A better solution is to ensure that when people pay online, their card details are really secure. But achieving this is much trickier than had been hoped. One big credit card company is now planning to introduce a new system. This works by splitting a card number into pieces which are transmitted separately. All the banks and retailers involved would have to introduce the appropriate software by October next year.

However, one of Britain's biggest banks complains that software and servers alone will cost it "millions". There are also fears that the system will have to be abolished in a few years because the Americans are not using it. What is required, the bank says, is a "truly global" solution.

Unit 11 Credit enquiries

Introduction

Credit enquiries

Some widely used terms of payment, such as 30 days net, open account, or documents against acceptance, actually grant the customer credit since the goods or services are supplied before payment is effected. That is why suppliers need information about the customer's financial standing and payment record.

Information on a company's creditworthiness can be obtained from

- credit agencies (US credit bureaus) which compile information from data which is publicly available, such as companies' annual reports. The credit agency establishes a company profile and assesses the credit risk. Large companies have online links to one or more credit agencies which provide them with information on prospective customers. Numerous big organisations exchange data on their customers' payment record on a regular basis.
- the customer himself, who fills in a questionnaire sent by the supplier
- trade references, i.e. other firms whom the customer has mentioned as a source of information
- banks, which, however, normally provide information to other banks only
- chambers of commerce
- consulates

Credit enquiries sent to trade references should be marked "(private and) confidential" and it should be emphasised that the company providing the information will not be held responsible for this information and that it will be treated in strict confidence. At the end of the letter requesting information the writer will underline his willingness to reciprocate this service, should the need arise.

Credit information

Giving information about a business partner is not without risks and companies may refuse to provide information. Especially when the information is not wholly positive, there is the danger of an action for libel. That is why even when giving favourable information you should – as a precaution -
- mark the letter as "private and confidential"
- stress that the information is given without any obligation
- request confidential treatment
- use cautious expressions like "we believe", "in our opinion", etc.

If the information you are giving is only lukewarm or is even unfavourable the following additional precautions should be taken:
- refer to the name of the company about which you are giving information indirectly ("the company in question") or type its name on a separate slip of paper.
- avoid mentioning the precise amount of the credit line by referring to it as, say, "the figure mentioned in your letter"
- use even more cautious expressions like "it is said", "as we have heard", "according to reliable sources", "apparently", "they are generally thought to be ...", etc.

When describing a firm's current financial position or the promptness with which it pays its bills, use the continuous form. By using the ordinary form you might imply that what you are saying is generally the case with this firm. "They pay their bills slowly" means they are generally slow to pay their debts, whereas "they are paying their bills slowly" does not imply a general habit but merely a present state of affairs.

■ **Study the above information and discuss with a partner whether the following statements are correct:**

1. Before a businessperson agrees to supply a customer he/she does not know on the basis of 30 days net, he or she ought to make enquiries concerning the prospective customer's creditworthiness.
2. A prospective customer may himself provide credit information by filling in a questionnaire.
3. A trade reference is information on the situation in a particular sector of industry.
4. Letters containing credit information should be marked "private and confidential".
5. When giving credit information you ought to avoid woolly expressions like "I believe", we have heard", etc.

A Activities

A1 Offering references

■ As Gino Giacomelli, the proprietor of Eurosport, intends to purchase official football kits from Sportwelt Fan-Artikel regularly, he applies for an open account with them. **Put these jumbled sentences in the correct order and rewrite the whole letter. Note that there is one inappropriate piece of information!**

1. Yours sincerely,
2. You may also check my credit rating with the following companies in Germany:
3. Badenbike, Draisstr. 342, 76189 Karlsruhe
4. Please let me know your decision regarding my credit status as soon as possible.
5. Sportwelt Fan-Artikel, Wertachring 93, 86153 Augsburg
6. Enclosed is my purchase order no. 42298 for 600 sets of official LFC football kit.
7. I would like to place this order on open account according to your regular terms.
8. I have been in business for more than 10 years, and you may check my credit rating with Ms Giulia Vitelli, branch manager of Banca di Bergamo, Via Garibaldi 50, 78038 Firenze, Italy.
9. Wedler & Co., Steilhang 45, 87527 Sonthofen
10. Dear Ms Springer,

A2 Making credit enquiries

a Having received Gino Giacomelli's application, Sportwelt Fan-Artikel sends a credit enquiry to the branch manager of Banca di Bergamo. **Read this letter and decide which of the words in brackets is correct.**

Sportwelt Fan-Artikel

Wertachring 93
86153 Augsburg
Tel +49 821 720473, Fax +49 821 720659
E-Mail sportwelt@comlink.de

Ms Giulia Vitelli
Branch Manager
Banca di Bergamo
Via Garibaldi 50
78038 (❶ Roma / Genoa / Firenze)
Italy   12 March 200_

Dear Ms Vitelli,
Mr Gino Giacomelli, the (❷ boss / director / proprietor) of Eurosport, 34 Via dei Banchi, Firenze, has placed an order with us for €4,800 worth of merchandise and given your (❸ name / banks / firms) as a credit reference.

We would very much appreciate any information (❹ of / regarding / that) Eurosport's credit rating, especially as to how long Mr Giacomelli has had an account (❺ at / for / with) you and whether or not any of his debts are past (❻ bad / due / increasing).

We will, of course, treat any information we receive in the (❼ strict / strictest / strictly) confidence.

Yours sincerely,

Denise Springer
Export Manager

➡ 203
➡ 206

b Use the letter on page 223 as a model and write a credit enquiry to be sent by Sportwelt Fan-Artikel to Hyflyer plc concerning Badenbike, who wish to be granted a quarterly credit line of €20,000.

A3 Giving credit information

I Favourable information

➡ 223
■ Giulia Vitelli from Banca di Bergamo sent Denise Springer the following reply to her request for credit information. **Choose the appropriate words for the gaps from the box.**

Banca di Bergamo
Via Garibaldi 50 • 78038 Firenze

Ms Denise Springer
Sportwelt Fan-Artikel
Wertachring 93
86153 Augsburg
Germany

20 March 200_

Private and confidential

Dear Ms Springer,

We are pleased to send you, in ❶, the credit ❷ you requested concerning Mr Gino Giacomelli, ❸ of Eurosport.

Mr Giacomelli, who took over Eurosport in 199_, has had a personal giro and savings account with us for more than twelve years. His accounts have always been in order, with adequate ❹ for all cheques drawn.

On the basis of our experience, we ❺ that Mr Giacomelli is ❻ and that you can ❼ accept an order for the ❽ you mention.

This information is given ❾ and without ❿ on our part.

Yours truly,

Giulia Vitelli

Giulia Vitelli
Branch Manager

> cover
> amount
> believe
> confidence
> confidentially
> creditworthy
> information
> proprietor
> responsibility
> safely

224 Unit 11 • Activities

11 Unfavourable information

214 ■ The Scottish firm, McGregor & Stornoway, has placed an order worth £42,000 with Wedler & Co. and has given McDermot Bros., 35 Redwood Crescent, East Kilbride G74 5PR, Scotland, as a reference. Wedler sent a credit enquiry to McDermot Bros., signed by Ms. M. Urban, and received the following reply. **Study the credit information and decide which of the alternatives in brackets is correct.**

McDermot Bros.

35 Redwood Crescent
East Kilbride
G74 5PR
Scotland
Tel.: 1620 89388
e-mail:mcdermot@sportslink.uk

Messrs Wedler & Co.
Steilhang 45
87527 Sonthofen
Germany

29 March 200_

Attn.: Ms M. Urban

Private and confidential

Dear Ms Urban

Credit reference on your prospective customer

In reply to your enquiry of 23 March (**❶** about / according to) a prospective customer in Scotland we should inform you that we are surprised that the firm in question has given our name as a reference. The last time (**❷** we have done /we did) business with this firm was two years ago. Since (**❸** than / then) we have heard that they have incurred heavy losses in connection with their involvement in a ski resort development in the Grampians but we are not sure about these rumours.

Therefore, we would (**❹** suggest that you proceed / suggest to proceed) with caution and initially do business on the basis of cash transactions only.

Please treat this information, which is given without any obligation whatsoever, (**❺** as strictly / as strict) confidential.

Yours sincerely

Fraser Stewart

Fraser Stewart
Chief Accountant

B Tool kit

B1 Structure of business communications: Credit enquiries

Credit enquiries should be structured like this:

Structure	Language to use
1. appropriate salutation	Dear Sirs
2. reference to the company about which information is required	Messrs. Tilney & Partners have given us your name as a reference.
3. reasons for enquiring	As we have had no previous dealings with this firm ...
4. information requested, e.g. • type of company • reputation of its owners • business conduct • financial standing • creditworthiness • credit line suggested • payment record • volume of business done with them • turnover, if appropriate • other relevant information	We would be most grateful if you could give us information on their financial standing and payment record. Above all, we would like to know whether you think it advisable to grant them a monthly credit facility amounting to €20,000. Any other information you are able to supply will be very much appreciated.
5. promise to treat the information confidentially and without obligation for the firm providing it	Any information you provide will, of course, be treated in strict confidence and without any obligation for you.
6. offer to render a similar service	We would be happy to be of assistance to you in a similar matter, should the occasion arise.
7. appropriate complimentary close	Yours faithfully

■ **What is the purpose of these sentences? Find the appropriate numbers in *structure of business communications* above.**

1. It goes without saying that we will at any time be prepared to render you a similar service.
2. We are particularly anxious to know whether they have been paying their bills promptly in the last few months.
3. Do you think that they are good for such an amount?
4. Please also indicate the volume of business you have been doing with them.
5. Your company has been given as a reference by Rosings Biosystems Ltd.
6. You may rest assured that any information you give us will be handled with the utmost discretion and that you will not be held responsible in any way.

B2 Building blocks for business communications: Credit enquiries

1 To refer to the company in question

| We have | been given | your address | by | Messrs. Wentworth & Sons as a reference. |
| | received
obtained | | from | |

| Mrs Palmer has | given us your name as a trade reference.
informed us that you are prepared to provide a reference.
has recommended your credit agency **to** us. |

2 To mention the reason for the enquiry

| As | this firm
this company | is not known to us ...
has never placed an order of that size ... |
| | they are now asking for open account terms ... | |

| Since we have not | done business with them so far ...
had any dealing with them before ... |

3 To ask for information

| We would be | pleased
grateful
obliged | if you could | give us
provide us **with**
supply | information **on** ... |

| | their
the company's
its | solvency.
financial standing.
creditworthiness.
business conduct.
payment record.
general performance. |

| Please | let us know
tell us | if they are solvent.
how promptly they meet their financial obligations. |
| | indicate the volume of your business dealings with them. | |

Do you think it would be	advisable reasonable in order	to grant them	credit amounting **to** ... this credit line? these credit facilities?

Any other	details particulars information	you may be able to supply will be appreciated.

4 To promise confidential treatment

You may be sure We assure you You have our word	that any information given will be	treated **as** strictly confidential handled with the utmost discretion

➡	and	without any obligation for you. that you will not be held responsible for it. with no liability **on** your part.

5 To offer to reciprocate

If we can	do you a similar service be **of** assistance to you in a similar case return the favour	we shall be glad to reciprocate. please let us know. we will be pleased to do so.

■ Use the building blocks to find the equivalents of these German sentences:

1. Sie wurden uns von Rushworth Industries als Referenz benannt.
2. Zu Gegendiensten sind wir stets gern bereit.
3. Da wir mit dieser Firma bisher noch nicht in Geschäftsverbindung standen, möchten wir über sie Erkundigungen einziehen.
4. Wir wären Ihnen dankbar für Auskunft über die finanzielle Lage des Unternehmens sowie über sein Geschäftsgebaren und seine Zahlungsmoral.
5. Welchen Umfang hatten Ihre Geschäfte mit dieser Firma und wie pünktlich wurden Ihre Rechnungen beglichen?
6. Sind Sie der Meinung, dass wir dieser Gesellschaft eine Kreditlinie in dieser Höhe einräumen sollten?
7. Wir versichern Ihnen, dass alle Auskünfte streng vertraulich behandelt werden.
8. Mr. James Allen hat uns wegen einer Referenz an Sie verwiesen.
9. Wir sind besonders daran interessiert zu erfahren, ob Rechnungen pünktlich bezahlt werden.
10. Selbstverständlich werden diese Angaben für Sie vollkommen unverbindlich bleiben.

B3 Structure of business communications: Credit information

Credit information should be structured like this:

Structure	Language to use
1. appropriate salutation	Dear Dr. Grant
2. reference to the company in question	In reply to your letter of 5 May we would like to say that the company in question ...
3. information on the company, e.g. • type of company • reputation of its owners • business conduct • financial standing • credit status • creditworthiness • credit line suggested • payment record • volume of business done with them • turnover, if appropriate • other relevant information	We are pleased to inform you that our dealings with this firm have always been entirely satisfactory. However, the volume of their orders has, so far, never quite reached the sum in question. We have every reason to believe that they are financially sound and good for the amount mentioned in your letter. I'm afraid that, according to reliable sources in the industry, their financial position is not as secure as one could wish.
4. recommendations, if applicable	We would, therefore, advise you to proceed with caution.
5. exclusion of liability	We would like to point out that this opinion is given without any obligation on our part.
6. request for confidential treatment	Please treat this information strictly confidentially.
7. appropriate complimentary close	Yours sincerely

■ What is the purpose of these sentences? Find the appropriate numbers in *structure of business communications* above.

1. We have received your letter dated 29 December and would like to point out that our last business transaction with the company in question was two years ago.
2. The owners enjoy an excellent reputation in local business circles.
3. In our opinion the credit facilities mentioned could safely be granted.
4. They have always paid our bills promptly, normally taking advantage of cash discounts.
5. We have it on good authority that they sometimes tend to commit themselves too heavily.
6. Please note that we cannot be held responsible for this information and that it must remain confidential.

B4 Building blocks for business communications: Credit information

1 To refer to the company in question

The company	mentioned **on** the enclosed slip ... referred **to** in your letter ... in question ...

2 To give favourable information

We believe We are informed There is no doubt	that the company	is financially sound. is in a good financial state. has sufficient capital resources.

The	proprietors owners directors	enjoy an excellent reputation. have a good track record. are respectable and trustworthy business partners of ours.

3 To give non-committal information

We have only been doing business with this firm	**for** a few months **on** a very modest scale **on** cash with order terms	and are **for** this reason not in **a** position to say anything specific.

4 To give unfavourable information

It is said We have heard It is generally known There are reports It seems Our impression is	that this company	is financially insecure. is experiencing financial difficulties. is in a precarious financial position. may not have sufficient resources. is finding it hard to meet its commitments. is more or less insolvent.

According to reliable sources	the firm	is settling its accounts only with delays. has suffered heavy losses. does not seem to have a sound financial basis.
	one of their major customers has gone bankrupt.	

5 To make recommendations

We would, therefore,	recommend **that** you advise you to suggest **that** you	perhaps demand that collateral is provided. do business **on** cash terms only. proceed with caution **in** your dealings with this firm. obtain further information **from** their bankers or a credit agency.

6 To exclude liability and request confidential treatment

Please note that this	opinion information recommendation	is given without any obligation **on** our part.

We would remind you We expressly point out	that this information must be treated confidentially.

We trust that you will Please We would ask you to	treat this information	with the utmost discretion. **as** confidential. in strict confidence.

■ Use these building blocks to find equivalents for the following German sentences.

1. Mit Bezug auf Ihr Schreiben vom 29. Dezember möchten wir Ihnen mitteilen, dass die genannte Firma seit fünf Jahren zu unseren Kunden zählt.

2. Wir bitten Sie, diese Angaben, für die wir keinerlei Verantwortung übernehmen, vertraulich zu behandeln.

3. Da wir erst seit wenigen Monaten mit dieser Firma in Geschäftsverbindung stehen, können wir leider keine fundierte Aussage machen.

4. Es heißt allgemein, dass sich das Unternehmen in einer äußerst schwierigen Lage befindet, nachdem einer seiner wichtigsten Kunden Konkurs angemeldet hat.

5. Wir würden Ihnen daher empfehlen, Sicherheiten zu verlangen, bevor Sie einen Kredit gewähren.

6. Wir sind der Meinung, dass das Unternehmen auf einer soliden finanziellen Basis steht.

C Additional practice

■ Study the building blocks and complete the following sentences.

1. Messrs Bates & Co. have given us your name as ...
2. Please let us know how promptly they ...
3. Any other information will ...
4. We assure you that we will treat this information as ...
5. We are of the opinion that the firm is in a good ...
6. There are rumours that this company may not have ...
7. We would suggest that you do business on cash ...
8. This information is given without any ...
9. According to reliable sources one of their major ...
10. If we can do you a similar ...

D Background information: Distribution channels

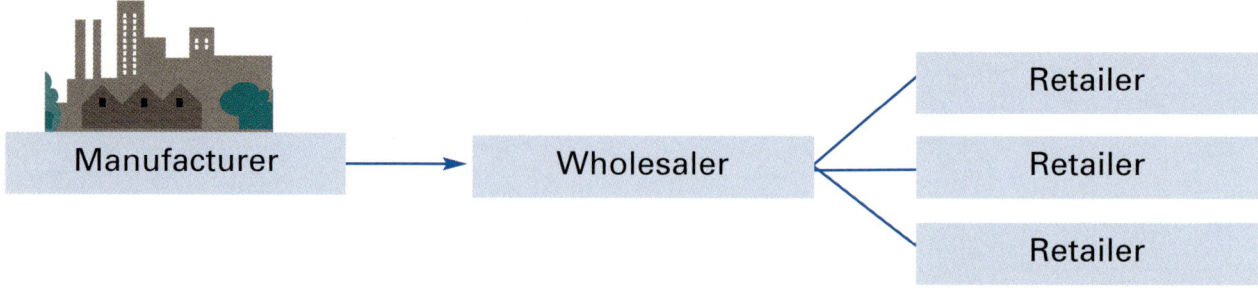

Traditional distribution channels have undergone major changes in recent years resulting from advanced communication technologies and more sophisticated logistics. Players at both ends of the distribution chain, manufacturing industry *and* the retail trade, have become more powerful in the ongoing concentration and globalisation process and are frequently in a position to bypass traditional intermediaries by direct purchasing or direct marketing. This development has been facilitated by electronic commerce, which is blurring the dividing lines between retailers, wholesalers and mail-order houses. This process of eliminating the middleman, who represents a substantial cost factor, is often called disintermediation.

Traditionally, **wholesalers** are the **links between manufacturers and retailers**. They "break bulk", i.e. they buy large quantities from the manufacturers, splitting them up into smaller quantities, sometimes repackaging them, and **distribute** these smaller units to the retailers. For this purpose they often maintain their own sales force and fleet of vehicles. An important function of wholesalers is **warehousing**, i.e. providing suitable storage for goods, for example under refrigeration. Wholesalers may also offer credit facilities to their customers. The wholesale trade is making use of the opportunities offered by modern technology with its own call centres and extranet links, enabling retail customers to place orders 24 hours a day. **Advising** customers on the nature and application of products and services remains one of the principal functions of wholesalers.

Retailers provide a local supply of goods and offer a personal service to the general public. They sell in small quantities and may provide after-sales service where necessary. There is a wide variety of different retail outlets. The number of individual **specialist shops** has been falling over the years with **chain stores** taking their place. Some chains specialise in a particular kind of merchandise, such as clothing, whereas the big grocery supermarkets offer some non-food items as well. **Department stores** sell an even wider range of articles and like modern chain stores try to provide a **one-stop service** for their customers. Generally, they are also operated by large chains. Other low-price retail chains offer a very basic service and range of goods to cut costs. Traditional **corner shops** have all but disappeared and there are fewer and fewer bakeries, greengrocer's or butcher's shops run by individuals. For small last-minute purchases kiosks, filling stations, and 24 hour stores provide a range of essential goods. "Armchair shopping" has a long tradition in the form of **mail-order houses** which accept orders not only by post but also by telephone, e-mail or the internet. **E-commerce** is, however, not restricted to mail-order houses, numerous internet businesses from travel agents to supermarkets – sometimes known as e-tailers - have gone online recently. E-commerce is an area of rapid growth but it is essential that logistics, i.e. the way the goods are delivered, are organised efficiently.

■ **Translate the second paragraph in writing.**

E IHK-Prüfungsvorbereitung

1. Fremdsprachenkorrespondent/in

Geschäftsbrief nach Angaben in Deutsch (Bearbeitungszeit 45 Minuten)	Hilfsmittel: zweisprachige Wörterbücher

Situation

Sie sind Barbara Wittig und arbeiten in der Abteilung Rechnungswesen der Firma Turbotechnologie AG, Erfurt. Ein Kunde aus den USA, Willoughby Corporation, Boston, wird von Ihnen seit zwei Jahren auf der Basis Kasse gegen Dokumente beliefert. Er hat nun um offenes Zahlungsziel mit einer vierteljährlichen Kreditlinie von 50 000 Euro gebeten und die amerikanische Firma Edward Ferrars Inc., 2002 Waterview Route, Parsippany, New Jersey 07054, als Referenz genannt.

Aufgabe

Bitte verfassen Sie die Kreditanfrage an Edward Ferrars Inc. und berücksichtigen Sie dabei folgende Punkte:
- Grund für die Anfrage
- Bitte um Auskunft über
  - Erfahrungen mit der Firma
  - finanzielle Lage
  - Umfang der Geschäftätigkeit
  - Art der Geschäftsführung
  - Zahlungsmoral
  - Ruf der Geschäftsleitung
- Frage nach der Vertretbarkeit der gewünschten Zahlungsbedingungen und Kreditlinie
- Bitte um weitere sachdienliche Informationen
- Zusicherung der Verschwiegenheit
- Angebot von Gegendiensten

2. Fremdsprachenkorrespondent/in

Geschäftsbrief nach Angaben in Deutsch (Bearbeitungszeit 45 Minuten)	Hilfsmittel: zweisprachige Wörterbücher

Situation

Sie sind Fanny Knight und leiten die Abteilung Credit Control der US-amerikanischen Firma Edward Ferrars Inc., Parsippany, New Jersey. Sie haben eine Kreditanfrage der Firma Turbotechnologie AG, Juri-Gagarin-Ring 27, 0361 Erfurt, bezüglich der Willoughby Corporation, Boston, erhalten, die von Barbara Wittig aus der Rechnungsabteilung unterschrieben war.

Aufgabe

Bitte beantworten Sie die Anfrage unter Berücksichtigung folgender Punkte:
- Geschäftsverbindung seit 12 Jahren
- regelmäßig – etwa vier bis fünf mal pro Jahr – Aufträge in Höhe der genannten Kreditlinie
- Zahlungen stets pünktlich
- finanzielle Lage anscheinend stabil
- Firma scheint effizient geführt zu werden, moderne Management-Methoden, aggressives Marketing
- offenbar ausreichendes Schwergewicht auf Forschung und Entwicklung: in regelmäßigen Abständen verbesserte oder neue Produkte
- die vier gegenwärtigen Geschäftsführer genießen ausgezeichneten Ruf
- Firma engagiert sich stark für gemeinnützige Projekte
- Auskunft völlig unverbindlich
- Bitte um vertrauliche Behandlung

Unit 12 Promoting sales

Introduction

There are many different ways of promoting sales and of attracting potential clients or customers. These include the various different forms of advertising. One popular form of advertising is mail shots. Depending on the product, it may be essential to have a mailing list which is both up to date and selective in order to target potential customers and not waste money sending the mail shot to a more or less random group.

In the last couple of years every self-respecting firm has acquired a website. However, it is important to invest in a well-designed website. If it takes too long to find the desired information or it is too complicated the customer will be left feeling frustrated, which is counterproductive. Websites also need updating regularly. Banner advertisements can be placed on a website such as Yahoo or Lycos to draw attention to your website. Again it is important to consider the target group.

In spite of modern means of communication face-to-face contact is still very important in business. Business trips are a feature of many executives' lives. A well-planned itinerary is essential and the objectives of the trip should be defined in advance. The schedule should be flexible enough to allow for unexpected problems (e.g. delayed flights or traffic congestion). If the trip takes in foreign countries it is important to check up on such things as local public holidays, the usual working hours and any major cultural or religious differences.

■ Write a short summary of this text in German.

A Activities

A1 Sales letters

■ First read the sales promotion letter on the next page. Then analyse the letter using the following questions:

1. What is the purpose of direct mail in general? What is the purpose of the letter on the next page?
2. How does the letter try to attract the reader's interest? Does the first line really catch the reader's attention?
3. What information does the letter provide? How does it build up interest in the product?
4. How does the letter stimulate the desire to buy? What benefits are promised?
5. Why is it necessary to stress that weight-lifting is completely safe?
6. How does the letter encourage the customer to buy the goods on offer? Is it easy to buy them?
7. Do you think it is a good idea to combine dumb-bells with a special discount on swimwear? Why or why not?

SPORTS UNLIMITED

76 The Mall   Stratford E15 1XD
Tel 020 8226 3112 Fax 020 8226 3112

Please visit our new web site at
www.sportsul.co.uk

Samantha Broadbent
61 Whiteoak Green
South Woodford
London
E12 7RF

28 February 200_

Dear Ms Broadbent,

What do Claudia Schiffer and Arnold Schwarzenegger have in common?

They both lift weights to keep in shape – with very different results, of course. And many women in Britain are discovering now that weight-lifting is an effective and fun way to better health and a good-looking body for next summer's beach activities.

Sports Unlimited has put together a special package for preferred customers to help you get started. We offer you a pair of dumb-bells and the fully illustrated Guide To Building Your Body, which tells you how to firm up every muscle in your body, from your deltoids to your calves.

Despite the myths about body-building, these exercises will not make a woman look like a man. Does Claudia Schiffer look like Arnold Schwarzenegger? The exercises are completely safe, and according to the latest Family Doctors' Association report, "…weight-lifting strengthens the cardiovascular system and shows results faster than any other form of exercise."

Our Get-Ready-for-the-Beach package includes two dumb-bells and the complete Guide To Building Your Body at the low low price of £19.95, and additionally entitles you to a 20 per cent discount on up to three pieces of swimwear that you purchase before 31 May.

Please note that this exceptional offer expires on 31 March. Store hours are 10am – 9pm, so you can shop at your convenience. And, of course, SAVVY, EXAM and BUSTER cards are always welcome.

Yours sincerely,

Trish Dewar

Trish Dewar
Store Manager

A2 Websites

a   With the popularity of the World Wide Web, most companies have their own websites. **Study the design of this home page and discuss it in class.**

b   **Now listen to the conversation between Toni Harding, the proprietor of Kaozsports, and Kate Paxton.**

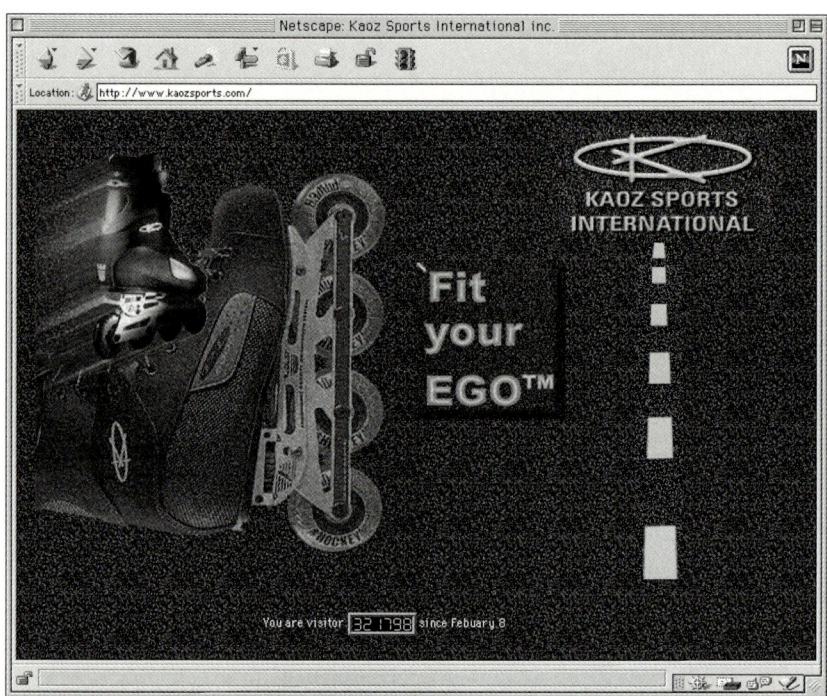

Take notes on these items:
- reasons for publishing via the Internet
- what is included in the electronic catalogue
- costs of transferring the catalogue to the Web
- annual costs of maintaining the website
- annual budget for security

c   **Then write a memo in German for Frau Springer from Sportwelt Fan-Artikel, Augsburg.**

d   As Sports Unlimited's web presence has not been very successful, Kate Paxton decides to gather independent information in order to rebuild the company's website. Read these excerpts from an article entitled "Things to consider When Doing Business on the Internet". **Work in groups of four. Two of you translate paragraph one of the article, the other two do paragraph two. Then compare your translations in the group.**

Build or lease?
Depending on the company's current technology applications, hardware resources and the skills level of its personnel, it may be more cost-effective to place the development and maintenance responsibilities with an outside agency. However, those who do so may find that they give up some control as well. Fees for consultants and service providers vary widely, and companies may be better off in the long run if they build their own site, using in-house personnel who can combine technical skills with an understanding of the company's needs.

Personnel costs
Labour costs account for 42% of the overall price of running a network, and that percentage is increasing. Network managers are in demand, with salaries ranging from £50,000 to £100,000 per year, depending on experience. The most sought-after candidates combine technical knowledge with excellent communication skills, and the flexibility to adapt to rapidly changing technologies. However, software manufacturers are promising tools to take over some of the work traditionally done by people.

Security costs
Companies should factor in security when they consider the cost of business on the Web. Security procedures must be monitored and upgraded. Policies must cover password access and updating, and systems prioritization. High personnel costs are involved in maintenance and end-user education. Security costs can vary dramatically depending on the size and focus of the company. While small companies may rely on routers to provide simple security through TCP/IP packet filtering, larger companies with many systems to protect will need to add a software-based application firewall.

Future costs
Relatively low start-up costs deceive many executives, who do not recognize the likelihood that they will need to add bandwidth to move information in and out of the server and over the Internet. A popular site requires a faster connection, and the site needs to be maintained, involving increased personnel costs. Improvements in service, capabilities, and multimedia applications are expected to continue, and it is difficult to predict what impact they will have on future costs.

A3 Agencies and Co-operation

1 Enquiry about co-operation

■ Wedler & Co, Sonthofen, Tel +49 8321 38790, manufacturers of winter sports equipment, are considering appointing an agent to handle their sales in the UK. The managing director, Toni Schäfer, E-mail: toni.schaefer@wedler.de, has been browsing the Internet trying to find an organisation he might approach for help. The Anglo-German Chamber of Commerce, London, Tel. +44 20 7929 0103, e-mail: jane.perrot@anglogermanchamber.com, seems likely to be able to assist him in his search for a suitable partner. **Study his e-mail and decide which of the alternatives in brackets is correct.**

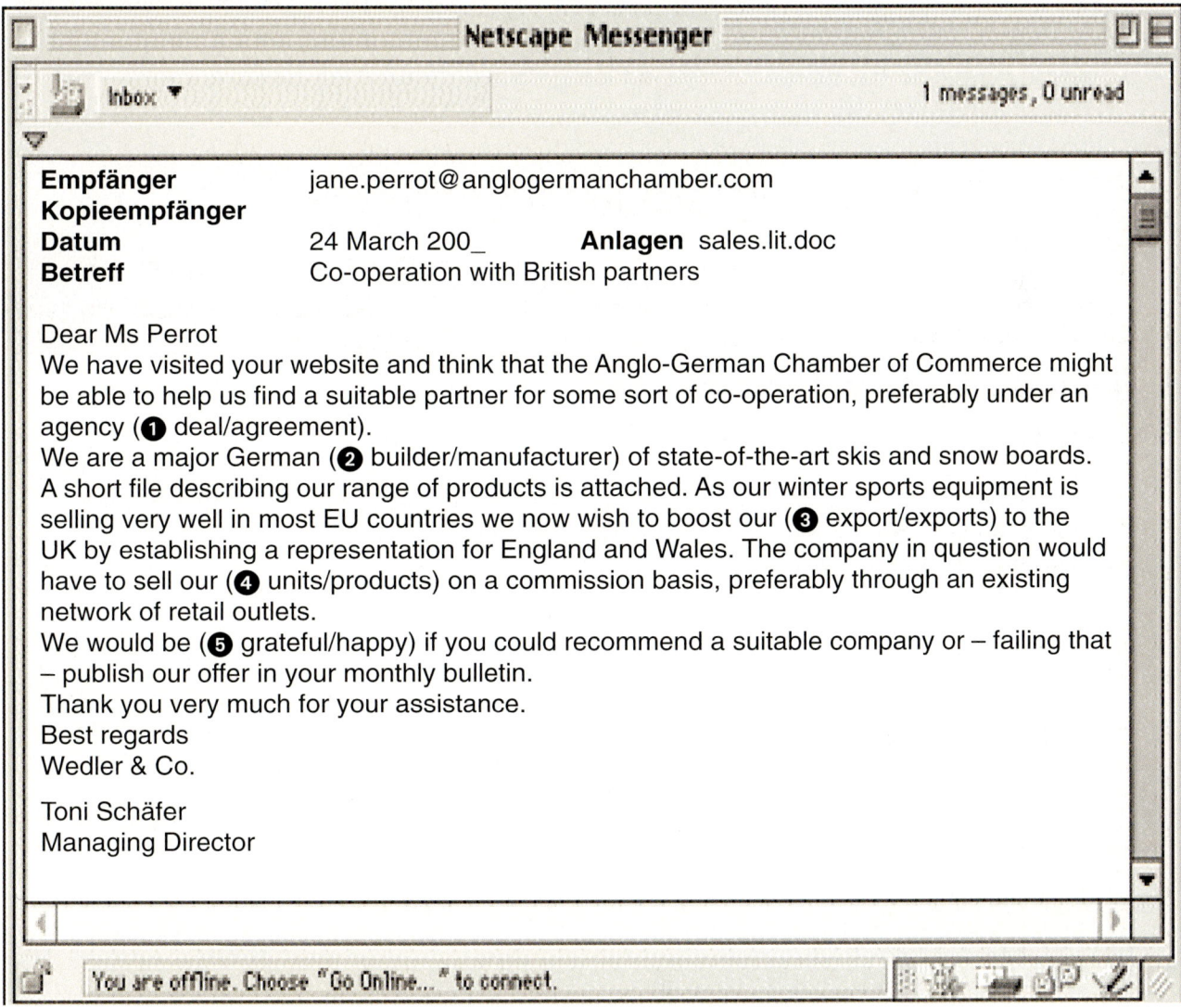

Empfänger	jane.perrot@anglogermanchamber.com
Kopieempfänger	
Datum	24 March 200_ **Anlagen** sales.lit.doc
Betreff	Co-operation with British partners

Dear Ms Perrot
We have visited your website and think that the Anglo-German Chamber of Commerce might be able to help us find a suitable partner for some sort of co-operation, preferably under an agency (❶ deal/agreement).
We are a major German (❷ builder/manufacturer) of state-of-the-art skis and snow boards. A short file describing our range of products is attached. As our winter sports equipment is selling very well in most EU countries we now wish to boost our (❸ export/exports) to the UK by establishing a representation for England and Wales. The company in question would have to sell our (❹ units/products) on a commission basis, preferably through an existing network of retail outlets.
We would be (❺ grateful/happy) if you could recommend a suitable company or – failing that – publish our offer in your monthly bulletin.
Thank you very much for your assistance.
Best regards
Wedler & Co.

Toni Schäfer
Managing Director

11 Offer to act as agent

→ 135
→ 136

a Sports Unlimited has been importing OSPEE swimwear for some time, and now they are interested in becoming the U.K. agent for OSPEE. **Read this excerpt and give the correct forms of the verbs in brackets.**

> Dear Mr Kim,
>
> Since we (**1** start) importing your products almost two years ago, interest in them has been increasing tremendously. As you know, we (**2** have) well-established business partners in all major cities of the U.K. and Eire, (**3** specialize) in top-quality brands, who (**4** enquire repeatedly) about the availability of your products.
> We are confident that there is a huge market potential throughout the United Kingdom, which we (**5** can exploit) to our mutual benefit. Therefore, we (**6** like to act) as the U.K. agents for your entire product line and suggest the following terms:
>
> - Our agency agreement is to start on 1 July 200_ and is to run for an initial period of two years.
> - Trading (**7** will do) on open account terms, with monthly statements payable within 30 days.
> - The goods (**8** will store) in our warehouses at our risk and expense.
>
> To cover our expenses, we suggest a 20 per cent commission on the invoice value DDP Stratford, and we (**9** appreciate) your support of our initial marketing efforts.
> You (**10** check) our credit standing with the following:
>
> > Mr Geoffrey Greenaway, Manager of Claybar's Bank International Services Branch, 134 Brooke Street, London W3 8DE, United Kingdom
> > Mr Taro Ichimura, Overseas Sales Manager of ISACS International, 5–39–18 Nishi-Shinjuku, Shinjuku-ku, 139 Tokyo, Japan
>
> We (**11** look forward) to hearing from you soon.
>
> Yours sincerely,

b Fax a credit enquiry to Mr Geoffrey Greenaway, Manager of Claybar's Bank International Services Branch, referring to Sports Unlimited's proposal.

Some time later, Kate Paxton receives this fax from South Korea.

> Thank you very much for your letter, in which you suggest acting as our general agent.
>
> We would indeed be very interested in expanding our business in the United Kingdom, and therefore I am planning to be in London from May 12 to 15. During this time we could work out all the necessary arrangements for a mutually beneficial agency agreement.
>
> I look forward to hearing from you soon.

III Agency agreement

a Work in groups of four. First revise the tips and phrases for successful negotiations in unit 5 page 88, then split into two sub-groups. Subgroup A studies the suggestions made by Sports Unlimited on page 238, sub-group B uses the notes on the right written down by Ospee's export manager. Then negotiate the terms of an agency agreement between Sports Unlimited and OSPEE. Remember: both sides are eager to reach an agreement, so be prepared to compromise!

- reply from Doyles Bank favourable
- great opportunity to expand business in U.K.
- open account okay, but only 10 days
- but: commission too high, suggest 10% on FOB Pusan
- appoint for a trial period of one year
- support: 25% of actual advertising expenditure

b Now use the terms you have negotiated to rewrite this agency agreement form.

1. **OSPEE SPORTSWEAR INTERNATIONAL**, 134 Imun-Dong, Dong Dae Mon-Ku, 123 Seoul, South Korea (hereinafter called the Principal) appoints **Sports Unlimited**, 76 The Mall, Stratford, E15 1XD, United Kingdom (hereinafter called the Agent) to be its sole agent in the United Kingdom and the Republic of Ireland for the period of …

2. During this term, the Agent shall endeavour to expand the sales of OSPEE branded products all over the area defined by the boundaries of the United Kingdom and the Republic of Ireland. The cost of an initial advertising campaign will …

3. All transactions shall be carried out on open account, and the Agent will receive monthly statements of account payable … days after the date of invoice. Consignments are to be stored at the Agent's risk and expense, and the goods remain our unrestricted property until they have been paid for in full at the prices invoiced.

4. The Principal will allow the Agent a commission of … per cent on the amount of invoice … The said commission is to be paid at the end of …

5. The above agreement expires on … unless extended for a longer period.

IV Communication between principal and agent

■ Read this agent's report by Sports Unlimited to the principal, Ospee Sportswear International. Imagine you are your company's agent in some foreign country and write a similar report on your company's products or services.

Dear Mr Kim,
I am pleased to report that overall sales in the first quarter of 200_ at GBP 259,000 were up by 11.3% compared with the final quarter of 200_. We have now established a network of regular customers including both specialist shops and department stores throughout England and Wales. At the same time private consumption is still very buoyant in the UK.

However, the performance of the Splashback two-piece model (23 8013/14/15) was disappointing. Sales actually fell by 15%. A number of our customers suggested that it was no longer really in keeping with the latest fashion trends. It clearly needs updating. The market for sportswear in Britain is as you know intensely competitive. We need to have the edge over our competitors both in price and in fashion. We suggest that you buy in professional know-how to anticipate trends, which we could arrange if you wish.

The Olympia one-piece model and the Aquablade striped model both sold very well and more than offset the drop in sales of the Splashback model.

I am pleased to say that we shall be passing on a number of large orders in the next two weeks as customers cover their requirements for the summer.

A4 Fairs and exhibitions

I Enquiry directed to fair organisers

a Hyflyer plc is planning to launch its products on the Hungarian Market by exhibiting its mountain bikes at the HUNGAROSPORT fair in Budapest. **Study Rob Sullivan's fax to the organisation committee and choose the correct prepositions.**

Telefax Message

Dear Sirs

From what I gather **(from/of)** the information provided in "The Bicycle World" next year's HUNGAROSPORT fair might be a promising venue **(to/for)** displaying our products in your country. We are a medium-sized British manufacturer of quality bicycles and are thinking **(at/of)** a stand of about 10 x 15 metres with an adjoining room for hospitality and discussions.

We require the usual facilities (electricity, water, telephone, fax and ISDN lines) and would appreciate being allocated space **(near/on)** the entrance to the main hall.

Please send us your full documentation **(on/over)** the fair, complete with application forms, prices, deadlines, list of stand-building firms and any other information that might be helpful.

Best regards

Hyflyer plc
Rob Sullivan

b Amanda Jones from Leisurecorp, Limavady, is planning to visit the ITB tourism fair in Berlin. Amongst all the information provided on the internet she finds the following application form.
Study the form and – with the help of your dictionary – make sure you understand every word.

Application Deadline: September 1, 2000			
Invoicing Address		Phone	Fax
Street		Town and postal code	
Country		Main Domicile	
Mailing Address for Invoice		Phone	Fax
Street		Town and postal code	
Country			
Person to contact		Phone	
E-Mail		Internet	
Required area:	Front: ___ m Depth: ___ m Total: ___ m²	Space rental:	Row-stand per sq.m. EUR 133.– Corner-stand 15% surcharge Peninsula-stand 40% surcharge Island-stand 65% surcharge
Stand open to 2 3 4 sides		AUMA-fee EUR 0.55/sq.m. + V.A.T.	
We will be building a two-storey stand		Yes	No
We have read and acknowledge the Conditions of Participation and the General Terms of Business for Trade Fairs and Exhibitions of Messe Berlin (see appendix).			
Place and date		Signature	
For non-registered firms, name of proprietor		Please, type signatory's name or write in block capitals	

11 Conversations at fairs

- Relating to other people and networking are most important in business. **First, listen to the conversation at the ITB tourism fair in Berlin. Then work with a partner and create dialogues for the following situations.**

1. At the CeBIT computer fair in Hanover: Partner A is a software developer. Partner B is a prospective customer looking for a solution to his e-commerce software problems.
2. At the BOOT fair in Düsseldorf: Partner A is working on the stand of a large surfboard-maker displaying the latest models. Partner B is a wholesaler interested in the new products.
3. At your industry's most important trade fair in Germany: Partner A represents his own firm. Partner B is a prospective customer interested in partner A's products or services.

A5 Personal assistants' communications

I Travel arrangements

a Although the Internet makes international contacts much easier, there is nothing like a face-to-face meeting with business partners. To connect with business partners, Amanda Jones from Leisure Corp is preparing to attend the Tourism Fair. **Complete this reservation fax to Hotel Europa.**

❶ reserve a single room with ❷ for Ms Amanda Jones, staying for ❸ nights from 29 April and departing ❹ morning of 3 May.

Ms Jones ❺ be on flight BA 836 arriving at 5:45 p.m. on 29 April. ❻ you arrange for airport pickup service?

❼ forward to receiving your confirmation, with details of cost, by ❽ ❾

b **Read this reply to Amanda Jones' reservation and choose the correct form of the verb.**

This fax is in confirmation of your reservation for a single room with bath for 29 April – 3 May. The room (❶ to be) available to Ms Jones after 2 p.m. on 29 April.

Our rate is EURO 129.00 per night, VAT included.

As Ms Jones (❷ to be) arriving by plane, we invite her (❸ to take) advantage of the Hotel Europa Shuttle. Our limousine (❹ to depart) from Terminal A every hour on the half hour, and the service (❺ to be) free for guests of the hotel.

Yours sincerely

II Invitations

- Computer Clinic will have been in business for 20 years next month. Will Duncan has asked his secretary to draft an invitation to a reception and dinner to mark the occasion. **Complete the text using the appropriate words from the box.**

> attend ❈ exactly ❈ guests ❈ pleasure ❈ some ❈ time

Dear Mr/Ms ...

20 years is a long ❶ in the EDP business. Computer Clinic has now been offering sophisticated networking solutions successfully for ❷ 20 years. We at Computer Clinic think that this calls for ❸ sort of celebration.

We, therefore, take ❹ in inviting you to a reception and dinner at the Pembroke Arms Hotel in Pembroke on 15 April 200_ , starting at 6 p.m. The Welsh Country Singers, under the direction of William Evans, will be entertaining our ❺

Accommodation will be arranged for you at the Pembroke Arms Hotel.

We very much hope that you will be able to ❻ our party. We look forward to receiving your confirmation on the enclosed fax reply slip.

Yours sincerely
Computer Clinic

Will Duncan

Encl. Fax reply slip

III Congratulations

- Kate Paxton from Sports Unlimited has just received the award "British Businesswoman of the Year", which is awarded annually by the business magazine "The Industrialist". Kim Chong Il from OSPEE SPORTSWEAR INTERNATIONAL in Seoul, South Korea, sends his congratulations. **Study his letter and express your opinion on the style of the letter.**

➡ 238

OSPEE SPORTSWEAR INTERNATIONAL
Kim Chong Il, Chief Executive

134 Imun-Dong, Dong Dae Mon-Ku
123 Seoul, South Korea

30 Dec 200_

Dear Ms Paxton

Having just read the latest issue of "The Industrialist" I wish to congratulate you most sincerely on your having received the award "British Businesswoman of the Year". The honour could not have been bestowed on a more deserving person. As a business partner of yours of long standing I am particularly aware of your merits both as a successful businesswoman and as a warm-hearted and friendly person.

With best wishes and kindest regards
Yours sincerely

Kim Chong Il

B Tool kit

B1 Structure of business communications: Agency agreements

Agency agreements should include the following:

Structure	Language to use
1. Names of principal and agent and type of agency	Messrs Denny & Co. of Gloucester are herewith appointed sole agents of Virtual Toys Ltd.
2. Subject matter and exclusion of competitive products	It is to be understood that Denny & Co. will sell our virtual toys and refrain from selling any competitive products.
3. Territory covered by agency	The territory covered is to be confined to England and Wales.
4. Commission and del credere commission, if applicable	We agree to a commission of 5 per cent for Denny & Co if regular list prices are realized. For standing surety Denny & Co. will be granted 2 per cent del credere commission.
5. Method and terms of payment for customers	All goods are invoiced by Virtual Toys Ltd. direct to the consignees. In principle, customers must open irrevocable letters of credit.
6. Sales support (advertising, showrooms etc.)	Virtual Toys Ltd. will supply advertising material free of charge. Denny & Co. will provide showrooms.
7. Consignment goods and/or after-sales service, if applicable	Virtual Toys Ltd. will keep a permanent consignment stock in Gloucester. The goods will remain Virtual Toys Ltd.'s unrestricted property until they have been fully paid for.
8. Commencement and expiry dates	The above agreement commences on 1 January 200_ and expires at the end of 200_, unless extended for a longer period.
9. Date and signatures	13 November 2000_ For Denny & Co. For Virtual Toys Ltd.

B2 Building blocks for business communications: Agencies

1 To apply for an agency

I have learned **from**	the Anglo-German Chamber of Commerce Mrs Harville of Harville & Partners your advertisement in *The Industrialist*

that you are looking for	an agent for your products		in	Scotland the North of Bavaria Romania and Bulgaria
	someone	to represent your interests to market your services		

and I would like to	inform you that I would be prepared to assume the sole agency. offer my services. say that I am interested in distributing your products as your agent.

2 To offer an agency

We are interested in	setting up an agency in your part of the country. finding a dynamic person to handle our sales in the Channel Islands. appointing a sole agent for our products.

3 To introduce yourself, your firm, your products or your services

I	have got excellent connections in our industry. have been working successfully in this line for 15 years. have always achieved excellent sales figures.

Our company has	spacious premises including a large showroom. an extensive network of sales outlets all over the country. a highly motivated sales force.

We are	well-known Germany's leading one of the major	suppliers of accessories **for** the car industry. manufacturers of kitchen utensils. providers of e-commerce services.

Our	sound systems will satisfy your most discerning customers. products are unsurpassed both **in** quality and price. financial services are sure to find a ready market **among** professionals **on** high incomes.

4 To appoint an agent

We are pleased to We herewith	appoint you sole agent entrust you **with** the sole agency	for the whole of Italy.

5 To report to the principal

We are enclosing our	report for the 2nd quarter. account sales for January. sales figures for articles NZ12 and 14.

May I point out that	the figures have never been better in the last 5 years. sales have increased almost 200%. this increase is the result of our good after-sales service.

| The decline in sales is due to | fierce competition **from** Malaysia and Taiwan. | |
| | the fact that | your prices are 20% above those of our competitors.
we had to recall 1000 scooters because they were not safe. |

The economic situation here	has unfortunately been deteriorating **over** the last few months. is now improving slowly. is still somewhat unsettled.

6 To ask the principal for support

I am afraid	sales will remain sluggish unless you cut your prices **by** at least 5%. I must ask you for another Euro 20,000 to finance the advertising campaign. this extremely valuable customer will have to be granted 25% discount.

In view of my	outstanding results excellent sales record lead over the competitors	I think it would be only fair to raise my commission **to** 12%.

7 To inform or instruct the agent

The new	prices will apply **as from** July 1st. improved version will not be introduced **before** March. advertising budget will have to be spread **over** 13 months.

Please bear in mind that	you must not handle systems of a competitive type. we require an accurate database of our customers at all times. your service engineers must be available day and night.

Tool kit · Unit 12   245

8 To modify or cancel the agency agreement

We are prepared to	increase your commission **by** 2.5%. extend your territory to include the state of Saxony as well. prolong the agreement **for** another two years.

We think it best	to terminate the agreement **as of** 1st September to grant you a del credere commission of 2%. to increase your advertising allowance **to** Euro 150,000 per year.

| We hereby give due notice of the termination of the agency agreement with effect **from** 1 January 200_. ||

■ Use these building blocks to find equivalents for the following German sentences.

1. Wir suchen eine zuverlässige Firma, die in der Lage ist, unsere Produkte auf dem deutschen Markt zu vertreiben.
2. Wir wären an der Übernahme der Vertretung interessiert, da wir über ein dichtes Vertriebsnetz und gut ausgebildete Mitarbeiter verfügen.
3. Wir ernennen Sie hiermit zu unserem Alleinvertreter für das Gebiet der Republik Irland.
4. Bitte senden Sie uns unverzüglich Ihre Verkaufsabrechnung für das vierte Quartal.
5. Der Rückgang der Absatzzahlen ist auf die unsichere politische Lage in unserem Land und die damit verbundene Rezession zurückzuführen.
6. Die für das Frühjahr geplante Werbekampagne kann nur durchgeführt werden, wenn Sie unser Werbebudget für das kommende Jahr um ein Drittel erhöhen.
7. Angesichts des geringen Umsatzes halten wir es für das Beste, den Vertretungsvertrag nicht zu verlängern.

B3 Building blocks: Fairs and exhibitions

1 To ask the organisers for information

We are interested in	introducing our software solutions displaying our latest innovations exhibiting our products	at	this year's PC Fair the Melbourne Fair the Motor Show in Detroit

	and would ask you to send us	your information package with application forms. information **on** your rates and deadlines. names and addresses of stand-constructors.

2 To book space or a stand

Our company wishes	to book a stand in the main exhibition hall. to reserve floor space for a stand covering 8x15 metres. to rent an outdoor area of about 250 square metres.

3 To organise the necessary equipment

| Our stand must be equipped with | a hot and cold water supply.
telephone and ISDN lines.
220 Volt sockets. |

| Competent interpreters (English/German)
First-class catering services
4 small tables and 16 upholstered chairs | will also be required. |

4 To have a stand built and dismantled

| Are you in a position to | build a stand for us according to the enclosed specifications?
design an eye-catching stand for us and erect it before May 15th?
help us remove the heavy exhibits and dismantle the stand? |

Use these building blocks to find equivalents for the following German sentences.

1. Da wir unsere Produkte auch dieses Jahr auf der Industriemesse in Shanghai ausstellen möchten, bitten wir Sie um Zusendung der Anmeldeformulare, Tarife und Bedingungen.
2. Unser Stand soll sich im Zentrum von Halle 8 befinden und mit Internetanschluss ausgestattet sein.
3. Könnten Sie uns zwei vorzügliche Dolmetscherinnen und ein zuverlässiges Verpflegungsunternehmen empfehlen?

B4 Building blocks: Secretarial communication

1 To enquire about, reserve, book or cancel hotel and conference rooms

| Please reserve for us
We require
We would like to book | a single room
a double room | with | for non-smokers
bath
shower and WC
en suite facilities |
| | an executive suite
a self-catering flat | | on a different floor
facing the sea
and parking facilities for 2 cars |

| | for | one of our senior executives
Mr Cole, our service engineer,
a group of representatives | for | three nights **from** 3 **to** 6 March.
the duration of the trade fair.
a period of at least 6 weeks. |

Tool kit · Unit 12 247

For	our annual general meeting a meeting of our distributors a project conference	we need	an assembly hall of at least 500 square metres a conference room seating about 50 persons a quiet meeting room
	equipped with		VCR, flip chart, overhead projector. all the usual facilities. a stage and a big screen.

Coffee, tea and soft drinks will be required at all times during the meeting.
A buffet lunch would be appreciated.
Lunch will have to be served at 12:30.

We regret having to	change cancel	the reservation the booking	at such short notice. because Mrs Osborne is unable to get a flight for that date. due to circumstances beyond our control.

2 To book flights and reserve train tickets

You are booked **on** flight no. LH 348, leaving Heathrow **at** 17:15, arriving (**at** the airport) **in** Cologne **at** 20:10 **on** 23 March.

Please reserve two seats for us	**by** the window **next to** the aisle **adjacent to** each other	in the	smoking non-smoking	section of a first class carriage.

3 To write invitations

The chairman	will be pleased to welcome you **at** invites you to attend	our annual dinner **at** the Park Hotel. a conference **on** the prospects of e-commerce.
	is looking forward to meeting you for an informal discussion **in** the VIP lounge.	

The	meeting reception presentation	will be held will take place	**at** the King George Hotel **at** the Conference Centre **in** our main hall	**on** Wednesday, June 7th. **from** 7 pm **to** 9 pm. **between** 10 am **and** 3 pm.

4 To express congratulations

I would like to congratulate you **on**	your company's 25th anniversary. the occasion of your 60th birthday. your appointment **to** your company's executive board.
Dot.Com. Ltd wishes all its loyal customers a Merry Christmas and a prosperous New Year.	

■ Use the building blocks on the previous pages to find the equivalents for the following German sentences.

1. Ich benötige ein ruhiges Einzelzimmer mit Bad sowie einen Parkplatz in der Hotelgarage vom 27. bis 31. Juli.
2. Der Konferenzraum muss mit Videorekorder und Overheadprojektor ausgestattet sein.
3. Da für den 27. August alle Flüge ausgebucht waren, müssen wir die Reservierung des Einzelzimmers für Frau Stellfeld leider ändern. Sie wird erst am 28. anreisen und, wie vorgesehen, am 30. abreisen.
4. Wir geben uns die Ehre, Sie zu unserem Neujahrsempfang am 9. Januar um 18 Uhr im Hotel Superior einzuladen.
5. Der Vorstand spricht Ihnen seine besten Glückwünsche zu Ihrer Beförderung aus.

B5 Useful phrases for welcoming a visitor

Good morning. Can I help you?

I'm afraid Herr Seydlitz hasn't got here yet. He's probably been held up by the traffic.

I'm expecting him to arrive at any moment.

Herr Seydlitz is sorry to keep you waiting.

He'll be here in about five minutes.

I've been trying to contact Herr Seydlitz on his mobile.

Would you just take a seat. I'll tell Herr Seydlitz you've arrived.

Herr Seydlitz will be down in a moment.

I'm afraid Herr Seydlitz is not at his desk. I shall have to ring round to find out where he is. It shouldn't take more than a moment.

Herr Seydlitz is expecting you. He'll be down in a moment.

The weather is ghastly, isn't it?

This is the first warm spring day we've had.

Have you got a heat wave like this in England?

What's the weather like in South Africa at this time of the year?

Can I get you anything? Would you like some tea or coffee?

I hope you had a pleasant journey/flight.

Is this your first visit to Berlin?

I hope that your hotel is comfortable.

It is very convenient for the city centre.

Perhaps you would prefer to wait in the visitors' lounge until Herr Seydlitz gets here. Would you like the Financial Times?

Would you just come this way, please.

I'll let you know the minute Herr Seydlitz gets here.

Is there anything else I could get you?

C Additional practice

a Choose the correct form of the verb.

1. (① to have) read in our local Trade Promotion Board's bulletin that you (② to look) for an agent to distribute your dust separation systems in Northern Ireland, I wish to express my interest in (③ to represent) your company.

2. My company (④ to do) business in the field of sports equipment for 20 years now and we (⑤ to have) 15 distribution centres spread all over Germany.

3. There is no doubt ELITE writing utensils (⑥ to find) a ready market in the Republic of South Africa, too.

4. Account sales for the quarter ending 30 June (⑦ to be enclosed) and you (⑧ to see) that we (⑨ to be able) to sell at list prices in every transaction.

5. If you wish to retain your market share, you (⑩ to have to adjust) your prices accordingly.

b Find the correct preposition.

1. We herewith entrust you ① the sole agency ② our visual aid systems.

2. As a result ③ the strong competition ④ Mexico we are finding it very difficult to maintain last year's level.

3. The new price will be valid ⑤ January 1st.

4. We are pleased to inform you that the board has decided to raise your commission ⑥ 1.5%.

5. As we intend to display our latest developments ⑦ the Microtechnology Fair, we would ask you ⑧ your assistance ⑨ the preparations.

6. Please be so kind as to book ⑩ Mrs Russel a single room ⑪ en suite facilities ⑫ 4 nights ⑬ 9 December ⑭ 13 December 200_.

7. Mr Benwick will be arriving ⑮ Gatwick ⑯ Tuesday ⑰ 11:15 ⑱ flight no. BA 341.

8. Please also reserve ⑲ us a single room ⑳ non-smokers ● a different floor.

9. I would prefer a seat ● the window ● the non-smoking section.

10. We would like to congratulate you ● your appointment ● your company's board.

c Mr Leigh from Cumbria Steel plc, Cumbria House, Dryslwyn Carmarthen, Dyfed SA32 7BY, tel. extension: 01558 769 323, e-mail: r.leigh@cumbria.aol.uk, is planning to fly to Düsseldorf for a meeting with Herr Rolf Lemmen from EISEN-STAHL EXPORT GMBH, Michel-Müller-str. 125, 40235 Düsseldorf, E-mail: rolf.lemmen@eisenstahl.com. **Study the timetable, the ticket and Mr Leigh's notes and write the e-mail.**

LONDON
LHR Heathrow H
LCY London City Y

→ **Düsseldorf** *DUS*   + *02:00*
  0815H – 1030   4627   320   0
  1440H – 1700   4577   737   0
  1905H – 2120   4521   320   0
  2005H – 2225   4509   737   0

| LONDON/LHR | LH | 4627 | K | 02AUG | 08:15 | OK | MHAP3M | 02AUG | 02AUG | 20K |
| DUESSELDORF | LH | 1933 | K | 02AUG | 18:10 | OK | MHAP3M | 02AUG | 02AUG | 20K |

Please send Herr Lemmen an e-mail with these details and dates and ask him not to bother to pick me up at the airport, I'll take a taxi.

 d Listen to the dialogues involving Kim Chong Il from OSPEE and take notes.   → 239

e Make up similar dialogues with a partner.

f   Work with a partner. Student A is Joe T. Wallis from Delta Games in Cupertino, California, an American manufacturer of board games. Student B is Rita Spielvogel from Gametoys in Spielberg, Bavaria, a company that has now been importing games from Delta Games for three years. Gametoys is interested in representing Delta Games in the EU. Mr. Wallis is planning a trip to Europe to visit wholesalers in Germany, Denmark and Poland. He rings Frau Spielvogel to arrange a visit to her company. **Act out the telephone conversation, then change roles.**

➡ 41
➡ 99

Information for Joe T. Wallis

Ask Mrs Spielvogel how she is, exchange a few personal remarks.

You are planning a trip to Europe to visit customers in Germany, Denmark and Poland in the course of the summer, preferably in August. You are thinking of setting up agencies in those countries.

September is a problem as you will be attending the Toys and Games Fair in Chicago between 7 and 10 September. After that date you would be free.

You accept the invitation. You will be contacting your Danish and Polish customers immediately and inform Mrs Spielvogel right away whether a visit to her company would be more convenient for you before or after the Fair in Munich.

Mrs. Spielvogel will be hearing from you very soon to finalise the arrangements. You are looking forward to meeting her.

Informationen für Frau Spielvogel

Sie freuen sich von Mr. Wallis zu hören. Machen Sie ein paar persönliche Bemerkungen.

Sie wären an der Übernahme der Vertretung von Delta Games interessiert. Im August hat Ihre Firma allerdings, wie viele andere auch, Betriebsferien. September wäre besser. Mr. Wallis könnte dann auch die Freizeitmesse in München besuchen. Sie werden dort einen Stand haben. Vor oder nach der Messe könnte ein Besuch bei Ihrer Firma in Spielberg arrangiert werden und man könnte über die Modalitäten der Vertretung sprechen.

Die Freizeitmesse in München findet erst vom 19-22 September statt. Sie laden Mr. Wallis zu einem Besuch auf der Messe und bei Ihrer Firma ein.

Sie freuen sich auf den Besuch. Sie wollen Mr. Wallis Ihre Firma und die schöne Umgebung mit herrlichen Wäldern zeigen. Auch die alten Städte Regensburg und Passau wären einen Besuch wert.

D Background information

D1 Intermediaries in foreign trade

A company wishing to increase its sales in a particular foreign country is faced with a wide range of options. It may employ an intermediary, establish a branch office or a subsidiary, sell its products or services via an import/export company, a distributor or the internet. Other possible channels are franchising, licensing and joint ventures.

Commission agents (sometimes also called representatives) try to obtain orders in the name and for the account of their principals, i.e. the suppliers. Agents are appointed because they know the language, local business conditions and practices of the country in question. They visit potential customers and introduce their principal's goods or services or exhibit and demonstrate them at their own showrooms. They may organise **advertising** campaigns, conduct market research and carry out maintenance and repair work as part of an **after-sales service** agreement. For their efforts they receive a **commission** from the principal, i.e. a percentage of the invoice amount. If they agree to guarantee payment by the customers, they are paid an additional **del credere commission**. An agent is said to "represent" his principal and must always perform his duties in the principal's best interest as skilfully and carefully as possible; and he must provide his principal with a financial account when called upon to do so. He must not sell rival products. An **agency agreement,** concluded for a certain period of time and covering a certain territory, forms the legal basis of the relationship between agent and principal. If the principal confers upon the agent the exclusive right of sale for a given territory, the agent becomes his **sole agent**.

For products that might be required at short notice, such as accessories and spare parts, or goods that are normally sold in small quantities or sell better in showrooms, it is advisable that agents keep a stock of the articles on a **consignment** basis. That means that the goods remain the property of the principal until the agent – now acting as **consignee** – has sold them. Unsold goods are returned to the principal. Consignees are sometimes also called factors or distribution agents.

Brokers are also agents acting as intermediaries between buyers and sellers but without any permanent arrangement with a particular principal. Brokers often deal in insurance policies, stocks and bonds or in commodities whose prices are subject to sudden fluctuations, such as agricultural produce and raw materials. The commission they receive is called brokerage.

Estate agents who sell or let properties (real estate) on behalf of clients play a similar role and also charge a commission for their services.

Distributors (also called authorised dealers) actually purchase the products from the suppliers and sell them in their own name to their customers, thereby assuming full responsibility for the condition and sale of the products and any outstanding accounts. They will typically require exclusive right of sale.

A **franchise** is an arrangement by which the producer of a branded mass article gives a company or a trader the exclusive right to produce and/or sell this product against payment of a royalty. The franchisee purchases the raw material, the ingredients or the finished product, possibly including such things as shop design, advertising material etc., from the franchisor and must comply with the franchisor's stipulations.

Import/export houses (also called export merchants) buy and/or sell goods in their own name and for their own account. They frequently specialise in a particular class of goods or in imports from and exports to a particular country. Their function is similar to that of wholesalers in domestic trade.

Whenever a company's business in a foreign country reaches a certain volume, setting up a **branch office** overseas may become a viable option. Branch offices are entirely under the control of the head office in the country of origin.

Unlike branch offices, **subsidiaries** are independent companies, run by their own management, even though at least more than half of their share capital (equity) is owned by the parent company. Companies wishing to promote their exports by setting up a subsidiary in a foreign country often do so by acquiring an existing firm in the same line of business.

E-commerce, i.e. buying or selling via the internet, is rapidly becoming one of the most important means of exporting and importing goods and services. There are numerous different ways of doing this and new ones are being created all the time. A company's website should be designed and updated with the utmost care and professional skill.

Licensing is a way of exporting know-how. A licence represents permission given to a manufacturer by the owner of a patent to use a process or to produce an article under licence against payment of a royalty.

Joint ventures are usually temporary partnerships between two or more companies co-operating in some special business activity, which involves risks but where there is also a reasonable expectation of profit. The installation of large-scale industrial plants, huge infrastructure projects, etc. could not be executed without joint ventures, sometimes involving a large number of companies.

In cases where a country imposes restrictions on transactions in foreign currencies, exporters may agree to accept goods or services of a given value in exchange for the goods or services they wish to sell, without money payments being involved. Such deals are called **barter transactions**.

■ **Study the above information and choose the correct terms from the box for the following transactions.**

> branch office ∗ consignment basis ∗ distributors ∗ estate agent
> franchising ∗ joint venture ∗ license ∗ sole agents ∗ subsidiary

- Leisure Corp are looking for new premises. They contact the firm of William Price who promises to find suitable rooms for them within a short time. Mr. Price is an ❶

- Sports Unlimited are the only company entitled to sell Ospee's branded goods in the UK and in the Republic of Ireland. They are ❷

- BMG Sports Cars are sold in Germany by dealers who first purchase them from the manufacturer in Great Britain. These dealers may also be called ❸

- Cumbria Steel has an outlet in Zwickau which must refer to the headquarters in Cardiff for even minor decisions. Their Zwickau unit is a ❹

- McChicken is a highly successful chain of identical fast food restaurants to be found in every major town. The legal pattern on which they operate is called ❺

- Shimada of Japan have developed a new type of brake. Shimada agrees to permit Hyflyer to manufacture this kind of brake using Shimada's patents. Hyflyer manufactures the brakes under ❻

- A new underground railway is to be built in Manila. Several German building contractors agree to co-operate for this project. They form a ❼

- Sports Unlimited keep a stock of Ospee's swimwear which remains Ospee's property until it has been sold. Sports Unlimited do business on a ❽

- Badenbike have been taken over by Hyflyer plc because Hyflyer wanted to gain a permanent foothold on the German market. Badenbike are Hyflyer's ❾

D2 Sales Promotion

I Marketing

Marketing comprises the activities required to create a profitable demand for a product. Before a product is launched or even before it is released for mass-production, **market research** is conducted to establish whether there is a market for it. Market research is carried out in the form of *field research* (interviews in the street or on the phone and questionnaires sent to relevant groups of consumers or companies) and *desk research* (evaluation of the material obtained by field research and from any statistical material available).

Once a company has decided to launch a product, its success on the market will largely depend on the appropriate **marketing mix**, i.e. choosing the right prices and discounts, conditions of payment and delivery and distribution channels. The positioning of the product in the right segment of the market, the batch sizes the firm is prepared to sell, the quality of its after-sales service, its delivery times, all contribute to a product's success or failure. The company's general image also plays a role. That is why many firms engage in **public relations** activities such as sponsoring sports or cultural events, inviting the public to visit their premises on open days, making donations to charities, funding ecological projects and getting involved in community affairs. These activities are designed to define and enhance the firm's overall image rather than promote a particular product.

II Advertising

Successful advertising may help promote the sale of a product more than most other marketing instruments do. Consumers are sometimes provided with useful information on products by advertising (*informative advertising*) but they may also be subjected to persuasion, often at a subconscious or subliminal level (*persuasive advertising*), which is intended to create a desire for a product. Having decided to launch an advertising campaign, a firm commissions an advertising agency to design suitable advertising material for the various media unless it has its own advertising department. The *advertising medium* to be chosen will depend on the kind of product to be promoted, the target group and the budget available.

For consumer goods there are plenty of suitable media, such as

- fliers and hand-outs
- TV and radio commercials
- posters on billboards or hoardings
- outdoor advertising on buildings, buses, lorries, etc.
- home pages and banners on the internet
- advertisements in newspapers and popular magazines
- distribution of samples

For capital goods there are other media, such as

- sales letters, faxes or e-mails,
- websites on the internet
- brochures, folders and other sales literature
- advertisements in trade journals
- presentations at fairs and exhibitions

III Fairs and exhibitions

Fairs are large commercial and industrial exhibitions held at given venues at regular intervals, where buyers and sellers meet to do business. They provide excellent opportunities for giving or obtaining information on recent developments and establishing contacts. Trade fairs either concentrate on one sector of industry, like the Frankfurt book fair, or on a wide range of industries
5 like the Hanover fair. Germany hosts a large number of industrial fairs that attract exhibitors and visitors from all over the world, the country's most important fair and exhibition centres being Hanover, Düsseldorf, Munich, Frankfurt, Berlin and Cologne, to name but a few. Most fairs are open to business people only. Some, however, are open to the general public, either all the time or at least on certain days.

10 Britain is one of the three leading countries in the world for international conferences. Among the most modern conference and exhibition centres are the International Conference Centre in Birmingham and the Queen Elisabeth II and Olympia Conference Centres, both in London. A number of medium-sized cities such as Brighton (East Sussex) and Harrogate (Yorkshire) are also important conference venues. In Scotland, there is a new International Conference Centre in
15 Edinburgh.

■ **Study the text on sales promotion and find out which statements are correct.**

1. market research
   a. means going abroad to find a market
   b. improves conditions on the market
   c. tries to find out whether there is a market for a product

2. public relations
   a. is the same as advertising a product
   b. concentrates on promoting a firm's image
   c. are a firm's relations with the press

3. persuasive advertising
   a. tries to inform consumers
   b. tries to obtain information on consumers
   c. tries to influence consumers

4. capital goods
   a. are shares and bonds
   b. are investment goods such as machinery, computers etc.
   c. are first-class goods

5. trade fairs
   a. provide entertainment for families
   b. serve to establish contacts between buyers and sellers
   c. are held to promote a city

E IHK-Prüfungsvorbereitung

1.	**Zusatzqualifikation Englisch für kaufmännische Auszubildende Fremdsprache im Beruf I**
Geschäftsbrief nach Stichworten (Bearbeitungszeit 45 Minuten)	Hilfsmittel: zweisprachiges Wörterbuch

Situation

→ 223 Die Firma **Sportwelt Fan-Artikel**, Wertachring 93, 86153 Augsburg, Tel.(0821) 720473, Fax (0821) 720659, E-Mail sportwelt@comlink.de, feiert ihr 25-jähriges Bestehen. Aus diesem Anlass sollen langjährige Geschäftspartner zu einer Veranstaltung eingeladen werden.

Aufgabe

Die Exportleiterin, Denise Springer, bittet Sie, für den Geschäftsführer Walter Gruber die personalisierte Einladung per E-Mail an die englischsprachigen Geschäftspartner zu formulieren. (Hier: personalisierte Einladung an Mr Giacomelli von **Eurosport**, Via dei Banchi 45, 78038 Firenze, E-Mail giacomelli.eurosport@italink.com)

- Datum: 4. Februar 200_
- Anlass: am 2. Juli 200_ besteht Sportwelt Fan-Artikel 25 Jahre
- Einladung an alle Geschäftspartner zur Mitfeier des Jubiläums an diesem Tag:
    - 11 Uhr Empfang in den Geschäftsräumen von Sportwelt, Wertachring 93
    - 12.30 Uhr Mittagessen in der Kantine mit der Geschäftsleitung
    - 14 Uhr Präsentation neuer Produkte, Besichtigung der Geschäftsräume und Vorstellung der Mitarbeiter
    - 15.30 Stadtrundfahrt per Bus
    - 19 Uhr Abendessen im Hotel Drei Könige,
- Unterkunft: alle Geschäftspartner sind eingeladen, zwei Nächte (1.-3. Juli) im Hotel Drei Könige, einem 4-Sterne Hotel, zu verbringen
- Bitte um Zusage bis 31.03.200_ .
- Hoffnung, Mr Giacomelli bei dieser Gelegenheit begrüßen zu können

2.	**Zusatzqualifikation Englisch für kaufmännische Auszubildende Fremdsprache im Beruf I***
Vermerk in Deutsch über ein englisches Telefongespräch (Bearbeitungszeit 20 Minuten)	Hilfsmittel: zweisprachiges Wörterbuch

Situation:

In dem folgenden Gespräch sind Sie Elisabeth Bornemann von der Firma Techno-Messgeräte GmbH in Köln. Heute ist der (heutiges Datum). Sie erhalten gleich einen Anruf von David Jones von der britischen Firma Precision Instruments Ltd in Rochester.

* Die Bearbeitungszeit beträgt bei Fremdsprache im Beruf 30 Minuten, die Dialoge sind dementsprechend etwas länger.

Aufgabe:

Verfolgen Sie das Gespräch und fertigen Sie anschließend für Ihre Geschäftsführerin, Frau Angela Fischer, eine entsprechende Gesprächsnotiz in Deutsch an. Gestalten Sie bitte ein Formblatt. (Sie werden das Gespräch zweimal hören).

> Bornemann: Techno-Messgeräte GmbH, Bornemann. Guten Tag.
>
> Jones: –
>
> Bornemann: I'm sorry, she's on a business trip and won't be back until tomorrow. Can I help you?
>
> Jones: –
>
> Bornemann: If you would like to give me the details I will pass them on to her and get you an answer as quickly as possible.
>
> Jones: –
>
> Bornemann: When are you expecting to arrive in Cologne?
>
> Jones: –
>
> Bornemann: That depends on what kind of train you take. I should take the Intercity. Don't forget to pay the supplementary charge. It is also the rush hour – you may want to travel first class. The actual travelling time is about 20 minutes.
>
> Jones: –
>
> Bornemann: I will confirm this as soon as possible. Which is the best number to reach you on?
>
> Jones: –
>
> Bornemann: Certainly, what kind of hotel would you prefer?
>
> Jones: –
>
> Bornemann: Certainly, I know just the thing. There are no fairs on at the moment so it shouldn't be a problem.
>
> Jones: –
>
> Bornemann: Thank you for your call. I'll arrange everything and confirm as soon as possible. I'm sure there won't be any problems.

3. Fremdsprache im Beruf I
Gelenkte Zusammenfassung in Deutsch eines englischen Textes

Schwerpunkte: Handel / Industrie / Werbung (Bearbeitungszeit 45 Minuten)	Hilfsmittel: zweisprachiges Wörterbuch

Situation

Sie arbeiten in der Marketingabteilung eines Konsumgüterherstellers. Zu Ihren Aufgaben gehört die Auswertung der englischsprachigen Presse.

Aufgabe

Bitte fassen Sie für Ihre Kollegen nachstehenden Artikel aus der Wochenzeitung *International Commerce* vom 7. Juni 200_ (228 Wörter) in Deutsch auf ungefähr ein Drittel der Länge zusammen. Gehen Sie dabei auf folgende Punkte ein:

- Sponsoren der Fußball-Europameisterschaft
- Begründung und Beweis von Super Cola
- Beteiligung und Erwartungen von Dairiona

Football? We love it, say sponsors

Football and coffee, football and computers, football and yoghurt, football and phone companies ... the list is endless.

Every day at the European Football Cup, international companies, banks and corporations, in other words dozens of official sponsors, flood the press centre with all kinds of fliers, stressing the undeniable connection between their products and the world's greatest game.

But is this just one giant public relations exercise or is there any proof that sponsoring football makes money? "No doubt whatsoever," says Super Cola's PR manager for worldwide sports. "Football is a huge marketing tool for any company that is truly global. For us, the European Cup is a perfect fit. Football is the most popular sport in the world and we do business in some 200 countries." To prove his point the PR manager says that in 1997 French sales of Super Cola went up by 18 per cent because of the company's sponsorship of the World Cup.

Some of the supposed connections between football and sponsors are, however, rather thin. What on earth, for instance, can the Dairiona dairy group, which admittedly makes tasty yoghurts, have to do with kicking a round ball into a net? Everything, according to the company which is sponsoring the European Cup with numerous promotional campaigns. With millions of viewers the European Cup will help boost the Dairiona brand.

---

4. Fremdsprache im Beruf I
Gelenkte englische schriftliche Beschreibung einer Grafik

Schwerpunkt: Banken (Bearbeitungszeit 30 Minuten)	**Hilfsmittel:** zweisprachiges Wörterbuch

Situation
Sie arbeiten bei einer internationalen Bank, deren Konzernsprache Englisch ist. Ihr Chef soll bei einer Tagung einen Überblick über das Geschäft mit Hypothekenkrediten in den skandinavischen Ländern geben.

Aufgabe
Bitte verfassen Sie hierfür eine schriftliche Beschreibung in Englisch der nachstehenden Grafik für Norwegen, welche zeigt, wie viel Prozent der Hypothekenkredite in den letzten fünf Jahren von einzelnen Kreditinstituten bereitgestellt wurden.

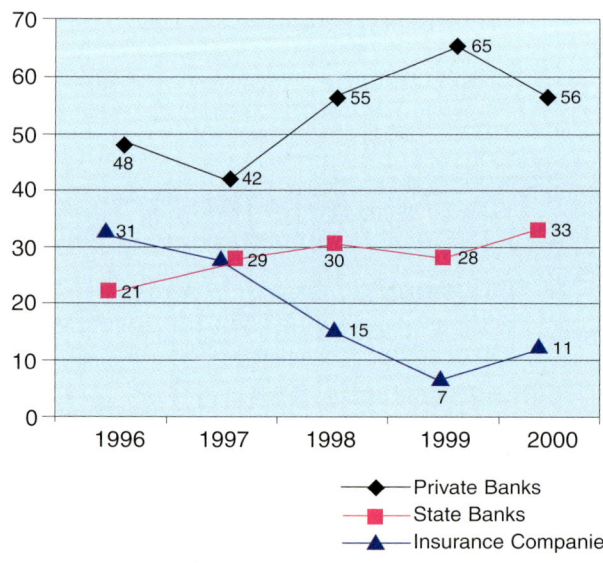

5. Fremdsprachenkorrespondent/in
Übersetzung Deutsch/Englisch

(Bearbeitungszeit 60 Minuten)	**Hilfsmittel:** zweisprachige Wörterbücher

Bei den deutschen Werbeagenturen herrscht weiterhin Optimismus. Eine Umfrage des Verbandes der Werbeagenturen ergab, dass gut drei Viertel der befragten Agenturen den Geschäftsverlauf im ersten Halbjahr dieses Jahres als zufriedenstellend oder sehr gut bezeichneten.

Knapp 70 Prozent der Agenturleiter rechnen für das zweite Halbjahr mit einem weiter günstigen Geschäftsverlauf. Die im Frühjahr vorhergesagte Umsatzsteigerung von 6 Prozent sehen 57 Prozent der Befragten als immer noch gültig an, 36 Prozent glauben sogar, diesen Wert übertreffen zu können. „Es würde mich nicht wundern, wenn das Umsatzwachstum am Jahresende mehr als 7 Prozent betragen würde", sagte der Präsident des Verbandes bei der Präsentation der Ergebnisse. Als Gründe nennt er die günstige Entwicklung der Konjunktur und die Tatsache, dass der Wettbewerb zwischen Unternehmen immer mehr auf der Kommunikationsebene stattfindet.

Qualifiziertes Personal wird auch bei den Werbeagenturen knapp. Immer mehr Mitarbeiter wandern zu Internet-Unternehmen oder nach Berlin ab. „Berlin übt eine gewaltige Sogwirkung aus", sagte der Verbandspräsident. „Wer an anderen Standorten sitzt, hat große Probleme, kreative Kräfte zu gewinnen."

6. Fremdsprachenkorrespondent/in Englisch
Geschäftsbrief nach Stichworten

(Bearbeitungszeit 45 Minuten)	**Hilfsmittel:** zweisprachige Wörterbücher

Situation

Sie sind der/die Assistent/in von Petra Mertens, der Exportleiterin der TESTCO GmbH, Stahlstr. 45, 26125 Oldenburg, eines Herstellers von elektronischen Prüfsystemen. Der Absatz in der Republik Irland hat sich in den letzten Jahren so positiv entwickelt, dass die Geschäftsführung erwägt, einen eigenen Repräsentanten mit der Vertretung ihrer Interessen zu betrauen. Von der Irish-German Chamber of Commerce in Dublin haben Sie Adressen irischer Firmen erhalten, die in Frage kommen könnten. Heute ist der 20. September 200...

Aufgabe

Verfassen Sie für Ihre Chefin, die selbst unterschreiben wird, eine Anfrage an LabEquip Ltd, Ballycasheen, Killarney, Co. Kerry, wegen einer Vertretung und berücksichtigen Sie dabei bitte folgende Punkte:

- Einleitung
- Vorstellung Ihrer Firma
    - Gegründet 1964
    - Marktführer in Deutschland
    - Marktanteil in Irland fast 9%

- Hauptsitz in Oldenburg, weitere Produktionsstätten in Gera (Thüringen) und in Brno (Tschechische Republik)
- Insgesamt 720 Mitarbeiter
- Kataloge, Produktbeschreibungen anbei
* Alleinvertreter für die gesamte Republik Irland gesucht
* Großzügige Provision, evtl. auch Delkredereprovision
* Kundendienst (Inspektion, Wartung, Reparaturen, Verkauf von Ersatzteilen) muss übernommen werden
* Ausstellungs- und Lagerräume erforderlich
* Bei Interesse Einladung nach Oldenburg zur Besprechung weiterer Einzelheiten
* Schlusssatz

7. Fremdsprachenkorrespondent/in Englisch
Beantwortung einer englischen Korrespondenz in Englisch

(Bearbeitungszeit 60 Minuten) | **Hilfsmittel:** zweisprachige Wörterbücher

Situation:

Sie (eigener Name) sind ein/e Mitarbeiter/in von Frau Christine Ziolkowski, der Exportleiterin des deutschen Herstellers von Sanitär-Armaturen, Bohe KG, Mutterstadter Str. 42-46, 67071 Ludwigshafen, Tel.(0621) 4670970, Fax (0621) 4670975. Ihre Chefin hat gestern beiliegendes Fax von Ihrer Vertretung in Kanada erhalten.

Aufgabe

Da Ihre Chefin einen auswärtigen Termin wahrnehmen muss, hat sie Ihnen das Fax mit folgender Notiz zur Beantwortung auf den Schreibtisch gelegt:

Veranlassen Sie bitte den Versand der zwei Akryl-Griffe umgehend, wie gewünscht, per Luftfracht. Lieferadresse: 22 Seguin St., Parry Sound, Ontario P2A 1B1.
Schicken Sie Mr Benwick ein Fax zur Bestätigung.
Fragen Sie ihn, ob er evtl. bereit wäre für uns ein Konsignationslager einzurichten. Einzelheiten müssten natürlich noch verhandelt werden.
Frage der Provisionserhöhung muss von der Geschäftsleitung entschieden werden.
Werbekampagne der geschilderten Art grundsätzlich eine gute Idee.
Ich werde versuchen ihn am Donnerstag anzurufen, um diese Punkte zu besprechen.
Unterschreiben Sie in meinem Namen.

Ziolkowski

Charles Benwick
Bathrooms

1421 Mayflower Drive, Mississauga, Ontario L5R 1T2
Tel.001416 5682314, Fax 001416 5682414

Telefax

From: Charles Benwick
To: Mrs Christine Ziolkowski, Bohe KG, Fax 0049 621 4670975
Date: July 14, 200_   **Pages:** 1
Subject: Consignment for CANADIAN HOMES; marketing strategies

Dear Christine
Thank you for shipping the consignment of 200 single-lever faucets and 500 2-handle faucets for the CANADIAN HOMES DIY-chain so punctually. However, their chief buyer, Tom Wood, has just called me and complained that two of the acrylic handles for the 2-handle faucets are missing. Would you please ensure that they are airfreighted to their delivery address as soon as possible. CANADIAN HOMES is one of Canada's most ubiquitous chains of DIY-stores and we should do our utmost to retain this valuable customer.

It has not been easy for us here to win this order in the face of stiff competition from the USA and Mexico. You will know that under the North American Free Trade Agreement, goods from both countries enjoy tariff-free access to the Canadian market. That is why we feel that your marketing strategies for Canada should be reviewed.

Firstly, we will only be able to maintain the growth rates in sales if we can agree on a modest increase in our commission of 2% as the cost of making sales has been increasing considerably in the last two years.

Secondly, advertising ought to be stepped up. We suggest launching a campaign in DIY magazines, positioning Bohe bathroom fittings as up-market products. Quality and prestige should be emphasised as the distinguishing features of the brand in order to gain market share against the competition from the south.

I await your comments.

Best regards
Charles

---

8. | **Fremdsprachenkorrespondent/in Englisch**
Zusammenfassung (in Deutsch) einer englischen mündlichen Nachricht

| (Bearbeitungszeit 30 Minuten) | **Hilfsmittel:** zweisprachige Wörterbücher |

Situation
Ihr Chef, Herr Friedrich von Ruhleben, hat folgende Nachricht auf seinem Anrufbeantworter vorgefunden.

Aufgabe
Er bittet sie, einen Vermerk in deutscher Sprache zu verfassen, den er an die zuständigen Sachbearbeiter weiterleiten kann.

Further reading: Job application

When looking for a job it is important to read the relevant advertisements carefully. When you have found a suitable vacancy it is useful to know something about the firm. Is it a large, well-known organisation? Have you seen any articles about it in the press? Do you know anything about its personnel policy? Does it provide training programmes? More specific information regarding the position itself includes the career prospects it offers and, of course, the salary. Are there any fringe benefits and/or a company pension scheme? The title of the job advertised may not correspond exactly to your qualifications. This may especially be the case if you are applying for a job in another country. The many job titles in Germany involving a particular type of training (e.g. apprenticeship) and an examination before the Chamber of Commerce or Handwerkskammer often have no direct equivalent in English. Here it is important to look carefully at the job description and consider whether the skills and duties required are covered by your qualifications and experience.

There are various ways of finding out what vacancies exist. Obviously, many firms publicise openings in the newspapers, often for specific professions on different days. There are also job exchanges on the internet such as eteach.com which specialises in teaching positions or jobsunlimited.co.uk. This is particularly convenient if you are applying abroad, as it obviates the necessity of buying expensive newspapers and periodicals which may not be readily available. It is also possible to look for a position through a specialist recruitment agency. If there are not enough positions advertised in a given field people often send out unsolicited applications to organisations which are likely to need to recruit staff.

When applying in English – and there are an increasing number of international companies in continental Europe whose company language is English – it is important to be aware of differences. For instance, in an English CV do not give your parents' profession(s) or your religious denomination. Do not send references if applying in Britain. A potential employer will ask you to give the names of referees and will then approach them direct to obtain a reference. It is as well to warn people in advance if you give their names! CV's do not generally include photographs. A modern CV often reverses the chronological order and starts with the most recent information on your career before giving details of previous employment, training and educational qualifications.

It should be emphasised that different countries have very different educational systems and traditions which are not always entirely comparable. The English equivalents in the following CV are only approximate paraphrases or explanations of the German terms.

a Work with a partner. Make a list of what you will have to find out about the firm and the position in question before and during the job interview. Compare your lists.

b Study the above text and the two CVs on the following pages and describe the differences between a German and an English CV.

c As its exports to the Continent are booming Hyflyer plc has published the job advertisement below in several French and German newspapers.
Read the advertisement and look up any words you don't know in a dictionary.

Would you be excited about working in an international environment with a leading manufacturer of bicycles?

If so, why not apply for the position of

ASSISTANT TO THE EXPORT MANAGER

Successful applicants will have
- **several years' experience in export management**
- **native speaker competence in French or German**

Successful applicants will be
- **familiar with EU export procedure**
- **highly self-motivated**
- **flexible and mobile**
- **resilient and hard-working**

We offer a challenging management role, a competitive salary, attractive fringe benefits, and excellent career prospects.

Apply with full CV to:
The Recruitment Officer, Hyflyer plc
438 Weltmore Industrial Park,
Warwick
CV43 6TS

---

d Dennis Schönhoff from Düsseldorf is interested in the vacancy and has asked someone with a good knowledge of English to help him with his CV. **Study Dennis' German and English CVs.**

Further reading · Unit 12   265

CV in German

Persönliche Angaben

Name	Dennis Schönhoff
Adresse	Rubensstr. 244
	40235 Düsseldorf
Staatsangehörigkeit	deutsch
Geburtstag	18. 01. 1978
Geburtsort	Wuppertal
Familienstand	ledig

Schulbildung

1988 – 1994	Realschule im Schulzentrum Nord, Wuppertal Abschluss: Fachoberschulreife
1994 – 1996	Höhere Handelsschule im Berufskolleg, Wuppertal Abschluss: Fachhochschulreife
1996 - 1997	Sprachschule Sebastian, Remscheid Abschluss: IHK-Prüfung „Geprüfter Fremdsprachenkorrespondent Englisch", Gesamtnote: „Befriedigend"

Ausbildung

1999-2001	Ausbildung zum Groß- und Außenhandelskaufmann bei KÄMPFER SPORTGERÄTE GmbH, Düsseldorf
Mai 2001	Abschlussprüfung: Note „Gut"

Tätigkeiten

1997 – 1998	Zivildienst bei der Johanniter Unfallhilfe
Juni 2001 – heute	Exportsachbearbeiter bei KÄMPFER SPORTGERÄTE GmbH, betraut mit der Abwicklung von Exporten von Hallensportgeräten in die englischsprachigen Länder Afrikas, zuständig für den Kontakt mit Vertretern, die Abwicklung von Exportaufträgen, die Ausfertigung von Versandpapieren sowie die Bearbeitung von Akkreditiven.

Sonstige Kenntnisse

Windows, Excel, Powerpoint
Grundkenntnisse in Spanisch
Personenbeförderungsschein

Interessen

Fußball, Tennis, Snowboardfahren, Science Fiction

II CV in English

Personal details

Name:	Dennis Schönhoff
Address:	Rubensstr. 244, 40235 Düsseldorf
Nationality:	German
Date of birth:	18 Jan. 1978
Place of birth:	Wuppertal
Marital status:	single

Work experience

June 2001 – the present — Export sales clerk at KÄMPFER SPORTGERÄTE GmbH, responsible for exports of indoor sports equipment to the English-speaking countries in Africa, involving liaising with agents, processing incoming orders, making out shipping documents and handling letters of credit.

1997 – 1998 — Social service (in lieu of military service) with the Johanniter Unfallhilfe (ambulance service)

Apprenticeship

1999-2001 — Practical traineeship as wholesale and export clerk at KÄMPFER SPORTGERÄTE GmbH, Düsseldorf; combined with continued theoretical training at vocational college

May 2001 — Final Chamber of Commerce examination
Overall grade: "gut" (A-B)

Education

1996 - 1997 — Sprachschule Sebastian (language school), Remscheid
Qualification: Chamber of Commerce Examination: Foreign language correspondent (English)
Overall grade: "befriedigend" (B-C)

1994 – 1996 — Vocational Training College (age 16-18), Wuppertal
Qualification: final school leaving examination qualifying for admission to polytechnic (Fachhochschulreife)

1988 – 1994 — Secondary school in the Schulzentrum Nord, Wuppertal
Qualification: final school leaving examination (age 16)

Other skills

Windows, Excel, Powerpoint
Spanish (working knowledge)
Large passenger vehicle driving licence

Personal interests

Football, tennis, snowboarding, science fiction

e   Now write an English CV for yourself.

Vokabelverzeichnis

(v) = Verb
(adj) = Adjektiv
(adv) = Adverb

A

abbreviation	Abkürzung
access	Zugang, Zutritt
accessories	Zubehör(teile)
accommodate (v)	entgegenkommen; auch: unterbringen
accommodation	Unterkunft, Hotelzimmer
accompany (v)	begleiten
according to	laut, gemäß
accordingly	demgemäß, folglich
account for (v)	ausmachen, auf ... entfallen
account holder	Kontoinhaber(in)
account sales	Zwischen- oder Schlussabrechnung eines Vertreters
account	Konto, Forderung, Verbindlichkeit, Abrechnung
accountancy	Rechnungswesen, Buchhaltungs- und Bilanzwesen
accountant	Wirtschafts-, Buchprüfer(in), (Bilanz)buchhalter(in)
accounting department	Rechnungsabteilung
accounting system	Buchführungssystem
accumulate (v)	(sich) anhäufen
accuracy	Genauigkeit
achieve (v)	erzielen, erreichen
acknowledge (v)	bestätigen
acquire (v)	sich aneignen, erwerben
action	hier: Klage
actual	tatsächlich, real (Achtung: *aktuell* heißt: *current, topical*)
actually	tatsächlich
adapt (v)	anpassen
additional	zusätzlich
adjoining	angrenzend, daneben liegend
adjust (v) a complaint	eine Beschwerde erledigen
adjustment	Anpassung, Angleichung, Beilegung
admission	Zulassung, Zugang, Eingeständnis
adopt (v) a measure	eine Maßnahme ergreifen
adult	erwachsen
advance (v) money	Geld vorstrecken, Vorschuss geben
advantageous	vorteilhaft
advertisement	(Werbe)anzeige
advertising allowance	hier: genehmigter Werbeetat
advertising	Werbung
advice of dispatch	Versandanzeige
advisable	ratsam, empfehlenswert
advise (v)	benachrichtigen, informieren; auch: (be)raten
advising bank	avisierende Bank (*Akkreditiv*)
affect (v)	beeinträchtigen, betreffen
affordable	erschwinglich
after receipt of your order	nach Erhalt Ihrer Bestellung
after-sales service	Kundendienst
agency agreement	Vertretungsvertrag
agency	Vertretung, Agentur
agenda	Tagesordnung, Plan
agent	Vertreter(in)
agree (v) to do s.th.	sich bereit erklären etwas zu tun
agricultural produce	landwirtschaftliche Produkte
aid	Hilfe, Hilfsmittel, Unterstützung
air waybill	Luftfrachtbrief (s. Unit 8)
aisle	Gang (*Flugzeug, Zug, Kirche*)
alert	Warnsignal
allocate (v)	zuteilen
allow for (v)	berücksichtigen, einkalkulieren
alteration	(Ab)änderung
amend (v)	ergänzen, abändern
amendment	(Ab)änderung, Ergänzung
amicable settlement	gütliche Einigung
ample	ausreichend, genügend
anger	Zorn, Wut
anniversary	Jahrestag, Jubiläum
annual general meeting	Jahreshauptversammlung
annual report	Jahresbericht
annual	jährlich
anticipate (v)	erwarten, vorhersehen, voraussehen, zuvorkommen
anxious	bestrebt, bemüht, besorgt
apart from	abgesehen von
apologise / apologize (v)	sich entschuldigen, um Verzeihung bitten
apparently	offensichtlich
appeal (v) to	appellieren an, gefallen
applicable	anwendbar, geltend
applicant	Antragsteller(in), Bewerber(in)
application form	Antrag(sformular), Bewerbungsformular
application	Bewerbung; auch: Anwendung
apply (v)	gelten, Anwendung finden; auch: sich bewerben
appoint (v)	ernennen, berufen
appointment	Termin(vereinbarung); auch: Ernennung
appreciate (v)	schätzen, zu schätzen wissen, begrüßen
apprenticeship	Lehre
appropriate	angemessen, passend, geeignet, entsprechend
approval	Beifall, Zustimmung
approve (v) the budget	den Haushalt/Etat genehmigen/bewilligen
approved lines	anerkannte Schifffahrtslinien
arbitrator	Schiedsrichter (*in kaufmännischen Angelegenheiten*)
area representative	Gebietsvertreter(in)
arise (v), arose, arisen	entstehen
arms and weapons	Rüstungsgüter
arrears in payment	Zahlungsrückstände
arresting	hier: ansprechend, ins Auge fallend

artificial	künstlich	be (v) aware of	sich bewusst sein
artwork	Design	be (v) bothered	hier: sich die Mühe machen
assembly hall	Versammlungssaal	be (v) in charge	zuständig sein
assess (v)	schätzen, einschätzen	be (v) compelled	gezwungen sein
assets	Vermögen(swerte)	be (v) incorporated	Körperschaftsstatus besitzen
assistance	Hilfe	be (v) in demand	gefragt sein
associate	Partner, Teilhaber	be (v) keen on s.th.	auf etwas versessen sein, etwas unbedingt wollen
association	Vereinigung, Verband		
assorted	ausgewählt	be (v) obliged	gezwungen sein; auch: jmdm. verbunden sein
assume (v)	annehmen, übernehmen, vermuten		
		be (v) short by	zu wenig enthalten, knapp sein an
assurance	Zusicherung		
assure (v) s.o.	jmdm. versichern	be (v) subject to controls	Kontrollen unterliegen, kontrolliert werden
at first glance	auf den ersten Blick		
at least	mindestens, wenigstens	be (v) weighted	gewichtet werden
at our risk and expense	auf unsere Kosten und Gefahr	bearer cheque	Überbringer-, Inhaberscheck
at regular intervals	in regelmäßigen Abständen	beaten track	ausgetretener Pfad; hier: Ziele für Massentourismus
at short notice	kurzfristig		
at the latest	spätestens	beneficial	vorteilhaft
at this stage	zu diesem Zeitpunkt, in diesem Stadium	beneficiary	Begünstigter, Nutznießer, Berechtigter
at your earliest convenience	sobald wie möglich	benefit	Nutzen; auch: Unterstützung
		bent	verbogen
attached	beiliegend, als Anlage	bestow (v) on	verleihen *(Preis, Titel)*
attachment	Anhang	beverage	Getränk
attend (v)	teilnehmen, auf Dauer besuchen	Bill of Exchange Act	Wechselgesetz
attention line	Zeile für „zu Händen von"	bill of exchange	Wechsel (s. Unit 5)
attest (v)	attestieren, beglaubigen	bill of lading	Konnossement (s. Unit 8)
authorised dealer	Vertragshändler	billboard	Reklamefläche, Anschlagbrett
automated teller machine / cash dispenser	Geldautomat	billing	Rechnungsausstellung, -erstellung
		binding	hier: Bindung
automotive components	Automobilteile	blame (v) for	verantwortlich machen für, Schuld zuweisen
availability	Vorhandensein, Verfügbarkeit		
available	verfügbar, erhältlich; hier: benutzbar	blank endorsed	blanko indossiert (s. Unit 5)
		blank line	Leerzeile
award (v)	verleihen	blank space	leeres Feld, freier Raum
award	Preis	blow (v)	hier: durchbrennen
awkward	ungeschickt, schwerfällig, peinlich	blueberry	Heidelbeere
		blur (v)	verwischen, verschwimmen lassen
		board of directors	Geschäftsleitung, Vorstand,
B		board	hier: Karton, Schiffsdeck, Board *(Leiterplatte)*
back (v) up	unterstützen, -mauern		
bad debts	faule/uneinbringliche Schulden	body	hier: Hauptteil (eines Briefes)
balance (v) an account	Konto ausgleichen	bold type	Fettdruck
balance	Saldo, Differenz, Restbetrag	bond	Anleihe, Obligation, Schuldverschreibung
ban	Verbot		
bank counter	Bankschalter	boost (v)	ankurbeln, Auftrieb geben
bank guarantee	Bankbürgschaft	both ... and	sowohl ... als auch
bank transfer	Banküberweisung	boundary	Grenze
banker's draft	Bankscheck (s. Unit 5)	brainstorm (v)	Einfälle sammeln
bankruptcy	Konkurs, Bankrott	brakes	Bremsen
bar chart	Balkendiagramm	branch manager	Filialleiter
barrier	Hindernis, Barriere	branch office	Filiale, Zweigstelle
barter transactions	Tausch-, Kompensationsgeschäfte	brand	Marke
		branded product	Markenerzeugnis
batch size	Liefer-, Produktionsmenge	breach of contract	Vertragsbruch
batch	(Liefer)menge, Partie	break (v) bulk	in großen Mengen kaufen und in kleineren Mengen verkaufen
BC (before Christ)	v.Chr., vor Christus		
be (v) at a loss	außerstande sein		
be (v) at fault	schuldig sein, Schuld haben	break	Pause, Unterbrechung

brief	kurz
briefly and concisely (adv)	kurz und bündig
bring (v) up the rear	das Schlusslicht bilden
brochure	Prospekt, Broschüre
broker	Makler(in)
brokerage	Maklerprovision, Courtage
browse (v) the internet	im Internet surfen
building contractor	Bauunternehmen
bulletin	Mitteilungsblatt
bundle	Bündel, Bund
buoyant	lebhaft, florierend
burden	Last
business conduct	Geschäftsgebaren
business facilities	Ausstattung für Geschäftsleute
business section	Wirtschaftsteil (einer Zeitung)
by and large	im Großen und Ganzen
bypass (v)	umgehen

C

calf, calves	hier: Waden
call (v) for	verlangen, erfordern
cancel (v)	stornieren, absagen, streichen
cancel (v) an order	Auftrag annullieren
capital goods	Investitionsgüter
capital letter	Großbuchstabe
cardboard box	Pappkarton
cardiovascular system	Herz-Kreislaufsystem
career prospects	Aufstiegschancen
cargo	Fracht, Ladung
carriage forward	unfrei, Fracht bezahlt der Empfänger
carriage	Fracht, Beförderung, auch: Waggon
carrier	Frachtführer, Transportunternehmen, Fluglinie
carry (v) a line of products	eine Produktreihe führen, anbieten
cartridge	Patrone
cash against documents	Kasse gegen Dokumente (s. Unit 7)
cash discount	Skonto, Barzahlungsrabatt
cash on delivery	per Nachnahme, Zahlung bei Erhalt der Ware
cash with order	Bezahlung bei Auftragserteilung/Bestellung
cashier	Kassierer(in), Kassenführer(in)
cater for/to (v)	befriedigen, sorgen für, verpflegen
catering	Gastronomie, Verpflegungswesen
caution	Vorsicht
cautious	vorsichtig
celebration	Feier
centre of gravity	Schwerpunkt
century	Jahrhundert
certificate of origin	Ursprungszeugnis (s. Unit 8)
certified technician	geprüfte(r) Techniker(in)
certify (v)	bestätigen
chain store	Ladenkette

challenging	herausfordernd
charge (v) a sum to an account	ein Konto mit einem Betrag belasten
charge (v) too much	zuviel berechnen / verlangen
charge (v) VAT	Mehrwertsteuer erheben
charge (v) with	betrauen mit
charge (v)	berechnen
charge	Gebühr
charge card	Kunden-, Einkaufskarte
chargeable weight	frachtpflichtiges Gewicht
charity	karitative / gemeinnützige Organisation
chief accountant	Leiter(in) des Rechnungswesens
chief executive officer (CEO)	Firmenchef(in), Vorstandsvorsitzende(r)
choice	Alternative, Wahl
circumstances	Umstände
claim (v)	behaupten, fordern, beanspruchen
claim	Forderung, Anspruch, Beschwerde, Behauptung,
clause (v) a bill of lading	ein Konnossement einschränken
clause	Klausel, Paragraph
clean bill of lading	reines Konnossement
clean on board B/L	reines Bordkonnossement
clear (v) for import	zur Einfuhr freimachen
clear (v) the balance	das Konto ausgleichen
clear (v) through customs	verzollen, zollamtlich abfertigen
client	Kunde, Kundin, Klient(in)
coding system	Kodiersystem
collapse (v)	zusammenbrechen
collateral	Sicherheit(en) (bei Krediten)
collect (v)	abholen, (ein)sammeln
collection	hier: Inkasso, Einzug, Einziehung
collection agency	Inkassobüro
collocation	Zusammenstellung (von Wörtern)
column	Spalte, Säule
combine (v)	verbinden
come (v) up to expectations	Erwartungen entsprechen
command (v) a majority	über eine Mehrheit verfügen
commence (v)	hier: in Kraft treten, beginnen
commercial invoice	Handelsrechnung (s. Unit 7)
commercials	Werbespots
commission (v) with	beauftragen mit
commission agent	Handelsvertreter(in)
Commission	(EU-)Kommission (s. Unit 9)
commission	Provision, auch: Kommission
commit oneself (v)	sich engagieren; auch: sich festlegen
commitment	Verpflichtung
commodity	Ware, Rohstoff (z.B. Kupfer, Kaffee, Baumwolle)
community	Gemeinde, Gemeinschaft
commute (v)	hier: ändern, umändern; auch: pendeln
company pension scheme	betriebliche Altersversorgung, Betriebsrente

company secretary	(keine deutsche Entsprechung, gesetzlich vorgeschriebene Position mit juristischen Funktionen)	contingencies	Eventualitäten, unvorhergesehene Umstände
comparable	vergleichbar	continuous	anhaltend, ununterbrochen
compare (v)	vergleichen	contract of carriage	Beförderungsvertrag
compensation	Entschädigung, Schadenersatz(leistung)	contribute (v)	beitragen
		contribution	Beitrag
competitive	wettbewerbs-, konkurrenzfähig, wettbewerbsintensiv, heiß umkämpft	convenience	Komfort, Annehmlichkeit, Bequemlichkeit
		convenient	passend, geeignet, bequem, angenehm
competitor	Konkurrent, Konkurrenz	convention	Konvention, Gepflogenheit
compile (v)	zusammenstellen	convey (v)	ver-, übermitteln, befördern
complaint	Beschwerde, Mängelrüge, Klage	conveyor belt	Förder-, Montageband
complimentary close	Grußformel am Schluss (Brief)	convince (v)	überzeugen
complimentary	gratis, Geschenk-	cordial	herzlich, freundschaftlich
comply (v) with	befolgen, entsprechen, nachkommen	corner store	Tante-Emma-Laden
		corporate customers	Firmenkunden
component	Bestand(teil), Bauelement	correspondent bank	Korrespondenz-, Partnerbank
composed	hier: gefasst, gelassen	cost estimate	Kostenvoranschlag
comprehensive	umfangreich, umfassend	Council of Ministers	(EU-)Ministerrat (s. Unit 9)
compulsory liquidation	Zwangsliquidierung	counter-offer	Gegenangebot
concept	Konzept, Begriff, Konzeption	coupon	Gutschein
concerned	betroffen, besorgt, beteiligt	courier service	Kurierdienst
concession	Zugeständnis, Konzession	courier	Bote, Kurier
concise	kurz, knapp	court action/proceedings	Gerichtsverfahren, Klage vor Gericht
conclude (v) contracts	Verträge abschließen		
confer (v) the exclusive right of sale	das Alleinverkaufsrecht übertragen	courteous	höflich
		cover (v)	hier: versichern
confidence	Ver-, Zutrauen, Zuversicht	cover / coverage	Deckung(sschutz) (s. Unit 8)
confident	zuversichtlich	cover(ing) letter	Begleitschreiben
confidential	vertraulich	cracked	gesprungen, rissig
confined to	beschränkt auf	craft	Handwerk, (Kunst)gewerbe
confirm (v)	bestätigen	craftsmanship	handwerkliches Geschick, handwerkliche Ausführung
confirmation	Bestätigung		
confirmed letter of credit	bestätigtes Akkreditiv (s. Unit 7)	create (v)	schaffen, erzeugen
conflicting views	widersprüchliche Ansichten	credit (v) to a bank account	einem Konto gutschreiben
conform (v) to/with	entsprechen, (sich) anpassen, übereinstimmen mit	credit agency	Auskunftei
		credit enquiry	Bitte um Kreditauskunft
conformity	Übereinstimmung	credit line	Kreditlinie
consent	Einverständnis, Zustimmung	credit note	Gutschrift(sanzeige)
consequently	folglich, infolgedessen	credit period	Zahlungsziel
consider (v)	überlegen, in Erwägung ziehen	credit rating	Kredit-Rating, Einschätzung der Kreditwürdigkeit
considerable	erheblich, beträchtlich		
consideration	Überlegung, Erwägung, Berücksichtigung	creditor	Gläubige(r)
		creditworthiness	Kreditwürdigkeit
consignee	Empfänger, Konsignatar	crew neck	runder Halsausschnitt
consignment goods	Kommissionsware (s. Unit 12)	crisp	knusprig, spröde, knackig, hier: gestochen klar
consignment note	Frachtbriefdoppel (s. Unit 8)		
consignment stock	Konsignations-, Auslieferungslager	crossed cheque	Verrechnungsscheck
		crucial	entscheidend
consignment	Lieferung, Sendung	cue	Hinweis
consistent	konsequent, gleichbleibend	currency	Währung
constant	ständig	current account	laufendes Konto, Girokonto
constitute (v)	darstellen, bilden	current	laufend, gegenwärtig, aktuell
construction industry	Bauindustrie	currently (adv)	zur Zeit, gegenwärtig
consular invoice	Konsulatsfaktura (s. Unit 8)	custom tour	Individualreise
consultant	Berater(in)	customary	gebräuchlich, üblich, gewohnheitsmäßig
consume (v)	trinken, verzehren, konsumieren		
consumer	Verbraucher	customs authority	Zoll(behörde)
contain (v)	enthalten, aufweisen	customs duties	Zollabgaben
contents	Inhalt, Gehalt	customs invoice	Zollfaktura (s. Unit 8)
		customs	Zoll; auch: Gebräuche, Sitten

D

damages	Schaden(s)ersatz
date of issue	Datum der Ausstellung
date of maturity	Fälligkeitsdatum
DDU, Delivered Duty Unpaid	Geliefert unverzollt (s. Unit 4)
deadline	letzte Frist, äußerster Termin
debit (v) an account	ein Konto belasten
debit note	Belastungs-, Lastschriftanzeige
debtor	Schuldner
deceive (v)	täuschen
declare (v) insolvency	Zahlungsunfähigkeit erklären
declare (v)	angeben, melden
decline (v)	zurückgehen, ablehnen
decline	Rückgang
deduct (v)	abziehen
default settings	Fehler bei den Einstellungen
defence	Verteidigung
degree	Grad, Ausmaß
delay (v)	verzögern
delay in payment	Zahlungsverzug
del credere commission	Delkredereprovision (s. Unit 12)
delicate	heikel, empfindlich, zerbrechlich, zart
delivery	Lieferung, Sendung; auch: Übergabe
deltoids	Deltamuskeln
demand (v)	verlangen, fordern
demand	hier: Nachfrage
dented	ver-, eingebeult
department store	Waren-, Kaufhaus
depend (v) on	abhängen von
deposit (v) money	Geld einzahlen
deputy	Stellvertreter(in)
derive (v)	herleiten
deserve (v)	verdienen
deserving	verdienstvoll
design (v)	gestalten, entwerfen, konstruieren, vorsehen
design features	Designmerkmale
designation	Bezeichnung, Kennzeichnung
despite	trotz
destination	Zielort, -flughafen, -bahnhof
deteriorate (v)	schlechter werden
determinable	bestimmbar
determine (v)	bestimmen
detriment	Beeinträchtigung, Nachteil
device	Gerät, Vorrichtung, Apparat
diary	Terminkalender, Tagebuch
differentiate (v)	unterscheiden
digest (v)	verdauen
dimensions	Abmessungen, Dimensionen
direct debiting	Lastschriftverfahren
directive	(EU-)Richtlinie, Vorschrift
dirty/foul/claused B/L	unreines/eingeschränktes Konnossement (s. Unit 8)
disappointed	enttäuscht
disappointment	Enttäuschung
discerning	anspruchsvoll
discontinue (v)	einstellen, unter-, abbrechen
discount (v) a B/E	einen Wechsel diskontieren / ankaufen (s. Unit 5)
discount	Rabatt, Diskont
discrepancy	Abweichung, Unstimmigkeit, Diskrepanz
dismal	trübe, trostlos
dismantle (v)	auseinander nehmen, zerlegen
dispatch (v)	versenden
dispense with (v)	verzichten auf
display (v)	ausstellen, präsentieren
dispose (v) of	veräußern, abstoßen, entsorgen
disregard (v)	hier: als gegenstandslos betrachten
dissatisfied	unzufrieden
distinctive	kennzeichnend, charakteristisch, auffallend
distribute (v)	vertreiben, verteilen
distribution channels	Vertriebswege, -einrichtungen
distribution of profits	Gewinnausschüttung
distribution	Vertrieb, Verteilung
distributor	(Vertrags)händler
document of title	Traditionspapier, Eigentumsurkunde
documentary letter of credit	Dokumentenakkreditiv (s. Unit 7)
documentation	Dokumente, Nachweis
documents against acceptance	Dokumente gegen Akzept (s. Unit 7)
documents against payment	Dokumente gegen Bezahlung, Kassa gegen Dokumente (s. Unit 7)
documents for collection	Dokumenteninkasso (s. Unit 7)
domestic	Inlands-, Binnen- ,(ein)heimisch, häuslich
donation	Spende
doubt (v)	zweifeln, bezweifeln
down payment	Anzahlung
down to the dot	bis auf's i-Tüpfelchen
downturn	Abschwung
dozen	Dutzend
draft (v)	verfassen, entwerfen, formulieren
draw (v) a B/E on	einen Wechsel ziehen (ausstellen) auf
draw (v) a cheque on a bank	einen Scheck auf eine Bank ziehen
drawee	Bezogener (s. Unit 5)
drawer	Aussteller (s. Unit 5)
drive	hier: Laufwerk
drop in sales	Umsatzrückgang
due date	Fälligkeitsdatum
due	fällig
dumb-bell	Hantel
duplex unit	Duplexvorrichtung *(zum Drucken auf beiden Seiten)*
duplicate waybill	Frachtbriefdoppel (s. Unit 8)
duration	Dauer
dust separation	Staubabscheidung

E

eager	bestrebt, bemüht, erpicht
earthquake	Erdbeben
ease	Leichtigkeit, Einfachheit
ecological	ökologisch, Umwelt-
economical	sparsam, kostensparend
edge	Rand, Kante; auch: Vorsprung
educational qualifications	hier: Schulbildung
educational system	Schulwesen
effect (v) payment	Zahlung anweisen / vornehmen
effective	wirkungsvoll, effektiv, tatsächlich
efficient	tüchtig, leistungsfähig
elect (v)	wählen
eliminate (v)	ausschalten
embarrass (v)	in Verlegenheit bringen
embody (v)	verkörpern
embrace (v)	umfassen, umarmen
emphasise / emphasize (v)	betonen, hervorheben
employ (v)	einstellen, benutzen
employees	Beschäftigte, Mitarbeiter
en suite facilities	eigenes Bad mit WC
enable (v) s.o.	jmdm. befähigen, es jmdm. ermöglichen
enabled	hier: aktiviert
enclosure(s)	Anlage(n) (*Brief*)
encourage (v)	ermutigen, fördern, anregen
endeavour (v)	sich bemühen
ending	hier: Schlusssatz
endorse (v)	indossieren (*Eigentum durch einen Vermerk auf der Rückseite eines Orderpapiers übertragen*)
endorsement	Indossament (*auf der Rückseite eines übertragbaren Wertpapiers angebrachte Erklärung (Unterschrift), mit der der jeweilige Inhaber das Recht aus dem Papier auf einen anderen überträgt*)
enforce (v)	erzwingen, durchsetzen
enhance (v)	verbessern, verschönern, vergrößern
enquire, inquire (v),	anfragen, sich erkundigen
enquiry, inquiry	Anfrage
ensure (v)	sicherstellen, dafür sorgen
entirely	gänzlich, vollständig
entitle (v)	Anrecht geben, berechtigen
entitled	berechtigt
entrust with (v)	beauftragen/betrauen mit
environment	Umfeld, Umwelt
environmentally friendly	umweltfreundlich
equip (v) with	ausstatten mit
equipment	Ausrüstung, Ausstattung, Anlagen, Geräte
equity	hier: Eigenkapital
erect (v)	aufbauen, aufstellen
error	Fehler, Irrtum
essential	wesentlich, von großer Bedeutung
establish (v) rapport	eine Beziehung herstellen
establishment	Errichtung, Gründung, Einrichtung
estate agent	Immobilienmakler
estimate	Kostenvoranschlag
evaluate (v)	auswerten
evaluation	Aus-, Bewertung
even	sogar
eventual(ly)	letztendlich, letzten Endes, schließlich (Achtung: *eventuell* heißt *possible bzw. possibly, perhaps*)
evidence	Beweis(material), Beleg, Hinweis
evil	Übel
ex stock	ab Lager
exacting	anspruchsvoll
exceptional	außergewöhnlich
excerpt	Auszug, Exzerpt
exchange rate	Wechselkurs
exclusion	Ausschluss
exclusive of VAT	ohne Mehrwertsteuer
execute (v)	durch-, ausführen
executive board	Vorstand
executive suite	Luxussuite für Geschäftsreisende
exhibit (v)	ausstellen
exhibition	Messe, Ausstellung
exhibits	Ausstellungsgegenstände, Exponate
expand (v)	ausdehnen, erweitern, expandieren
expandability	Ausbaufähigkeit
expenditure	Ausgaben, Aufwendungen, (Un)kosten
expertise	Gutachten, Fachwissen
expire (v)	ablaufen
expiry date	Verfallsdatum
explicit	ausdrücklich
export declaration	Ausfuhrerklärung
export permit	Ausfuhrgenehmigung
export procedure	Ausfuhrverfahren, Exportabläufe
expose (v)	aussetzen, exponieren
expressly (adv)	ausdrücklich
extend (v)	ausdehnen, erweitern, sich erstrecken
extension	Verlängerung; auch: Nebenstelle, Durchwahl
extensive	ausgedehnt
EXW, Ex Works	ab Werk (s. Unit 4)
eye-catching	ins Auge springend, auffallend

F

face value	Nennwert
face	hier: Vorderseite
facilitate (v)	erleichtern, ermöglichen
facilities	Einrichtungen, Möglichkeiten
factor	Kommissionär (s. Unit 12)
factor (v) in	mit einrechnen

factoring	Factoring (s. Unit 10)
factual	sachlich, tatsächlich
fail (v) to do something	etwas unterlassen
fail (v) to meet obligations	Verpflichtungen nicht nachkommen
failure	Versagen, Versäumnis, Nichterfüllung
faithful(ly)	gewissenhaft, getreu
fallback position	Rückzugsposition
fare	Fahr-, Flugpreis, Fahrgeld
faucet	Wasserhahn
fault	Schuld
faulty	fehlerhaft, schadhaft, mangelhaft
favourable	günstig, positiv
feature (v)	herausstellen; hier: als Besonderheit bieten
feature	Merkmal, Eigenart, Besonderheit
feeder	Papierkassette, -zuführung
fees	Gebühren, Honorare
field research	Feldforschung
fierce competition	harter Wettbewerb
fidelity discount	Treuerabatt
file (v) for bankruptcy	Konkurs anmelden
files	Akten, Dateien, Unterlagen
fill (v) an order	einen Auftrag ausführen
finalise (v)	endgültig festlegen, zum Abschluss bringen
financial standing	finanzielle Lage, finanzieller Status
find (v) a ready market	sich gut verkaufen
findings	Feststellungen, Befund, Ergebnis
first and foremost	vor allem
first name	Vorname
flavour	Aroma, Geschmack
fleet of vehicles	Fuhrpark
flier	Flugblatt, Reklamezettel
floating policy	Abschreibe-, Pauschalpolice (s. Unit 8)
fluctuation	Schwankung, Fluktuation
fluent	fließend, gewandt
flush	bündig, ohne Einzug
focus	Brenn-, Mittelpunkt
folder	Mappe, Faltblatt
for the account of	auf Rechnung von
foreign affairs	auswärtige Angelegenheiten
foreign currency	Devisen
form	Formular, Formblatt
forward (v)	(nach)senden, befördern, weiterleiten
forward exchange dealings	Devisentermingeschäfte
forwarder's certificate of receipt	Spediteurübernahmebescheinigung (s. Unit 8)
frame tubes	Rahmenrohre
franchisee	Franchisenehmer (s. Unit 12)
franchising	Franchise-, Konzessionsvergabe
franchisor	Franchisegeber
free collective bargaining	Tarifverhandlungen (s. Unit 6)
freight forwarder	Spediteur
freight rates	Frachtkosten
frequent	häufig
friction	Reibung
fringe benefits	freiwillige / zusätzliche Leistungen
frontier	(Staats)grenze
full board	Vollpension
furnish (v)	beibringen, vorlegen, ausstatten
fuse	Sicherung (elektrisch)

G

gain (v) a foothold	Fuß fassen
gains	Einnahmen, Einkommen, Gewinne, Erträge
garment	Kleidungsstück
gather (v)	sammeln, zusammentragen, sich versammeln
gathering place	Treffpunkt, Versammlungsort
gears	Gänge, Getriebe
gender	Geschlecht
general average	gemeinschaftliche Havarie (s. Unit 10)
gentle	sanft
genuine	echt
ghastly (adj)	scheußlich
give (v) due notice	hier: in aller Form benachrichtigen
given	angesichts, in Anbetracht
glamorous	bezaubernd, prächtig
glow	glühen, leuchten
go (v) without saying	selbstverständlich sein
go (v) bankrupt	bankrott gehen, in Konkurs gehen
goal	Ziel; auch: Tor
goodwill	Wohlwollen, ideeller Firmenwert
gradually	schrittweise, allmählich
graduate	Hochschulabsolvent(in), Akademiker(in)
grant (v) a discount	einen Rabatt gewähren
grant (v) an adjustment	eine Regulierung gewähren
grateful	dankbar
greengrocer	Gemüsehändler
grid	Raster, Gitternetz
groceries	Lebensmittel
gross	brutto
gross domestic product	Bruttoinlandsprodukt (s. Unit 9)
gross national product	Bruttosozialprodukt (s. Unit 9)
growth industry	Wachstumsbranche
guide	(Fremden)führer, Reiseführer

H

habit	Gewohnheit
hair clip	Haarspange
half board	Halbpension
half-timbered cottages	ländliche Fachwerkhäuser
handle (v)	hantieren, handhaben, umgehen mit, bearbeiten
handling fees	(Konto)führungsgebühren

handling	Bearbeitung, Handhabung, Behandlung	implications	Auswirkung, Folge, Konsequenz
hand-out	Handzettel, Prospekt, Werbegeschenk	implicit	stillschweigend einbegriffen, unausgesprochen enthalten
handy	handlich	imply (v)	beinhalten, besagen, stillschweigend voraussetzen
hard disk drive	Festplatte	import duty	Einfuhrzoll
hard-working	fleißig	import licence	Einfuhrgenehmigung, Importlizenz
haulage	Beförderung, Transport(kosten)	import quota	Einfuhrkontingent, -quote
have (v) an edge	einen Vorteil, Vorsprung haben	impose (v)	verhängen, auferlegen
have (v) in common	gemeinsam haben	in advance	im Voraus
have (v) in stock	auf Lager / vorrätig haben	in due course	zu gegebener Zeit
head buyer	Chefeinkäufer(in)	in keeping with	in Übereinstimmung mit
head of department	Abteilungsleiter(in)	in money terms	in Geld ausgedrückt
head office	Zentrale	in our favour	zu unseren Gunsten
heading	Überschrift	in quadruplicate	in vierfacher Ausfertigung
heavy-duty	hochleistungsfähig, strapazierfähig	in return	im Gegenzug, dafür
hedging	Kurs-, Preissicherungsgeschäft, Risikoabsicherung (*Versuch der Vermeidung zukünftiger Verluste durch Abschluss von Temingeschäften, bei denen die Erfüllung des Vertrages (z.B. die Abnahme der Devisen) erst zu einem späteren Zeitpunkt, aber zum Kurs des Abschlusstages erfolgt.*)	in stock	vorrätig, auf Lager
		in strict confidence	streng vertraulich
		in the event that	falls
		in the foreseeable future	in absehbarer Zeit
		in the meantime	in der Zwischenzeit
		in transit	auf dem Transport / Transit, unterwegs
		in triplicate	in dreifacher Ausfertigung
		in view of	angesichts
		inadequate	unzureichend
		inappropriate	unangemessen, unangebracht
hence	daher, folglich	incident	Vor-, Zwischenfall, Ereignis
hereinafter	nachstehend	inclination	Neigung
hesitate (v)	zögern	incompatible	nicht kompatibel
hidden	versteckt	inconvenience (sg.)	Unannehmlichkeiten
hire (v)	einstellen	incorporate (v)	einbeziehen, eingliedern, auch: als AG eintragen
hoarding	Plakatwand, -tafel		
hold (v) liable	haftbar machen, zur Verantwortung ziehen	incredible	unglaublich
		incur (v) damages	Schadenersatz leisten müssen
holding company	Holding(gesellschaft) (s. Unit 2)	incur (v) debts	Schulden machen
holiday entitlement	Urlaubsanspruch	incur (v) losses	Verluste erleiden
honour (v) a B/E	einen Wechsel honorieren, einlösen	indemnify (v)	entschädigen
		indentation	Einrückung
hook	Haken	indicate (v)	angeben, anzeigen
horizontal axis	waagerechte Achse	industrial plant	Industrieanlage, -betrieb
hospitality	Gastfreundschaft, Bewirtung	inexpensive	preiswert
host (v)	Gastgeber sein, ausrichten	inflow	Zufluss
host country	Empfänger-, Gastland	ingredients	Zutaten
hostile take-over bid	feindliches Übernahmeangebot	inherent in	innewohnend, zugehörend
hot rolled stainless steel	warm gewalzter Edelstahl	inherit (v)	erben
hotel lounge	Hotelhalle	initial (v)	mit Handzeichen versehen
however	jedoch	initial order	Erstauftrag
hub	Nabe	initial	anfänglich, erst/e/er/es
huge	riesig	initiate (v)	in die Wege leiten, beginnen
		inland waterway transport	Binnenschifffahrt
I		inspection authority	Prüf-, Teststelle
		installation	Aufstellung, Montage, Einbau
imaginary profit	imaginärer Gewinn	instalment	Teil-, Ratenzahlung, Rate
imaginative	phantasievoll	instance	Fall, Beispiel
impact on	Auswirkung, Einfluss auf	instant access	sofortiger Zugriff (*auf das Guthaben*)
impair (v)	beeinträchtigen		
impediment	Hindernis	instant	Augenblick
impending	bevorstehend	institute (v) legal proceedings	gerichtliche Schritte einleiten
implement (v)	aus-, durchführen, durchsetzen		

Wörterverzeichnis

instruct (v)	anweisen, anleiten, instruieren	(the) latter	letztere/r/s, zuletzt genannt
instructions	Anweisungen	launch (v)	auf den Markt bringen, starten
insurance certificate	Versicherungsschein, -zertifikat	leading-edge (adj.)	auf dem neuesten Stand der Technik
insurance policy	Versicherungspolice	leaflet	Broschüre, Faltblatt
interest rate	Zins(satz)	league	Liga
interference	Interferenz, Einmischung, Störung	legal department	Rechtsabteilung
interior decoration	Raumausstattung	legal entity	juristische Person
intermediary	Vermittler, Mittelsmann	legal tender	gesetzliches Zahlungsmittel
interpret (v)	auslegen, dolmetschen	legalise (v)	beglaubigen, rechtskräftig machen
interpreter	Dolmetscher(in)	legislation	Gesetz(gebung)
introductory discount	Einführungsrabatt	lend (v)	(aus)leihen, Darlehen gewähren
investigate (v)	untersuchen, ermitteln	less a discount	abzüglich eines Diskonts/Abschlags
invisible trade	unsichtbarer Handel; hier: Dienstleistungen	letter of credit	Akkreditiv (s. Unit 7)
invoice	Rechnung	letter of indemnity	Konnossementsgarantie (s. Unit 8)
involve (v)	mit sich bringen, nach sich ziehen, involvieren	letterhead	Briefkopf
involvement	hier: Beteiligung, Engagement	level of formality	Grad der Förmlichkeit
irrevocable	unwiderruflich	lever	Hebel
issue (v) a letter of credit	ein Akkreditiv eröffnen / ausstellen	liability	Haftung
issue (v)	ausstellen, herausbringen, -geben	liable	haftbar
		liase (v)	als Kontaktperson fungieren
issue date	Eröffnungs-, Ausgabedatum	libel	Verleumdung
issue	Ausgabe einer Zeitung; auch: Frage, Problem	licensing	Lizenzvergabe
		limited liability	beschränkte Haftung
itinerary	Reiseplan, Reiseroute	limited partnership	in etwa: Kommanditgesellschaft (KG) (s. Unit 2)
		line graph	Liniendiagramm
		line of business	Branche, Sparte
J		line	Produktsparte, Sortiment
		link	Verbindung
jam (v)	(sich) stauen	linking words	Binde-, Verbindungswörter
job description	Stellenbeschreibung	litigation	Rechtsstreit, Prozess
job exchange	Stellenbörse	loan	Darlehen, Kredit
job title	hier: Position	location	Standort
jog pant	Jogginghose	lock (v)	(ab)schließen, verriegeln, blockieren
join (v)	beitreten, sich anschließen		
joint stock companies	Kapitalgesellschaften (s. Unit 2)	logistics	Logistik, Nachschubwesen
joint(ly)	gemeinsam	long-standing	langjährig
judge (v)	beurteilen, urteilen	lounge	Warte-, Hotelhalle, Aufenthaltsraum
jumbled	durcheinander geraten/gemischt		
justified	gerechtfertigt, berechtigt	loyal	loyal, treu
just-in-time delivery	Just-in-time-Anlieferung	lukewarm	lauwarm
		lump sum	Pauschal-, Einmalbetrag
K			
		M	
keep (v) track	verfolgen, sich auf dem Laufenden halten		
		made out to order	an Order ausgestellt (*Vermerk, der die Verfügungsberechtigung bestimmter Personen kennzeichnet*)
keep in shape	in Form bleiben		
key interest rates	Leitzinsen		
kit	Ausrüstung		
		mail-order house	Versandhaus
		mail shot	Postwurfsendung
L		mailing list	Adressenverzeichnis
		maintain (v)	aufrechterhalten, beibehalten, behaupten
labour costs	Arbeits-, Personalkosten		
labour	Arbeit, Mühe; auch: Arbeitskräfte	maintenance	Wartung (technischer Geräte)
		make (v) arrangements	Vorkehrungen treffen
lasting	dauerhaft	make (v) out to	ausstellen auf (*jem. als Begünstigten eintragen*)
lately	in letzter Zeit		

276 Wörterverzeichnis

malfunction (v)	schlecht funktionieren
management	Geschäfts-, Unternehmensleitung/führung
managing director	geschäftsführende(r) Direktor(in), Geschäftsführer(in)
manually	von/ mit der Hand
manufacturer	Hersteller(firma), Produzent, Fabrikant,
manufacturing industry	verarbeitende Industrie
marine insurance policy	Seeversicherungspolice (s. Unit 8)
marine insurance	(See)transportversicherung
marine risks	Seetransportgefahren
marital status	Personenstand
mark of origin	Ursprungsbezeichnung
marked	deutlich, markiert
marketing	Marketing, Absatzwesen
marking	Markierung
maturity	Fälligkeit(sdatum), Verfallsdatum, Laufzeit
means of payment	Zahlungsmittel
medieval	mittelalterlich
meet (v) a deadline	eine Frist einhalten, einen Termin einhalten
meet (v) an order	Auftrag ausführen
meet (v) commitments	Verpflichtungen nachkommen
meet (v) halfway	auf halben Wege entgegenkommen
meet (v) requirements	den Anforderungen entsprechen
membership fee	Mitgliedsbeitrag
memo	Aktenvermerk, -notiz
merchandise	Ware(n)
merchant	Kaufmann
merely	lediglich, bloß
merger	Fusion (s. Unit 2)
merits	Verdienste
message	Botschaft, Mitteilung, Meldung
Middle Ages	Mittelalter
minor	kleiner, untergeordnet
misleading	irreführend
mobile (phone)	Handy
mode of transport	Transportart
modest	bescheiden
monetary union	Währungsunion
monitor (v)	überwachen, beobachten
mortgage	Hypothek
motor insurance	Kfz-Versicherung
movement certificate	Warenverkehrsbescheinigung (s. Unit 2)
multimodal transport	multimodaler Verkehr/Transport (*mehrere Transportarten*)
multiple	viel-, mehrfach, mannigfaltig
mutual	gegenseitig, beiderseitig
myth	Mythos, Märchen

N

nail polish	Nagellack
native speaker	Muttersprachler(in)
navy	dunkelblau
negotiate (v)	ver-, aushandeln, negoziieren
negotiation	Verhandlung
network (v)	Netz aufbauen
nevertheless	dennoch, nichtsdestoweniger
no matter how	ganz gleich wie
non-performance	Nichterfüllung
not ... at all	überhaupt nicht
note (v)	zur Kenntnis nehmen
note of appreciation	kurzes Dankschreiben
note to this effect	diesbezüglicher Vermerk
notice (v)	feststellen, beobachten, anzeigen
noticeable	spürbar
notification	Benachrichtigung
notify (v)	benachrichtigen, melden
notify address	Meldeadresse (*bill of lading*)
nuclear risks	atomare Risiken

O

objective	Ziel, Absicht, Zweck
obligations	Verpflichtungen, Verbindlichkeiten
observer	Beobachter
obviate (v)	hinfällig machen, vorbeugen
obvious(ly)	offensichtlich, offenbar
occasion	Anlass
occurrences	Vorfälle, Vorkommnisse
of long standing	langjährig
offer without engagement	unverbindliches Angebot
offset (v)	ausgleichen
omission	Unter-, Auslassung, Versäumnis
omit (v)	aus-, weglassen
on behalf of	im Auftrag/Namen von
on demand	auf Verlangen
on favourable terms	zu günstigen Bedingungen
on good authority	aus informierter Quelle
on the debtor's part	seitens des Schuldners
on your part	Ihrerseits
on-board bill of lading	Bordkonnossement (s. Unit 8)
one-off	einmalig
one-stop	hier: alles unter einem Dach
on-site	am/vor Ort
open account terms	Kontokorrentbedingungen, Lieferantenkreditklausel, offenes Zahlungsziel (s. Unit 7)
open (v) an L/C	ein Akkreditiv eröffnen
open cheque	Barscheck
open credit	offener Kredit, offenes Zahlungsziel (s. Unit 7)
open day	Tag der offenen Tür
open policy/cover	offene Police, laufende Versicherung
opening	offene Stelle, Einleitung
operating costs	Betriebskosten
operation manual	Bedienungshandbuch, -anleitung
operator	hier: Telefonvermittlung, -zentrale

opportunity	Möglichkeit, günstige Gelegenheit, Chance	performance	Leistung, Ausführung, Abschneiden, Aufführung
optional	wahlweise, fakultativ	periodicals	Zeitschriften
options	hier: Alternativen, Wahlmöglichkeiten	person in charge	Sachbearbeiter(in), zuständige Person
order cheque	Orderscheck (s. Unit 5)	personnel	Personal
order form	Bestellschein	persuade (v)	überreden, zureden
order on call	Abrufauftrag	persuasive	suggestiv
ordinary partnership	in etwa: offene Handelsgesellschaft (OHG)	phase (v) out	(schrittweise) abbauen, auslaufen lassen
origin	Ursprung, Herkunft	pick (v) up	sich erholen, abholen
out of court	außergerichtlich	pie chart	Tortendiagramm
out of stock	vergriffen	place (v) an order with s.o.	jmdm. einen Auftrag erteilen
outflow	Abfluss	place (v) in danger	gefährden
output	Leistung, Ausstoß, Produktion	place (v) to account	in Rechnung bringen/stellen, berechnen
outstanding	ausstehend; auch: hervorragend	plywood	Sperr-, Furnierholz
overbearing	überheblich, anmaßend	point of sale	Kasse, Kassenterminal
overdeliver (v)	zu viel liefern	policy	(Versicherungs)police
overdraft	Kontoüberziehung	pool of money	Kapitalstock
overdue	überfällig	port of destination	Bestimmungshafen
overlook (v)	übersehen, außer Acht lassen	port of discharge	Entladehafen
overly	übermäßig	port of shipment	Verschiffungshafen
overseas	im Ausland	positioning	Positionierung
oversight	Versehen	possession	Besitz
overwhelming	überwältigend	postage	Porto
owe (v)	schulden	postal order	Postanweisung
ownership	Eigentum(srecht)	postcode/zip code	Postleitzahl
		postpone (v)	aufschieben, verschieben
		poultry	Geflügel

P

package	Packung, Packstück, Kollo, Paket	power cord	Elektrokabel
packing list	Packliste	precarious	prekär, unsicher
padding	Polster(material)	precaution	Vorsichtsmaßnahme
paragraph	Absatz (*im Text*)	precede (v)	voranstehen, -gehen, -stellen
parent company	Muttergesellschaft	predicament	missliche Lage, schwierige Lage
partial shipment	Teillieferung	predict (v)	voraussagen
participant	Teilnehmer(in)	preferential duties	Vorzugszölle
particle	Teilchen; hier: Partikel	premises	Geschäftsräume, Firmengelände
particular average	Teilhavarie (s. Unit 8)	premium	Prämie
particulars	Einzelheiten	prepaid	vorausbezahlt
partner	Partner, Teilhaber, Gesellschafter	preprinted form	Vordruck
partnership	Partnerschaft, in etwa: Personengesellschaft (s. Unit 2)	preprinted	vorgedruckt
		presentation	Präsentation, Vorlage
part-time	Teilzeit	previous	vorherig, vorangegangen
party to a contract	Vertragspartei	pricing	Preisgestaltung
past due	überfällig	principal	hier: Prinzipal, Auftraggeber
patience	Geduld	printer setting	Einstellung des Druckers
pattern	Muster, Vorlage, Struktur	private consumption	privater Verbrauch
payable at	zahlbar bei	private limited company	in etwa: Gesellschaft mit beschränkter Haftung (GmbH)
payee	Zahlungsempfänger	private sector companies	private Unternehmen
payment by instalments	Ratenzahlung	pro forma invoice	Proformarechnung (s. Unit 7)
payment in advance	Vorauskasse, Vorauszahlung	proceed (v)	vorgehen, verfahren
payment record	bisherige Zahlungsmoral	proceeds	Erlös, Ertrag, Einnahmen
peak	Gipfel, Spitze	process (v)	be-, verarbeiten, behandeln
penalty	Vertrags-, Geldstrafe	product liablility	Produkthaftung
pending your instructions	bis zum Eintreffen Ihrer Anweisungen	professions	Berufe (*gehobener Art*)
		profit margin	Gewinnspanne
perception	Wahrnehmung	project (v) a value	eine Wertvorstellung vermitteln
		prolong (v)	verlängern
		promote (v)	hier: fördern

pronounce (v)	aussprechen	range of products	Produktpalette, -reihe, Sortiment
proof	Beweis	range	Bereich, Reichweite, Auswahl, Sortiment
property	Immobilie, Besitz, Eigentum	ranking	Rangfolge
proposal form	hier: Antragsformular	rash	vorschnell, übereilt
proposal	Vorschlag	raspberry	Himbeere
proprietor	Inhaber(in), Eigentümer(in)	rate of exchange	Wechselkurs
prospective customer	mögliche(r)/potenzielle(r) Kunde/Kundin, Interessent(in)	reach (v) an agreement	eine Vereinbarung treffen
prosperous	wohlhabend	realize (v)	feststellen, einsehen
provide (v)	liefern, bereitstellen	realize (v) list prices	Listenpreise erzielen
providing / provided	vorausgesetzt	reasonable	vernünftig, in Ordnung, angebracht, angemessen
provision of services	Bereitstellung von Dienstleistungen	rebate	Bonus, Rückvergütung, Nachlass
provisions	Vorkehrungen, Vorsichtsmaßnahmen	receipt of order	Auftragseingang
public holidays	gesetzliche Feiertage	receipt	Quittung, Beleg, Empfangsbestätigung
public limited company	in etwa: Aktiengesellschaft (AG)	received for shipment B/L	Übernahmekonnossement (s. Unit 8)
public relations	Public Relations (*Maßnahmen zur Förderung des Ansehens einer Firma*) (s. Unit 12)	reception	Empfang
publication of accounts	Veröffentlichung des Jahresabschlusses	recharge (v)	aufladen
		recipient	Empfänger(in), Adressat(in)
punctual	pünktlich	reciprocate (v)	sich revanchieren, dem anderen einen ähnlichen Dienst erweisen
punctuation	Zeichensetzung, Interpunktion		
purchase order	Materialanforderungsschein, Auftragsformular	recommend (v)	empfehlen
purchasing	Einkauf	recommendation	Empfehlung
put (v) through	verbinden, (am Telefon) durchstellen	reconstruction	Wiederaufbau
		records	hier: Akten, Unterlagen
put (v) off	verschieben, aufschieben	recover (v)	hier: einziehen; auch: erholen
puzzling	verwirrend	recruit (v)	anwerben, einstellen
		recruitment	Personalbeschaffung, -einstellung

Q

		rectify (v)	richtigstellen, berichtigen
qualifcation	Qualifikation, berufliche Eignung	refer (v) s.o. to	jmdm. verweisen an
		reference	Bezug, Bezugszeichen
qualified majority	qualifizierte Mehrheit	refrain (v) from	unterlassen
qualify (v) for	in Frage kommen, berechtigt sein, Voraussetzungen erfüllen	refrigerated truck	Kühltransporter
		refrigeration	Kühlung
quantity discount	Mengenrabatt	refund	Nachzahlung, Rückerstattung
quarterly settlement	vierteljährlicher Kontenausgleich	refuse (v)	ablehnen, sich weigern
		registrar of companies	in etwa: Handelsregister
quarterly	vierteljährlich, Quartals-	registration number	Anmelde-, Zulassungsnummer, Autokennzeichen
quay	Kai		
queries	Fragen	regret (v)	bedauern
questionnaire	Fragebogen	regular customer	Stammkunde, -kundin
quotation	(Preis)angebot; auch: Zitat	regulation	Vorschrift, Regelung
quote (v)	angeben, zitieren	relate (v) to	hier: eine Beziehung finden
		related products	verwandte Produkte
		release (v)	frei-, übergeben, herausgeben, veröffentlichen, entbinden

R

		reliable	zuverlässig
		religious denomination	Konfession
rail consignment note	Eisenbahnfrachtbrief	rely (v) on	sich verlassen auf
rail	Reeling	remainder	Restbetrag
raise (v) capital	Kapital aufbringen, -nehmen, beschaffen	remedy	Abhilfe, Heilmittel
		reminder	Mahnung
rally (v)	sich erholen; auch: sich versammeln	remit (v)	überweisen, bezahlen, senden
		remittance slip	Überweisungsbeleg, Einzahlungsschein
random group	nach dem Zufallsprinzip ausgesuchte Gruppe		
		remote access	Fernzugriff

Wörterverzeichnis

removable	transportabel, heraus-, abnehmbar	**S**	
render (v) impossible	unmöglich machen	safeguard (v)	sicherstellen, garantieren, schützen
render (v) services	Dienstleistungen erbringen	salary	Gehalt
renowned	renommiert	sales contract	Kaufvertrag
rent	Miete	sales force	Verkaufsmannschaft, Außendienstorganisation
repeat order	Nachbestellung	sales literature	Prospektmaterial
replacement	Ersatz(teil) *(etwas Identisches)*	sales representative	Vertreter(in)
reply slip	Antwortcoupon	sales	Umsatz *(bei Geldbeträgen)*, Absatz *(bei Stückzahlen)*
report	Bericht	salutation	Begrüßung; hier: Anrede
representative	Vertreter(in)	sample kit	Mustersatz, -kasten
reprint	Nachdruck, Neuauflage	samples	Proben, Muster
reputation	Ruf	satisfaction	Zufriedenheit
request (v)	(er)bitten, verlangen, anfordern	satisfactory	befriedigend, zufriedenstellend
request	Bitte	save (v)	sparen, ersparen; hier: speichern
require (v)	benötigen	savings account	Sparkonto
research (v)	forschen, untersuchen, recherchieren	scale	Maßstab, Umfang
research and development	Forschung und Entwicklung	scarf, pl. scarves	Schal
reservation	hier: Vorbehalt	schedule	Zeitplan
reserve (v) the right	sich das Recht vorbehalten	scope of cover	Umfang des Deckungsschutzes
resilient	widerstandsfähig, elastisch	scope	Umfang, Bereich, Spielraum, Rahmen
resolution	hier: Auflösung	scratched	zerkratzt
resolve (v) a problem	ein Problem lösen	screen	Leinwand, Bildschirm
resort	Urlaubs-, Ferien-, Badeort	seafood	Meeresfrüchte
resources	Ressourcen, Quellen, Geldmittel	seaworthy	seetüchtig, seefest
respectable	solide, angesehen, seriös	second (v)	abordnen, zeitweilig versetzen
respective	jeweilig, einschlägig	sector of industry	Branche, Industriezweig
respite	Zahlungsaufschub	secure (v)	sichern
respond (v)	reagieren, antworten	select (v)	(aus)wählen, herausgreifen
response	Antwort, Reaktion	self-catering flat	Ferienwohnung
rest (v) assured	versichert sein, sicher sein	self-respecting firm	Firma, die etwas auf sich hält
restore (v)	wiederherstellen	sell (v) at a discount	mit Diskont/Abschlag, unter Nennwert verkaufen
resume (v)	wieder aufnehmen	senior executive	leitende(r) Angestellte(r), Führungskraft
retail chain	(Einzel)handelskette	sequence (v)	gliedern
retail outlets	Einzelhandelsgeschäfte	service (v) debt	Schuldendienst leisten, Zins- und Tilgungszahlungen vornehmen
retailer	Einzelhändler	service engineer	Kundendiensttechniker, -ingenieur
retain (v)	behalten, ein-, beibehalten	set (v) out	darlegen; auch: anfangen
retain (v) the custom of s.o.	jem. als Kunden behalten	set off (v) against	anrechnen, abziehen
return (v) a call	zurückrufen	set up (v) a business	eine Firma gründen
reveal (v)	aufdecken, bekannt geben	setting	Einstellung
reverse (v)	umkehren, umdrehen	settle (v) a matter	eine Angelegenheit regeln
review	Nach-, Überprüfung, (Buch)besprechung, Kritik	settle (v) an invoice	eine Rechnung begleichen
revise (v)	revidieren, überarbeiten	settle (v)	abrechnen, bezahlen, erledigen
revocable	widerruflich	settlement	Begleichung, Bezahlung
rim	Felge	set-up	Aufstellung, Aufbau, Montage
riots and civil commotion	Aufruhr und innere Unruhen	share (v)	teilen, sich teilen, sich beteiligen an, teilhaben
rival products	Konkurrenzfabrikate	shareholders	Aktionäre, Anteilseigner, Gesellschafter
rough handling	unsachgemäße Behandlung	shares/stocks	Aktien
router	Router *(EDV)*		
royalties	Nutzungs-, Lizenzgebühren, Tantiemen		
rude	grob, unerzogen		
rummage (v)	durchwühlen		
rumour	Gerücht		
run (v) a business	eine Firma leiten		
run (v)	hier: betreiben		
rustic fare	ländliche Küche *(Speisen)*		

sheet	Blatt, Bogen, Platte; hier: Feinblech	staggered payment	gestaffelte Zahlung
shifter	Schaltmechanismus	staggered prices	Staffelpreise
shipper	Versender, Ablader (*Exporteur*)	stained	fleckig, verschmutzt
shipping advice	Versandanzeige	stand (v) surety	Bürgschaft leisten
shipping rate	Frachttarif	stand (v) to lose	mit Sicherheit verlieren
shortage in weight	Fehlgewicht	stand constructors	Standbauunternehmen
shortage	Mangel	stand (v) out	auffallen, sich abheben
shortcomings	Unzulänglichkeiten	standards	Normen
shortly	in Kürze, demnächst	standing order	Dauerauftrag
shuttle	Pendelbus, -verkehr	standstill	Stillstand
sight draft	Sichttratte, -wechsel (s. Unit 5)	start-up	Firmengründung, Neugründung
signatory	Unterzeichner(in)	state-of-the-art	auf dem allerneuesten Stand (der Technik)
signature	Unterschrift	statement of account	Kontoauszug
significant	erheblich, deutlich, wesentlich	statement	Erklärung, Aussage
simultaneous	gleichzeitig	stationery	Briefpapier, Schreibwaren
sincere	herzlich, aufrichtig	steady	stetig
single market	europäischer Binnenmarkt	steamy	feuchtheiß, dampfend
single with business facilities	Einzelzimmer für Geschäfts- leute	steel plate	Stahlblech
		steep	steil
skill	Fertigkeit, Fähigkeit, Geschicklichkeit	step (v) in	eingreifen, sich engagieren
		stipulate	(vertraglich) festsetzen, vereinbaren, bestimmen
skilled	geschult, gelernt		
skills level	Ausbildungsniveau	stock exchange	(Wertpapier)börse
slice	Anteil, Scheibe, (Kuchen)stück	stocks /shares	Aktien
slight	gering, geringfügig	stopgap letter	Zwischenbescheid
slip of paper	Zettel	storage capacity	Speicherkapazität
slope	Abhang, Hügel	store (v)	lagern
slowdown	Verlangsamung, Abschwächung	straight	gerade, ordentlich
sluggish	schleppend, stagnierend	strategy	Strategie
slump (v)	(ab)stürzen, zusammensinken	strawberry	Erdbeere
smooth out (v)	ausgleichen, überbrücken	stress (v)	betonen
smooth	glatt, reibungslos	stricly net	ohne jeden Abzug
socket	Steckdose	striped	gestreift
softer regulations	weniger strenge Vorschriften	stuffy	verstaubt, muffig, steif
softly tailored	bequem geschnitten	sturdy	stabil, fest, kräftig
software failure	Software-Defekt	style sheet	Formatvorlage
soiled	verschmutzt, schmutzig	subconscious	unterbewußt
sole agent	Alleinvertreter (s. Unit 12)	subject line	Betreff
sole trader	Einzelkaufmann/-kauffrau	subject to	unterliegend, abhängig von, vorbehaltlich
sole(ly)	ausschließlich, allein		
solicitor	Rechtsanwalt, Rechtsanwältin	subject to change without notice	Änderungen vorbehalten
solidly reliable	hier: solide und zuverlässig		
solvency	Zahlungsfähigkeit, Solvenz	subject to confirmation	freibleibend, unverbindlich
solvent	zahlungsfähig, liquide	subject to prior sale	Zwischenverkauf vorbehalten
sophisticated	hochentwickelt, technisch raffiniert, anspruchsvoll	subliminal	unterschwellig
		submit (v)	unterbreiten, vorlegen, einreichen
sound business judgment	sicheres geschäftliches Gespür		
		subsequent	nachträglich, anschließend, darauffolgend
sound	solide, seriös, gesund		
source	Quelle	subsidiary	Tochterunternehmen, Konzerngesellschaft
spacious	geräumig		
spare parts	Ersatzteile	subsidies	Subventionen, Zuschüsse, Beihilfen
spark (v) the customer's interest	das Interesse des Kunden wecken		
		subsist (v)	bestehen, existieren, fortdauern
specialist shop	Fachgeschäft	substitute	Ersatz (*etwas Ähnliches*)
specific	bestimmt	subtotal	Zwischensumme
specifications	(technische) Angaben, Spezifikationen	sue (v)	verklagen
		sufficient	genügend, ausreichend, genug
sports equipment	Sportartikel, Sportausrüstung	suggest (v)	andeuten, erkennen lassen, vorschlagen
spray dryer	Zerstäubungstrockner		
spread (v)	ver-, ausbreiten	suggestion	Vorschlag, Andeutung
stage	Bühne		

Wörterverzeichnis

summarize (v)	zusammenfassen
summary	Zusammenfassung
summit	Gipfel(treffen)
supervisory board	Aufsichtsrat
supplier	Lieferant, Zulieferer
supply and demand	Angebot und Nachfrage
supply	Vorrat, Angebot, Versorgung
support (v)	unterstützen, belegen
surety	Sicherheit, Bürgschaft
surge (v)	anschwellen, stark ansteigen
surname	Familienname
surplus	Überschuss
surrender (v)	aushändigen, überlassen, abtreten
surround (v)	umgeben
survey report	Schadensgutachten
suspicious	verdächtig, argwöhnisch, misstrauisch
swimwear	Badebekleidung, -mode
switch (v)	hier: wechseln
styrofoam-padded	mit Styropor gepolstert

T

table top games	Brettspiele
table	hier: Tabelle
tactful	taktvoll
take (v) for granted	als selbstverständlich voraussetzen
take (v) legal steps	gerichtliche Schritte einleiten
take (v) on a risk	ein Risiko übernehmen
take (v) out insurance	Versicherung abschließen
take (v) precedence	Vorrang haben
take (v) up documents	Dokumente aufnehmen/annehmen (s. Unit 7)
take in (v) impressions	Eindrücke aufnehmen
take in (v)	einschließen
take notes (v)	Notizen machen
target (v)	anpeilen, zielen auf, gezielt ansprechen
target group	Zielgruppe
target language	Zielsprache
target	Ziel(vorgabe), Richtwert
tariffs	Tarife, hier: Zölle
tax consultant	Steuerberater(in)
tax	Steuer
teal	blaugrün
tear (v) (up)	auf-, zerreißen
tear-off coupon	Kupon, Bezugsschein *(zum Abreißen)*
tear-off section	Teil zum Abreißen
technician	Techniker(in)
telephone extension	Durchwahl
temporary	vorübergehend, zeitweise
temporary staff	Aushilfskräfte
tenacious	hartnäckig, beharrlich, zäh
tend (v) to	dazu neigen ... zu sein, häufig sein
tentative	zögernd, vorsichtig
terminate (v)	beenden
terms of delivery	Lieferbedingungen
terms of payment	Zahlungsbedingungen
territory	Gebiet
texturally enhanced	strukturell angereichert
theft	Diebstahl
thereof	davon, dessen/deren
third-party insurance	Haftpflichtversicherung
thorough	gründlich, sorgfältig
throughout	durch ... hindurch, überall in ...
thus	auf diese Weise, folgendermaßen
tiers of management	Ebenen der Geschäftsleitung
tighten (v) regulations	Vorschriften verschärfen
time bill	Nachsicht-, Zeit-, Zielwechsel, Wechsel mit Laufzeit (s. Unit 5)
time deposit account	Festgeldkonto
tips	hier: Hinweise
tissue paper	Seidenpapier
title	hier: Recht(sanspruch)
to date	bisher, bis heute
to the full extent	in vollem Umfang, bis zur vollen Höhe
to the order of	an die Order von *(Vermerk auf Wertpapieren, durch den diese durch Indossament übertragen werden können)*
topic	Thema
total (v)	zusammenzählen, addieren
trace (v)	verfolgen, nach-, aufspüren
track record	bisheriger geschäftlicher Erfolg, Erfolgsbilanz
trade (v) in	in Zahlung nehmen
trade discount	Handels-, Wiederverkaufsrabatt
trade fair	Fachmesse
trade journal/magazine	Fachzeitschrift
trade reference	Referenz, Empfehlung von einer anderen Firma
trade terms	Vertrags-, Handels-, Lieferbedingungen
trade union	Gewerkschaft
traffic congestion	Stau
trainee	Trainee, Auszubildende(r)
transaction slip	Transaktionsbeleg
transmission	Übermittlung, Übertragung
travel agent	Reisebüro
tray	Tablett
treat (v)	behandeln
trial order	Probeauftrag
triple	dreifach; hier: mit drei Betten
trough	Tiefstand, Talsohle, Trog
trust (v)	hier: davon ausgehen
trustworthy	vertrauenswürdig
turnover	Umsatz
typeface	Schriftart, Font
tyres	Reifen

U

unanimity	Einstimmigkeit
unattended	unbeaufsichtigt
unconditional	uneingeschränkt, vorbehaltlos, nicht an Bedingungen geknüpft
unconscious	unbewusst
underline (v)	unterstreichen
underpromise (v)	zu wenig versprechen
understanding	verständnisvoll
undertake (v)	sich verpflichten, über-, unternehmen
undertaking	Verpflichtung, Zusicherung, Unterfangen
underwriter	Versicherungsgeber (s. Unit 8)
unfavourable	ungünstig
unforeseen	unvorhergesehen, unerwartet
unfortunate	unglücklich, unglückselig
unfounded	unbegründet, grundlos
uniform customs and practice	einheitliche Richtlinien und Gebräuche
unique	einmalig
unless	außer wenn, es sei denn, wenn nicht
unreasonable	unvernünftig, unangebracht
unreliable	unzuverlässig
unrestricted	uneingeschränkt
unsettled	unsicher, instabil
unsolicited application	Initiativbewerbung
unsolicited	unaufgefordert, nicht angefordert
unsurpassed	unübertroffen
unvalued policy	Police ohne Wertangabe
update (v)	aktualisieren
upholstered	gepolstert
upmarket	am oberen Ende des Marktes, elegant, nobel
urgent	dringend
usage	Ver-, Anwendung, Gebrauch
user's manual	Benutzerhandbuch
utensils	Geräte

V

vacancy	freie Stelle, Stellenangebot
validity	Gültigkeit, Geltung
valley	Tal
valued policy	Police mit Wertangabe
VAT – value-added tax	Mehrwertsteuer
vehicle	Fahrzeug
venue	Veranstaltungsort, Treffpunkt
verification	Überprüfung
verify (v)	nachprüfen, Echtheit feststellen, beglaubigen
vertical axis	senkrechte Achse
vessel	Schiff; auch: Gefäß
via modem	über, mittels Modem
viable	gangbar, machbar, praktikabel
vineyards	Weinberge
vintage	Jahrgang, Spitzenwein
vintners	Weinbauer, -händler
vip-very important person	prominente Persönlichkeit
visible trade	Warenhandel, Güterverkehr
visual aid	optisches Hilfsmittel
viz.	nämlich
volume buyer	Großabnehmer, -kunde
voyage policy	Einzelpolice
voyage	Seereise

W

warehouse	Lager(haus) (Achtung: *Warenhaus* heißt *department store*)
warehousing	Lagerhaltung
warm-up suit	Trainingsanzug
warranty (=guarantee)	Garantie
waste (v) money	Geld verschwenden
waste	Abfall, Müll
waybill	Frachtbrief
wealthy	wohlhabend, reich
website	Internet-Adresse
weight certificate	Gewichtszertifikat
weight	Gewicht
weight-lifting	Gewichtheben
whereas	wohingegen, dagegen
wholesaler	Großhändler
width	Breite
wiggly	zuckend, wackelnd
willingness	Bereitschaft
wine tasting	Weinprobe, -verkostung
wiring	Verdrahtung, Kabel
with compliments	zur gefälligen Kenntnisnahme, mit freundlicher Empfehlung
with respect to	mit Bezug auf
withdraw (v) money	Geld abheben
withhold (v) payment	Zahlung zurückhalten
without any obligation	ohne Verpflichtung, unverbindlich
without engagement	freibleibend
without further delay	umgehend
witness	Zeuge, Zeugin
wooden crate	Lattenverschlag, -kiste
woolly	unklar, ungenau
word order	Wortstellung
wrap (v)	einwickeln
wrong entry	falsche Eintragung

Y

yield (v) interest	Zinsen abwerfen, Verzinsung erzielen

Z

zip	hier: Reißverschluss
zip code/post code	Postleitzahl

Carrier: Hapag-Lloyd Container Linie GmbH, Hamburg

Bill of Lading

Multimodal Transport or Port to Port Shipment

Hapag-Lloyd

Shipper:

Carrier's Reference: | **B/L-No.:** | **Page:**

Consignee or Order:

Export References:

Forwarding Agent:

Notify Address (Carrier not responsible for failure to notify; see clause 20 (1) hereof):

Consignee's Reference:

Place of Receipt:

Precarrying Vessel: | **Voyage-No.:**

Ocean Vessel(s): | **Voyage-No.:**

Place of Delivery:

Port of Loading:

Port of Discharge:

Container Nos., Seal Nos.; Marks and Nos.	Number and Kind of Packages, Description of Goods	Gross Weight:	Measurement:

Shipper's declared Value [see clause 7(1) and 7(2)]		Above Particulars as declared by Shipper. Without responsibility or warranty as to correctness by Carrier [see clause 11(1) and (2)]		
Total No. of Containers received by the Carrier:	Packages received by the Carrier:	RECEIVED by the Carrier from the Shipper in apparent good order and condition (unless otherwise noted herein) the total number or quantity of Containers or other packages or units indicated in the box opposite entitled "Total No. of Containers/Packages received by the Carrier" for Carriage subject to all the terms and conditions hereof (INCLUDING THE TERMS AND CONDITIONS ON THE REVERSE HEREOF AND THE TERMS AND CONDITIONS OF THE CARRIER'S APPLICABLE TARIFF) from the Place of Receipt or the Port of Loading, whichever is applicable, to the Port of Discharge or the Place of Delivery, whichever is applicable. One original Bill of Lading, duly endorsed, must be surrendered by the Merchant to the Carrier in exchange for the Goods or a delivery order. In accepting this Bill of Lading the Merchant expressly accepts and agrees to all its terms and conditions whether printed, stamped or written, or otherwise incorporated, notwithstanding the non-signing of this Bill of Lading by the Merchant. IN WITNESS WHEREOF the number of original Bills of Lading stated below all of this tenor and date has been signed, one of which being accomplished the others to stand void.		
Movement:	Currency:	^		
Charge	Rate	Basis	Wt/Vol/Val	P/C	Amount	^
						Place and date of issue:
						Freight payable at:	Number of original Bs/L:
Total Freight Prepaid	Total Freight Collect	Total Freight			

Spediteur-Übernahmebescheinigung
Shipping and Forwarding Receipt

Positions-Nr. ....

Kontrakt-Nr. ....

Ich/wir bescheinige/n hiermit, erhalten zu haben
I/We herewith certify having received

von der Firma ....
from Messrs.

in ....

folgende Sendung:
the following consignment:

Zeichen und Nummern marks and numbers	Zahl und Art der Packstücke Quantity and description of the packages	Laut Angabe des Absenders: as per senders declaration:		
		Inhalt contents	Bruttogewicht gross-weight	Nettogewicht net-weight

in äußerlich guter Beschaffenheit
in apparent good order and condition

*) { zur unwiderruflichen Weiterbeförderung an
for irrevocable reforwarding / reshipment to
zur unwiderruflichen Weiterbehandlung gemäß Instruktionen der
for irrevocable handling as per instructions of

Firma ....
Messrs.

in ....
at

Besondere Angaben (Transportmittel, Abgangsdatum, Versand der Dokumente, Deckung der
spezial remarks Transportversicherung, besondere Akkreditivbestimmungen, Wert laut Angabe des Absenders und ähnliches):

....
....
....
....
....

Ort .... Datum ....
dated at this   (Stempel und Unterschrift)
                              (stamp and signature)

*) nicht Zutreffendes streichen.
Es gelten die Allgemeinen Deutschen Spediteurbedingungen (A D Sp) und außerdem die Bedingungen der in Anspruch genommenen Transportanstalten oder sonstiger an der Ausführung beteiligter Dritter entsprechend der §§ 2d und 52 der ADSp.

Nr. 114

FORMULARVERLAG CW NIEMEYER 31789 **Hameln,** Walter-von-Selve-Str. 6, Tel. (0 51 51) 98 93-0, Fax 98 93-93
Auslieferungslager: 42283 **Wuppertal,** Carnaper Straße. 28, Tel. (02 02) 50 20 31, Fax 50 19 92
63075 **Offenbach a. M.,** Rohrmühlstraße 5, Tel. (0 69) 86 26 82, Fax 86 96 00
71263 **Weil der Stadt,** Glemsweg 17, Telefon (0 70 33) 3 49 40, Fax 3 48 42
39167 **Hohendodeleben,** Matthissonstr. 26, Tel. (03 92 04) 54 47, Fax 6 0179

1 Absender - *Consignor - Expéditeur - Expedidor*	**Y** 528254 **ORIGINAL**
	EUROPÄISCHE GEMEINSCHAFT EUROPEAN COMMUNITY - COMMUNAUTE EUROPEENNE - COMUNIDAD EUROPEA **URSPRUNGSZEUGNIS** *CERTIFICATE OF ORIGIN - CERTIFICAT D'ORIGINE - CERTIFICADO DE ORIGEN*
2 Empfänger - *Consignee - Destinataire - Destinatario*	**3** Ursprungsland - *Country of origin - Pays d'origine - País de origen*
4 Angaben über die Beförderung - *means of transport - expédition - expedición*	**5** Bemerkungen - *remarks - observations - observaciones*
6 Laufende Nummer; Zeichen, Nummern, Anzahl und Art der Packstücke; Warenbezeichnung *Item number; marks, numbers, number and kind of packages; description of goods*	**7** Menge *Quantity*

8 DIE UNTERZEICHNENDE STELLE BESCHEINIGT, DASS DIE OBEN BEZEICHNETEN WAREN IHREN URSPRUNG IN DEM IN FELD 3 GENANNTEN LAND HABEN
The undersigned authority certifies that the goods described above originate in the country shown in box 3
L'autorité soussignée certifie que les marchandises désignées ci-dessus sont originaires du pays figurant dans la case No. 3
La autoridad infrascrita certifica que las mercancías arriba mencionadas son originarias del país que figura en la casilla no. 3

Handelskammer Hamburg
Hamburg Chamber of Commerce
Chambre de Commerce de Hambourg
Cámara de Comercio de Hamburgo
i. A.:

Wertmarke hier aufkleben

Hamburg, den

Genehmigt durch Erlaß des Bundesministers der Finanzen vom 22. 5. 1969 III B/8 – Z 1351 – 23/69
Bestell-Nr. 1 (ECE-Rahmenvordruck). Zu beziehen durch die Handelskammer Hamburg (2.95)   C. Mahnkopp - Hamburg

Shipper's Name and Address		Shipper's Account Number	Not negotiable **Air Waybill*** Issued by
			Member of International Air Transport Association
			Copies 1, 2 and 3 of this Air Waybill are originals and have the same validity
Consignee's Name and Address		Consignee's Account Number	It is agreed that the goods described herein are accepted in apparent good order and condition (except as noted) for carriage SUBJECT TO THE CONDITIONS OF CONTRACT ON THE REVERSE HEREOF. ALL GOODS MAY BE CARRIED BY ANY OTHER MEANS INCLUDING ROAD OR ANY OTHER CARRIER UNLESS SPECIFIC CONTRARY INSTRUCTIONS ARE GIVEN HEREON BY THE SHIPPER, AND SHIPPER AGREES THAT THE SHIPMENT MAY BE CARRIED VIA INTERMEDIATE STOPPING PLACES WHICH THE CARRIER DEEMS APPROPRIATE. THE SHIPPER'S ATTENTION IS DRAWN TO THE NOTICE CONCERNING CARRIER'S LIMITATION OF LIABILITY. Shipper may increase such limitation of liability by declaring a higher value for carriage and paying a supplemental charge if required.
Issuing Carrier's Agent Name and City			Accounting Information
Agent's IATA Code		Account No.	
Airport of Departure (Addr. of First Carrier) and Requested Routing			

To	By First Carrier	Routing and Destination	To	By	To	By	Currency	CHGS Code	WT/VAL PPD COLL	Other PPD COLL	Declared Value for Carriage	Declared Value for Customs
Airport of Destination			Flight/Date				Amount of Insurance		INSURANCE – If Carrier offers insurance, and such insurance is requested in accordance with the conditions thereof, indicate amount to be insured in figures in box marked 'Amount of Insurance'			

Handling Information

SCI

(For U.S.A. use only) These commodities licensed by USA for ultimate destination .... Diversion contrary to USA law prohibited.

No. of Pieces RCP	Gross Weight	kg lb	Rate Class Commodity Item No.	Chargeable Weight	Rate / Charge	Total	Nature and Quantity of Goods (incl. Dimensions or Volume)

Prepaid	Weight Charge	Collect	Other Charges
	Valuation Charge		
	Tax		
	Total Other Charges Due Agent		Shipper certifies that the particulars on the face hereof are correct and that **insofar as any part of the consignment contains dangerous goods, such part is properly described by name and is in proper condition for carriage by air according to the applicable Dangerous Goods Regulations.**
	Total Other Charges Due Carrier		
			Signature of Shipper or his Agent
Total Prepaid		Total Collect	
Currency Conversion Rates		CC Charges in Dest. Currency	Executed on (date) at (place) Signature of Issuing Carrier or its Agent
For Carrier's Use only at Destination		Charges at Destination Total Collect Charges	

* Luftfrachtbrief (nicht begebbar) – eine verbindliche Übersetzung dieses Frachtbriefformulars (einschließlich der Vertragsbedingungen) in die deutsche Sprache liegt bei allen Lufthansa Frachtbüros aus.

ORIGINAL 3 (FOR SHIPPER)

Quellenverzeichnis

S. 7:	l. & r. PhotoDisc; Mi. MEV FAC7/8
S. 8:	Computer Clinic logo: Canvas Clip Art
S. 9:	o. MEV FAC 2; u. MEV PC 10
S. 11:	MEV FAC7/8
S. 16:	PhotoDisc
S. 18:	MEV AFA 2
S. 20/21	Canvas Clip Art
S. 23	Klett-Archiv
S. 39:	o. MEV AFA19; u. MEV FAC11/12
S. 44:	PhotoDisc
S. 66:	Corel
S. 81:	Corel
S. 83:	PhotoDisc
S. 115:	l. – r. MEV FAC 2; MEV PC10; MEV PC6
S. 127:	Europäische Zentralbank
S. 157:	Fotos: Hermann Wolter, Bad Schwartau; Zeichnungen: Graphikbüro Böttcher& Bayer, Stuttgart
S. 158:	HHVW, Port of Hamburg Marketing and Public Relations, Hamburg
S. 217:	l. – r. MEV PC3; MEV FCC3; MEV FAC9/10; MEV FAC17
S. 251:	Corel
S. 256:	MEV FAC 7/8
S. 257:	CeBit Hannover
S. 264:	PhotoDisc

Dank und Anerkennung

Wir danken Frau Sabine Johänntges von der Firma ThyssenKrupp, Frau Pia Gessner von der Stadtsparkasse Wuppertal, Herrn Michel Markus, vormals Firma Toepfer, Hamburg, und den Prüferkollegen von der IHK Düsseldorf für Anregungen und Kritik sowie zahlreichen Auszubildenden und Mitarbeitern der Firmen Krupp-Hoesch Stahlexport und ThyssenKrupp für ihre Rolle als kreative Versuchskaninchen.